JULIA VELVA
A ROMAN LADY FROM YORK
Her Life and Times Revealed

For my dear sons Ned and Bart, with much love

JULIA VELVA
A ROMAN LADY FROM YORK
Her Life and Times Revealed

PATRICK OTTAWAY

AN IMPRINT OF PEN & SWORD BOOKS LTD.
YORKSHIRE – PHILADELPHIA

First published in Great Britain in 2021 by
Pen and Sword History
An imprint of
Pen & Sword Books Ltd
Yorkshire - Philadelphia

Copyright © Patrick Ottaway, 2021

ISBN: 978 1 52671 097 0

The right of Patrick Ottaway to be identified as Author of this Work has been asserted by him in accordance with the Copyright, Designs and Patents Act 1988.

A CIP catalogue record for this book is available from the British Library

All rights reserved. No part of this book may be reproduced or transmitted in any form or by any means, electronic or mechanical including photocopying, recording or by any information storage and retrieval system, without permission from the Publisher in writing.

Typeset in 11.5/14 pts Ehrhardt by
SJmagic DESIGN SERVICES, India.

Printed and bound in India by Replika Press Pvt. Ltd.

Pen & Sword Books Ltd incorporates the Imprints of Pen & Sword Atlas, Pen & Sword Archaeology, Pen & Sword Aviation, Pen & Sword Discovery, Pen & Sword History, Pen & Sword Fiction, Pen & Sword Maritime, Pen & Sword Military, Pen & Sword Military Classics, Pen & Sword Politics, Pen & Sword Select, Pen & Sword True Crime, Air World, Frontline Publishing; Leo Cooper, Remember When, Seaforth Publishing, The Praetorian Press, Wharncliffe Local History, Wharncliffe Transport, Wharncliffe True Crime and White Owl.

For a complete list of Pen & Sword titles please contact

PEN & SWORD BOOKS LIMITED
47 Church Street, Barnsley, South Yorkshire, S70 2AS, England
E-mail: enquiries@pen-and-sword.co.uk
Website: www.pen-and-sword.co.uk

Or
PEN AND SWORD BOOKS
1950 Lawrence Rd, Havertown, PA 19083, USA
E-mail: Uspen-and-sword@casematepublishers.com
Website: www.penandswordbooks.com

Contents

List of Illustrations vi

Preface xi

Chapter 1 Introduction 1

Chapter 2 The making of Julia Velva's York: legionary fortress and civilian settlement 17

Chapter 3 Julia Velva's York: 'the summit of sublunary grandeur' 67

Chapter 4 Producers and traders 127

Chapter 5 Provincial society and daily life 165

Chapter 6 Religious belief and practice 205

Chapter 7 Cemeteries and burials 228

Chapter 8 A Roman lady from York 251

Notes 256

Bibliography 278

Index 293

List of Illustrations

1.1 An outline plan of Roman York and its environs.
1.2 Aerial view of York from the south-west.
1.3 Conjectural reconstruction of Roman York from the south-west.
1.4 The discovery of Julia Velva's tombstone on The Mount in 1922.
1.5 Julia Velva's tombstone.
1.6 Julia Velva's tombstone: detail of Julia Velva's head.
1.7 An artist's impression of Julia Velva.
1.8 Julia Velva's tombstone: Aurelius Mercurialis.
1.9 Julia Velva's tombstone: the girl.
1.10 Julia Velva's tombstone: the servant boy.
2.1 Map showing the York region with Roman roads and other Roman sites.
2.2 Plan of the legionary fortress at York with sites referred to in the text.
2.3 Plan showing the location of sites referred to in the text north – east and south-west of the Ouse.
2.4 Relief map of the York area with the principal Roman roads.
2.5 Simplified cross-section across the valley of the Ouse at York (with location plan).
2.6 The banks of the River Ouse upstream from York at Clifton.
2.7 Outline plan of the late first century fortress.
2.8 Reconstruction of the headquarters basilica of the Roman fortress.
2.9 Reconstruction of the interior of the headquarters basilica of the Roman fortress.
2.10 Column from the headquarters basilica of the Roman fortress.
2.11 The apse of the fortress baths *caldarium* at the Roman Bath public house.
2.12 The main channel of the Roman sewer, which served the legionary fortress.
2.13 The reconstructed Roman west gate of the fort at South Shields.
2.14 The exterior of the Multangular Tower.
2.15 The tile cornice at the top of the Roman fortress wall.
2.16 A reconstruction drawing of the Multangular Tower.

List of Illustrations vii

2.17 The interior of the Multangular Tower.
2.18 A reconstruction drawing of the south-west front of the legionary fortress showing the Multangular Tower and Interval Tower SW6.
2.19 Gladiators in relief on a ceramic lamp from York.
2.20 Cross-section of the main Roman road from the south-west at Wellington Row.
2.21 Heslington East: plan of the lattice pattern of late Iron Age – early Roman ditched enclosures.
2.22 A reconstruction drawing of an enclosure with roundhouses.
2.23 Altar dedicated to the goddess Fortuna.
3.1 Coin of Julia Domna.
3.2 An illustration of a soldier of the early third century.
3.3 A baldric fitting with an eagle in relief.
3.4 Third-century iron dagger.
3.5 Painted wall plaster from centurions' quarters in the First Cohort Barracks.
3.6 Reconstruction of the fortress buildings found in the *praetentura* at 9 Blake Street.
3.7 Reconstruction of the late second-century legionary fortress defences.
3.8 The east corner of the legionary fortress.
3.9 The base of the late Antonine fortress wall in the Parliament Street sewer trench.
3.10 Sarcophagus of Julia Victorina
3.11 Sarcophagus of Aurelius Super.
3.12 The medieval city walls south-west of the River Ouse.
3.13 Wellington Row: late second-century magnesian limestone surface of the main Roman road from the south-west.
3.14 5 Rougier Street: surface of a late second-century street.
3.15 The street fountain from Bishophill Junior.
3.16 Isometric drawing of the timber-lined well at 58 – 9 Skeldergate.
3.17 Plan of archaeological sites in the Rougier Street and Tanner Row area.
3.18 Wellington Row excavation 1988 – 9: plans to show the sequence of building.
3.19 Wellington Row: remains of the mid- to late second-century stone building.
3.20 Wellington Row: south-east corner of the building.
3.21 5 Rougier Street: plan showing the Roman stone pillars and street.
3.22 5 Rougier Street: stone pillars.
3.23 24 – 30 Tanner Row: showing site during machine clearance.
3.24 24 – 30 Tanner Row: Building 1 looking south-west.
3.25 24 – 30 Tanner Row: plan showing Buildings 1 and 2.
3.26 24 – 30 Tanner Row: detail of the front wall of Building 1.
3.27 1 – 9 Micklegate: walls of early third-century bath house.

3.28 Reconstruction of the interior of a Roman bath house.
3.29 Reconstruction drawing of the apsed building found in 1939.
3.30 St Mary Bishophill Junior: plan of the Roman building found in 1961 – 3.
3.31 St Mary Bishophill Junior: detail of the Roman building showing a stone-lined drain.
3.32 Plan of the Roman buildings found at 37 Bishophill Senior and at St Mary Bishophill Senior.
3.33 Reconstruction drawing of Roman houses at 37 Bishophill Senior and St Mary Bishophill Senior.
3.34 Sandstone slabs arranged as on a roof.
3.35 Ceramic flue vent and roof finial found in Bishophill in 1872.
3.36 Millstone grit blocks re-used in the south-west wall of St Michael Spurriergate.
3.37 Millstone grit drum, probably from a Jupiter column.
4.1   Reconstruction drawing of a man ploughing with cattle.
4.2   Drawings of an iron coulter and share found in Parliament Street.
4.3   Reconstruction drawing of a beehive quern in use.
4.4   Dexter cattle.
4.5   Dump of kiln waste from Peasholme Green.
4.6   Ebor Ware jar.
4.7   Ebor Ware candle-holder.
4.8   A smithing scene showing Vulcan at work.
4.9   Tools from 24 – 30 Tanner Row.
4.10 Drawing of a woman spinning.
4.11 Reconstruction drawing of a warp-weighted loom.
4.12 Two bone knife handles.
4.13 Mason's square and hammer incised on the side of Flavia Augustina's tombstone.
4.14 A hunt cup.
4.15 Samian jar.
4.16 Samian bowl with chained captives in relief.
4.17 Pieces of a green-glazed cup.
4.18 Rhenish ware beaker.
4.19 Cross-section drawing of a Gallic amphora.
4.20 Board of silver fir from 24 – 30 Tanner Row.
4.21 Faceted glass bowl.
4.22 Marble statuette of an athlete.
5.1   The opium poppy.
5.2   Two pierced bone spoons.
5.3   Cross-section drawings of 'casserole' dishes.

List of Illustrations   ix

5.4   Sarcophagus of Aelia Severa.
5.5   Skeleton of an executed male with iron rings around his ankles.
5.6   The tombstone of Corellia Optata.
5.7   Roof tile with XX (20) scored into it.
5.8   Tombstone of Flavia Augustina.
5.9   Tombstone of Julia Brica.
5.10 Reconstruction illustration of women with early third-century hair and dress styles.
5.11 Tombstone of Aelia Aeliana.
5.12 Incomplete relief of a female figure, probably from a tombstone.
5.13 Roman shoes.
5.14 Drawing of the sole of a sandal and a reconstruction drawing.
5.15 Male head from the tombstone of Aelia Aeliana.
5.16 Reconstruction drawing of the head of Aelia Aeliana.
5.17 A balsamarium in the form of an infant bust.
5.18 Plate brooch in the form of a crow.
5.19 Bracelet made of gold and silver wire.
5.20 Roman gold objects from York.
5.21 Drawings of intaglios from the fortress baths sewer in Church Street.
5.22 Intaglio depicting Minerva.
5.23 A tettine.
5.24 Glass bottle from the grave of Corellia Optata.
5.25 Drawing of a fragment of a glass bowl from 37 Bishophill Senior.
5.26 Drawing of black rats.
6.1   Inscribed copper alloy plaques from the old station.
6.2   Reconstruction drawing of a sacrifice scene.
6.3   Altar dedicated to Arciacus.
6.4   Sheep tibia with incised representations of human figure, dog and building facades.
6.5   Statue of the god Mars.
6.6   Pipe clay figurine of Venus Anadyomene from 24 – 30 Tanner Row.
6.7   Incomplete relief of a cockerel with bags across his back, probably representing Mercury.
6.8   Head thought to be from a statue of the god Bacchus.
6.9   Altar dedicated to the Matres.
6.10 Silver ring inscribed TOT.
6.11 Relief of the god Attis.
6.12 Tablet referring to construction of a temple of Serapis.
6.13 Relief showing Mithras slaying the bull of life.
6.14 Reconstruction drawing of the Mithras relief.

6.15 Statue dedicated to Arimanius.
6.16 Ceramic antefix showing the head of Mithras.
6.17 Pot in the shape of a female head.
6.18 Jet pendant with the head of Medusa.
6.19 Greek sphinx.
7.1   Illustration of the cemetery south-west of the Roman town.
7.2   Fishergate House: cremation burial.
7.3   Drawing of an inscribed lead ossuarium.
7.4   Cremation burial under excavation at Driffield Terrace.
7.5   Child's burial from The Mount cemetery.
7.6   Tile cists from Roman cemeteries in York.
7.7   Sarcophagus with gypsum burial, from The Mount cemetery.
7.8   Sun symbol at the head of Hyllus's tombstone.
7.9   Plan of the burials at 1 – 3 Driffield Terrace.
7.10 Driffield Terrace decapitated skeleton.
7.11 Roman vault discovered 1807 on The Mount.
7.12 Furnished burial at Driffield Terrace.
8.1   An artist's impression of a Roman banquet.

Preface

Julia Velva's tombstone has been a part of my life for almost forty years. It has been my opening image in innumerable lectures on Roman York that I have given around the country. On many occasions I have stood in front of it in the Yorkshire Museum and described its finer points. Julia Velva's tombstone is my favourite object from Roman Britain and is the inspiration for this book. This is because it not only allows us to learn a little about two real, named, people in the past, Julia Velva herself and Aurelius Mercurialis, her heir, but also because it shows them to us in at least a version of their home environment, a rare contemporary representation of Roman daily life. Moreover, as I hope will become clear in the course of this book, Julia Velva's tombstone is a starting point for many different messages from York's Roman past. Finally, although it was found in 1922, nearly 100 years ago, as I write this, I can claim a direct connection with the tombstone's discovery – a sort of apostolic succession – in that an elderly gentleman who attended one of my first evening classes in the early 1980s told me that, as a small boy, he had himself seen the tombstone being raised from the ground.

The popular image of the Romans in York, as in Britain as a whole, has a strong military flavour. Mention the Romans and most people will immediately envisage men in steel body armour, wearing helmets and armed with swords and shields. Although it cannot be denied that the legionaries were a critical component of Roman York, so were families and communities made up of people occupying many different stations in life as craftworkers, labourers, shopkeepers, artists, dancers, musicians, gladiators, fortune-tellers, and so on. Some of them were, like Julia Velva herself, members of a wealthy elite similar in their outlook and values to elites all over the Roman Empire. Others belonged to the humblest and most impoverished levels of society, like a girl whose skeleton I found buried face-down in a ditch in one of my excavations. She must have been more-or-less contemporary with Julia Velva but had died aged about 14. We can only speculate about how she met her end and why she was placed with little ceremony in a remote resting place on the edge of a field. But however short a time she spent on this earth, Julia Velva's York was hers as well.

I have written about Roman York before, but this book adopts a slightly different approach in being concerned largely with the century or so between the mid-second and mid-third centuries, which would have encompassed the fifty-year lifespan of Julia Velva. This allows me to consider in a bit more detail some of the archaeological evidence from the city, especially rich for this period, than would be possible in a work that attempted to cover the whole of the Roman era.

I refer extensively to material from the excavations by York Archaeological Trust (YAT), for whom I worked for twenty-five years, and I am grateful to the trust and the current chief executive, David Jennings, for permission to use a number of illustrations from its publications and archives. Adam Raw Mackenzie and Louis Carter kindly sent those I did not already have in hand. I am also grateful to their supervisor Christine McDonnell, head of curatorial services at YAT. The book benefits from a project ('Old Collections – New Questions') at the Yorkshire Museum (part of the York Museums Trust) for which, in 2017, I compiled an overview of its huge and remarkable Roman collections. I am particularly grateful to Emily Tilley and Andrew Woods at the museum for their assistance with this book and to the York Museums Trust for permission to reproduce images of some of the more interesting and exciting objects it holds. For sending me documents and other information about their work or the work of their organisation, I am grateful to Graham Bruce (On Site Archaeology), Malin Holst, Lauren McIntyre, Ian Milsted (YAT) and Paula Ware, Malton Archaeological Projects (MAP). The plans were drawn by Lesley Collett to her usual high standard. Cecily Spall of FAS Heritage (Field Archaeology Specialists) kindly supplied three images of burials. Anthony Crawshaw supplied the splendid aerial view of the city in 1.2. Natalie Toy, York Minster, facilitated the use of 3.5 and measured the head. Images not specifically acknowledged are my own copyright. Photographs of items in the Yorkshire Museum collections taken by me are captioned 'Yorkshire Museum'.

Margaret Rogers drew my attention to the relief in her possession, appearing as 5.12. Penny Walton Rogers advised me on matters to do with the Roman loom. At Pen & Sword, thanks are due to Charlie Hewitt and Philip Sidnell for commissioning the book, and to Diane Wordsworth who did a great job as copy editor. Finally, I am enormously grateful to my friend Nick Hodgson of Tyne and Wear Museum Service who gallantly read through the whole text. Nick made many useful comments and saved me from some gross errors of fact and interpretation – those that remain are, of course, entirely my own responsibility.

This is not a book about Roman Britain as a whole. It sticks largely to themes for which York has produced good evidence. Bibliographical references for points made in the text are indicated by superscript numbers that can be cross-referred to the 'notes' section at the end of the book, along with a list of all the references. These references are not intended to be exhaustive, but are, I hope, sufficient to allow the reader to at least make a start on further research into any matters that may be of interest.

Patrick Ottaway
1 January 2020
In honour of Janus – looking back and looking forwards

Dates and periods
All dates are AD unless stated.
The dates of the principal periods referred to are:

Trajanic	98 – 117
Hadrianic	117 – 138
Early Antonine	138 – 161
Late Antonine	161 – 192
Severan	192 – 235

Chapter 1

Introduction

Julia Velva's tombstone
This is a book about Roman York (*Eburacum* or *Eboracum*), which takes as its starting point the tombstone of a lady named Julia Velva, today on display in the Yorkshire Museum.[1] As the site of a legionary fortress and a town that became a provincial capital, as well as being where two emperors passed into the next world, York was one of the most important places not only in Roman Britain but in the western empire. A summary plan of Roman York appears as 1.1, an aerial view of the modern city as 1.2 and, based on it, a reconstruction in the early third century as 1.3.

Julia Velva's tombstone is thought to date from the early third century and we would probably not be too far off the mark in saying that she died somewhere between the years 210 and 240. The inscription on the tombstone tells us that she was aged 50 at death and so she was probably born between the years 160 and 190. We can therefore think of the 'Julia Velva period', as I will call it on occasions, as having a time-span of up to about eighty years, during which time York underwent many marked changes in both its military and civilian character. From the study of her tombstone, we can say, or infer, a number of things about Julia Velva herself. By using archaeological evidence and contemporary written sources we can also say a lot about the place she lived in, about the people she might have known and about what they thought, did in their work, ate for dinner, etc. In other words, we can get a good impression of the sort of 'life' Julia Velva might have led and the sort of 'times' she might have experienced.

I am not going to confine myself to the Julia Velva period entirely, because to understand what York was like when she was alive we have to understand its history from the time a Roman Army arrived in about the year AD 71 with the intention of conquering the whole of the north of Britain. This is not only of interest to us looking back from York today, but also relevant for understanding how Julia Velva and her contemporaries thought about their own times. Just like us, the Romans took a great interest in their history, or what they believed to be their

2 Julia Velva, A Roman Lady from York

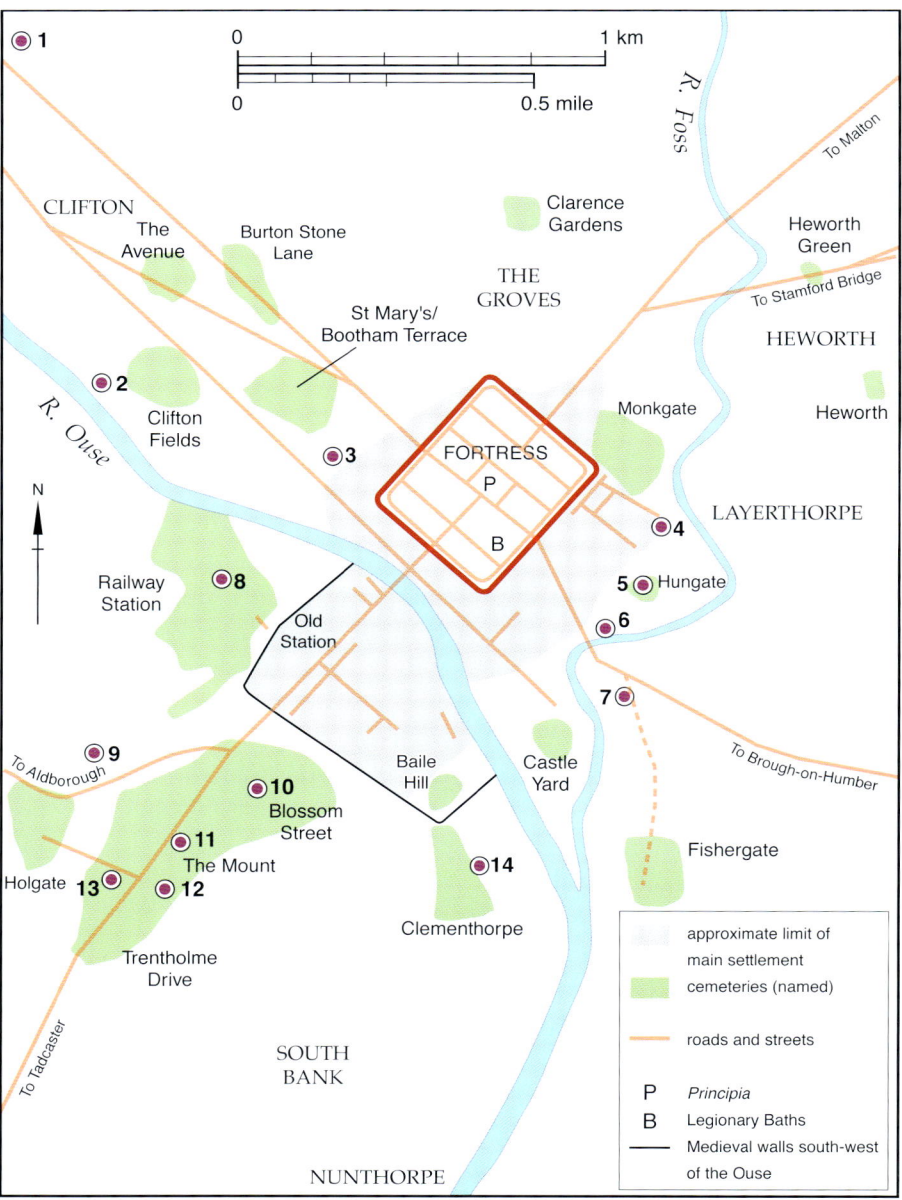

1.1: An outline plan of Roman York and its environs showing the principal areas of settlement, recorded cemeteries (named), and roads and streets, known and conjectured. Key to sites: 1, tomb of Titus Flavius Flavinus; 2, Sycamore Place (ironworking site); 3, nave of St Mary's Abbey (Roman buildings); 4, Peasholme Green (pot and tile making); 5, Hungate (cemetery); 6, Garden Place (structures); 7, St Denys Church, Walmgate (altar to Arciacus); 8, Royal York Hotel (cemetery); 9, St Paul's Green, Holgate (water pipe) and Holgate Cattle Dock (trackway); 10, 35–41 Blossom Street (cemetery); 11, 104 The Mount (burial vault); 12, Julia Velva's tombstone; 13, Driffield Terrace (cemetery); 14, Clementhorpe (Roman house).

1.2: Aerial view of York from the south-west. The River Ouse runs across the centre of the image from left to right. It is crossed by Lendal Bridge (mid-nineteenth century) on the left and by Ouse Bridge (in origin probably ninth- or tenth-century) in the centre. The Roman bridge was a little to the right of Lendal Bridge, opposite the Guildhall. York Minster, in the centre of the Roman legionary fortress, is top left. The River Foss can be seen upper right. The medieval city walls south-west of the Ouse can be seen in the lower half of the image and Micklegate Bar (city south-west gate) is lower left approached from the south-west by Blossom Street. (© A. Crawshaw)

history (although we would call some of it myth), and drew upon its example to shape their future. The works of Livy and Tacitus and other Roman authors who addressed historical subjects may well have been on the bookshelves of *Eboracum*. Important events recorded in them were no doubt commemorated. For example, one can envisage the people of York having their own version of the celebrations in Rome for the 900th anniversary of what was believed to be the foundation date of the city (in our terms 753 BC), which took place in the year AD 148.

Julia Velva's tombstone was discovered on 11 July 1922 during road-widening near the junction of The Mount and Albemarle Road on the south-west side of

4 *Julia Velva, A Roman Lady from York*

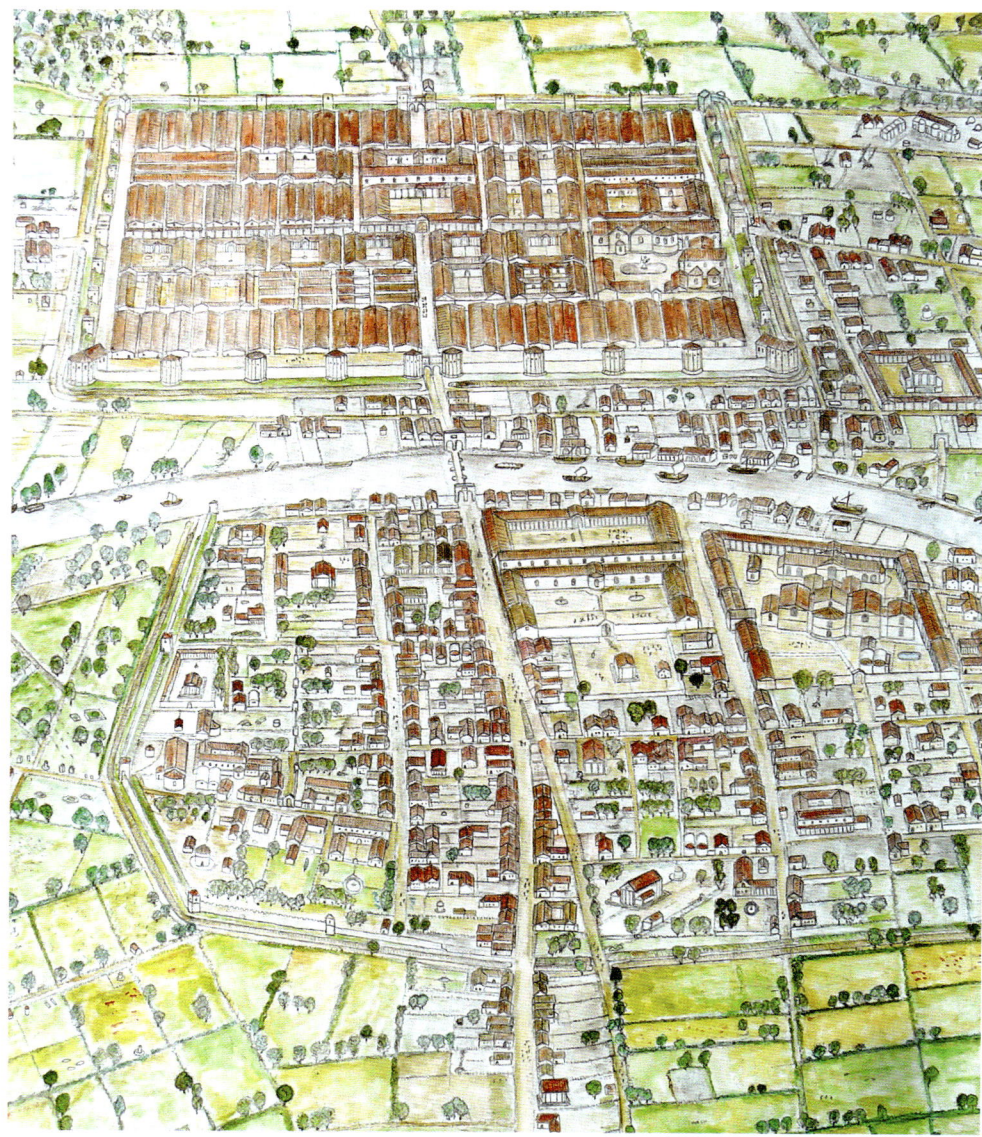

1.3: Conjectural reconstruction of Roman York from the south-west based on the photograph in 1.2. This imagines the town on the south-west bank of the Ouse at the beginning of the third century, when defences were under construction and the line of the main road from the south-west had just been moved south-eastwards onto slightly higher ground to run up to the site where Micklegate Bar now stands.

York (1.1, 12; 1.4; 2.4, 5). According to the report in the *Yorkshire Philosophical Society Annual Review*, it was '15 yards from the present highway, 3 ft 6 ins down, lying face down in two pieces'.[2] In Roman times this was a very prominent place, close to a local high point, on the south-east side of the main Roman approach road

1.4: The discovery of Julia Velva's tombstone on The Mount in 1922. (© York Museums Trust)

to York from the south-west. At some time in the past, the tombstone was either deliberately pushed over or had fallen over, fortunately before it could be defaced to any great extent as so many Roman tombstones were, probably by iconoclastic Christians.

The tombstone is 1.63m high, of which 0.23m served as a base set into the ground, 0.99m wide and 0.23m thick (1.5). It is made of millstone grit, a type of sandstone found to the west of York, which was popular with the Romans for tombstones and other monuments as well as for major buildings.[3] Originally, Julia Velva's tombstone would have caught the eye even more than it does today because, in line with usual practice, it would have been painted in bright, gaudy colours. The display face is divided into two near equal-sized parts. The upper part has a dining scene in relief and the lower part the dedicatory inscription. The dining scene, a popular subject on Roman tombstones, although there are only a few examples in Britain, may be taken to represent a version of the *silicernium*, a funeral feast given in honour of a deceased person, either at the funeral itself or a few days after it. It is shown taking place in the dining room, or *triclinium*, of a typical Roman

1.5: Julia Velva's tombstone (height 1.63m). (© York Museums Trust)

elite dwelling – *triclinium* because it would typically have accommodated three couches arranged around a semi-circular or rectangular space. The *triclinium* shown here is framed by an arch supported on either side by half-columns. In an adjoining anteroom food and drink, brought from the kitchen, would have been prepared by slaves to take into the diners. While the hosts and their guests ate and drank, musicians and dancers might have performed for their entertainment.

Julia Velva is shown, as one did in polite Roman society, reclining to dine, leaning on her left elbow. This can also be a pose expressing mourning and it may be compared with that of the god Attis on a funerary monument from York (6.11)[4] and other monuments from Gaul and the Rhineland.[5] Attis was the consort of the goddess Cybele – *Magna Mater* (the great mother) – but by the second century AD, he appears to have acquired an independent role as a protector and comforter of the dead. The pinecones at the top of the tombstone allude to Attis as he was turned into a pine tree after betraying the goddess (see p 216). The sculptor has taken trouble with Julia Velva's head and shoulders (1.6), but her lower body has been omitted. She has rather large eyes – 'windows on the soul'. Her hair is parted in the centre, and on either side one can just see surviving undulations to suggest it fell in waves over her ears before being gathered into a plait. This would have been wound around the back of her head and can just be seen projecting above it. Her hairstyle bears a resemblance to a style seen on images of Empress Julia Domna, wife of Emperor Septimius Severus (reigned 197 – 211). A similar style can be seen on the head of Aelia Aeliana, another lady of York, whose tombstone also has a dining scene (5.11).[6] An artist's impression of Julia Velva based on her image on the tombstone appears in 1.7. Usually, a couch in the *triclinium* would accommodate three people. But what is shown on Julia Velva's tombstone is probably a bed with a head and foot board – perhaps representing the bed in which she died. It stands at some height from the ground and would probably have required steps to get onto. The frame would have been strung with a web of cords that supported the thick mattress, clearly visible here.

In addition to Julia Velva herself, there are three other figures portrayed on her tombstone, making four altogether. As many as four figures is rare on Roman tombstones in Britain, but in this case may have been deliberately intended to allude to her initials IV, the Roman numeral for 4. Standing on the right of Julia Velva (her left), in front of a table, is a male figure. This is presumably Aurelius Mercurialis, named in the inscription as the person who set up the tombstone (1.8). His relationship to Julia Velva is not stated, but he was probably her husband and heir.

The face of Mercurialis is also shown with over-large eyes and he clearly has a beard and moustache. His hair is shown coming to a peak at the front in the manner of Emperor Gordian III (238 – 44) on some of his busts. On the right side of his head (visible on 1.8) his ear is much too near the top of his head, although on the left side it is anatomically correct. Mercurialis's body appears somewhat deformed in having legs rather short in relation to his torso. He wears a form of tunic with long sleeves that comes down to his knees. This is sometimes known as a 'Gallic coat' which, by the second century, was routine attire in the western empire.[7] Wrapped around Mercurialis's shoulders is a thick, heavy shawl or mantle. Here is a man prepared for a York winter. In his over-sized

(*Above*) 1.6: Julia Velva's tombstone: detail of Julia Velva's head.

(*Below*) 1.7: An artist's impression of Julia Velva based on the image on her tombstone (by Bart Ottaway)

1.8: Julia Velva's tombstone: Aurelius Mercurialis.

right hand, Mercurialis holds a scroll that may represent the will of Julia Velva and may also have been intended to proudly indicate he was literate.

On the left side of the scene a female child, perhaps about 12 years of age, is shown seated in a high-backed basketwork chair. Children sat, rather than reclined, to dine (1.9). The girl holds a bird, a symbol of childhood – the 'sweet bird of youth' to quote Tennessee Williams. Her hair is also shown parted in the centre, waved and falling to her shoulders in another style adopted by Julia Domna. To the girl's left, in the centre of the scene, is a small male figure holding a large jug in his left hand (1.10). He is clean-shaven, indicating his youth, and wears an unbelted tunic that comes to his knees. Slung across his shoulder running diagonally to the waist is a strap, perhaps to hold a bag or purse. This was an era when clothes did not have pockets. This person is probably a household slave. In the conventions of the figural art of the period, people of inferior social status were shown small in relation to their masters.

What is shown here is a high-status Roman family group from York in a room in their fine house, a semi-public room that would have been used for receiving not only friends and other guests, but clients seeking favours and assistance. The viewer is, in a sense, a guest as well, asked to pay respect to this little group who look straight out at you confident in the knowledge that they are people of some account in their community. A statement is being made not just for the time when Julia Velva's passing was commemorated, but for the future when the girl, and her siblings perhaps, will grow up and raise their own families. Tombstones like this speak about family and dynasty as much as about a particular individual. They do not, in any sense, give us accurate portraits but conform to an accepted

(*Above left*) 1.9: Julia Velva's tombstone: the girl.

(*Above right*) 1.10: Julia Velva's tombstone: the servant boy.

manner of representing people of high social status, in this case in a style that has its origins in parts of Gaul and the Rhineland from where it probably arrived in York with the army.[8]

We learn a little more about Julia Velva, and the circumstances in which the stone was set up, from the inscription in the lower half:

DM
IVLI(A)E – VELV(A)E – PIENTISSI
M(A)E – VIXIT – AN(NOS) – L – AVREL(IVS) –
MERCVRIALIS – HER(ES) – FACI
VNDVM – CVRAVIT – VIVVS –
SIBI – ET – SVIS – FECIT

Letters omitted from the words as they would have been spelled out in full are in brackets, and letters running together into one – ligatured – are underlined.

The inscription begins with the standard invocation to the Manes, spirits of the dead, with whom Julia Velva now resides, in the abbreviated form DM (DIS MANIBVS). In the first line is her name, in the dative case, followed by PIENTISSIM(A)E (also in the dative case) meaning 'very dutiful'. This is a stock epithet, found on other Roman tombstones, intended to show that the deceased conformed to a certain sort of Roman ideal of womanhood and thereby added lustre to her surviving family. The duties that a woman, in an elite household at least, was expected to perform were focused on the domestic sphere in which she catered to the needs of her husband and children. She also participated in the cult of the household *lares* (presiding spirits) and family deities (*penates*) – and so calling a woman 'dutiful' had both a secular and religious significance. If one says the words JVLIAE VELVAE PIENTISSIMAE out loud, one finds they have a certain rhythmic quality that must surely be deliberate – perhaps they were chanted at her funeral.

In the second line we are told that Julia Velva died aged 50 years. This represents quite a respectable lifespan for Roman Britain in which relatively few people lived beyond about 40. Whether Julia Velva was actually 50 is, of course, not known and in the absence of the sort of systematic recording of births we have today, some approximation may have been made. The rest of the inscription tells us that Aurelius Mercurialis set the stone up 'for himself and his heirs' (SIBI ET SVIS FECIT) while he was still alive (VIVVS). The implication is that he would be buried in same place.

Their names tell us that Julia Velva and Aurelius Mercurialis were both Roman citizens, and hence members of the upper echelons of society in *Eboracum*, because they have a family name (*nomen gentilicium* or *nomen*) followed by the familiar name (*cognomen*) by which they were known to friends and family. There was a time when male citizens usually had three names, *tria nomina*, with a *praenomen* before the family name (as in Titus Flavius Flavinus, a York centurion). However, as there were relatively few *praenomina* (hence often written as just the initial letter), their use for distinguishing one man from another was limited and so they had largely, if not entirely, fallen out of use by the end of the second century. Julia Velva's family name is Julia, the female form of Julius, a distinguished name indeed having been that of the great, and deified, Julius Caesar, although she is highly unlikely to have been his direct descendant. It is more likely that she was the descendant of someone who had become a citizen in Julius Caesar's time, perhaps as a freed slave. Alternatively, she might have been someone who had, herself, been freed from slavery, becoming a 'freedwoman' and taken her master's family name. In any event, Julia Velva may well have known, and taken pride in the fact, that the Julii claimed to be descended from Venus through Aeneas, son of the goddess, who, as Virgil's *Aeneid* tells us, played a key role in the foundation of Rome. Velva, Julia Velva's *cognomen*, is thought to be a British ('Celtic') name, which suggests she was a local girl, quite possibly the daughter of a native woman and a legionary veteran.[9]

Aurelius Mercurialis's family name, Aurelius, suggests he, or his father, had acquired citizenship, probably following army service, in the reign of either Marcus Aurelius (161 – 80) or his son Commodus (177 – 92). It was common practice for anyone receiving citizenship to take the family name of the ruling emperor of the time, considered, in a sense, as their patron. If he had acquired citizen status, rather than inheriting it, Mercurialis would have been born with just this one name, being what the Romans referred to as a *peregrinus*, literally a 'foreigner'. Once a citizen, he would have still been known to friends as Mercurialis, but he would have proudly used his two names in the public arena. By naming him Mercurialis his parents had probably hoped to put him under the protection of the god, Mercury, from whom he might acquire some of his qualities as messenger of the gods and the patron of commerce.

Finally, we might look at how the inscription as it is displayed on the tombstone has been structured in terms of numeric patterns based on square numbers. Julia Velva's name – IVLIE VELVE – is displayed as nine (3^2) letters and there are eighty-one (9^2) letters altogether (if the DM formula is ignored and ligatured letters are counted as 1). There are sixteen (4^2) words and the letter I, first letter of Julia Velva's name in Latin, occurs sixteen times. Why these patterns were included is not clear, but it may be to do with the desire to create an inscription with the sort of harmonious character that would appeal to the gods.

Although it might appear quite crudely executed ('provincial') when compared to some of the beautifully carved Roman examples from the Mediterranean world, Julia Velva's tombstone is, nonetheless, a complex and sophisticated composition in terms of what it tells us in visual and written form about the society of which the people depicted were members and about the values and aspirations that governed how they saw themselves and how they behaved. The tombstone is, therefore, an ideal starting point for an investigation of Roman York in the late second and early third centuries, when our couple was amongst its residents.

In the next chapter (2), I shall describe how the York that Julia Velva and Aurelius Mercurialis knew had developed since the Ninth Legion arrived in AD 71. This requires, first of all, a consideration of York's natural environment, critical to our understanding of why the Romans chose York as a base in the first place and of what role it adopted subsequently in the economy and society of its region and of Britain as a whole. This is followed by a summary account of the first century or so of Roman York's history and a description of its topography and built environment, both military and civilian in this period. In Chapter 3, we look at the York in which our couple grew up and lived their lives, beginning with historical background, and then returning to the themes of topography and buildings. In Chapter 4, I shall cover aspects of the economy of Roman York, in terms of both production and trade, the latter illustrating its particularly extensive connections with the wider world in the Julia Velva period. The next chapter (5) discusses the character and composition of Roman provincial society in *Eboracum* and looks at aspects of daily life such as education, dress and hairstyles, and diet and health. Worthy of a chapter on its own is the subject of religion in Roman York. We have already seen that Julia Velva's tombstone has its sacred aspect and, as such, it is a good starting point for reviewing the abundant evidence for belief and cult practice. The links between religion and burial take us back once more to the place where Julia Velva's tombstone was discovered in the heart of one of Roman York's great cemeteries (1.1, 12). Starting from here we will look at the history of the cemeteries and at what we know about burial practice. Finally, in my last chapter, I will draw together some of the themes of the book and speculate on what our lady of Roman York might be like if we were to meet her.

Sources of evidence

In its role as a contemporary written document and as an archaeological artefact, Julia Velva's tombstone is an important piece of evidence for Roman York. However, before concluding this chapter, a brief review of all the sources of evidence, and how they have been studied, is in order to remind us of how we know what we know about the city in the Julia Velva period itself – and in earlier and later times as well.

The earliest contemporary written source directly relevant to Roman York (as *Eburacum*) is in the form of the addresses on two wooden writing tablets, which date to *c*. 95 – 105, from the fort at Vindolanda on the northern frontier.[10] York itself has produced a number of inscriptions of various dates, largely on stone, but also on other media. The inscriptions on stone are usually funerary, on tombstones and sarcophagi, or religious, mostly on altars dedicated to the gods and goddesses, some classical, others local. Other common forms of inscription from York include stamps on the tiles made in the legionary kilns, and makers' names, or initials, on pottery vessels and other artefacts. There are also examples of owners' names and there are some informal graffiti, some in the form of names, others less readily intelligible.

More generally relevant to York, although hardly ever mentioning it by name, is a great range of contemporary literary sources, notably the works of some of the Roman historians. They include Cornelius Tacitus (*c*. 55 – 120), author of *The Annals*, *The Histories* and *The Agricola* (biography of his father-in-law and governor of Britain c. 78 – 84), which cover the first century AD from the reign of Augustus until about the year 84. Also important is Cassius Dio (c.150 to 235), who wrote a history of Rome from its foundation to the year 229, although much of his work is lost and we rely largely on an eleventh-century 'epitome' (abstract) of his text. Belonging to a similar period as Dio is another Greek speaker, Herodian, who wrote a history of the Roman Empire for the years 180 – 238, i.e. from the death of Emperor Marcus Aurelius to the reign of Gordian I. Like Dio, Herodian did not know Britain first-hand but makes some references to events here. The reliability of Tacitus, Dio and others for events in Britain and elsewhere is usually difficult to assess, although they do create a very compelling picture of the imperial court and its violent and unpredictable character. The same may be said of *The Augustan History* (*Historia Augusta*), probably written in the fourth century and structured as biographies of all the Roman emperors from Hadrian to Numerian (117 to 284).[11]

If we move on from historical to geographical sources, we should note the work of the Greek-speaking Egyptian, Ptolemy, active in the years c.140 – 60, who compiled a geography of the Roman Empire, which includes Britain.[12] Ptolemy provides a list of place names, including York as *Eboracum*, and is one of the principal sources for the names and locations of the territories occupied by the native peoples of Britain. Also of a geographical character are itineraries, or 'road books', intended for use by the army and imperial postal service, the *cursus publicus*. The most comprehensive, as far as Britain is concerned, is the early third-century *Antonine Itinerary* (named after Emperor Antoninus – usually known as 'Caracalla').[13] It lists place names in the empire arranged along the main roads and gives distances between them. For Britain there are fifteen itineraries. Roman York's importance as a centre for communications is shown by its location on four of them.

As far as other Roman literature is concerned, one might reasonably ask how relevant much of it is for the study of York or indeed for Britain as a whole. *Britannia* was, after all, a province that was very different in terms of its culture, economy and society from the lands around the Mediterranean. However, York, more than most other places, either in its region or in Britain as a whole, apart from London and a few other towns, had a population in the Roman period that included many people who originated and/or had lived and travelled in the imperial heartlands whether as soldiers, administrators and merchants or as their wives and families. References to the works of Ovid, Petronius, Pliny the Elder, Virgil and other classical authors can therefore, I suggest, contribute meaningfully to the story of Roman York in a way that they would not, perhaps, to that of the rural farmsteads in the region where life went on much as it had before the conquest.

As far as the archaeology is concerned, all that survives above ground today to represent Roman York are a few remains of the fortress defences. Most important are the west corner tower, the Multangular Tower, and associated stretches of fortress wall to be seen in the Museum Gardens (2.14 and 2.17). Another fragment of wall can be seen nearby in St Leonard's Place and a bit of the north-west gate is visible below the floor of a café close to the medieval Bootham Bar. At the east corner of the fortress one can see the wall and remains of an interval tower, which were exposed in excavations in 1926 (3.8). Everything else archaeological that bears on the history of Roman York has been found below ground, whether in formal excavation, during digging by workmen for cellars, sewers and other utilities, or as chance finds in a variety of circumstances.

The buried remains are made up firstly of abandoned stone and timber structures in varying states of incompleteness, secondly of features such as ditches, pits and graves dug into the ground, and thirdly of a vast number of superimposed deposits, or strata, composed variously of such things as building debris, domestic and industrial refuse, garden soil and naturally accumulating silts and sands. All of this material is testimony to the intensity of human activity in the city in the Roman period and to the intervention, from time to time, of natural forces. Within the historic core of York, i.e. within much of the city that was walled in medieval times, there is typically a depth below modern ground level of about 3m to 5m, and in places more, of archaeological remains of which, roughly speaking, the lowest 1m to 3m is Roman. In peripheral parts of the historic core and in suburban areas there is usually rather less depth and sometimes all that survives are features – pits, ditches, etc. – that have been cut into the natural geology.

Where the remains of the Roman period are deeply buried, they have usually been well-protected from damage by modern intrusions. In addition, a factor favouring the preservation of archaeological deposits and the material they contain arises from the city's low-lying situation, which means that it has been greatly affected by a gradual rise in the water table. In certain parts of the city, especially close to the rivers, the ground has therefore become subject to waterlogging. This inhibits the usual processes of decay, which require oxygen, and allows the remarkable and unusual survival of organic materials from timber buildings to leather shoes as well as human and animal bones, plant material and even insects. In addition, the Roman deposits at York produce vast quantities of the sort of artefactual material one would expect from any settlement of the period. In terms of bulk, the principal components are pottery, building materials (such as stonework, tiles and plaster), and industrial waste (such as metalworking slag). Small finds occur in all the metals (although rarely gold) as well as in bone and ivory, wood, glass, jet, stone and ceramics.

Roman York has been the subject of study since the seventeenth century, often by scholars of national as well as purely local reputation. Any artefacts recovered in the early years usually ended up in private collections. However, in 1827 the Yorkshire Museum was opened by the Yorkshire Philosophical Society for the edification of the general public by the display of antiquities, many of them Roman. Today the museum is the principal archive in the city for archaeological material of all periods as well as having extensive galleries devoted to the Roman period.

The first history of Roman York, *Eboracum or the History and Antiquities of the City of York*, was written by a York surgeon, Francis Drake (1696 – 1771) in 1736. It includes material previously published by others and new material arising from his own observations. Just over 100 years later, in 1842, the subject was revisited by Charles Wellbeloved, a Unitarian minister and first honorary curator of the Yorkshire Museum. His *Eburacum or York under the Romans* was based both on previous discoveries and his own first-hand observations in the city at the beginning of a great period of redevelopment stimulated, in part at least, by the arrival of the railways. A few line drawings from Wellbeloved's *Eburacum* are reproduced in this volume. In 1924, Gordon Home published his *Roman York*, a useful survey of the evidence, primarily the material in the Yorkshire Museum collections. Home also made an appeal for proper archaeological excavations in the city that might, for example, solve the problem of whether there were Roman defences around the town south-west of the Ouse. This remains an unanswered question (see pp 88–9), but the first formal excavations in York took place shortly after Home's book appeared, in 1925 – 7 under the direction of Stuart Miller (1880 – 1952), a lecturer in Roman History and Archaeology at Glasgow University, on behalf of the newly formed York Excavation Committee.[14] Miller's work had as its principal objective the study of the Roman fortress defences with a view to determining the sequence of their construction.

Since Miller (except during the Second World War), there has been a regular programme of archaeological excavations in York which, in the 1950s and 1960s, were largely focused on investigating the Roman period. A great landmark in the study of the subject arrived in 1962 when the Royal Commission on Historical Monuments for England (RCHME) published *Eburacum*. This was the commission's first volume of its great inventory of York's historic monuments, which tells us in its own words (p xxv):

> ... *we have recorded the remains of 61 monuments including the legionary fortress with its defences, streets and internal buildings as one monument. Further we have described 154 Roman inscriptions, sculptured stones and architectural fragments and listed some 500 Roman burials.*

Ten years later, the pace of excavation picked up considerably following the foundation of the York Archaeological Trust in 1972. Research arising from the trust's work at sites including 9 Blake Street in the legionary fortress, and 24 – 30 Tanner Row and Wellington Row in the Roman town south-west of the Ouse, forms the basis for much of this book. In addition to excavation, the trust was involved in many of the developments in research methods that are now standard in archaeology, including environmental archaeology or the study of biological material preserved in archaeological deposits.[15] The trust has also pioneered the study of artefacts and human remains with cutting-edge scientific techniques. Most recently, in connection with the remarkable burials, largely of decapitated males, found at Driffield Terrace on The Mount (1.1, 13), the trust sponsored the examination of dental enamel and relict DNA, which has cast new light on the origins of the population of Roman York (pp 176–9).

In 1990, Planning Policy Guidance Note 16, a new government policy statement on how archaeology should be dealt with in the local authority planning process, reiterated most recently as the revised National Planning Policy Framework in 2018,[16] has resulted in a further surge in the amount of archaeological excavation in York. Some form of fieldwork can now be expected in advance of almost all new developments in the city. Compared to what RCHME had available to it in 1962, the database we now have for the study of Roman York is hugely increased. Some of the highlights of recent work will appear in our pursuit of Julia Velva's York.

Chapter 2

The making of Julia Velva's York: legionary fortress and civilian settlement

A map of the York region showing Roman roads and the location of other Roman sites and places may be found on 2.1. Sites referred to in the legionary fortress may be found on 2.2 and in the civilian settlements north-east and

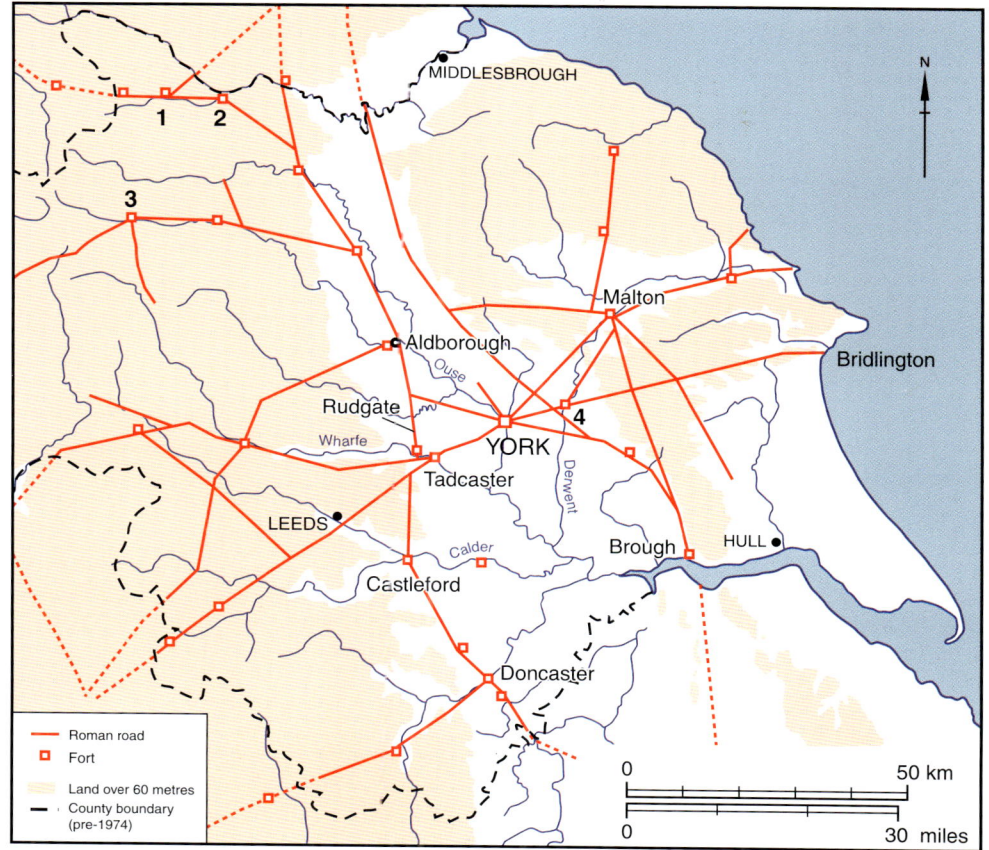

2.1: Map showing the York region with Roman roads and other Roman sites (Hull, Leeds and Middlesbrough shown for location only). Key: 1, Bowes; 2, Greta Bridge; 3, Bainbridge; 4, Stamford Bridge.

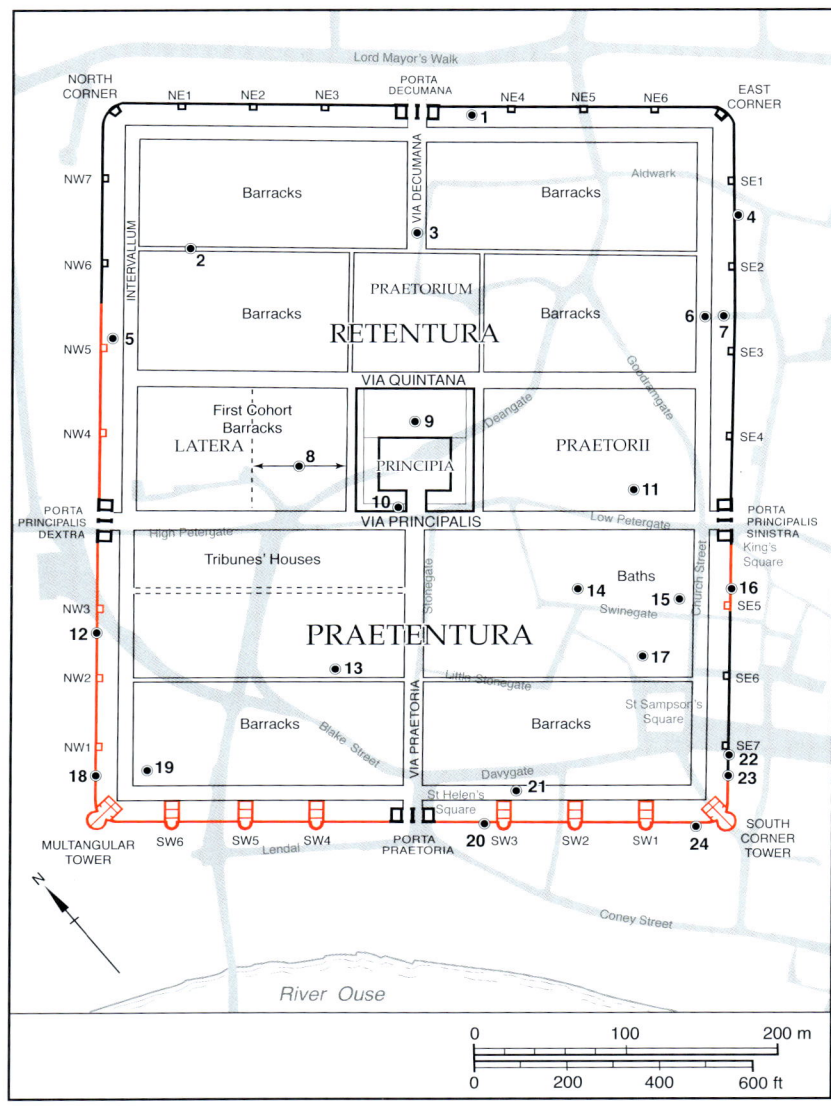

2.2: Plan of the legionary fortress at York with sites referred to in the text (date of discovery in brackets). Note that the numbering of the stone interval towers is taken from RCHME'S *Eburacum*. Key: 1, Gray's Court (*intervallum* building, 1860 – 1); 2, minster library (street and barracks, 1997); 3, treasurer's house (*via decumana*, 1954); 4, Hawarden Place (defences,1925); 5, Dean's Park (defences and *intervallum* building, 1927); 6, Bedern (*intervallum* street, 1974 – 5); 7, Bedern well (1975); 8, minster excavations (first cohort barracks, 1966 – 73); 9, minster excavations (headquarters building, 1966 – 73); 10, St Michael le Belfry Church (column bases, 1892); 11, Low Petergate (buildings, 1957 – 8); 12, St Leonard's Place (defences, 1835); 13, 9 Blake Street (barracks and other buildings, 1975); 14, 12 – 18 Swinegate (baths, 1989 – 90); 15, 4 – 5 Church Street (baths building and sewer, 1972); 16, King's Square (defences, 1957 and 1963); 17, Roman Bath pub (baths,1930 – 1); 18, defences near NW1 (1970); 19, public library (barrack building, 1925); 20, Coney Street (defences, 1955); 21, Davygate Arcade (defences and barracks,1955 – 8); 22, Parliament Street sewer trench (defences, 1976); 23, 16 Parliament Street (defences,1987); 24, Feasegate (defences,1955 – 57).

The making of Julia Velva's York: legionary fortress and civilian settlement

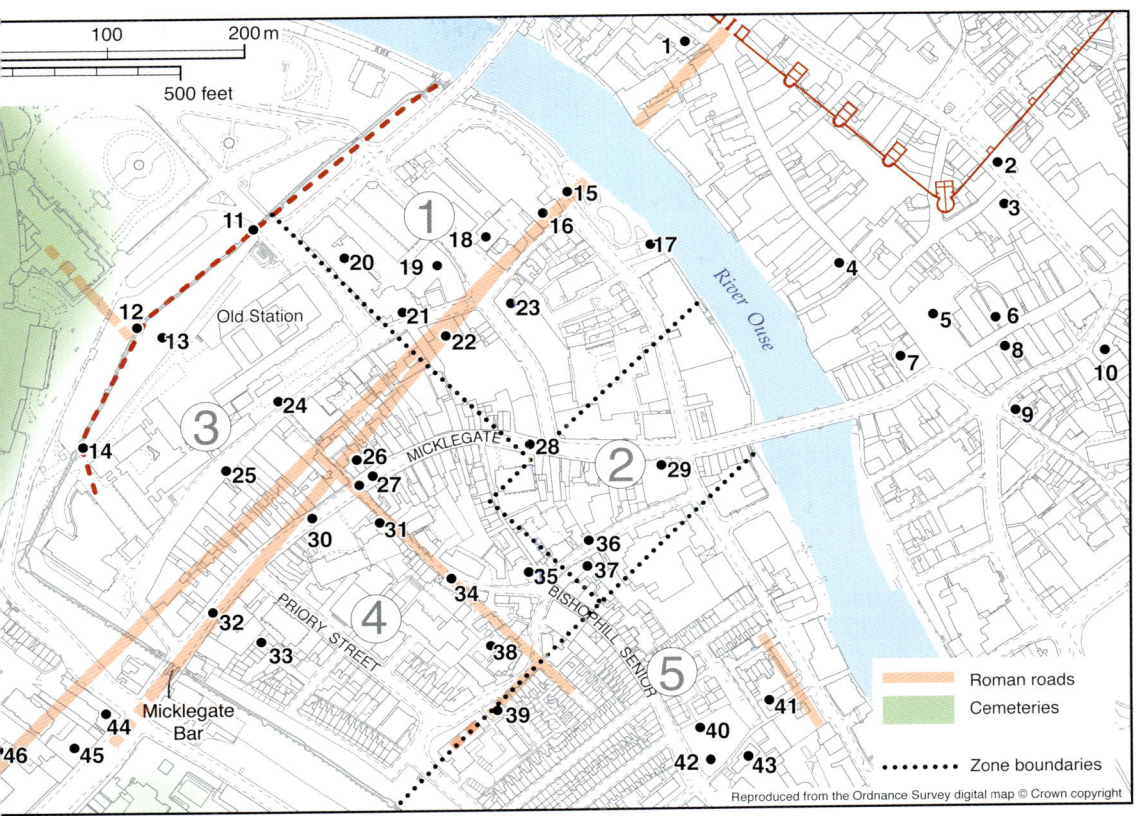

2.3: Plan showing the location of sites referred to in the text north-east and south-west of the Ouse (date of discovery in brackets; base map © Crown Copyright). Key: (**NE**) 1, Lendal Post Office (building, 1883); 2, Parliament Street sewer trench (fortress defences, 1976); 3, corner of Parliament Street and Market Street (building, altar,); 4, 39 – 41 Coney Street (warehouse, street); 5, Spurriergate (buildings, 1959, 2000 – 05); 6, High Ousegate (building, 1977); 7, St Michael Spurriergate; 8, 25 – 7 High Ousegate (buildings, 1902 – 3); 9, 1 – 3 Nessgate and street Nessgate (inscriptions and column, 1839 and 1925); 10, 16 – 22 Coppergate (glassmaking, 1976 – 81); (**SW**) 11, Roman town wall (1874); 12, Roman town wall (1939); 13, Roman building at LNER wartime facility (1939); 14, Roman town wall (1839); 15, North Street (Roman bridgehead, 1893); 16, Wellington Row (Roman road and buildings, 1987 – 90); 17, North Street pumping station (waterfront structure, 1993); 18, 5 Rougier Street (street and buildings, 1981); 19, 24 – 30 Tanner Row (buildings, 1983 – 4); 20, Grand Hotel, Trench 1 (2013); 21, North-Eastern Railway offices and Grand Hotel (buildings, 1901 and 2013); 22, 27 Tanner Row (Roman road, 1971); 23, Co-op, George Hudson Street (column bases, 1898); 24, Toft Green (buildings, 1770, 1840 and 2011); 25, Toft Green (Roman house, 1853); 26, 78 – 82 Micklegate (street, 1821); 27, sewer trench at 78 Micklegate (buildings, 1946); 28, Micklegate (relief of Mithras, 1747, and building, 1853); 29, 1 – 9 Micklegate (bath house, 1989); 30, 88 – 90 Micklegate, (street and altars, 1752); 31, Jacob's Well (column bases, 1895 – 1901); 32, opposite 138 Micklegate (street metalling, 1992); 33, former Kennings Garage (building, 2000); 34, Trinity Lane (street, 1995); 35, 12 St Martin's Lane (building, 1947 and 1993 – 4); 36, Fetter Lane (baths, 1852); 37, Fetter Lane (building and terrace, 2000); 38, St Mary Bishophill Junior (building, 1961 – 3 and 1967); 39, Bishophill Junior (building and street, 1961 – 2); 40, 37 Bishophill Senior (house and terrace, 1973 – 4); 41, 58 – 9 Skeldergate (street and well, 1973 – 4); 42, St Mary Bishophill Senior (house, 1964); 43, Friends' Burial Ground (building, 1973); 44, corner Queen Street and Blossom Street (buildings, 1826); 45, 14 – 20 Blossom Street (buildings and road, 1991 and 1994); 46, 18 – 22 Blossom Street (road and building, 1953 – 4).

south-west of the Ouse on 2.3. Other sites in and around York appear on 1.1 and 2.4. Another source of geographical information on Roman York is the York *Historic Town Atlas* published in 2015.

Landscape and environment

By the time Julia Velva was born, probably sometime after the year 160, York had been Roman for about 100 years. It had become well-established as a military base and was about to become a major urban centre. Originally York, about 300km north of London, was most likely chosen by the Roman Army for its strategic location. It lies in the middle of a lowland zone, the Vale of York, which continues northwards becoming the Vale of Mowbray, extending as far as the River Tees. York is also about 60km from the sea to the east, which is reached by means of the River Ouse and the Humber Estuary. Today the journey from London to York can take just under two hours by train but in Roman times, even at what became a communications hub of roads and rivers, York would have been quite isolated by its distance from other towns and military bases. On the swiftest horse, or by ship, it is unlikely that *Londinium* (London) could have been reached in much less than two or three days. Nevertheless, York, as we shall see, was in touch with the rest of the Roman world, its ideas and pre-occupations, and had access to its material culture in a way denied to almost all of the rest of northern Britain except the Hadrian's Wall zone. At the same time, however, most of *Eboracum*'s day-to-day needs had to be supplied locally and understanding the advantages, and challenges, of the local landscape was critical for the legionary commanders and provincial governors based here.

The landscape of York: its ups and downs

Illustration 2.4 shows the relief geography of the York area. It will be immediately apparent that the landscape is largely low-lying. At the top of what we know today as The Mount, where Julia Velva's tombstone once stood (2.4, 5), we are, as the name implies, almost as high as it gets in the city at *c.* 21m above sea level. Extending to the north-west and south-east is a ridge from which the land falls away towards the medieval walled city and River Ouse to the north-east, and to some of York's outer suburbs to the south-west. This ridge is part of the York moraine, composed of material deposited by retreating glaciers at the end of the last Ice Age about 10,000 years ago.[1] An outlier of the moraine, on which the legionary fortress once stood, lies on the north-east bank of the Ouse where natural ground level is at mostly between *c.* 12m and 14m above sea level. A simplified cross-section of the valley of the River Ouse through the centre of York appears in 2.5. It is on the line of the main Roman approach road from the south-west, between a point near Micklegate Bar and York Minster, showing natural and modern ground levels and Roman and modern river levels. The cross-section shows, in particular, how the land, in what

The making of Julia Velva's York: legionary fortress and civilian settlement 21

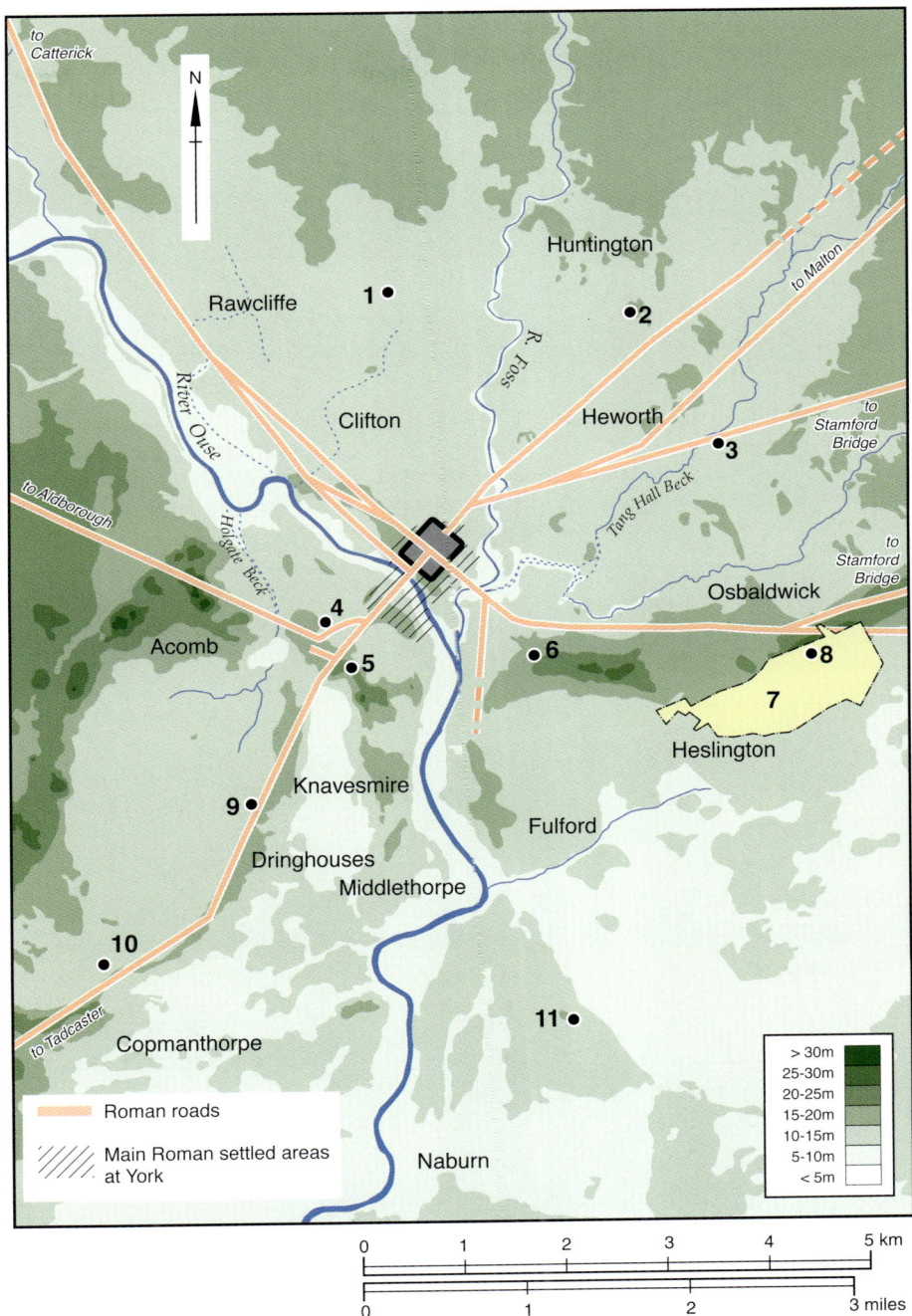

2.4: Relief map of the York area with the principal Roman roads (© York Archaeological Trust). Key: 1, Roman camps on Bootham Stray; 2, Roman camps on Huntington South Moor; 3, Appletree Farm, Heworth (Roman road); 4, St Paul's Green (water pipe); 5, site of Julia Velva's tombstone; 6, Belle Vue Street (trackway); 7, Heslington East; 8, Kimberlow Hill; 9, Starting Gate, Dringhouses (buildings); 10, Askham Bog; 11, Lingcroft Farm, Naburn.

22 *Julia Velva, A Roman Lady from York*

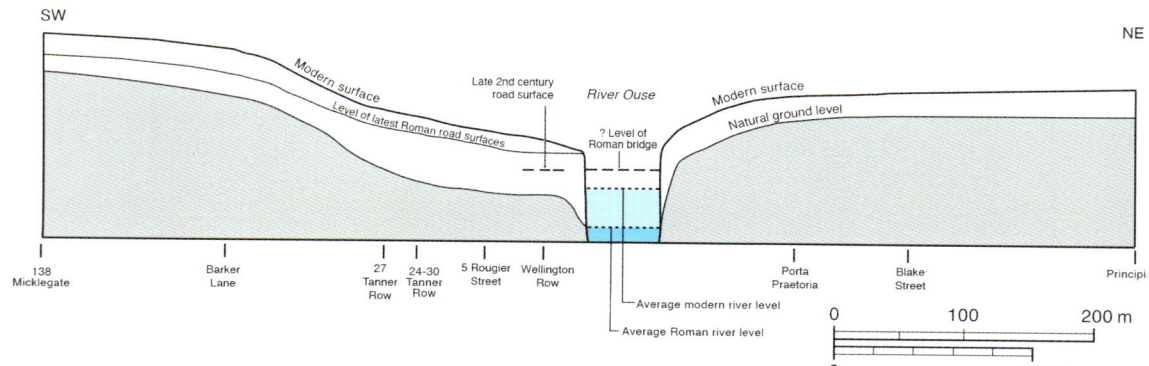

2.5: Simplified cross-section across the valley of the Ouse at York (with location plan) from near Micklegate Bar (south-west) to York Minster, legionary fortress headquarters basilica (north-east), along the (original) line of the main Roman road from the south-west and the *via praetoria* showing approximate ground and river levels in the Roman period and present day. Levels were taken from sites shown on the plan with open circles. (© York Archaeological Trust)

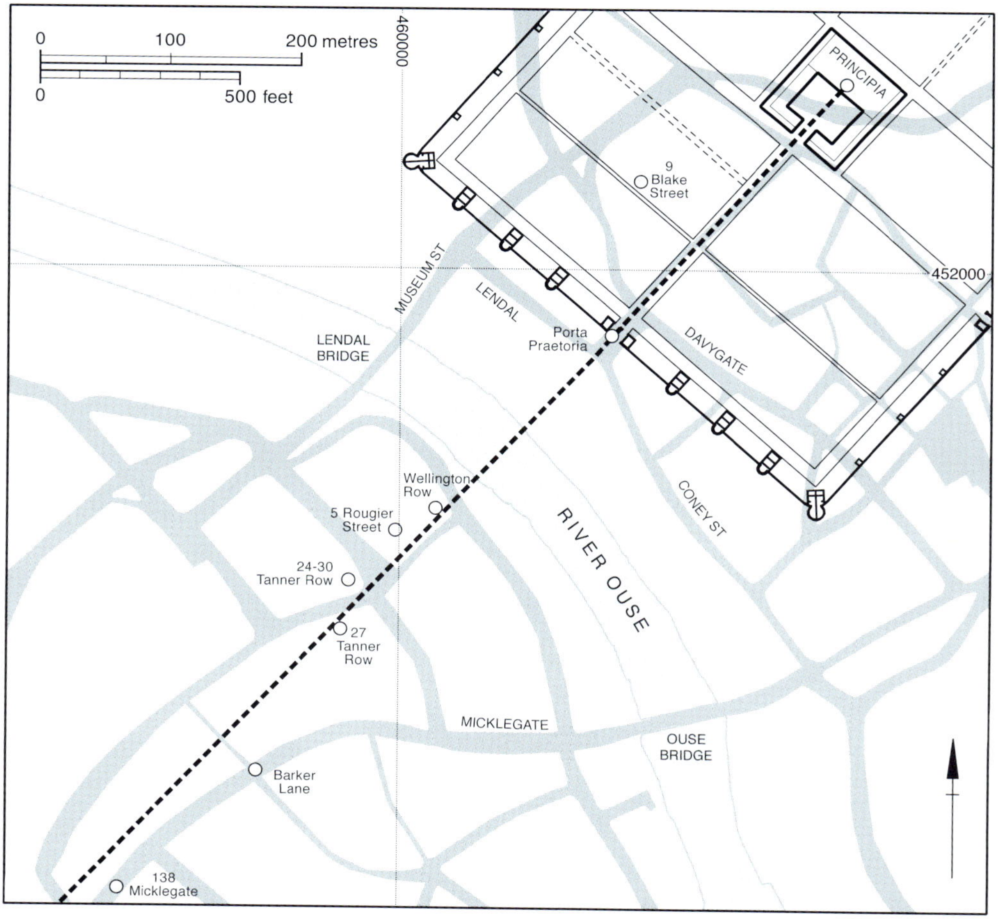

would become the principal urban area (see p 87) rises fairly sharply from a river terrace on the south-west bank of the Ouse. Some comments on the river level follow.

The moraine is cut by the River Ouse just to the south of its confluence with the River Foss. The moraine then runs eastwards for *c.* 3.5km, reaching a high point of 32m above sea level at Kimberlow Hill (2.4, 8). Beyond here the moraine runs as far as Stamford Bridge on the River Derwent, 12km to the east of York (2.1, 4). To the north-west of The Mount the moraine runs for *c.* 700m before it is cut by Holgate Beck and it then picks up again to run on to Acomb, now a York suburb. Another arm of the moraine runs south-west to Dringhouses then to the village of Copmanthorpe before continuing towards the town of Tadcaster, thereby providing suitable raised ground for the main Roman road to York (see pp 54–6).

The York moraine, and the Escrick moraine to the south of the city, were formed at the southern edge of the Vale of York glacier by 13,000 BP (before present – late in the Devensian period).[2] Beyond the ice limit lay Lake Humber, created by ice blocking the Humber Estuary. The lake survived until about 11,000 BP, after which it drained into the Humber leaving thick deposits of glacio-lacustrine clay overlying the Triassic sandstone that forms the solid geology of much of the Vale of York.[3] In addition to clay there is, as a result of glacial action, a varied pattern of Quaternary ('drift') deposits in the York area including sands and gravels that were more suitable than the clay for early arable agriculture. In the river valleys there are alluvial deposits of clay, silt and sand. The moraine itself is quite variable in its geological character. In excavations (2007 – 11) at the site of a new university campus at Heslington East (2.4, 7), *c.*3km east of the city centre, it was shown that impermeable boulder clay is overlain by sands and gravels and at the junction between them there are springs that account for a long history of settlement in the prehistoric and Roman periods.[4] In places on the moraine there are kettle holes where buried blocks of ice melted leaving a void that filled up with peat. This formed a resource used for fuel in Roman times.[5] Peat would also have been found in a raised bog south-west of York, immediately to the north of the moraine at Askham, which was formed in a lake left behind by the retreating glaciers (2.4, 10).

The picture we now have of the York area as a result of aerial photography and archaeological fieldwork is one of a well-populated landscape in the late prehistoric period in which the population adopted an agricultural regime based on arable and stock rearing. There would also have been extensive areas of woodland in the Vale of York in both the prehistoric and Roman periods. What was known in medieval and later times as the Forest of Galtres to the north-west of York, lying between the Ouse and upper reaches of the Foss, came, until fairly recently, to within a few kilometres of the city.[6] However, 'woodland' does not mean impenetrable forest, but a varied landscape of pasture, used for grazing stock, and stands of trees that were actively managed for timber and other materials.

Rivers and floods

Fertile alluvial deposits in the valleys of the Rivers Ouse and Foss were composed of silty material washed down from higher ground upstream. Areas close to the rivers might have been at risk of flooding, especially in winter, but rather different environmental and topographical conditions in the York area may mean that this was less of a hazard in Roman times than it has been recently.[7] Average rainfall in the city today is *c*. 600mm per annum, perhaps not much different to what it was in the Roman period. But it is, and was, much greater in the Pennine Dales to the west. Today the level of the River Ouse rises rapidly after heavy rainfall, primarily because of the volume of water flowing down to York from the dales where there is now relatively limited tree cover to impede run-off. Another factor in the history of the river regime at York is that, although its course is much the same, the channel of the Ouse is more confined than it once was as a result of encroachment by riverside facilities and buildings. This process began in Roman times and continued in the medieval and later periods and so is another reason why, today, any excess water comes up over the riverbanks whereas in earlier times it could spread out into a flood plain.

As far as the River Foss is concerned, its course through the city in the Roman period is uncertain due to two major post-Roman developments. In the first it was dammed at the castle after the Norman conquest, creating a great area of open water, the King's Fishpool, and secondly, it was canalised at the end of the eighteenth century.[8] Nonetheless, it is likely that the Roman river's course in the city centre is not that different from what it is today, although it was probably wider.

Finally, when we attempt to compare the rivers at York today with what they were like in earlier times we must remember that, until the mid-eighteenth century, they were tidal. Since then the river level has been artificially maintained at an average mean summer level of *c*. 5m above sea level by locks *c*. 6km downstream at Naburn.[9] However, Julia Velva would have seen rivers that had an average summer level as much as 3.5m below the present-day average. We know this because archaeological excavations on sites adjacent to the south-west bank of the Ouse, in the centre of the city, have produced evidence for Roman structures at as low as 2 – 2.5m above sea level. On the Foss, on a site opposite the castle, a Roman cobbled surface was found at only *c*. 1.50m above sea level, at a depth of 8.70m below the modern ground surface.[10]

Environment and climate

While rainfall in Roman York may have been about the same as it is today (*c*. 600mm), average summer temperatures could have been a bit higher. In recent times (1981 – 2010) Met Office data shows that the warmest months,

July and August, had an average temperature of 20 – 21°C. However, several species of bug (the term used in its correct entomological sense) found in a well filled up in the late second century – the 'Bedern well' (2.2, 7) – on the fortress defences would (in 1986) have been outside their present range in Britain.[11] This suggests that the average July temperature in Roman York was at least 1° higher, making the city more like the south-east of England in terms of climate.

Whether flooding was a problem or not, the banks of the Ouse were, when the Roman Army arrived, probably either pasture for sheep and cattle or simply left untended. The evidence comes from the well-preserved organic remains of plants, insects and molluscs found in the earliest deposits on archaeological sites. South-west of the river at 58 – 9 Skeldergate (2.3, 41)[12] and 24 – 30 Tanner Row (2.3, 19),[13] *c.* 50m and *c.* 120m respectively from the present bank, extensive deposit sampling produced remarkable data sets that suggested the existence of a natural ecology very like that which prevails upstream of the city today (2.6). Many of the plant taxa represented at Tanner Row were rather low-growing, indicating trampled or grazed land. Small mollusca were consistent with damp meadows

2.6: The banks of the River Ouse upstream from York at Clifton in May 2018.

or well-drained pasture. There were also aquatic insect species usually found in sluggish streams or muddy pools, and beetles that lived on herbivore dung, probably deposited by cattle grazing in the vicinity. Pollen preserved in a buried soil at 58 – 9 Skeldergate, radiocarbon-dated to the late first century AD,[14] suggested plants of rough pasture on land not close-cropped by sheep. Close to the opposite bank of the Ouse a buried soil at 39 – 41 Coney Street (2.3, 4) produced pollen of grassland and of hazel and alder, suggesting areas of scrub.[15] In amongst the trees on the river banks there may well have been an appreciable number of yews (*Taxus baccata*), as one interpretation of the place name for York (*Eboracum* or *Eburacum*) is that it derives from a native name meaning the 'place of the yew trees'.[16] Alternatively, the name may refer to a local leader named 'Eburos'.

The Roman conquest and the legionary fortress at York

It was into a landscape of small farming settlements, scattered largely on the better land for agriculture, that the Roman Army arrived in about the year AD 71. However, it was while sheep tended by native shepherds were still safely grazing on the banks of the Ouse that the conquest of Britain by the Romans had begun in AD 43, in the reign of Emperor Claudius (AD 41 – 54).

In Claudius's reign there had, according to Tacitus, been two sorties into the north of England, in AD 48 and then in AD 51 – 2.[17] In the latter the Roman governor Didius Gallus may have set up a temporary base at York, thereby giving the army some advance information about the site ahead of the conquest twenty years later. By the beginning of the reign of Emperor Nero (54 – 68), most of Britain south of a line roughly between the River Mersey and Humber Estuary had become part of the Roman province of *Britannia*. In the north the two native peoples named in Ptolemy's Geography, the Brigantes, who occupied most of the land as far as the Scottish Lowlands, and the Parisi, in what is now the East Riding of Yorkshire, remained nominally independent, although probably as client kingdoms. A client kingdom was a very particular sort of political entity cultivated and sponsored by the Roman Empire on its frontiers during the expansionist phase of the late republican and early imperial periods. In exchange for remaining independent and benefitting from Roman protection, a client ruler was expected to agree that on his/her death Rome would succeed to and incorporate the kingdom into the empire.

In AD 60 – 1 the Roman imperial enterprise in Britain nearly came to a halt following the forced and violent annexation of the East Anglian client kingdom of the Iceni, which resulted in the revolt of Queen Boudicca. Eventually she was defeated by a Roman Army under the general Suetonius Paullinus.[18] However, there was no further Roman advance in Britain until the reign of Emperor Vespasian (69 – 79). Like Claudius before him, Vespasian needed a victory or two to gain legitimacy as emperor in the eyes of other leading families and potential rivals in Rome. His eye fell upon northern Britain, where he presumably thought that conquest would be relatively easy as the Britons were not regarded as very sophisticated militarily in terms of armaments or organisation. Furthermore, there was merit to be acquired by finishing a project left incomplete by previous emperors, a project that was, moreover, associated with Julius Caesar himself.

As we understand it from Tacitus, the occasion of the Roman invasion of the north was a flare-up of a dispute in the royal house of the Brigantes between Queen Cartimandua, a client ruler who had good relations with Rome, and her former consort Venutius, who opposed the Roman advance.[19] However, the danger of a hostile leader in the north would only have been a pretext for further imperial expansion in Britain. Unfortunately, we know little about Cartimandua, apart from three references in Tacitus's works. But she was unusual in being, like Boudicca, a woman with political authority, an authority that derived, presumably, from her lineage in one of the native aristocratic houses. Nevertheless, Cartimandua seems to have been a very different proposition from women of the Roman world who usually played little formal part in public affairs. Her residence, or one of them, is thought to have been at Stanwick, near Richmond (North Yorkshire), where there is a massive enclosure, *c*. 300ha in extent, surrounded by a bank and ditch.

Vespasian sent the newly appointed governor of Britain, Petillius Cerialis, with the legion he commanded at the time of Boudicca, the Ninth *Hispana* (so named because of a long stay in Spain early in Emperor Augustus's reign), north from the fortress at Lincoln (*Lindum*). The main body of the legion, accompanied by other units, probably took a route which, in due course, became the main Roman road to York and the north-east (2.1). From Doncaster, where a fort (*Danum*) would be established, the army then stuck closely to a ridge of slightly elevated ground formed by the narrow magnesian limestone belt that runs through this part of England. The men crossed the Calder at Castleford, which would become another fort site (*Lagentium*), and headed towards Tadcaster (*Calcaria*) on the River Wharfe. Just before Tadcaster the legion would have turned to the north-east, leaving the magnesian limestone for the final 20km to York but, where possible, following slightly raised ground on the York moraine (2.4). In addition, some of the troops probably headed due north from Lincoln up the Roman road, now Ermine Street (A15), and crossed the Humber to Brough on Humber where there is an early fort (*Petuaria*), although tides and other hazards in the estuary would have made this a difficult exercise.[20]

The Roman Army
The arrival of the army and its many camp followers would lead to a major change in the make-up of the population in the York area. In view of this, and in order to

understand the character and layout of the Roman fortress, it is necessary to have in mind an outline of the army's structure, personnel and equipment in the late first and early second centuries.

The invasion in AD 43 had brought four legions to Britain and there may have been detachments of others and an equivalent number of auxiliaries. After about the year 87 there were only three legions remaining, which would form the permanent garrison of the province for the rest of the Roman period. They were based in the fortresses at Caerleon (*Isca*, near Newport in Monmouthshire) and Chester (*Deva*) as well as York. Throughout the Roman period, except perhaps when it was out on campaign, local residents like Julia Velva would have been only too aware of the army's presence. They would have seen great columns of men marching in and out of the fortress gateways, they would have seen them being trained in the use of weapons and equipment, and they would have seen and heard the men entertaining themselves in the taverns and streets when off duty.

A legion was made up of about 5,200 infantrymen plus a small number of cavalry. All the men were Roman citizens, meaning they were privileged and wealthy members of imperial society who had a direct stake in the defence and, if possible, expansion of the empire. Late first-century legionaries serving in the west were usually recruited in colonies in Italy and Gaul, but local recruitment in the provinces, including Britain, gradually became more common. Auxiliary regiments, who formed the fort garrisons, were made up into units about 500- or 1,000-strong, whether infantry, cavalry or a mixture of the two. They were raised from subject peoples throughout the empire, hence they were (except for their officers) usually non-citizens. Unit names, such as the Fourth Cohort of Gauls, based at Castleford (*Lagentium*), often reflect their origins. The principal function of both the legionary fortresses and forts was to provide accommodation for the men and their equipment. Although they had defences to prevent sudden attacks by hostile forces or intrusion by wild animals, they were not like medieval castles, primarily designed for defence, but were bases from which the Roman Army would go out to fight in the field where its superior discipline and weaponry could be brought to bear on the enemy.

Weaponry for both legionaries and auxiliary infantrymen consisted of a short sword, worn on the right side, used for close combat, a dagger worn on the left, and a shield.[21] They also had a *pilum*, a form of javelin, which was usually thrown at the enemy in the early stages of a battle to soften them up. Cavalrymen were equipped with a spear as well as a sword and dagger. The army's artillery included large iron-framed, torsion-powered *ballistae*, which fired iron-tipped wooden bolts or stone balls.[22] In addition, stone balls might simply be thrown at or dropped on an enemy. Examples of both the iron bolt tips and stone balls have been found in York.[23]

By way of body armour, both infantry and cavalry often wore chainmail, but infantry might also wear so-called *lorica segmentata*, overlapping elongated plates of iron, or *lorica squamata*, made of overlapping iron scales. Surprisingly perhaps, York has produced little in the way of Roman armour, although there are a few fragments from the excavations and in the Yorkshire Museum's collection.[24]

In the late first century, soldiers usually signed on for twenty-five years of service. Although this might seem unduly long, especially given average life expectancy (p 168), an army career, whether as a legionary or an auxiliary, was much sought after as it was seen as a route to wealth and social advancement. Soldiers not only had a salary, paid partly in money and partly in grain and other commodities, but they also had opportunities for enriching themselves from the spoils taken in conquered territories. On retirement, legionaries received land on which they could set themselves up as gentlemen farmers. Possession of wealth in the form of land, and its resources, agricultural, mineral and human, was the key to entering the upper echelons of society. For auxiliaries there was the benefit of acquiring Roman citizenship.

As far as their personal circumstances were concerned, officers were free to contract officially recognised marriages, but (until the early third century) other ranks were not. By refusing to recognise a soldier's marriage as legal, the authorities avoided assuming any responsibility for his children. Only on retirement could a soldier marry legally and any existing, as well as subsequent, children became legitimate.[25] This does not mean that soldiers led celibate lives while in service. Arrangements were made for lady-friends and children, not considered legitimate until their fathers retired, to live in settlements adjacent to the fortresses. For the womenfolk of the Roman world, a legionary veteran without an existing attachment was probably considered a good match, although he might be rather long in the tooth. Such a man was, perhaps, Gaius Aeresius Saenus, named as a veteran on the York tombstone of his wife Flavia Augustina (5.8).[26]

The organisation of a Roman legion explains, in large part, the way a fortress was laid out. The basic unit was the *contubernium* of eight men, who shared a tent when on campaign and a pair of rooms in a fortress barrack. Ten *contubernia* made a century of eighty men, who occupied a barrack block and were commanded by a centurion who had rooms at one end where he could live with his wife and family. Now lacking its inscription is the tombstone of a York-based centurion (found on The Mount), showing him holding in his left hand the vine staff, symbol of his office, with which he was allowed to correct indiscipline in the men.[27] Three groups of two centuries made up a cohort of 480 men and there were ten cohorts in a legion. However, by the late first century, the first cohort is thought to have been composed of five centuries each of 160 men, i.e. it was of almost double the strength of the other cohorts.[28]

The command structure of a legion was closely integrated with the career paths of men in the upper echelons of imperial society, paths that would take them into senior military and governmental positions. The post of legionary commander, the legate (*legatus*), was reserved for a man of the senatorial order (see p 180 for the 'orders'). He was usually in his 30s and would have been destined for the highest offices in the empire. The second-in-command, known as the *tribunus laticlavius* (i.e. with a broad stripe on his toga), would also have belonged to the senatorial order, but was probably in his 20s. The other five senior officers, *tribuni angusticlavii* (with a narrow stripe), were from the equestrian order. These senior officers usually served for no more than three years in a post like York before moving on. The highest ranking officer in a more permanent position was the camp prefect (*praefectus castrorum*) who would have risen through the ranks. His role was to take charge of engineering and construction work by the soldiers and of their training, munitions and equipment. There were other men with special responsibilities such as the standard-bearers who would provide rallying points on the battlefield. A standard-bearer from the Ninth Legion based at York is Lucius Duccius Rufinus, whose tombstone can be seen in the Yorkshire Museum.[29]

The legion and auxiliaries who arrived in the north in the late first century were, of course, engaged in conquest that involved 'battles, some of them bloody', as Tacitus puts it[30] (and some not?). However, integral to the process was the construction of fortifications and roads linking them and at the centre of the network was the fortress at York. It occupied *c.* 20ha on the north-east bank of the River Ouse with the smaller River Foss on its south-east side. Its slightly elevated site would have been very apparent in the late first century when the river level was lower and there had not yet been nearly 2,000 years of settlement-derived material accumulated in the river valleys.

The fortress plan

The fortress at York had the playing card-shaped plan (rectangular with rounded corners), which was fairly standard in the late first century (2.2). There were defences around the perimeter, and the interior, very like a Roman town, was divided up by a grid of streets creating spaces (*insulae* – islands) for the buildings. York was similar in plan to Caerleon (*Isca*), built by the Second Legion about two years after York in 73 – 4,[31] although Chester (*Deva*), where construction began in about 74 or 75, was larger and had a rather different plan.[32] The line of the defences and the location of the main gates which stand at the end of the principal streets provide a framework for our understanding of the fortress at York, although the buildings and streets are still not well-understood in any detail. Because of the presence of a modern city on the same site, opportunities for archaeological excavation have largely been restricted to small trenches in advance of new development (except in the minster excavations of the headquarters and barracks in 1966 – 73) and watching briefs on service trenches for public utilities. The considerable depth of Roman levels also impedes access to them.

Adjacent to the legionary fortress at Inchtuthil in Scotland, built c. 83, temporary accommodation for the construction workers has been identified.[33] Nothing similar has been found at York, but must have existed as it would have taken some time to clear and level the ground and assemble the materials for construction. Surveying the site was the work of specialists (*agrimensores*) on the strength of the Ninth Legion. They would have been highly skilled men who, unusually in the Roman world, were highly numerate. To assist them in their work they probably had a manual that gave them at least the basic principles of how a fortress should be laid out, although each legion's surveyors would leave their own signature in the details. An example of such a manual, thought to date to the reign of Marcus Aurelius (161 – 80), although for a camp rather than a permanent fort or fortress, was written by the surveyor Hyginus Gromaticus.[34]

With the Roman surveyors' renowned good eye for the lie of the land, they chose a site at York on fairly level ground. Only at the south corner is there a bit of a dip down towards the river. The corners were placed almost exactly at the cardinal points. This may have been done for purely practical reasons to do with the topographical conformation of the site. However, one might also see this arrangement, found at Caerleon as well, as deliberately intended to symbolise Rome's control over the four corners of the earth. The foundation of the fortress would have been accompanied by appropriate rituals and sacrifices seeking favour from the gods. Particular reverence would have been directed not only to Jupiter, principal protector of Rome, but also perhaps to Apollo, a god especially appropriate for a construction project since he is said to have raised the walls of Troy by the music of his harp alone.[35] It was, as the poet Virgil tells us in the *Aeneid*, from the ruins of Troy, following Aeneas's journey to Italy, that Rome itself would eventually emerge.

The surveyor's principal instrument was the *groma*, which consisted of an iron cross-piece with its arms at 90° to one another from each of which a plumb-line was suspended.[36] The cross-piece was attached by a bracket to a staff in such a way that the surveyor could sight through opposing plumb-lines and set out straight lines marked out by rows of poles set vertically into the ground. He could survey right angles easily enough, although other angles might be more difficult. For the purposes of measurement, the surveyors probably used rods and chains marked out as appropriate. The standard unit of measurement was the Roman foot, the *pes Monetalis* (1pM = about 0.296m or 0.97 imperial feet – the length of a sheet of A4 paper), so-called after the standard that was found in the temple of Juno Moneta in Rome. The main problem with using a *groma* was keeping the plumb-lines still in windy conditions. But all the evidence suggests that the Roman Army surveyors achieved a considerable degree of accuracy in setting out their forts and fortresses, including York. One might even say there was an obsessiveness about the pursuit of accuracy, suggesting that the surveying and setting out process had a ritual element to it, another facet of the attention to detail that characterised so much of Roman religious observance.

Forts and fortresses often faced towards the direction from which an enemy was thought most likely to approach. For example, on Hadrian's Wall the forts usually face north, but at York the river, as a major communications artery, was probably the critical determining factor for its orientation from which the rest of the plan followed. Archaeologists often adopt the terminology in Hyginus's manual (shown on 2.2). He describes the part that lay between what he refers to as the *praetorium*, in the centre of his camp, and the *porta praetoria* as the *praetentura*. The areas on either side of the *praetorium* are described as the *latera praetorii*, and that part of the camp behind the *praetorium* as the *retentura*. In Hyginus's camp the *praetorium* was the commander's living quarters, but in a fort or fortress it was not usually the same building as the unit headquarters – not on Hyginus's plan. An inscription found at Rough Castle fort on the Antonine Wall in 1903 identified the headquarters as the *principia*, and this is the term that is now generally used.[37]

Although the Roman system of numerals might seem cumbersome to us, the local Britons had nothing like it and sophisticated numeracy was as important as literacy as a basis for control of a population with little skill in either respect. We get a good impression of how the Romans used numbers for measurement in the plan of the York fortress (2.7). The dimensions of the rectangular space within the defences appears to have been 1600pM (473.6m) north-east/south-west by 1360pM (402.56m) north-west/south-east.[38] These dimensions were probably chosen to allow for easy setting-out and internal subdivision. It had to be possible to check the plan easily for accuracy and overcome just about the biggest problem in laying out a large rectangle on somewhat uneven ground with simple instruments, namely getting the corners at as near to right angles as possible. The dimensions 1600pM and 1360pM allowed the surveyors to bring Pythagoras's theorem into play. As we all learn at school, this states that in a right-angled triangle the square of the hypotenuse equals the sum of the square of the other two sides. A rectangle 1600pM x 1360pM has a hypotenuse, or diagonal, of almost exactly 2100pM, a round number that could easily be checked such as to ensure that the sides were indeed parallel to one another and the corners did have right angles. Once they were happy with the rectangle it was then divided up, using units of the Roman foot, into spaces for the streets and the *insulae*.

The making of Julia Velva's York: legionary fortress and civilian settlement   33

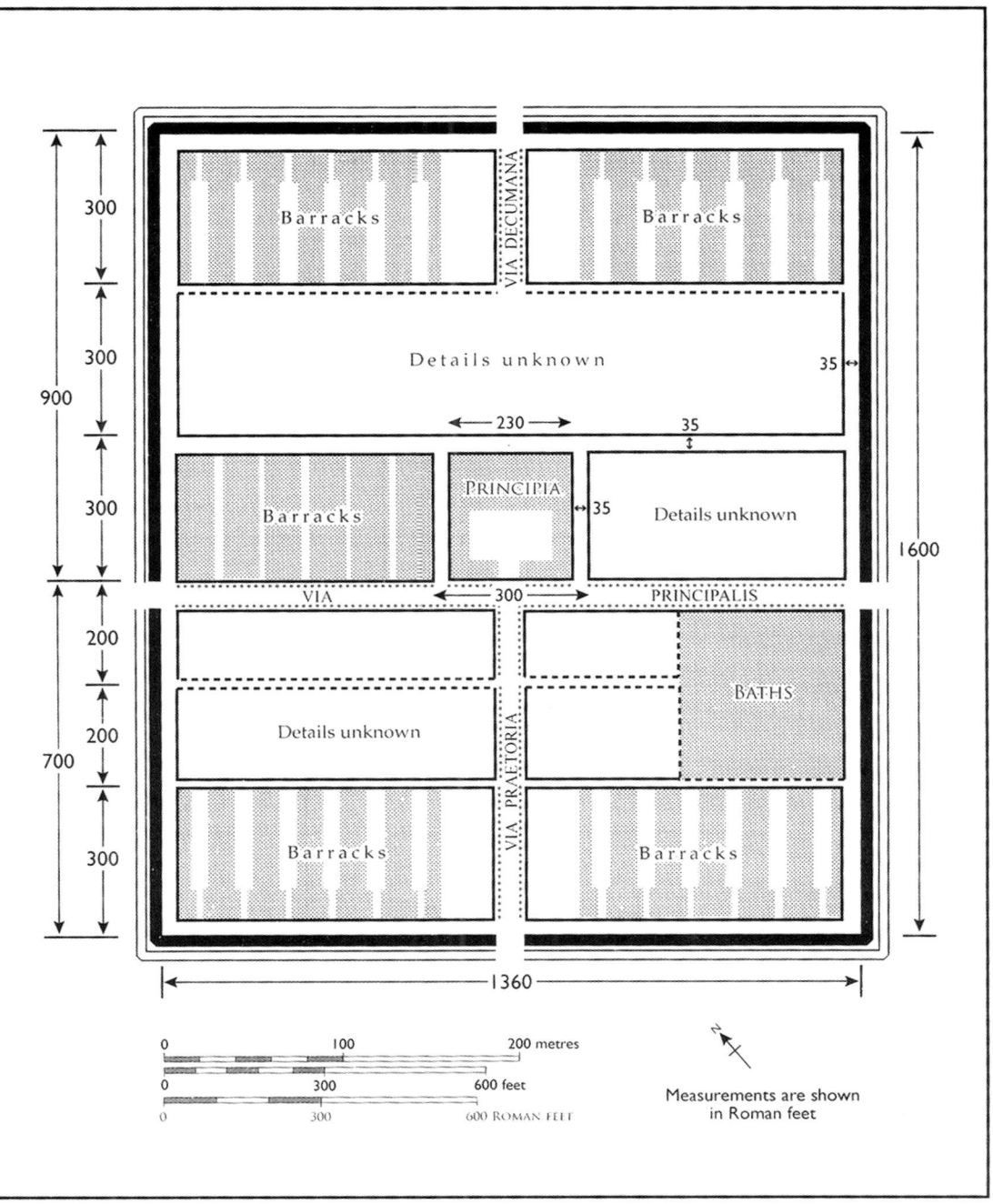

2.7: The late first century fortress: outline plan showing its metrology, principal streets and buildings. (From *York*, Historic Town Atlas, 2015)

Streets in the fortress

The *via praetoria* linked the headquarters building and the main south-west gate (*porta praetoria*). Much of the *via praetoria* lies underneath modern Stonegate, recorded with a central drainage channel, in the late nineteenth century (exact location unknown), at a depth of *c*. 2m.[39] Observed at the south-west gate (St Helen's Square) in 1847 was a stone-built drain or sewer running beneath the Roman street and heading for the river.[40] Crossing the *via praetoria* at 90° was the *via principalis*, which connected the north-west gate (*porta principalis dextra*) and south-east gate (*porta principalis sinistra*). The former lies partly under medieval Bootham Bar and the latter partly under King's Square. The street itself is now followed closely, although not exactly, by Petergate. The cobbled surface of the *via principalis* was observed in 1893 somewhere in High Petergate and, at a depth of 4m, at the junction of King's Square and Church Street (near the south-east gate) in 1912 and 1915.[41] This corresponds to the depth at which I recorded a hard-packed gravel surface and a central channel in a series of sewer repair trenches in Low Petergate in 1997.[42] Continuing the line of the *via praetoria* behind the headquarters building was the *via decumana*, followed for part of the way today by Chapter House Street, which ran up to the north-east gate. The *via decumana* was discovered in 1898 in a cellar of the Treasurer's House on Chapter House Street, where an excavation took place in 1954 (2.2, 3).[43] This found a sequence of three superimposed street surfaces, the latest of which now forms the cellar floor. The other named street, the *via quintana*, which is the street running north-west/south-east behind the headquarters, was recorded in the minster excavations. Around the perimeter of the fortress, between buildings and the defences, there was a wide space known as the *intervallum*. This served to lessen the chance that any enemy missiles that cleared the defences would damage the buildings and it allowed troops to be moved quickly around the perimeter to any point of attack.

The first fortress buildings

York would have had the suite of buildings common to more-or-less all late first-century fortresses, although little is known about many of them. The earliest buildings so far recorded in excavations are the barracks. They were long, low buildings, for the accommodation of the men, ranged around the perimeter of the fortress, except for those of the first cohort, which were next to (north-west of) the headquarters. The men's barracks, *c*. 78.5m long, were arranged in pairs facing each other which, including the alley between them, were *c*. 23.5m wide.[44] In 1925, near the west corner of the fortress (2.2, 19), Miller found a row of four 'upright oak stumps' (0.30m x 0.22m and 1.52m apart) which had been mortised into a timber sill beam.[45] This was probably an internal partition wall of a timber barrack block next to the north-western fortress *intervallum*. Otherwise, traces of the buildings are represented in the ground by post-holes and the shallow slots in which ground beams were laid. Vertical posts would have been mortised into them.

The barracks, like most Roman (as opposed to native British) timber buildings, whether military or civilian, would have employed a frame in which the members were jointed and sometimes nailed together. The roofs would usually have been supported on A-shaped trusses (3.7). Between the uprights the walls were formed from interwoven willow or hazel reds ('wattles'), which were covered with clay ('daub'). Inner wall surfaces were often plastered and painted. In the case of the York barracks, fragments found in excavations show they had simple white panels surrounded by red and black borders.[46] Roofs may have used wooden shingles, but more common in military buildings were ceramic tiles manufactured in the legionary kilns (see p 138).

The early defences

Although they had long since been covered over by later works by the time Julia Velva was around, understanding both why the fortress defences developed as they did and what can still be seen today depends on knowing what the earliest phase looked like. The first circuit of defences was similar to those at first-century forts and fortresses elsewhere in Britain. They consisted of a ditch up to $c.$ 5m wide and 1.5m deep, and behind it a rampart, $c.$ 6m wide and $c.$ 3m high, made largely out of the material dug from the ditch.[47] In addition, the rampart was strengthened with timber strapping and bands of turves also used for facing. There was a timber fence, or 'palisade', on the top of the rampart and timber gates (four in all) would have stood at the end of the main fortress streets. In addition, there were timber interval towers between the gates. Traces of towers have been found in a couple of places, both on the south-west side of the fortress, at Davygate, near the later stone Interval Tower SW3, and below stone Interval Tower SW5. They were probably 6.8m x 4m and supported on six posts.[48] At Davygate the bases of four them were found, taken from oak trees which, as the excavator Peter Wenham is pleased to tell us, were growing at the time Julius Caesar was in Britain and Jesus Christ was alive. The distance between the two recorded towers suggests there were originally ten on the south-west front.

Buildings of the Trajanic period

What we know about the origins of the headquarters and legionary baths probably takes us to the reign of Emperor Trajan (98 – 117), in which we have the first Roman stone buildings at York, buildings that would have still been standing in Julia Velva's time. The techniques used in their construction would remain more-or-less unchanged throughout the Roman period in both military and civilian contexts. Stone walls in Britain, as elsewhere in the north-western provinces of the empire, were not usually built directly on the ground surface but had a construction trench – in York, filled with a mixture of clay and cobbles or, for more substantial structures, Roman concrete. What we describe as 'mortar' or, if particularly hard, as 'concrete' were both made from lime and aggregate (sand, gravel or cobbles), mixed with water, in different proportions as appropriate to the task in hand.[49] Walls usually had a mortared rubble core to which small facing stones, *saxa quadrata*, were added, a construction technique sometimes known by the French term *petit appareil*. Each stone was tapered to fit snugly into the wall and was just big enough for a man to lift in one hand. This did away with the need for heavy lifting gear. The lower courses of the walls of larger buildings sometimes employed large blocks of millstone grit, which has good load-bearing properties, although a crane would have been needed to move them around. These blocks were often held together by iron cramps set in lead-lined sockets.

The mortared stone wall, introduced to Britain by the Romans, allowed for a much greater architectural ambition than anything seen here previously. Features like colonnades, arches and vaults would have been widely employed in Roman York, although the surviving evidence for them is limited to the small number of architectural fragments that have come to light from time to time. For the most part, roofs in stone buildings would have been similar to those in their timber counterparts with a cladding of ceramic tiles, at least until the end of the second century, after which thin sandstone slabs were preferred.[50] There is some evidence for external decoration with relief carving on, at least, the more monumental buildings. But in Roman architecture the principal decorative effort was usually focused on interiors. As Sir Mortimer Wheeler succinctly puts it, the journey of Classical architecture can be seen as running from the Parthenon, which is decorated solely on the exterior (think Elgin Marbles, the external frieze) to the Pantheon (Hadrian's temple of all the heavenly deities in Rome), conceived almost entirely in terms of its interior design.[51]

The headquarters building (principia)

In the centre of the legionary fortress stood the headquarters building (2.2, 9). There may have been an early version built of timber, but no clear trace of it was found in the minster excavations. What was found was a building, at least partly of stone, erected in *c*. 100, which would have formed a dominant feature on York's skyline from every point of the compass throughout the Roman period (2.8).[52] On the north-east side of a central courtyard stood the 32.50m-long 'cross-hall' or 'basilica', the latter a term usually used to describe a building with a wide central space – 'nave' – flanked by aisles (like a church). The nave was divided from the aisles by rows of great millstone grit columns, eight on each side, which also supported the clerestory walls in which windows provided light for the interior (2.9). A complete column was found where it had fallen, probably in

The making of Julia Velva's York: legionary fortress and civilian settlement 37

2.8: Reconstruction of the headquarters basilica of the Roman fortress looking east in *c.* 160. A first cohort barrack is under construction, in stone, at the bottom.

2.9: Reconstruction of the interior of the headquarters basilica of the Roman fortress looking north–west towards the tribunal at the far end.

the ninth century, and has been re-erected outside the south door of the minster (2.10).[53] It stands 7.75m high overall, including the block at the base, which would have been set into the ground such that its upper surface was at floor level. One can clearly see the way the column expands slightly in the centre, employing a technique known as 'entasis'. This is intended to correct the optical illusion of concavity in columns that taper slightly towards their tops when they are set out in rows. The base and lowest drums of another column can be seen today, where they were found, in the minster undercroft. They bear traces of whitewash, which may well have been applied to all the columns in the building, perhaps done in honour of Jupiter, protector of Rome, whose sacred colour was white. Another *in situ* column base, found in 1930, can be found below the floor of the minster crypt.

The space in each row between the basilica columns was at *c.* 4.9m (although probably rather more between the central pair) *c.* 4 x width of a column base (1.25m measured over the lower torus – the round projecting part). This made the basilica what the Roman architect Vitruvius (first century BC) refers to as an 'araeostyle' building. The architrave (the beam that sits on top of the columns) and walling above it would have to be timber as stone would have been too heavy to be supported on columns so far apart.[54] However, some suggestion of masonry in the clerestory walls comes from two pieces of plaster-rendered *petit appareil*, found in post-Roman contexts, which are thought to have fallen from them.[55] Had the walls above the columns at York have been made entirely of stone then arches would probably have been needed to support them, although they were not usually employed in Roman aisled buildings of the first or second century AD. The height of the basilica is difficult to estimate, but about 25m to the top of a gabled roof is not impossible. By way of comparison, the height of the nave vault in York Minster today is about 30m and so, perhaps, only slightly higher than the Roman building.

Behind the hall there would have been a row of five rooms used for administration except for the one in the centre, opposite the main door, which was the shrine, the *aedes principiorum* as it was identified on an inscription from the fort headquarters at Richborough, Kent.[56] In the shrine there would have been cult statues of the main protective deities of Rome and of deceased emperors, themselves considered divine. When they were not on campaign, the legion's standards were kept here. Below, or to one side of, the shrine there would have been a strong room, as can still be seen at forts such as Chesters and Vindolanda in the Hadrian's Wall zone. Here the legion's pay, soldiers' savings and other valuables were kept. Anyone who broke in to steal the contents would not only risk punishment in this world but would also face the wrath of the gods.

At the north-west end of the basilica nave at York remains of the tribunal were found,[57] a raised platform, probably embellished with larger than life statues and architectural flourishes, from which the legate or senior officers would

2.10: Column from the north-eastern colonnade in the headquarters basilica of the Roman fortress found collapsed in the minster excavations and re-erected outside the minster south door.

have addressed the men, administered justice and conducted the celebrations at official festivals. This is presumably what is referred to in the biography of Septimius Severus in *The Augustan History* when, having arrived in Rome newly acclaimed emperor by his legions in Syria, he summoned the praetorian guard ' … to his tribunal with armed men placed all around on all sides'.[58] A surviving early third-century calendar (probably of 225 – 7), on papyrus, lists the festivals celebrated by an auxiliary cohort stationed at Dura-Europos on the Euphrates frontier in Syria.[59] The same festivals and accompanying rituals would probably have been observed by the army at its bases all over the empire, including York.

On the other three sides of the headquarters courtyard, fully enclosing it, there would have been buildings used as stores and offices, and facing the junction of the two streets, *via principalis* and *via praetoria*, there was no doubt a grand entrance. In summary, the legionary fortress headquarters at York would have been a most impressive building in its overall dimensions, substantial nature of its construction, and architectural splendour. To a native Briton of the time who had never seen anything but round houses, it must have been almost unbelievable, something built by superhumans or aliens against whom any resistance was clearly useless.

The legate's house

Behind or next to the headquarters one would usually find the legate's residence (*praetorium*). This would have been a version of the traditional luxurious dwelling of the Roman elite, transplanted, more-or-less, unaltered from the Mediterranean region to Britain. Designed to keep the inmates cool in hot countries, it would have had thick outside walls, with few windows. And on the inside, rooms and other spaces ranged around a central courtyard surrounded by a covered walkway. Well-preserved *praetoria* can still be seen today at the Roman forts of Housesteads and Vindolanda in the Hadrian's Wall zone. The south-west corner of what was probably the York *praetorium* was found in the minster excavations,[60] located, as it probably is in the fortress at Caerleon also, behind the headquarters. The other senior officers, the tribunes, were accommodated in smaller versions of the legate's house ranged along the *via principalis*.

The legionary baths

Another very sophisticated and architecturally ambitious building in the legionary fortress was the bath house, which lay in the *praetentura*. It would have been constructed in stone from the start because of the dangers its furnaces and abundant running water would have posed to a timber building. Although relatively little is known of the York legionary baths, it was probably very similar to those at Chester and Caerleon, which have been more extensively explored. There would have been a range of rooms and outdoor spaces for the accommodation of social activities, sports and games, as well as the complex process of bathing in Roman style. This involved working up a sweat to open the pores of the skin by engaging in exercise of some sort and/or by sitting in a hot and steamy room, the *caldarium*, or in a hot and dry room, the *sudatorium*. Suitably sweaty, one was oiled, lubricated one might say, by a slave and then one scraped off the sweat, dirt and oil with a sort of metal scoop known as a strigil. A quick dip in the plunge bath of the *frigidarium* (cold room), or even in an outside pool, was then in order to close the pores again. Afterwards came a massage from a slave equipped with something sweet-smelling contained in glass 'unguent bottles', or little globular glass flasks carried on a chain attached to the wrist. Examples of both have been found in York.[61] Both gentlemen and ladies would have visited the fortress baths, the latter including the wives of officers who lived in the fortress. Other women were probably allowed in on certain occasions. However, a dim view of mixed bathing was taken by the authorities because it was thought to encourage immoral conduct. Emperor Hadrian (117 – 38) himself is said to have banned it in the city of Rome, meaning that men and women had henceforth to bathe at different times.

A few remains of the York fortress baths have been found in excavations at what is now the Roman Bath public house (2.2, 17), at 4 – 5 Church Street (2.2, 15) and at 12 – 18 Swinegate (2.2, 14),[62] although nothing approaching an overall plan of the building can be attempted. The walls found at 12 – 18 Swinegate, including one possibly marking the north-western perimeter of the baths, appear to have been largely late first-century (*c.* 90+) suggesting an episode of construction in the baths at about the same time as the headquarters building was going up. At the pub, visible in a dedicated display area, the remains include those of an impressive apse, which was probably part of the *caldarium*. Its floor has gone but some of the little columns (*pilae*) of tiles in the hypocaust below it survive (2.11). A Roman hypocaust was a heating system in which hot air, generated in a furnace, passed under the floors of a building and also, on occasions, up the walls in so-called 'box tiles'. Other walls under the pub are thought to belong to the *frigidarium*. The date of what can be seen here is uncertain, but it seems most likely that the walls are contemporary with those found at 12 – 18 Swinegate, i.e. very late first- or early second-century (and not late Roman as previously believed).

At 4 – 5 Church Street, the remains of a small room with a hypocaust were found but were not closely datable. Much more spectacular was the great sewer that still survives today several metres below Swinegate (2.12) – leaking modern sewers nearby mean it is very smelly. A channel was traced for *c.* 44m running north-west/south-east before it returned to the north-east at its south-east end. It has walls constructed of blocks of millstone grit and was capped with slabs of the same. But the floor was made from slabs of a Jurassic sandstone, probably from the Howardian Hills near Malton, otherwise rarely recorded in Roman York.[63]

2.11: The apse of the fortress baths *caldarium* at the Roman Bath public house.

2.12: The main channel of the Roman sewer (under Swinegate), which served the legionary fortress baths. (© York Archaeological Trust)

At intervals there are arches across the main channel that would have carried the walls of the rooms above. These rooms, served by side passages, included the latrines, as the sediments examined in one of the passages clearly derived from human waste represented by puparia of flies, which feed on faeces ('poo'), and fragments of sponge used as loo paper.[64] This is commented on by the first-century poet Martial in a line about mushrooms which, once eaten, leave no trace on 'the sponge at the end of a stick'.[65] The abundant remains of insect species that live inside buildings showed that the passages were not fed by exterior drains, but by the baths themselves. At some stage the main channel was blocked near its south-east end and it was routed into a second one coming in from the south-west. Pottery found in the silt which had built up after the main channel was abandoned suggests that it may have fallen out of use during the third century.[66] But whether the baths themselves had ceased to function before the late Roman period is not known. When in operation, the sewer would have carried a great volume of water and sewage, perhaps as much as the 318,000 litres (70,000 gallons) per day calculated for Exeter's fortress baths.[67] The sewer presumably disgorged into the River Ouse, although the route it took to get there remains unknown.

Lead water pipes serving the baths were found in a drain trench in Church Street in 1854,[68] but the original source of the water itself poses an interesting question. The pollen surviving in the silt in the sewer was not representative of vegetation in the immediate York area, but of the sort of mixed oak and lime woodland found on a well-drained calcareous substrate, such as the magnesian limestone found west of York.[69] How water was brought, perhaps as much as 14km from its source, is not clear, although by the late second century some of it probably came across the river, on a bridge, after flowing through the water main found at the Wellington Row site (2.3, 16 and see p 89).

The only other early stone buildings in the fortress lay in the *intervallum*. The walls of four examples have been found, one near Tower NE4 (2.2, 1), one in Dean's Park on the north-west side of the fortress (2.2, 5), and, on the south-west side, one adjacent to Interval Tower SW3 and another, apparently short-lived, replaced by Tower SW5.[70] These buildings may have been stores or army kitchens, which replaced earlier outdoor ovens set into the ramparts. Examples of the latter have been found near the Multangular Tower and Interval Tower SW3.[71] The Roman Army did not have a specialist catering corps providing meals for all. Instead, cooking was organised by the men themselves in each barrack block.

The defences rebuilt in stone

Without regular attention an earthen rampart will soon start to degrade, and the timber works also needed constant maintenance. Keeping the York defences in good condition was easily manageable if the fortress was only to be held for a short time. But once it was determined, probably by the reign of Emperor Trajan (98 – 117), that York was to be a military base for the foreseeable future, it became sensible to make the investment in stone structures. They would require less day-to-day upkeep but, more important, would give the fortress the imposing dignity appropriate to the imperial project in Britain.

It was probably in the reign of Trajan that on the north-east side of the defences, between the north-east gate and east corner, a halfway house solution to reconstruction in stone was adopted, with freestanding stone towers added to the late first-century earthen rampart.[72] It was only later, in the late second century, that the towers were connected by a wall. Between the east corner and the south-east gate, excavations have identified a stretch of fortress wall represented only by foundations of clay and cobble over timber piles, except in one place (2.2, 4) where a few courses of the wall itself survived.[73] At the east corner the clay and cobble were overlain by concrete of the late second-century wall, suggesting the stretch just described to the south-west of it was earlier and was, one suspects, also Trajanic.

The fortress gates – which remained standing throughout the Roman period – may also have been part of the Trajanic programme of construction in stone. As far as the north-west and south-east gates are concerned, excavations and observations have shown that little survives above their foundations.[74] However, they appear to have had the usual ground plan seen elsewhere in Britain at this time with a rectangular tower on each side of two arched portals. The ground floor of the tower housed guard chambers, from which passage in and out of the fortress could be supervised. The original height of the towers is unknown, but between them there would have been a walkway above the portals and perhaps further storeys above that. This sort of gate can be seen today in reconstructed form at South Shields Roman fort (2.13). A Trajanic date for the south-east gate may be inferred from the inscription on a great stone tablet found in 1854 while digging a drain in King's Square.[75] It had probably fallen, or been thrown down, from its original place in a prominent position on the gate. In beautifully executed lettering the inscription sets out all Emperor Trajan's titles, which allow the tablet to be dated to the years 107 – 108. This is the last datable reference to the Ninth Legion. Some remains of the south-west gate have been found in St Helen's Square, but are difficult to interpret in terms of its plan.[76] Nothing is known of the north-east gate, which presumably still lies below the rampart of medieval times on Lord Mayor's Walk.

Although evidence for them is limited, these gates would have been most impressive structures. But what was constructed on the south-west side of the fortress, overlooking the River Ouse, would have dominated the local landscape known to Julia Velva, Aurelius Mercurialis and every other resident of, and visitor to, Roman York. Even what still survives today more than catches the eye.

2.13: The reconstructed Roman west gate of the fort at South Shields (*Arbeia*; Tyne and Wear).

The Multangular Tower and contemporary walling

Those readers who are familiar with what is still a widely accepted narrative of the York fortress may wonder why I am now about to describe and discuss the Multangular Tower, at the west corner of the legionary fortress, and stretches of contemporary walling thought by RCHME to be early fourth-century.[77] We now know that a date some 200 years earlier, in the reign of either Trajan or Hadrian, is much more likely.

The Multangular Tower and curtain wall south-east of it, now standing in the Museum Gardens, formed part of the medieval city defences (2.14). A wall to the north-east of the tower, incorporating the remains of an interval tower (NW1), was exposed in 1970 (2.2, 18).[78] Walling constructed in a similar manner has also been found in excavations elsewhere, on the south-west side of the fortress, on the north-west side at Dean's Park (2.2, 5) and on the south-east side at Kings Square (2.2, 16).[79] What is known of the extent of this walling, or can be reasonably inferred, is shown on 2.2, but it may well have occupied a much larger proportion of the circuit.

The towers and curtain wall have concrete foundations in trenches up to 1.4m deep with timber piles usually *c*. 0.75m long driven into the base. Above the foundations the wall is *c*. 1.50m (*c*. 5pM) thick and constructed with a mortared rubble core that has courses of small stones on the outer face. The stones on the inner face (which would have been partly hidden by the earlier rampart) were less neatly cut, as can be seen today in a short stretch of the wall on St Leonard's Place near the Art Gallery (2.2, 12). At a height of about 2.30m above Roman ground level there are five courses of tiles that run back into the core of the wall, although not through its complete thickness. North-east of the Multangular Tower, at a height above Roman ground level of *c*. 5.20m (17.5pM), up to five courses of tiles survive near what was once the top of the wall. They are stepped out to form a cornice (2.15). This kept rainwater from running down the wall face. Above the cornice there had, presumably, once been a parapet in front of a narrow wall walk, although the main means of communication along the line of the defences would have been a walkway on the top of the rampart. The parapet may be estimated as a maximum 1.48m (5pM) high, probably with crenellations as shown in the reconstruction in 2.16. The original finish of the wall (and towers) is difficult to determine. However, it may have been plastered or rendered, a perfectly sensible precaution against the weather adopted elsewhere by Roman buildings. In some cases, these plastered walls were painted as if to appear made of large blocks of masonry.

2.14: The exterior of the Multangular Tower in Museum Gardens. The small facing stones of the Roman masonry in the lower part are clearly distinct from the large blocks of the medieval enhancement in the upper part.

The making of Julia Velva's York: legionary fortress and civilian settlement 47

2.15: The cornice formed from tiles at the top of the Roman fortress wall immediately north-east of the Multangular Tower.

2.16: A reconstruction drawing of the Multangular Tower looking north-west.

The Roman work in the Multangular Tower itself survives today to a maximum height of 5.80m. Above this is medieval enhancement. The tower projects from the western corner of the fortress defences, just like the matching tower at the south corner, which still stands to a height of *c.* 3m but lies entirely below ground.[80] The plan of these towers embodies an imaginative and complex design, carefully measured out in terms of the Roman foot, which has no exact parallel anywhere else in the Roman Empire. The projecting part is based on a fourteen-sided figure (hence 'multangular'), of which four segments were omitted for the entrance to a substantial structure at the rear, rectangular in plan. The overall length of the towers at ground level was *c.* 25.16m (85pM). Quite why a fourteen-sided figure was chosen is not clear, but given the ritual aspect of so much construction in the Roman world, including that with a military purpose, one should not rule out the possible symbolic significance of the number fourteen as twice seven, the number of the planetary deities in the Romans' earth-centred cosmos. Alternatively, there may have been a reference intended here to the fourteen regions into which, as Pliny the Elder tells us, Rome was divided for administrative purposes.[81]

The wall of the projecting part of each corner tower is 2.10m thick at the base, and the outer face is sloped in at a height of *c.* 1.12m to become *c.* 1.50m thick, the same as the curtain wall. The original height is not known but 13.32m (45pM), about twice the height of the curtain wall, would answer the requirements of symmetry and, perhaps, be as much as the walls could support. These are the dimensions used in the conjectural reconstruction in 2.16. Each tower was bisected by a spine wall at ground-floor-level – and probably on the upper floors also – and on each floor there were probably two small rooms at the rear. On the ground floor there were probably arches either side of the spine wall that carried the rampart walkway through the tower at first-floor-level.

The corner towers' walls are neatly faced on the interior and, unlike in the curtain wall, the tile courses come through the full wall thickness. Visible also on the interior of the Multangular Tower (2.17), at a height above ground level of *c.* 1.50m, is a facing course in which there is a series of voids where stones have been omitted. These are 'putlog holes', which originally accommodated the ends of horizontal poles forming part of the wooden scaffolding used during erection of the tower. At the time of the 1831 clearance of the tower two stones, which can no longer be found, were seen built into the wall referring to the century of Antonius Primus, although whether they were in their original position, thus commemorating the men responsible for construction of the tower itself, is not clear.[82] At a height of *c.* 4.45m (15pM) the inner face is stepped and the wall becomes 1m thick. The step was presumably intended to support a first floor. It was thought in making the model for the reconstruction that there was a second floor a further *c.* 4.45m high above the first, which was itself below a third, *c.* 2.20m high. At the top of the

The making of Julia Velva's York: legionary fortress and civilian settlement 49

2.17: The interior of the Multangular Tower. The putlog holes, band of tiles and step in the wall near the top of the Roman masonry below the medieval masonry can be clearly seen. On the ground are Roman stone coffins from various parts of the city.

tower the reconstruction shows a parapet 1.48m high, the same as estimated for the curtain wall. It is suggested (though not visible in the reconstruction drawing) that there was a low-pitched roof sufficient to divert rainwater into pipes that disgorged beyond the wall face.

There may have been ground-level-access to the corner towers, although as part of a defensive system in which they served as strong points, access may have been at first floor level from the rampart walk only. Still visible at the Multangular Tower are parts of two narrow windows, one on each side of the projecting part close to where it joins the curtain wall. As the reconstruction shows, they were for overlooking the junction between curtain wall and tower, an otherwise blind spot for defenders. There were presumably other windows but no evidence for them survives.

Between the two corner towers there were six interval towers (SW1 – 6), with six-sided projections going beyond the fortress wall, three each side of the south-west gate, which may itself have been flanked by projecting towers.[83] These towers were substantial structures that were 20.70m long and presumably the same height as those at the corners. In a military sense, the purpose of projecting towers was to allow defenders to shoot along the line of the walls at any hostile force attempting to scale or undermine them – 'enfilading' as it is known.

2.18: A reconstruction drawing of the south-west front of the legionary fortress showing the Multangular Tower and Interval Tower SW6 imagined looking north-east from close to the Ouse river front.

However, the Roman Army was not really expecting to be attacked in York, and one should probably see the whole of the stone-built south-west front of the fortress as intended to make an impression of impregnable grandeur on anyone approaching whether by river or road (2.18). Nonetheless, one might still ask why these towers were so large. If there were two storeys above ground in the Multangular Tower, then its total floor area was $c.$ 470m², and that of each of the six interval towers $c.$ 270m² (a barrack block was $c.$1050m²). The ground floors probably received little daylight and so they were, perhaps, used for storage or the confinement of prisoners. The upper floors could have been accommodation for any extra troops in York, reception rooms of some sort or, again, used as stores.

Interval towers contemporary with those on the south-west front on the other three sides of the fortress were relatively small (6m x 4.6m), on a rectangular plan and, like NW1, visible behind the public library, stood entirely behind the wall line.[84] Tower NW2, found at St Leonard's Place in 1835, seems, to judge by a drawing made by Wellbeloved at the time, to have survived to a good height above the curtain wall, and an original height (13.32m) matching the Multangular Tower would seem likely.

In order to accommodate the new projecting towers on the south-west front, the early fortress ditch was filled in and a new one dug outside it. This was seen in a complete cross-section of the sequence of fortress ditches at Interval

Tower SW6 in 1957 – 9 and at SW5 in 1960 and 1972.[85] Pottery in the early ditch suggested it was infilled by *c*. 100. The 'second ditch', accompanying the towers, *c*. 6m wide and 2m deep, contained pottery (which dates its infilling rather than cutting) that was dated to the late second to mid-third century, after which it was re-cut ('third ditch').

The date of the ditch is just one aspect of the tortuous story of establishing the date of the Multangular Tower and associated walling, a story that provides us with a good illustration of how archaeologists have moved on from an era when the dates ascribed to great Roman buildings were usually based on associating them with documented historical events to one in which more objective stratigraphic and scientific methods have begun to play a greater part.

When Stuart Miller began his excavations in the 1920s, it was axiomatic that projecting towers on Roman fortifications were late third- or fourth-century, even though there are projecting towers of early imperial date on the defences of towns such as Arles or Turin.[86] In Britain, projecting towers can be seen on forts on the south and east coast thought to have belonged to a system often referred to as 'the Saxon Shore', on account of the reference to a 'Count of the Saxon Shore' in *Notitia Dignitatum*, a list of officials usually thought to be early fifth-century. This in itself implied a late Roman date for the shore forts, which has been largely confirmed in excavation.[87] However, *all* the towers of these forts project forward of their wall lines whereas at York the interval towers, other than those on the south-west front, do not and are of normal early Roman type. Moreover, the walls of the Saxon Shore forts are much thicker (up to 3m) and higher (8 – 9m) than the fortress wall at York.

The problem that Miller encountered at York was that, on the one hand, he could identify no fortress wall at the Multangular Tower, or adjacent to it, which was earlier in date (a date he believed must be fourth-century) and, on the other hand, it did not seem likely that the defences on the north-west and south-west sides of such an important place as York had been left as earth and timber for 200 years or more after the Roman conquest. Miller therefore suggested that the fortress was originally larger and the earlier defences lay on a different line.[88] Uncertainty on the matter persisted until RCHME undertook an excavation of the fortress defences on the south-west side of the circuit at Coney Street in 1955 (2.2, 20).[89] The excavator concluded that the fortress had *not* originally been larger, but (erroneously in my view) that an early stone curtain wall (and towers) had been demolished more-or-less to its foundations, or lowest courses, on which the later Multangular Tower-type wall with the projecting towers was built. Subsequently, in 1957 a complete cross-section of the wall of this type at Feasegate produced no hint of more than one phase (2.2, 24).[90] Nevertheless, in 1962 RCHME felt able, in *Eburacum*, to state that the Multangular Tower and associated walling was indeed late Roman and, moreover, was 'Constantinian', i.e. of the reign of Emperor Constantine (ruled 306 – 37) who was acclaimed emperor in York. Having accepted this fixed point, a sequence of fortress defences was set out that introduced a Trajanic wall and a Severan wall. One effect of assigning an episode of construction on the fortress defences, with the monumental towers on the south-west front, to the early fourth century, is that it has conditioned thinking about the rest of the fortress at York in the late Roman period. This has led to claims, firstly about the date of buildings in similar style to the walls and secondly the character of the fortress as a whole, which are quite misleading.

In 1996 I published a report on excavations on the fortress defences which had taken place since RCHME's *Eburacum*, in which I concluded (agreeing with Miller) that there had been no earlier (Trajanic or Severan) fortress wall at the Multangular Tower – or in other places where wall of similar style occurs. I suggested, however, a late second- or early third-century date for construction based on the date of a few poorly stratified pottery sherds in rampart deposits that might have been contemporary with the wall.[91] It remained curious, nonetheless, that much of the fortress at York, of all places, seemed to have retained defences largely of earth and timber for more than 100 years after the conquest.

There the matter rested until the YAT training excavation of 2001 – 03 in the precinct of St Leonard's Hospital, a medieval institution in the western corner of the fortress. The project involved excavation of Interval Tower SW6, the rampart behind the fortress wall and the interior of the Multangular Tower. Within the Multangular Tower it was shown, as Miller had done, that there was no earlier fortress wall. From below the foundations of the tower it was possible to recover two of the timber piles – here made of alder rather than the usual oak – which were radiocarbon-dated using a high resolution method and a mathematical algorithm for greatest accuracy.[92] There is no reason to suppose that these piles had been re-used from another, earlier, structure and so the range of dates returned can probably be accepted. They suggest a construction date for the tower – and associated walling – between AD 80 and 110, a much earlier range than any previously suggested, but of a piece with the date of pottery in the ditch that had been infilled to allow construction of Interval Tower SW5, and also in a small stretch of the construction trench for the wall excavated in 1970 near Tower NW1.[93]

It would appear, in conclusion, that the Multangular Tower-type wall was employed in reconstructing most, but not all, of the fortress defences in stone at York, probably early in the second century, most likely in the reign of Trajan. The work should be set alongside the contemporary reconstructions of defences in stone at the sister fortresses of Caerleon and Chester.[94] On the south-west front at York, however, there was an architectural ambition of a rather different order than at the other two, involving towers quite different from any seen in Britain or, perhaps, at any other fortress in the empire at the same time.

Notwithstanding the argument summarised above, I suspect it will remain difficult for many archaeologists and historians of Roman Britain, raised on the apparent lapidary certainties in RCHME's *Eburacum*, to accept that one of the cornerstones of what was once thought about the archaeology of not only Roman York but of Roman Britain itself in the early fourth century rests, in fact, like the Multangular Tower itself, on very unstable ground. Nevertheless, I believe there are now fascinating questions to ask about why York was different and where the legionary architects got their ideas about the great projecting towers. Furthermore, the story I have outlined also shows how a great historic monument about which we thought we knew so much can still have secrets to reveal.

A Roman amphitheatre at York?

One of the great unsolved mysteries of York's archaeology is the Roman amphitheatre. Where did Victor, whose name appears on a small bone plaque, found in a York burial, wishing him a 'lucky win', suggesting he was a local gladiator, actually perform?[95] No trace has been found, although one would have thought it was an essential amenity for soldiers and civilians alike being used for military exercises as well as for the sort of robust entertainments popular all over the Roman world (2.19).

At Caerleon, an amphitheatre was constructed in earthwork and stone in *c.* 80 AD and has remained a prominent feature of the landscape.[96] At Chester, the first amphitheatre was constructed at about the same time with a stone outer wall retaining earthen banks for seating.[97] This was enlarged on a massive scale in, perhaps, the early third century. The amphitheatre was rediscovered in 1929 and its location was then seen to be visible in the distinctive pattern of roads south-east of the fortress, which clearly respected a large oval structure.

2.19: A pair of gladiators in relief on a ceramic lamp from York (YORYM 2010.326, Yorkshire Museum).

No landscape feature, as at Caerleon, or road pattern, as at Chester, exists in York to betray the site of an amphitheatre. If it had been a largely timber structure it would probably have left little visible trace in the modern townscape, but something along the lines of the other two employing massive amounts of monumental stonework seems more likely. If its remains are in fact buried, the most likely site, by analogy with other fortresses, is land north-west of the fortress *praetentura* encompassing what are now the Museum Gardens and King's Manor. So where did the stone go? One possibility is that if the amphitheatre was indeed in Museum Gardens, conveniently close to the river, it was shipped downstream to build the Anglo-Saxon churches of east Yorkshire and north Lincolnshire, in which there is abundant millstone grit, often large blocks, which must surely have come from a Roman building in York.

Another form of entertainment one would like to think was also available in Roman York, home today of one of Britain's foremost racecourses, is chariot racing. No equivalent of Colchester's circus, the only one known in Britain, has been found here, but the traditional equipage of the Ben Hurs of *Eboracum*, the quadriga, can be seen as a maritime version, with Neptune and a sea chariot, on a stone relief that may have adorned the north-west gate of the fortress.[98]

Roman roads around York

When travelling out into the country from her home in York, Julia Velva would have been able to take advantage of a fine system of well-made roads (2.1, 2.4). We have seen that the Roman Army arrived in York by means of routes approaching from the south (via Doncaster) and from the south-east (from Brough on Humber). In due course, these routes were converted into proper metalled roads, but they were just two of those the Ninth Legion was tasked with constructing to allow the army to move around the region quickly.

Roman roads in and around York are known largely from observations in utility trenches and building work and rarely from controlled excavation.[99] One can also spot straight stretches of Roman road lines in the city today, where they are followed by modern streets like Bootham and Clifton north-west of the fortress. Where they have been recorded, Roman roads were similar in the way they were constructed. The base (the *agger*) was usually made of large cobbles, often set in stiff clay, which were mounded slightly to allow a camber on each side to aid drainage of rainwater off the surface. Over the base were laid layers of fine gravel that were hard-packed to give a good wearing surface. Initially, at least, there were usually drainage ditches on either side of a road to collect water run-off, although, as time went on, they were often left to silt-up.

The Roman road that approached York from the south-west, on Iter II in the *Antonine Itinerary* (p 13), ran from a crossing of the River Wharfe at Tadcaster,

15km distant, on a line closely, if not exactly, followed by the modern A64, which crosses over it at Street Houses *c*. 10km from the city. From Street Houses, the line of the Roman road is followed today by a field path and then by a minor road known as the Ebor Way as far as the village of Copmanthorpe. After Copmanthorpe, the Roman road is closely followed once more by the A64 as far as Dringhouses, now a York suburb, 3.25km from the Ouse crossing. The road then runs a little to the north-west of the A64 (Tadcaster Road, Mount Vale, The Mount and Blossom Street). From where it has been recorded a little to the north-west of Blossom Street (2.3, 46),[100] the road presumably crossed the line of the city's medieval walls at a point a little to the north-west of Micklegate Bar before continuing, on a straight line, to the river crossing where, by Julia Velva's time, if not before, there was probably a bridge (see below). This line was not, however, necessarily retained throughout the Roman period, as is described on p 91.

In 1989 at the Wellington Row site, close to the river bank (2.3, 16), a sequence of road-related deposits 4m thick was carefully excavated (2.20).[101] The first gravel surface, probably late first-century, was about 10m wide and cambered on each side for drainage. It sloped gently down towards the river, which may imply that

2.20: Part of the cross-section of the main Roman road from the south-west at Wellington Row (1989) looking north-east towards the River Ouse. The earliest gravel surface is at the bottom, above it to the right is dark silt from a late first-century flood event, succeeded by a cobble mound (*agger*) and further gravel layers. Scale 1m. (© York Archaeological Trust)

there was no bridge at this time. Overlying the early surface was a deposit of clean water-deposited silt, up to *c.* 200mm thick, which must be late first-century. This silt may be the result of a flood but, if so, the river level had risen as much as 3m, an exceptional event as no other evidence has yet been found in York for a flood at any time in the Roman period. Subsequently, the road level was raised by about 1m with a mound of large cobbles, which was then covered by further layers of gravel. The lack of mud and refuse between the gravel layers gave the impression that, hereabouts at least, the road must have been swept clean on more-or-less a daily basis.

The only other road to be investigated by archaeological excavation in the immediate York area originated in the Roman fort and settlement at Stamford Bridge. Near Appletree Farm, Heworth, 2.5km east of York city centre, the road was recorded in 1959 and it still shows up as a low mound in fields by Tang Hall Beck (2.4, 3).[102] A sequence of road metalling had, remarkably, survived ploughing. The first phase, presumably of the late first century, i.e. the conquest period, was 10m wide with ditches on each side. In a second phase, dated to the early second century, the road width was increased to 13m. The new metalling covered over the former north ditch and a new one was cut. A third phase of metalling followed in the late third or fourth century.

Civilian settlement: Romans and natives

The people who lived in the scattered rural settlements of the York area before the Roman Army arrived were the Britons whose ancestors had, for the most part, probably lived here for many centuries. In turn they were, themselves, the forebears of people who continued to intermingle with the Romans throughout the imperial period and, in some cases, may have reached the upper echelons of local society, although in others they were reduced to slavery.

Aerial photography has identified numerous sites in the York area that are likely to be native British settlements of the late prehistoric and/or Roman period, defined for the most part by groups of ditched enclosures, usually known by archaeologists as 'field systems'. The evidence suggests that the area was well-populated when the Ninth Legion arrived, especially on the sand or gravel deposits that support soils particularly suitable for arable agriculture.[103] For example, *c.* 5km south of the city centre, aerial photographs revealed ditched enclosures and roundhouses on a 'sand island' at Lingcroft Farm, Naburn (2.4, 11), excavated by Bradford University.[104] Not visible on aerial photography, however, were large areas of ditched enclosures at Heslington East (2.21).[105] There were also remains here of a number of roundhouses of which the remains had largely been ploughed away leaving only shallow gullies, probably for catching water off the roofs. They included one large example, 11.10m in diameter, in its own

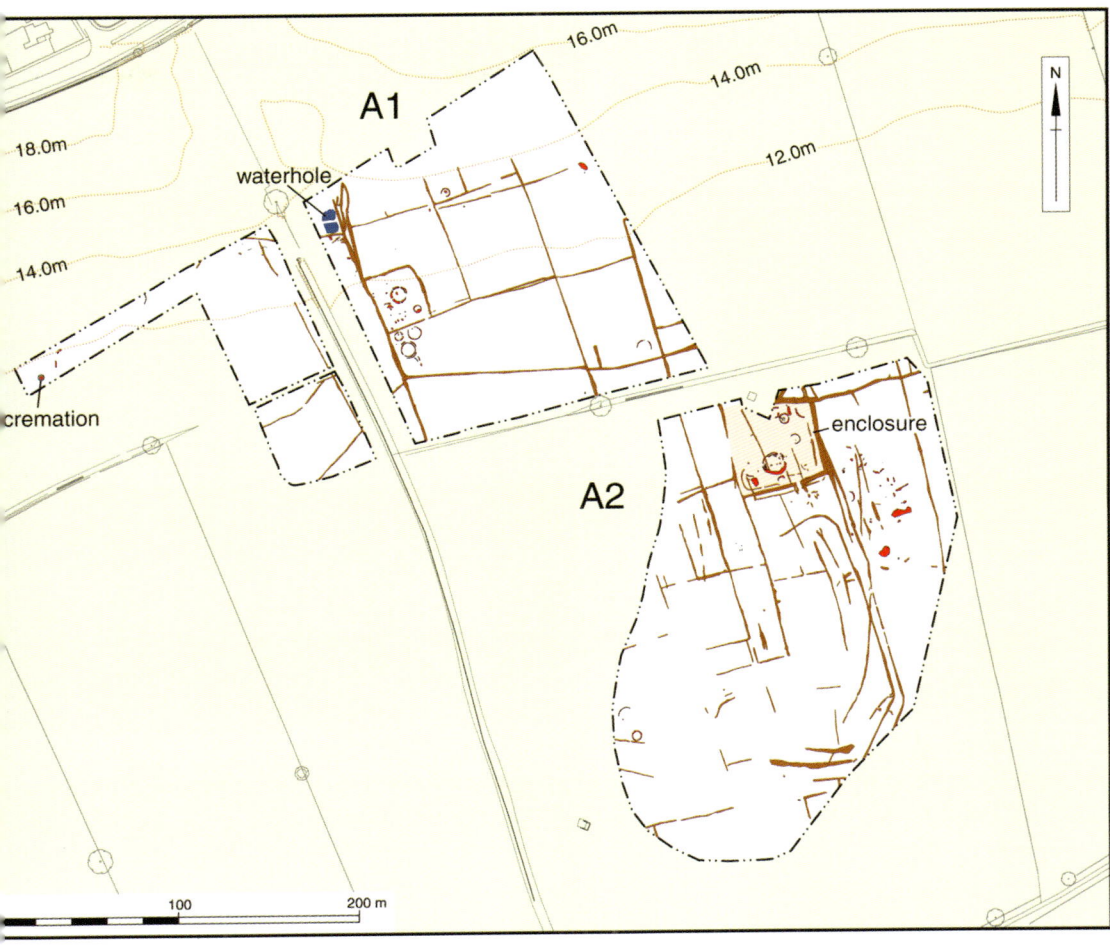

2.21: Heslington East: plan of a lattice pattern of late Iron Age to early Roman ditched enclosures. A possible elite residence and enclosure lies at the north end of Area A2. (© York Archaeological Trust)

ditched enclosure that had, perhaps, belonged to a local elite household. Although roundhouses are usually thought of as typical of the prehistoric period, in the York region they remained the all-purpose building for many country-dwellers throughout the Roman period (2.22).

There is no clear evidence for the Roman conquest having an immediate impact on sites like Heslington East. However, by the early second century, the field system at the site appears to have been abandoned perhaps, if now in the legionary *territorium* (see below), because of changes in the agricultural regime occasioned by the demands of the army. At the same time, typically Roman material culture, notably pottery, including local Ebor Ware, imported samian (red earthenware with a shiny surface) and amphorae, as well as coinage, began to find its way to

2.22: A reconstruction drawing of an enclosure with roundhouses in the hinterland of York as it might have appeared in the Roman period.

Heslington East and other sites in the hinterland suggesting perhaps that some form of trade was taking place between the Romans and the locals.

One impact of the new roads built by the Romans was to improve communications and interaction with the people in the surrounding countryside. One context in which this took place was probably the seizure of land to create what is often referred to as the *prata legionis* ('legion's meadow') or, by the second century, the *territorium legionis*, which was managed directly under military control.[106] Evidence from elsewhere in the empire suggests a legionary *territorium* could have been as much as 500km², and it would have encompassed a variety of landscape types and ecological zones suitable for arable, pasture and extraction of minerals. The location and size of any *territorium* around *Eboracum* is unknown, but one area which, it has been suggested, *did* lie within it is Bramham Moor, on the

The making of Julia Velva's York: legionary fortress and civilian settlement

magnesian limestone west of Tadcaster, at a distance of *c*.15km from York. Here, running east-west, two branches of the York to Ilkley (*Olicana*) Roman road have been identified from aerial photography and, in addition, five secondary Roman roads or tracks up to *c*. 700m apart.[107] The latter appear to be later than cropmarks representing field systems thought to be of Iron Age date and later than or contemporary with a major north-south Roman road now known as the Rudgate.[108] It has been suggested that these tracks are evidence for a Roman, perhaps legionary, re-organisation of the land into strips, each one perhaps assigned to a farm. This area is on good agricultural land and would have been an abundant source of grain for the army in York. Just 5km to the west, extensive excavations at Wattle Syke, near Wetherby, produced nearly 150 quern and millstone fragments testimony to intensive grain production in the Roman period,[109] although whether this site was in the *territorium* or not cannot be said.

The canabae

In addition to any rural settlements, regarded as also part of the *territorium*, was a settlement immediately outside the legionary fortress. This would have included infrastructure related to communications, warehousing, manufacturing and other ancillary activities associated with the legion. In addition, it provided accommodation for partners, slaves and other camp followers. In due course, their numbers would have included retired soldiers as well as local people who provided the military with goods and services of one sort and another. In other words, the Roman garrison at York formed part of a larger community from the earliest years of its presence here. As elsewhere in the empire this settlement outside the fortress defences may have been referred to as the *canabae*, the Latin word meaning the 'huts' in which the residents lived. Over time, legionary *canabae* often developed a measure of independence from army control and were administered by officials of their own. This may have been the case at York, as will be discussed below.

Unfortunately, our knowledge of any *canabae* settlement at York between the late first and mid-second centuries remains very limited, but we can get some general idea of its extent from data on pottery distribution. In Jason Monaghan's great survey of Roman pottery from York (published 1997), he divided the Roman period into a series of six 'ceramic periods' (CP) relating to the time-span over which certain key pottery types were produced and in circulation.[110] As far as this chapter is concerned, we may focus on the first two of these periods. CP1 runs from *c*. 71 to *c*. 120 (just after the beginning of Hadrian's reign), and CP2a from *c*. 120 to *c*. 160. Although patterns in the data are dependent on where archaeological investigation has taken place, and there are many parts of the city that remain unexplored, they do allow some inferences to be drawn about where people were living and dumping their refuse (including broken pots) – not necessarily the same places, although usually not far from one another. In both CP1 and CP2a the data shows, as would be expected, a concentration of pottery in the legionary fortress. Otherwise, there is a certain amount of material from immediately outside the fortress on all sides and along the line of the main approach road from the south-west but little else. As we shall see in Chapter 3, the picture will change markedly in CP2b (c. 160 – c. 200) – within the Julia Velva period.

The distribution of coins can also give some impression of settlement patterns. No major study of York's Roman coinage has yet been published, although a few lists by various hands are available in print.[111] Lists also exist in archives to which access is not generally available. For the purpose of this book, I have compiled a database of 842 Roman coins from lists available to me from forty-three archaeological excavations scattered over the whole of the Roman settled area at York. The vast majority do not come from contexts contemporary with either their minting or their loss. Many do not even come from Roman contexts. However, it may be assumed that, although redeposited on one or more occasions, coins do not, by and large, move far from the original place of loss, so it is possible to gain some idea of what was circulating in various parts of the settled areas. Of the 842, 216 come from the first twelve of the twenty-one time periods (i.e. up to the year 260) used by Richard Reece for study of the coinage of Roman Britain.[112] The sample is quite small and somewhat biased in that almost half of the coins come from only three sites, one in the fortress at York Minster (forty-one specimens) and two outside the walled town south-west of the Ouse at The Mount School (thirty-four) and Trentholme Drive (twenty-three). However, in spite of the limitations of the data, they suggest that as soon as the Roman Army had arrived, coinage began to circulate locally. There are fifty-six issues of emperors from Vespasian (69 – 79) to Trajan (98 – 117) as well as a small number of coins that had been minted in pre-Roman times, or in the years after AD 43 but before the conquest of the north. They were presumably lost after AD 71. These coins come from all parts of York, although almost half come from the fortress. In addition (not in the database), there is a hoard of thirty-five silver denarii from 9 Blake Street (2.2, 13) in the fortress in which the latest coins date to the year AD 74.[113] Otherwise coins of the early emperors come largely from sites close to the fortress or on the line of main road from the south-west.

Immediately outside the fortress, the north-east bank of the River Ouse would have been in use throughout the Roman period for the movement in and out of troops and supplies. At 39 – 41 Coney Street (now WH Smiths) (2.3, 4), some remains of two successive timber granaries were found – there were probably many others in this area.[114] Evidence was also found for what was probably a common problem of grain storage throughout the Roman period. In remains of the first building large quantities of grain pest insects suggested an infestation had probably led to its demolition.¹¹⁵ The second building had fallen victim to a fire. Little structural detail of the two buildings was found, other than slots that would have held low timber walls supporting raised floors typical of Roman granaries. Raised floors were intended to allow circulation of air and, thereby, some control over temperature and humidity. The second building was succeeded by the mid-second century by a riverside street. Another timber structure, also early Roman in date, was found nearby at Spurriergate in 1959, replaced by the same street (2.3, 5).¹¹⁶ North-west of the fortress a few traces of early buildings have been found, but north-east of it and further away, east of the River Foss, there was probably just open farmland in the early Roman period.¹¹⁷

Originally, land south-west of the River Ouse may have been considered another part of the *canabae*.¹¹⁸ However, very little evidence for human activity earlier than the late Antonine period has been found except on higher ground, overlooking the fortress, at the site of the old station (2.3). Unfortunately, what was found here in 1839 – 40 is difficult to date, to locate accurately or to interpret. Some remains of timber buildings were thought by RCHME, on no obvious evidence, to be of 'late 1st century date', also, perhaps, the date of a few beam slots found in an excavation of 2012 (p 111).¹¹⁹

Of greater interest from the old station was a Roman altar (2.23) found re-used in a later bath building but probably set-up in an earlier one in this same area. The altar bears a dedication to the goddess Fortuna, commonly found in bath houses, by Sosia Juncina, the wife of the legionary legate Quintus Isauricus, probably in

2.23: Altar dedicated to the goddess Fortuna from the old station. It was dedicated by Sosia Iuncina, wife of Quintus Antonius Isauricus, legate of the Sixth Legion, in the mid-130s, height 0.69m. (From Wellbeloved 1842)

York in the mid-130s (in the reign of Emperor Hadrian).[120] Religious dedications by women are rare in the Roman world, but Sosia Juncina was a woman of high social status for whom they would have been considered quite proper. Also thought to be early Roman were remains found in the same area in 1939 (in advance of the construction of an LNER – London and North-eastern Railway – wartime facility) of the plaster and wattle walls from timber buildings, as well as a 4m-length of a stone wall.[121] Some early activity is suggested by the samian sherds from the excavation. Of seventy-one samian vessels represented, Rob Perrin identified nineteen (27 per cent) as of South Gaulish origin (imported largely before *c.* 100).[122]

What I have described here does not amount to much, but in light of the construction later in the Roman period of a very substantial building on the site of the LNER wartime facility (p 111), possibly part of a governor's palace, the status of any earlier buildings poses the question of whether there was a military or official establishment south-west of the river from the time of the arrival of the Ninth Legion. In this case, a cemetery reserved for its residents might account for a few early Roman burials on the old station site which included two cremations and an unburnt body buried with a coin of Hadrian (117 – 38).[123]

A change of legion and the reign of Hadrian

Roman emperors from Augustus onwards were treated as semi-divine beings, existing halfway between men and gods. On their death they underwent their apotheosis, becoming fully divine, and were then worshipped like other deities. An empire-wide imperial cult was actively promoted, and it was part of a Roman citizen's duty to participate in it. As citizens themselves, Julia Velva and Aurelius Mercurialis would undoubtedly have been well aware of the emperors who had preceded those of their own time and now residing with the gods, but few of them were as well-known as P. Aelius Hadrianus – 'Hadrian' – whose reign lasted from 117 to 138 and had a major impact on Britain. A marble bust found in Stonegate in York, thought to represent Emperor Constantine (306 – 37) may, it has been suggested, be a reworked bust from a monumental statue of Hadrian which, in light of its findspot, had stood in the fortress headquarters.[124]

It was just before, or at about the time of, the visit of Hadrian to Britain in the year 122 that the Ninth Legion left York. The destination of the legion remains something of a mystery, but the legend that has grown up about its destruction in Scotland, embraced by novelists and film-makers alike, has no basis in fact. A stamped tile and a stamped pottery vessel of the Ninth Legion have been found at Nijmegen (Netherlands), where there is a legionary fortress at the mouth of the Rhine.[125] However, these items may be evidence for only a detachment – a vexillation – of the legion, the rest of the men being elsewhere.

We do not know whether Hadrian visited York when he came to Britain, but it is quite possible that he did so before continuing northwards over land, or perhaps by sea, to the frontier zone that really interested him. Hadrian brought with him to Britain the Sixth Legion *Victrix* (victorious) and *pia fidelis* (dutiful and loyal), which was to form the new garrison at York. Its badge was the bull, which represented strength and virility. Many of the men were probably taken straight to the frontier for a few years, where they were involved in construction of the wall that now bears the emperor's name. An indication of unusual military activity at York that should probably be dated to the Hadrianic period is a group of Roman camps on the northern side of the city, as many as seven or eight on Bootham Stray (2.4, 1) and two or three on Huntington South Moor, which were probably intended to accommodate troops for a short period before moving on (2.4, 2).[126] By Julia Velva's time, there would only have been mysterious humps and bumps in the fields to betray their presence, but it is amazing how persistent the camp ramparts remained until they were recorded in the twentieth and twenty-first centuries.

Hadrian's reign has been seen as a turning point in the fortunes of the Roman Empire because he realised that it could no longer continue to expand as it had done in the later Republican and earlier Imperial periods. Hadrian abandoned untenable conquests of Trajan in the east and then undertook two great journeys in which he visited all the armies of the empire, developing his policy for peaceful, stable and controlled frontiers manned by a well-trained and disciplined army. As far as Britain was concerned, Hadrian may have found a dangerous situation in the northern frontier zone. His fourth-century biographer in *The Augustan History* states: 'The Britons could not be kept under Roman control.' Furthermore, a tombstone of a legionary centurion, thought to date to the early second century, found at the fort at Vindolanda, refers to the deceased being 'killed in the war' – presumably with the Britons.[127] However, having imposed peace and built the wall, Hadrian could allow the north of England, or part of it at least, to assume a measure of self-government. The usual imperial policy was that, once pacified, a pre-Roman tribal area would become an autonomous region, or *civitas*, usually within pre-existing boundaries, which the local elite was expected to administer according to Roman law. In particular, they were charged with collecting taxes for the imperial treasury and recruiting soldiers for the army. To carry out their tasks effectively the elite were encouraged to build themselves a town, usually referred to today as a '*civitas* capital'. Some part, at least, of the north-east of England became the *civitas* of the Brigantes with its capital at Aldborough (*Isurium Brigantum*) on the River Ure, 25km north-west of York.[128]

The early Antonine period

In 138, Hadrian was succeeded by Emperor Antoninus Pius. He founded a dynasty, the 'Antonines', whose first two members (but not Commodus, the third) earned high praise from the great eighteenth-century antiquary and historian of the Roman Empire Edward Gibbon who, in his magisterial *Decline and Fall of the Roman Empire* (published 1776), declared:

> *The two Antonines governed the Roman world forty-two years, with the same spirit of wisdom and virtue … their united reigns are possibly the only period of history in which the happiness of a great people was the sole object of government.*

Modern scholarship usually takes a less sanguine view of how the empire into which Julia Velva was born was governed. The historian Colin Wells, writing of the same period, concludes: 'The Roman order was based partly on consent, partly on custom and partly on institutionalised terror unsurpassed until the dictatorships of the twentieth century', which was, he goes on, 'the price paid by the outcast, the dispossessed, or simply by those, like the Christians, who subscribed to a different set of values.'[129]

Still seen by emperors as critical to maintaining 'the Roman order' was successful conquest, even if they no longer aimed at the 'empire without limit', promised to the Romans by Jupiter, their supreme deity, as reported in Virgil's *Aeneid*.[130] Antoninus Pius, like Claudius and Vespasian before him, saw Britain as a place where a conquest could be easily achieved, and his prestige thereby enhanced. The only time Pius took the title *imperator* – 'victorious general' – was in reference to Britain following his movement of the frontier of the province northwards again, back into Scotland, to the Antonine Wall between the Rivers Forth and Clyde. The Sixth Legion, or some part of it, headed north again to the new frontier, leaving behind numerous inscriptions on the wall and in its forts commemorating their work, whilst references to individual legionaries appear on their altars and tombstones.

Only one of the legates of the Sixth Legion in the early Antonine period is recorded on an inscription from York itself, but others are known from inscriptions elsewhere in the empire.[131] The *curricula vitae* of these men give us a good impression of the way that members of the Roman elite gained empire-wide military and political experience during their working lives and spread the culture of that elite even to places remote from Rome, like York, at the same time. The first Hadrianic legate was P. Tullius Varro, from Etruria (in Italy), who had commanded the Twelfth Legion in Cappadocia (Turkey) and then, unusually, was moved sideways to the Sixth Legion. Anthony Birley suggests that his experience was needed to bring the legion from the fortress at Vetera,

Lower Germany, to York. L. Aninius Sextius Florentinus, whose CV appears on his tomb at Petra, Jordan, served with the Ninth Legion before going on to be governor of Arabia in 127. L. Minucius Verus, a native of Barcino in Italy, became legate of the Sixth Legion in *c.* 130. The man recorded in York itself is Quintus Antonius Isauricus, legate in the mid-130s, whose name appears on the altar found at the old station (see above) dedicated to Fortuna by his wife. The next York legate after Isauricus, in 135 – 8, was P. Mummius Rutilianus, probably son of the governor of Britain in 135, P. Mummius Sisenna. Rutilianus went on to become Proconsul of Asia in about 160 – 1. Other men of the Sixth Legion are described in the next chapter, although one who probably belongs to the Hadrianic period is Sollius Julianus whose name is scratched on a leather tent panel found at 24 – 30 Tanner Row (2.3, 19). He may well be the same man, with the *praenomen* Marcus, referred to on a stone commemorating building work by his men at Hare Hill on Hadrian's Wall.[132]

A Brigantian revolt?

Widespread credence was once given by archaeologists to a revolt of the Brigantes against the Romans in the middle 150s. This was contrived by the eminent archaeologist Francis Haverfield at the beginning of the twentieth century after the discovery of an inscription in the River Tyne, which was read as recording the arrival from Germany of reinforcements for the British legions under the governor Julius Verus (*c.* 155 – 158).[133] Also recruited to support the theory was a reference in a description of Greece by the author Pausanias, which appeared to refer to an attack by a people described as the Brigantes on the 'Genounian District'. But this is not now thought to refer to Britain. A coin issue of 155 depicting *Britannia* was said to show her with her head bowed as if indicating her shame at a revolt. But this may simply be the imposition of a modern interpretation onto a perfectly innocent depiction of the goddess. In addition, it was thought that the sequences in the Antonine Wall forts, and others in Scotland, included an episode of abandonment or destruction by hostile forces. However, re-examination of the evidence conclusively shows this is not the case.[134]

The 'Brigantian revolt' can now be safely consigned to archaeological mythology, but an amusing coda from the time when it was still orthodoxy is a story told to me by the late Peter Wenham, one-time head of history at St John's College. He recalled digging a small trench in the Bishophill area of York in 1962 (2.3, 39) where he encountered a burnt deposit, probably dateable to the late second century, within a Roman building. It so happened that on the day it was uncovered the site was visited by Sir Mortimer Wheeler, Britain's most prominent archaeologist at the time. Never shy of making a snap judgement, Sir Mortimer looked down into the trench and immediately announced that here was evidence for the Brigantian revolt – such is the way that history is sometimes made.

The late 150s saw the abandonment of the Antonine Wall shortly before the death of its creator in 161. Some forts in Scotland remained in commission after the mid-second century as outposts, but an inscription recording the rebuilding of Hadrian's Wall dated to 158, during the governorship of Julius Verus, implies re-occupation of the original frontier.[135] Following abandonment of the Antonine Wall, some of the forts in northern England were re-occupied and any involvement of the Sixth Legion with the frontier was largely concluded. It now turned its attention to new construction in the fortress at York, which is discussed in more detail below. Also clearly visible in the archaeology of the late Antonine period is evidence, in the form of new streets, buildings and other infrastructure, for the rapid growth of the civilian settlements on both sides of the River Ouse. The population clearly increased considerably, probably as a result of migration both from the local area and further afield in Britain and beyond. It was into this melting pot that Julia Velva and Aurelius Mercurialis would be born.

Chapter 3

Julia Velva's York: 'the summit of sublunary grandeur'

Historical background: the late Antonine period

The beginning of what was to be an exciting and important period in Roman York's history coincided with the reign of the emperor Marcus Aurelius, who succeeded Antoninus Pius in the year 161 and reigned until 180. Born Marcus Annius Verus at Rome in 121, the future emperor gained the approval of Hadrian and was betrothed to the daughter of another imperial protégé, Aelius Caesar. After the death of Aelius, Marcus was adopted by Antoninus Pius and took the names Marcus Aelius Aurelius Verus. In 139, he received the title of Caesar and in 145 married Faustina (Junior), daughter of Antoninus Pius. Marcus Aurelius took Lucius Verus as his partner emperor, but the latter died in 169. Marcus Aurelius is perhaps best remembered for his devotion to the Stoic school of philosophy as expressed in his celebrated *Meditations*. His reign was not entirely peaceful, being disturbed by many frontier wars. Moreover, the legions returning from Parthia in 166 brought back a devastating plague to Rome. On the northern frontier of Britain, there may have been some hostile incursion in the early 160s, referred to in *The Augustan History*,[1] which required action from the governor of Britain, Calpurnius Agricola. It was, perhaps, another crisis in the 170s which, according to Cassius Dio, occasioned the despatch to Britain of 5,500 cavalry recruited from nomadic tribesmen on the lower Danube (Sarmatia).[2]

Marcus Aurelius was succeeded by his son Lucius Aelius Aurelius Commodus (177 – 92), a man, according to Cassius Dio, 'of a weak rather than a wicked disposition'. He had been made co-emperor in 177 before assuming sole command at his father's death in 180. Early in Commodus's reign there was, according to Dio, a further attack on northern Britain.[3] He writes:

> *His greatest struggle was the one with the Britons. When the tribes in that island, crossing the Wall* [i.e. Hadrian's Wall] *that separated them from the Roman legions, proceeded to do much mischief ...*

Apparently 'a general' was killed, quite possibly a legate of the Sixth Legion. In any event, it is likely that York's legion was involved in military operations against the Britons under the direction of the governor Ulpius Marcellus, who served in 184 – 5. The next governor of Britain was Publius Helvius Pertinax (185 – 7), a former *tribunus angusticlavius* (equestrian tribune) of the Sixth Legion, who would have served in York in the 160s. Pertinax was a strict disciplinarian and this led to a mutiny by British troops. Although this was quelled, he had to resign his command. A higher destiny would now summon Pertinax after Commodus was murdered on 31 December 192. In his later years, Commodus had become insane and disgraced the imperial crown by fighting wild beasts in the arena. His megalomania caused him to believe he was the reincarnation of Hercules and some of his coins show him with his head covered with the skin of the Nemean lion slain by that hero. By contrast, Pertinax was 'excellent and upright', according to Dio. He reluctantly accepted the throne from Commodus's assassins. However, only eighty-six days later, Pertinax himself was murdered by mutinous praetorian guards who then, in effect, sold the crown to the highest bidder. This was Didius Julianus, who lasted a mere sixty-six days before he too was murdered.

Septimius Severus: the African emperor (192 – 211)

There are two great Roman emperors who have a special place in the history of York. One of them is Constantine (306 – 37) and the other is Septimius Severus (192 – 211) – 'conqueror of Arabia, conqueror of Adiabene [ancient Assyria] and most great conqueror of Parthia', as he is described on a great stone tablet at the fort of Bowes (*Lavatris*; formerly North Yorkshire, now County Durham).[4] With his impressive military reputation on the one hand, and his interest in astrology and exotic religious ideas represented, in particular, by the cult of Serapis (pp 217–18),[5] on the other, it is, I think, Severus who comes across as a more interesting and complex character than the leviathan of the early fourth century.

After the death of Severus's friend Pertinax, the Roman governor of Britain, Decimus Clodius Septimius Albinus, originally from Hadrumetum in the Roman province of Africa (now Tunisia and the northern part of Libya), was proclaimed emperor by the three British legions. At the same time that Albinus staked his claim, Septimius Severus, the governor of Upper Pannonia (now parts of Austria, Hungary and Slovenia), was hailed as emperor by legions under his command and moved west to secure Rome for himself. Initially Albinus was offered a role as a junior co-emperor, but once Severus had defeated another claimant, Pescennius Niger, a civil war with Albinus became unavoidable. This was settled in Severus's favour in 197 by a battle at Lyon, in Gaul, in which Albinus was killed, along with many soldiers from the army of Britain, including, presumably, men of the Sixth Legion based in York.

Lucius Septimius Severus was, like Albinus, born in the province of Africa, in his case at Lepcis Magna, now in Libya, in 146. Severus relied to an even greater extent than emperors before him on the support of the army. His attitude is epitomised in his reported dying words to his sons: 'enrich the troops and never mind the rest.'[6] Severus did as much as he could to secure the army's loyalty, for a start by giving them only their second pay rise since Augustus's time, although it may have been largely eaten up by price inflation. In addition, Severus allowed soldiers to regularise their private lives by contracting legal marriages whilst in service, which meant that any children were legitimate and, in the event of his early decease, able to inherit their father's estate.[7]

It used to be thought that, because Albinus took much of the army of Britain with him to fight in Gaul, the Britons who lived north of Hadrian's Wall would have taken the opportunity to attack the Roman province. Cassius Dio seems to suggest that in about 197 there was a threat to Britain from the Caledonians, in what is now Scotland, who gave assistance to a people he refers to as the *Maeatae*, living near the wall, from whom peace was purchased 'for a large sum'.[8] Archaeological evidence for reconstruction in the Hadrian's Wall zone, for example at Corbridge (Northumberland) and in the Pennine forts in Yorkshire, was once claimed as evidence of a Roman response to an attack on northern Britain in the early part of Severus's reign. In RCHME's *Eburacum*, Sir Ian Richmond describes 'the devastation of the north' and claims hostile forces had even got as far as York itself where: 'As a result of their destruction, the Trajanic [fortress] wall seems to have been removed to its foundations almost everywhere...'[9]

We now think that this sort of conclusion implies far more than a native British army was able to do or, indeed, had any intention of doing. Prevailing opinion today would see the northerners as simple tribesmen looking for loot, cattle, and slaves and not in the slightest bit interested in knocking down stone walls. In any event, there is no archaeological evidence that any stretch of the fortress wall at York was destroyed by enemy action or that any of it was rebuilt after the year 197. There was, however, reconstruction in the Hadrian's Wall zone and at the Pennine forts, including Bainbridge, Bowes, and Greta Bridge (2.1, 1-3), under Virius Lupus, governor from 197 to 200. This is no longer seen as restoration after hostile action, but more as the routine maintenance and modification of buildings and fortifications.

In the years 205 to 208, Lucius Alfenus Senecio, yet another African, in his case from Cuicul (Djemila) in the province of Numidia (now the eastern part of Algeria), was governor of Britain. It has been inferred from a remark by Cassius Dio that he had a military success, presumably somewhere in the north.[10] According to Herodian, Senecio made an appeal for reinforcements, which may have been what led to Septimius Severus visiting Britain in person.[11] Both Dio and Herodian claim that the emperor welcomed the opportunity to campaign here because he saw it as good training for his sons, Caracalla and Geta, who had become idle and unruly in the decadent environment of Rome.[12] Before Senecio moved on in 208, he was probably charged with making York ready for the emperor and his retinue, although a *domus palatina* (palace), referred to in passing in *The Augustan History*,[13] is likely to have been the commanding officer's house in the fortress rather than a completely new building.

Severus was accompanied to Britain not only by his sons but by his empress, Julia Domna (3.1). Formerly a priestess at *Emesa* (now Homs) in Syria, she was evidently a capable and intelligent woman and a style-icon whose clothes, jewellery and hairstyles would have been closely observed by the women of York. A hint of her interest in the province in which she now found herself, and of a certain salty sense of humour, comes from the famous exchange, recorded by Cassius Dio, between her and the wife of Argentocoxus, a Caledonian chief, following the signing of a treaty, probably in York.[14]

> *When the empress was jesting with the British woman after the treaty, about the free intercourse of her sex with men in Britain, she [the latter] replied "We fulfil the demands of nature in a much better way than do you Roman women; for we consort openly with the best men, whereas you let yourselves be debauched in secret by the vilest."*

Even though neither Cassius Dio nor Herodian specifically mention York, a legal document concerning the ownership of a slave, sent to a lady named Cecilia, states that it was written 'at *Eboracum*'.[15] In effect, the empire's seat of government was wherever the emperor happened to be. Therefore, when in York, Severus would, as well as his family, have had with him a large staff of courtiers and civil servants. Most important of these was the praetorian prefect, Aemelius Papinianus ('Papinian'), one of the most distinguished of all Roman lawyers. In addition, according to Herodian, Severus 'mustered troops from all parts and having raised a powerful army, he made ready for the war'.[16] These troops included Severus's new Second Legion *Parthica* (raised to fight in the east),

3.1: Silver denarius of the empress Julia Domna. (YORYM 2000.4381, © York Museums Trust)

members of the praetorian guard and other legionary detachments.[17] Quite where this 'powerful army' was accommodated when it first got to Britain is not at all clear, but much of it probably descended on York at least for a short while. For the local traders there must have been opportunities for making a bit of a killing out of all those new customers. At the same time the local girls would probably have found themselves even more at the centre of attention than was usual in a garrison town.

The weaponry, armour and dress of the soldiers of Severus's army now seen in York were, up to a point, similar to those of the army of Vespasian, but there were also important differences. The infantry now had a sword (*spatha*), rather longer than that of the first century, used for slashing rather than stabbing. The *spatha* was worn on the left side (previously a sword had been worn on the right). Its scabbard was suspended from a baldric, a wide strap made into a loop that hung over the right shoulder, as shown in 3.2.[18] The loop was closed by a metal fitting and below it there were very distinctive two-part terminals. A fine example from York of a baldric fitting with an eye for attachment, bearing the eagle, emblem of the Roman legions,

(*Right*) 3.2: An illustration of an early third-century Roman soldier showing how the baldric and sword were worn.

(*Below*) 3.3: A baldric fitting with an eagle in relief, emblem of the Roman legions (width 0.55m). (YORYM 2010.309.1, © York Museums Trust)

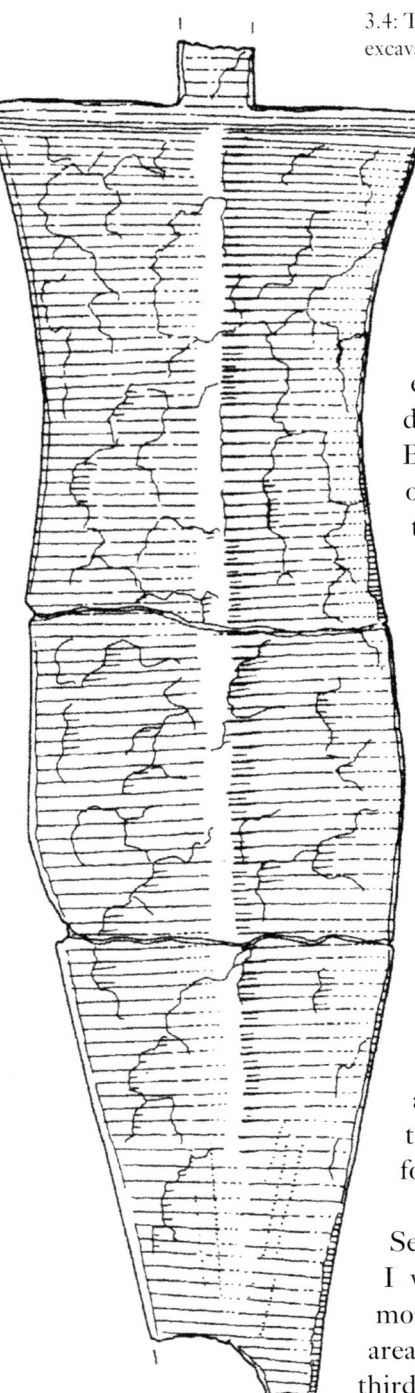

3.4: Third-century iron dagger from the minster library excavations, surviving length 267mm. (© FAS Heritage)

is shown in 3.3. Daggers had become proportionally wider in respect of length by the third century and an example from York was found at the minster library (3.4).[19]

During his three years based in York, while engaged in what an altar from Corbridge describes as a 'most happy' expedition to Britain,[20] Severus's armies campaigned north of Hadrian's Wall. Whether the intention was to incorporate the whole of Scotland into the empire is uncertain and we shall never know because of the emperor's death in 211, although a legionary fortress established at Carpow, near Perth, on the banks of the River Tay, looks like a statement of intent for some sort of permanent conquest. Striking archaeological evidence for the campaign has also been found in excavations at the fort at South Shields (*Arbeia*), at the mouth of the Tyne, which was extended in the early third century and much of the interior devoted to granaries, presumably to make a dedicated supply base nearer to the action than York.[21] In 210 the Sixth Legion was given the honorific title *Britannica*, which appears on tile stamps from York. This was the last occasion of such an award to a legion for its achievements in the field.[22]

We shall return to the archaeology of Severan York in the following chapters, but I would suggest that Roman York was at its most prosperous, extended over its greatest area, and had its largest population in the early third century. Although he knew a good deal less about the archaeological evidence than we do today, one can, nonetheless, agree with William Hargrove who, in his *History and Description of the City of York* of 1818, declared that:

> *It was during this residence of Severus, that our city shone in its full splendour. The prodigious concourse of tributary kings, foreign ambassadors, and other persons of distinction, who crowded the court of the sovereigns of the world, at this period, when the Roman Empire was near the zenith of its power; in addition to the emperor's own magnificence, his numerous retinue, the noblemen of Rome, or the officers of the army, all which would necessarily attend him; must have exalted* Eboracum *nearly to the summit of sublunary grandeur.*

Particular 'sublunary grandeur' would have surrounded Severus's funeral, which took place shortly after his death in York in February 211. This was probably as impressive a public spectacle as the people of Roman York, perhaps including Julia Velva and Aurelius Mercurialis themselves, had ever witnessed, although the emperor's formal apotheosis, when he joined the gods in the life eternal, took place later in Rome. The funeral pyre appears on commemorative coins of 211 and the ceremony is briefly described by Cassius Dio.[23]

> *After this* [death] *his body arrayed in military garb, was placed upon a pyre, and as a mark of honour the soldiers and his sons ran about it; and as for the soldiers' gifts, those that had things at hand to offer threw them upon it and his sons applied the fire.*

Severus's ashes were returned to Rome in a porphyry urn according to Dio (an alabaster urn according to Herodian, a gold urn according to *The Augustan History*) for burial in the mausoleum of the Antonine dynasty, although Severus was, of course, completely unrelated to it. According, again to *The Augustan History*, various omens predicted Severus's death, some arising from events in York itself. Whilst they may have been made up after the event for dramatic impact, Severus was apparently very superstitious and so one can well imagine his anxiety if he had, as *The Augustan History* tells us, been presented with some sacrificial animals that were black – the colour of death – when wishing to make a sacrifice to the gods. Worse still, even though the emperor rejected them, the animals, it is said, followed him back to the imperial residence.[24]

The heirs of Severus: Caracalla to Severus Alexander (211 – 235)

Severus's heir, Emperor Caracalla (Marcus Aurelius Antoninus, sole ruler 211 – 17) gets a very bad press from Cassius Dio, rightly so as he was the murderer of his brother and of many other prominent Romans. Caracalla's reign did, however, have an important impact on York as a result of his division of the province of *Britannia* into two. Presumably he feared that a single province, with its three legions, might become the base, once more, of a powerful rival claimant to the imperial throne, a claimant like Albinus, whom his father had defeated. Henceforth, therefore, Upper Britain (with legions at Caerleon and Chester) – *Britannia Superior* – was ruled from London whilst Lower Britain – *Britannia Inferior* – had its new capital, and only legionary base, at York. From now on, York's destiny was to become a centre for the administration of a province and for the ceremonial and pageantry that went with upholding the legitimacy of a great empire.

It was not only York but the Roman Empire as a whole that was impacted by another of Caracalla's decrees, the *constitutio Antoniniana*, which extended citizenship to all free-born people (i.e. non-slaves).[25] One of these new citizens may have been a certain Mercurialis who became the Aurelius Mercurialis of Julia Velva's tombstone, although his citizen status probably had rather earlier origins. Following the *constitutio*, many newly enfranchised persons also adopted Aurelius (the family name inherited by Caracalla) as their own. A proliferation of Aurelii on funerary monuments dedicated to soldiers in Britain suggests that at the beginning of the third century the legions began to recruit from local men who now had the required citizen status to be accepted.[26]

One other result of the extension of citizenship was that distinctions between the various types of self-governing communities in the empire, largely based on the extent of their residents' status as Roman citizens and other legal privileges, were, in effect, dissolved. The most prestigious of these communities had been the colonies (*coloniae*), settled by citizens, which in Britain had been founded for legionary veterans at Colchester, Gloucester and Lincoln in the first century. Their residents were charged with upholding Roman values and providing a focus of loyalty in newly conquered territory. Following the *constitutio*, *colonia* became a largely honorific title, although York residents may, nevertheless, have taken some pride in having it bestowed upon them. This probably took place at the same time as the division of Britain and promotion of York to provincial capital, although the only inscription referring to York as a *colonia* that can be dated is an altar, dedicated in 237 at Bordeaux by Marcus Aurelius Lunaris, a *sevir augustalis* of the *coloniae* of both York and Lincoln, to the *Tutela Bourdigalae*, a local goddess.[27] A reference to the *Colonia Eboracensis* (abbreviated to COL EBOR) can also be found at York itself in three funerary inscriptions for decurions (members of the town council; see below p 108).[28]

As a provincial capital, York became the seat of a governor (a praetorian legate) who also remained the commander of the Sixth Legion. This is confirmed in an inscription from Vieux (*Viducasses*), in Normandy, which refers to Tiberius Claudius Paulinus, governor in 220, as *legato Augusti pro praetore in Britannia ad legionem sextam*.²⁹ This powerful official probably continued to reside in the legate's house in the fortress. However, it has been suggested that the large, late second- or early third-century Roman building found at the site of the LNER wartime facility south-west of the Ouse (2.3, 13; see p 111) belonged to a gubernatorial palace.³⁰ Found in the same area, during construction of the old station, were two small, silvered copper alloy 'ansate' (from Latin meaning 'handle') plaques bearing punched inscriptions in Greek (6.1). One of them refers to the 'gods of the governor's *praetorium*', i.e. his 'residence' or 'headquarters'.³¹ These plaques were dedicated by a Scribonius Demetrius, who has been ingeniously identified with a Demetrius whom the author Plutarch met at Delphi in 83 – 4 and to whom he recounted his experiences of travelling in the west. However, although there are earlier buildings on the old station and LNER wartime facility sites, there is no evidence that they were part of a late first-century 'governor's *praetorium*' and there is no obvious context for such a building. The plaques were probably hung up in a shrine in a *praetorium* by a later Demetrius who had, after all, a common enough Greek name.³² Nonetheless, following the creation of the new province, there may have been an official imperial establishment of some sort sited prominently on the elevated ground (formerly the old station) facing the fortress on the other side of the River Ouse.

The first governor of Lower Britain may have been Marcus Antonius Gordianus Sempronianus Romanus ('Gordian'), who will reappear in our story shortly. A building stone found at the minster bears an incomplete inscription apparently referring to him. It appears to be a dedication by a group of his *beneficiarii* (legionaries with special duties) belonging to a *collegium* (society) which, perhaps, served some religious cult in York.³³

Caracalla was murdered in April 217, aged 29. He was succeeded by Marcus Opelius Macrinus, who had been party to the murder before being raised to the purple by the men under his command in the praetorian guard at Rome. However, an unfavourable peace agreement with the Parthians in the east led to his declining popularity – Rome despised a loser. Macrinus also fell foul of a conspiracy fostered by Julia Maesa, sister of Julia Domna, which led to a revolt by the army in Syria. In the ensuing struggle, Macrinus was put to death and Maesa's grandson, Bassianus, was raised to the purple.

Varius Avitus Bassianus was born in *Emesa* (Homs) like his grandmother and great-aunt. He was the son of one Sextus Varius Marcellus and Julia Soaemias, daughter of Julia Maesa, the third of the powerful Syrian women who had such a strong influence on the empire's affairs in the early third century. In his boyhood, Bassianus was appointed priest of the sun god, Elagabalus, and is usually known by that name as emperor. His brief four-year reign (218 – 222) was notorious for religious fanaticism alongside cruelty, bloodshed and excesses of every kind at the imperial court. There was general satisfaction at his murder.

The last of the imperial house founded by Septimius Severus was Marcus Aurelius Severus Alexander, born 208, son of Julia Mamaea, niece of Julia Domna, and Gessius Marcianus. Severus Alexander was adopted by Elagabalus in 221 and succeeded him in 222. He ruled well enough, but the army resented the influence his mother had over him. Severus Alexander's rise to power coincided with the governorship of Lower Britain of the Paulinus, referred to on the Vieux inscription. In York itself an inscribed tablet, found at Clementhorpe (1.1, 14), was set up in 221 by Lucius Viducius Placidus, a merchant – *negotiator* – from the territory of the Veliocasses (around Rouen) in northern Gaul, commemorating his gift of an arch and vaulted passage, probably part of a temple, which was dedicated *genio loci* (to the spirit of the place) and to the numen (divine spirit) of the emperors, meaning Elagabalus and his junior colleague Severus Alexander.[34] Had it been set up just a year later there would have been only one imperial dedicatee. It is possible that Placidus is the same man as a Placidus, son of Viducus, before he became a citizen under the terms of Caracalla's grant, who dedicated an altar near the mouth of the River Scheldt in the Netherlands.[35] He also describes himself as from the territory of the Veliocasses and a merchant trading with Britain.

In 232, Severus Alexander's armies had to face the Persians and there were disturbances on the German frontier. However, before fighting began the soldiers proclaimed one of their commanders, Maximinus the Thracian, as emperor. Severus Alexander and Julia Mamaea were murdered at Mainz (*Mogontiacum*) in Upper Germany. With the accession of Maximinus, a series of about fifty short-lived soldier-emperors began that would only come to an end with Diocletian's reign, which began in 284.

A bloody conclusion: the year 238

The last dated inscription relating directly to Roman York, on the Bordeaux altar described above, was set up just a year before further imperial bloodletting in 238. Marcus Antonius Gordianus, who had known York as governor of Lower Britain, was proconsul in Africa. When a rebellion broke out in his province against what was regarded as the tyranny of the emperor Maximinus, Gordian was petitioned to assume the purple, although he was in his 81st year. This was a very advanced age for Roman times but, presumably, he was a man of unusually sound constitution. Gordian took his son, also Marcus Antonius Gordianus, as joint ruler and sought the approval of the senate in Rome. However, although this was granted, the governor of the neighbouring province, Numidia, remained faithful to Maximinus and marched on Gordian at his base at Carthage. The younger Gordian was killed in battle. His father then committed suicide after a reign of only twenty-one days. Meanwhile in Rome, Decimus Caelius Balbinus and Marcus Claudius Pupienus Maximus were chosen by the senate to be joint emperors. Maximinus invaded Italy to reassert his claim, but after an unsuccessful siege at Aquilea (at the head of the Aegean), his troops mutinied. They murdered Maximinus and his son, also Maximinus. It was still the year 238 when Balbinus and Pupienus were both murdered. Gordian III (238 – 44), grandson of Gordian I, then became emperor.

As we reach the reign of Gordian III, we probably come to the limit of Julia Velva's possible lifespan, and so we shall now leave the history of imperial politics to continue on its bloodthirsty journey. However, it must have already been the case that the political instability and accompanying economic problems of the mid-third-century empire had begun to have an impact on York. One might say that Julia Velva was fortunate indeed to have lived in a golden age in which Rome's enemies remained largely beyond the frontiers, and internal peace led to a measure of prosperity for its people.

The Sixth Legion Victrix in York

The Sixth Legion's construction work in the late second-century fortress at York must have been very evident to all the local residents while it was ongoing. They would have seen stone, timber and other materials arriving in some quantity, by land and water, and would have seen and heard gangs of men, both soldiers and local conscripts, at work from morning to night.

As far as work on the streets is concerned, we know little about any refurbishment of the main thoroughfares, although this must have taken place. We do know, however, that between the rear of the rampart and the internal buildings, the *intervallum* street was resurfaced, or in some places given a cobble and gravel surface for the first time.[36] This street was known as the *via sagularis* (from the word *sagum*, a type of cloak often worn by soldiers, made from a rectangular piece of cloth – see p 189). Evidence from 9 Blake Street (2.2, 13) suggests that some of the minor fortress streets were also given proper surfaces for the first time and others, as at the minster library (2.2, 2) were resurfaced.[37] Along the main street frontages, the porticos were now supported on stone rather than timber pillars. Three stone pillar bases, nearly 1m in diameter, were found in a line by St Michael le Belfry church (2.2, 10) in 1892, 3m below modern level.[38] They had presumably supported the portico in front of the headquarters building. At the Treasurer's House, two adjacent column bases for the portico on the south-east side of the *via decumana* have been found. One can still be seen *in situ* (2.2, 3).[39]

The best evidence for reconstruction in stone in the late Antonine period comes from the barracks. In those of the first cohort, found in the minster excavations (2.2, 8), the walls, 0.60m thick, survived up to a maximum *c.* 1m high above their clay and cobble foundations.⁴⁰ Within the rooms of the centurions' quarters, numerous fragments of painted plaster were found that showed the walls were painted with elaborate decorative schemes.⁴¹ For example, there was a design, originally on a timber partition wall, that featured an attractive three-quarters view of a male face posed against a leafy garland or frieze (3.5). Other fragments indicate elaborate patterns based on depictions of vegetation as well as variously coloured bands and stripes. These wall paintings were, as was usual in all York's Roman buildings, realised in the fresco technique in which the pigments were applied when the plaster was still wet to ensure they did not fade. Although the pigments in the first cohort barracks were not analysed, those found elsewhere in Roman York have been shown to be based mostly on minerals readily available locally. Red and brown came from red ochre (haematite), yellow from yellow ochre (limonite), black from carbon (soot or charcoal), white from lime, and green from 'green earth' (glauconite). Blue was a compound known as Egyptian Blue (calcium-copper tetrasilicate). This was once thought to be an import to Britain, but pellets found at 24 – 30 Tanner Row (2.3, 19) south-west of the Ouse, suggest it may have been made in York itself.⁴²

As far as the barracks for the other cohorts are concerned, enough has been found of the new stone versions, for example in the *praetentura* at the former Davygate Arcade (2.2, 21) at sites nearby between Little Stonegate and Davygate, in the *retentura* at the minster library (2.2, 2), and in the Aldwark and Bedern area near the fortress east corner, to show that they were slightly different in size from

3.5: Painted wall plaster from the centurion's quarters of First Cohort Barrack 2 found in the minster excavations. The face measures *c.* 150 x 150mm. (© Chapter of York, reproduced with kind permission)

the earlier timber barracks, being now *c.* 71m long as opposed to 78m.[43] This is because the *intervallum* space itself, i.e. the distance between the buildings and the back of the rampart, was widened from 10.5m to *c.* 15 – 16m. As the rampart was also widened (see below), the overall distance between the building line and what had been the front of the early rampart, now the fortress wall, increased from *c.* 16.5m to *c.* 26.25m. In compensation, these stone barracks appear to have been wider than the earlier ones at *c.* 31.5m a pair, as opposed to *c.* 25m. However, the wider *intervallum* also meant that there was no longer space for the same number ranged side-by-side as before. The archaeological evidence is clearest on the south-west side of the fortress where instead of twelve pairs, six each side of the *via praetoria*, there was only room for five-and-a-half. Six pairs (twelve blocks) were originally required for two cohorts, i.e. 960 men, but five-and-a-half suggests accommodation for only 880, although how they were divided up between an odd number of blocks is unclear. In any event, there would seem to have been some reduction in the strength of the legion from what it had been in Vespasian's time.

Also replaced in stone were timber buildings facing the *via principalis*, found in Low Petergate (2.2, 11), and at 9 Blake Street in the *praetentura* (2.2, 13).[44] At the latter, the new buildings adopted a plan that was probably similar to that of their earlier timber forebears (3.6). Once again they were presumably some form of accommodation, but for whom remains unclear. There were two ranges, aligned north-west/south-east. In the 'main' range, parts of two buildings were found. One was only a fragment, but in the other there was a large room (internally *c.* 7.5m square) and an enclosed courtyard. In a later phase the room was divided into four small ones. An unusual discovery in an inserted cross wall was a hoard of thirty-five silver denarii (see p 60).[45] The latest coins were minted 100 years-or-so before construction of the wall, which suggests that the hoard was originally buried in an earlier timber building but, on being discovered, was then reburied. It seems strange that temptation to appropriate such a valuable cache was resisted by the wall builders, but perhaps a fear of divine retribution for disturbing an offering to the gods played a part in their restraint.

South-west of the main range there was a passage and then a 'narrow' range in which two rooms were found and then the street separating it from the north-east end of two barrack blocks. An early feature in the north-western room was the burial of an infant under 3 months old, which may have been another form of offering to propitiate the gods. Infant burials in Roman buildings, military and civilian, are quite a common phenomenon in Britain and thought to have a ritual aspect, although not necessarily associated with infanticide. On the floor of the same room there were fragments of painted plaster in the late Roman demolition debris. As in the first cohort barracks, there was evidence of a colourful interior. There had been two decorative schemes, one of red stripes and mustard-coloured

80 *Julia Velva, A Roman Lady from York*

3.6: Reconstruction of the fortress buildings found in the *praetentura* at 9 Blake Street (looking north), with the roof of a barrack building lower left. The roof of the nearer building is cut away to show the likely method of construction.

blocks on a white background, and a second of maroon, green and crimson stripes and blocks on a white background.[46]

On the fortress defences the reconstruction in stone, largely undertaken in the early second century, was completed in the late Antonine period. Between the north-east gate and the east corner, a curtain wall joined up the earlier freestanding stone towers, including that at the east corner. The wall can still be seen standing up to its full original height of *c*. 5m at the corner where it was uncovered in 1926, having been buried, and protected from stone robbers, in the medieval rampart (3.7 and 3.8).[47] A projecting cornice survives at the top and only the corner tower walls, which would originally have risen above this, are missing. The wall has the usual rubble core but there are neat facing stones surviving on both sides, a feature not seen on the Multangular Tower-type wall described above. At the base of the wall there is a substantial plinth of three blocks. This is another feature that is absent on wall of the Multangular Tower-type.

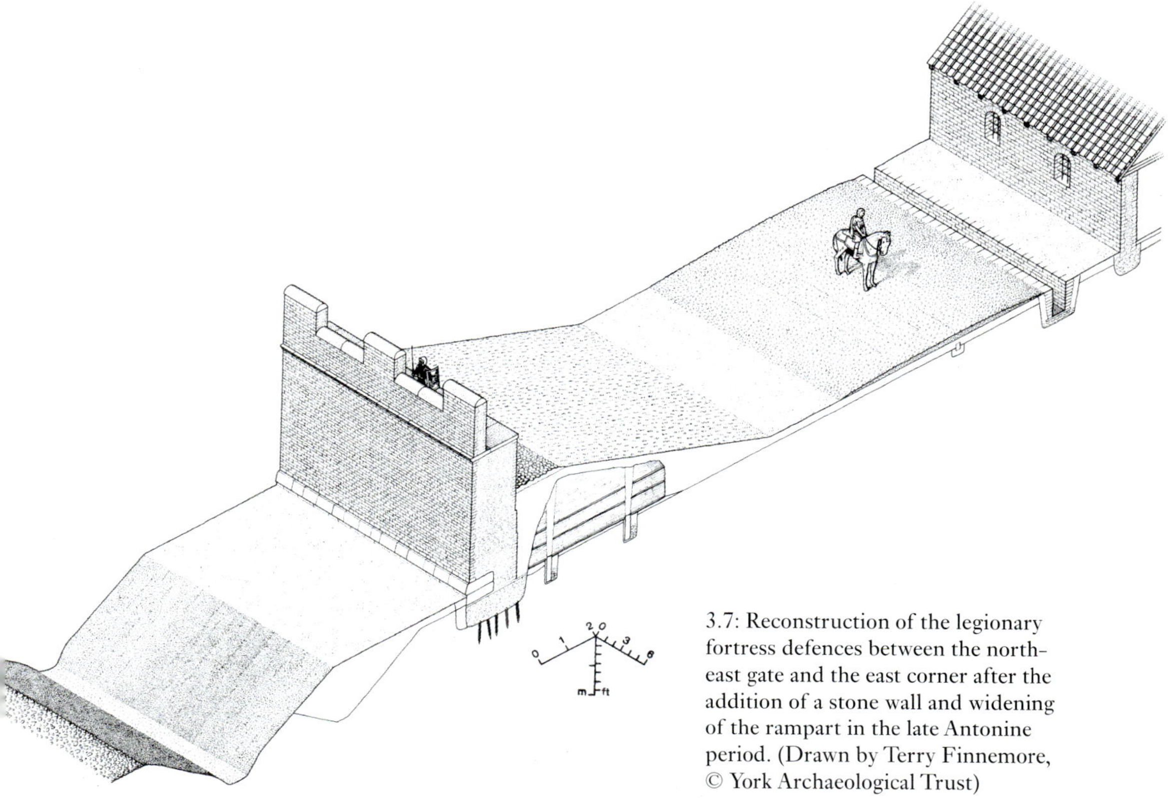

3.7: Reconstruction of the legionary fortress defences between the north-east gate and the east corner after the addition of a stone wall and widening of the rampart in the late Antonine period. (Drawn by Terry Finnemore, © York Archaeological Trust)

3.8: The east corner of the legionary fortress showing the wall of the late Antonine period and base of the earlier (Trajanic) stone tower, looking west.

A fortress wall, also of the late Antonine period, characterised by a similar, if not identical, plinth to that at the east corner, has been found near and just to the north-east of the south corner of the fortress. It was seen surviving to a height of 2.10m, a remarkable fourteen courses high above the plinth, in a sewer trench in Parliament Street in 1976 (2.2, 22; 3.9).[48] Close by, below the cellar floor of 16 Parliament Street (2.2, 23), a stretch of the same wall was recorded abutting (but *not* bonded to) what was thought to be the earlier Multangular Tower-type wall running towards the south corner tower.[49]

3.9: The base of the late Antonine fortress wall (exterior face) in the Parliament Street sewer trench looking north-west. The 1m scale stands on the upper course of the plinth. Below the plinth is the mortared rubble foundation. (© York Archaeological Trust)

Another aspect of the late Antonine work on the defences was a refurbishment, all around the circuit, of the rampart behind the fortress wall. It was widened to c. 9 – 10m but kept to its original height of c. 3m. This involved great dumps of earth and stones that must have been scraped up from a considerable area.⁵⁰ On top of the rampart, by the east corner, a cobbled walkway was found. This would have linked up all the gates and interval towers. Some impression of the rather varied ecology of the fortress rampart in the early third century comes from the timber-lined well dug into it near the east corner – the 'Bedern well' (2.2, 7).⁵¹ The infilling produced plant and insect remains characteristic of grassland, albeit disturbed by humans and grazing, and also of waste or cultivated ground. There were abundant grass caryopses as well as seeds of purging flax (*Linum catharticum*), a plant typical of short turf, as well as numerous seeds of leguminous plants, such as clovers and trefoils, and the ruderals docks (*Rumex* sp.) and stinging nettle (*Urtica dioica*). Whether the rampart was actively grazed by sheep or goats or not cannot be said, but it would have been a good way of keeping it tidy as well as adding to what was on the dinner menu.

Men of the Sixth Legion

It seems likely that amongst the men involved with supervising the construction work I have just described was the Helvius Pertinax tribune at York in the 160s who, in due course, became emperor for a very brief period (p 68). There is no inscription from York mentioning Pertinax, but a number of Sixth Legion men are named on local monuments, many of whom were probably around in Julia Velva's lifetime and even, perhaps, belonged to her coterie of acquaintances.

Late Antonine legates include Claudius Hieronymianus, who is named on a tablet that commemorates his construction of a temple of Serapis (see below). His legionary command is thought to belong to the 190s. Later he became governor of Cappadocia (northern Turkey), where he persecuted the Christians, apparently after his wife had become one.⁵² The only member of the equestrian order, from which officers below the rank of legate were drawn, who is described as such on a York inscription, is the camp prefect Antonius Gargilianus. Part of his tomb monument was found re-used in a post-Roman cemetery at York Minster.⁵³ It had been set up by Claudius Florentinus, who was his son-in-law and a decurion.

Centurions of the Sixth Legion known by name from their funerary monuments include Septimius Lupianus, a man whose *nomen* (family name) suggests he or his father had become a citizen under Septimius Severus.⁵⁴ Lupianus is named as the dedicator of York's finest stone coffin, adorned with cupids, in which his wife, Julia Victorina, and infant son, Constantius, were buried (3.10). The inscription tells us he is '*ex evocato*', meaning he had served in the praetorian

3.10: Stone sarcophagus of Julia Victorina, who lived 29 years, 2 months and 15 days, and her son Constantius, who lived 4 years, 21 days and 11 months, dedicated by the centurion and former *evocatus* (member of the praetorian guard) Septimius Lupianus. Found in 1956 in Castle Yard (containing an adult male) (length 2.24m).

guard based in Rome and was charged with protecting the emperor, before being promoted to centurion. Titus Flavius Flavinus is named on a millstone grit slab that must come from his tomb monument. This was found on Rawcliffe Lane 1.5km north-west of the fortress, where it had probably stood close to one of the main approach roads, perhaps on the edge of an estate acquired by Flavinus on his retirement (1.1, 1).[55] The monument had been the responsibility of his heir, Gaius Classicius Aprilis, who is known as a centurion himself from the inscription on a bronze urn, or camp kettle, found in the River Ouse.[56] Aurelius Super was a centurion whose stone sarcophagus, provided by his wife, was found in a cemetery in Castle Yard, about 500m south-east of the fortress (3.11).[57] His family name may indicate he was a man of native stock who, like Aurelius Mercurialis perhaps, had received citizenship under Marcus Aurelius or Commodus. Other centurions include a man with the *cognomen* Vitalis and an incomplete *nomen* surviving as MAT – possibly Maternus. Referred to in the third-century manner as an *ordinatus*, he was the dedicator of an altar to an otherwise unknown deity, Arciacus, linked with the imperial numen, found in Walmgate (1.1, 7; 6.3).[58]

Ordinary legionaries of the Sixth Legion, whose names we know from funerary monuments, include Lucius Baebius Crescens, whose fine millstone grit tombstone standing 1.83m high – a monument indeed – was found quite

3.11: Stone sarcophagus of the centurion Aurelius Super, who lived 38 years 4 months and 13 days (length 2.26m). The coffin was sponsored by his wife Aurelia Censorina. Found in Castle Yard in 1835.

near to Julia Velva's, but on the opposite side of the Roman road from the south-west, during construction of The Mount School in 1911.[59] Crescens, who we are told had served for twenty-three years, came originally from the Roman colony at *Augusta Vindelicorum*, capital of the province of Raetia, now Augsburg, in southern Germany. Another man of the Sixth was Felicius Simplex, who dedicated a stone sarcophagus to his 10-year-old daughter Simplicia Florentina.[60] This had probably been placed in a family mausoleum near where it was found, in 1838, on Holgate Road, also south-west of the Ouse. Finally, a most interesting member of the legion was Marcus Minucius Mudenus, whose name appears on a small altar that he set up to the mother goddesses of Africa, Italy and Gaul.[61] He was not only a soldier but a specialist river pilot – *gubernator* – the only Roman member of this distinguished profession known by name in Britain. He would have ensured the safe passage of ships up the Ouse to York from those parts of the empire he names, and others besides. Here is a man who would have been thoroughly familiar not only with the Ouse itself, but also the Humber Estuary and its various hazards.

Legionary veterans whose names we know include, from his tombstone, Manlius Crescens,[62] and Gaius Aeresius Saenus, the latter's name appears on the tombstone of his wife, Flavia Augustina, and two infant children (5.8).[63] Some of the other males referred to on tombstones and other inscriptions from York may have served in the legion, but this is not explicit.

A civilian metropolis

The location of sites south-west and north-east of the Ouse referred to below may be found on 2.3.

The presence of the legion in York, and its need for supplies, must have been an important factor in promoting the development of Roman civilian settlement on both sides of the River Ouse at York in the late Antonine period. This was represented by new infrastructure, including streets, a water supply, drainage, and terracing, as well as, although little is known about them, the public buildings. In addition, York now assumed a more prominent role than hitherto as a centre for manufacturing and trade. One need only look at the pottery from archaeological excavations in the city to get an impression of what was happening. First of all, there is simply a much greater quantity dated to Monaghan's Ceramic Period 2b (160 to 200) than to previous ceramic periods.[64] Secondly, sites producing pottery of this period are much more widely distributed through the city than those of earlier periods.

Originally, the civilian settlement at York, known perhaps as the *canabae* and under military control, was located largely north-east of the Ouse (see p 59). Whilst this continued to expand, it is on the south-west bank where, to judge by the abundant archaeological evidence, there was rapid development. This must, I suggest, imply the deliberate foundation, initially probably distinct in legal terms from the *canabae*, of a new settlement.

It is convenient to describe the civilian settlements at York from the late Antonine period onwards as a 'town' and so similar to the other Roman towns of Britain and, to some extent, to towns generally throughout history. This is because, although details are sketchy in some respects, York clearly had a relatively large and dense population compared to other places in the region and had at least some of the facilities and infrastructure we associate with a town. We also know that York, like other towns, played a prominent and distinctive role in the economy of the region (discussed further in Chapter 4), and was a centre for characteristically Roman forms of religious observance (see Chapter 6). However, in the ancient world, what really made a settlement distinct from others and determined its character was who its people were, in terms of their origins and legal status, rather than simply their absolute numbers or any particular physical form in terms of buildings, etc. As Thucydides tells us in *The Peloponnesian War*, when addressing the Athenians, their leader Nicias tells them: 'Reflect that you yourselves, wherever you settle down, are a city already … It is men that make the city, and not walls or ships with no men inside them.'[65] We find these ideas again in how Roman citizenship was conceived in that wherever a Roman citizen found himself, he remained, in some sense, a part of the city of Rome. The *coloniae*, populated by citizens, were all modelled on

Rome and, most important, were founded with the sanction of the gods of Rome and protected by them.

New settlements of citizens did not always gain *colonia* status straight away and York south-west of the Ouse may initially have been what was known as a *municipium*. This is how York is referred to by the mid-fourth-century historian Aurelius Victor in his account (in *De Caesaribus*) of the death of Septimius Severus, although he is not necessarily a reliable source for a period more than 200 years earlier. A *municipium* at York would have had a charter sanctioned by the emperor granting the inhabitants full 'Roman' rights, because they were probably, for the most part, Sixth Legion veterans and their families, and therefore all citizens, as opposed to the lesser 'Latin' rights given to settlements in which only the elected officials and their families were citizens. If not at the time of foundation, the settlement south-west of the river was probably united with that to the north-east, after Caracalla's *constitutio* removed most legal differences between the free-born people of the empire and Roman York had received *colonia* and provincial capital status.[66] Similar rapid progression in terms of status can be found at places with legionary fortresses on the Danube frontier in the late second and early third centuries, including *Singidunum* (Belgrade) in Serbia, and in Hungary at *Brigetio* (Komárom) and *Aquincum* (Budapest). At the latter a *municipium* was promoted to *colonia* in 194, and this status was subsequently extended to the *canabae* around the legionary fortress.[67]

The town south-west of the Ouse

On the south-west bank of the River Ouse there may have been some early Roman settlement on the high ground overlooking the Ouse, close to the main approach road from the south-west (see p 61). However, we are now concerned with areas that, previously unoccupied, witnessed rapid development after about 160. It was in this special and fortunate era of York's history that Julia Velva and Aurelius Mercurialis would have grown up and come to maturity.

The new settlement must have had formal limits, but they are not entirely certain. However, there would presumably have been a foundation ritual in which the space for the new settlement was marked out. This may well have taken a form similar to that said to have been employed in Rome itself when, as described by the Greek writer Plutarch in his *Life of Romulus*:

> *The founder fitted a brazen ploughshare to the plough, and, yoking together a bull and a cow, drove himself a deep line or furrow round the bounds … With this line they described the wall and called it* pomoerium *… and they consider the whole wall as holy, except where the gates are* [the gates were polluted by the passage of the dead and all manner of refuse].[68]

It has usually been assumed that the settlement limits south-west of the Ouse corresponded, at least in part, to the area enclosed by the medieval walls (1.1; 2.3).[69] The walls stand on top of earlier earthen ramparts (3.12) which, by analogy with the similar ramparts north-east of the Ouse, are probably medieval (late eleventh-century, and later) in origin. North-east of the Ouse, the medieval ramparts cover the Roman defences on the north-east and north-west sides of the legionary fortress, and so it has been suggested that the medieval ramparts south-west of the Ouse must also cover Roman defences. Furthermore, it would seem entirely appropriate that a Roman town at York, with a charter based on that of Rome itself, would be dignified by defences. This matter is of no small importance. As Sir Mortimer Wheeler put it:

> *The moments at which a town built or rebuilt its defences were manifestly of special importance in its life-history ... Fortifications ... not merely outline the town-plan (or some part of it) but may focus and express the city's vicissitudes and something of its sociology.*[70]

3.12: The medieval city walls south-west of the River Ouse looking north-east from between points 11 and 12 on the plan 2.3. York Minster, in the centre of the Roman legionary fortress, is in the background.

Unfortunately, what may be evidence for Roman town defences at York is limited to three observations of a stone wall, all on the north-west side of the medieval walled circuit. In 1839, Wellbeloved recorded what he thought was probably a Roman wall with a 'double facing of worked stone', when the northerly of the two arches on Queen Street was cut through the medieval defences for the railway (2.3, 14).[71] In addition, 'a very massive Roman wall' was found here running south-eastwards. If this was part of a town wall, the south-west corner of the medieval town lay beyond its Roman predecessor. In 1874, the foundations of a wall, probably Roman, were discovered below later ramparts during construction of the southern (but not northern) of two arches for the road that leads from the railway station to the city centre (2.3, 11).[72] Between the two locations just described, a substantial wall was observed, but not recorded in detail, when a tunnel was made in the medieval rampart for cables in connection with the LNER wartime facility in 1939 (2.3, 12).[73] There may perhaps have been a gate nearby to admit a minor Roman road approaching from the north-west, but it did not survive into later times.

Within the south-eastern part of the medieval walled city there was a Roman cemetery in the Baile Hill and Falkland Street area (1.1), which included burials with tile-built tombs (see p 232), the tiles themselves bearing Sixth Legion stamps that would make them later than *c.* 120.[74] Traces of Roman buildings were found at the Friends' Burial Ground (2.3, 43),[75] but there is as yet little evidence for Roman settlement any further from the urban core and the cemetery may have remained external rather than being (as at the old station) incorporated into the Roman town.

The main road from the south-west

The main Roman approach road to York from the south-west, laid out at the time of the conquest, may originally have had a military purpose, but subsequently became one of the main streets of the Roman town as well. At Wellington Row (2.3, 16), in about the year 160, the early road make-up of cobbles and gravel (pp 55–6) was replaced by a new and unusual surface made of crushed and hard-packed magnesian limestone (3.13). On the south-eastern side of it there was a trench lined and capped with large limestone blocks for the protection of a water main. This had been composed of lead pipes, of which one had survived. It had an internal diameter of 150mm, the largest of any lead pipe in Roman Britain, witness to a considerable flow of water.

It was not possible to excavate to the south-east of the water main, but it is possible that the main road was doubled in width at this time (to more than 20m), the pipe trench running down its centre rather than along one side. If, as it seems, water was being piped across the river, then this is good evidence that by the late Antonine period, if not before, there was a bridge. In 1893, stonework interpreted

3.13: Wellington Row: late second-century magnesian limestone surface of the main Roman road from the south-west looking north-west with the trench for a water pipe, lined and capped with limestone blocks, on its south-east side, in the foreground, scale 1m. (© York Archaeological Trust)

as the south-western bridgehead was found in sewer trenches at a depth of 6m to 9m, immediately north-east of the Wellington Row site (in North Street, 2.3, 15).[76]

The unusual use of limestone rather than gravel for the road, even though it was probably more expensive and perhaps less hard-wearing, prompts the thought that it was waste from some other officially sponsored construction project, perhaps walling on the fortress defences that we know was going on at much the same time (p 82), or even town defences. It has been suggested that a change from gravel to limestone rubble in the streets of Roman Cirencester (*Corinium*) in the early third century was related to the construction of its town walls.[77] Whether limestone was a suitable material for a street surface or not was not really tested, however, because before any significant wear could occur the level of the road was raised again with a deposit containing a lot of burnt material, probably derived from clearing up a fire in the adjacent building to the north-west (described below). This deposit was succeeded by up to 2m of cobbles and gravel, which by the fourth century had created a causeway standing some way proud of the contemporary ground surface.

Very little is known of the Roman waterfront south-west of the Ouse, which is a great pity as there may well be, still surviving if well-buried, the sort of very substantial timber wharf structures that have been so extensively examined in London. The only opportunity to check this arose in 1993 in a circular shaft of 6m diameter excavated on North Street in advance of construction of a water pumping station (2.3, 17).[78] A timber structure, possibly a river-front wall, was found, but insufficient to understand it properly.

Hitherto it has been assumed that the main approach road to York from the south-west remained on the line described on p 55 above throughout the Roman period, but there is evidence that this was not the case. It was proposed in RCHME's *Eburacum* that there was a Roman street within the walled medieval city parallel to the approach road (still shown on 1.1), represented by observations of a street at Micklegate Bar in 1910, at 88 – 90 Micklegate (possibly) in 1752 (2.3, 30) and at 78 – 82 Micklegate in 1821 (2.3, 26).[79] A more recent record of a street, initially thought to be on this same line, was made in 1992 in a sewer repair trench in Micklegate, in which there was more than 2m of Roman gravel street metalling (2.3, 32).[80] However, if this site is lined up with the observation at Micklegate Bar, it seems more likely that the street was not parallel to the main approach road but was, in fact, heading towards the river crossing, as I have shown on 2.3. At 27 Tanner Row (2.3, 22, 3.17, 7), nearer the river crossing, what were probably the latest Roman surfaces of the main road were recorded in 1972 in two narrow trenches.[81] It is difficult to be exact about the road's alignment here, but it did appear to be heading towards Micklegate Bar. Moreover, on such a line, about halfway, there is clear hump in Barker Lane (just off Micklegate, immediately left of 2.3, 26), suggesting a Roman street lies below.

Back at 18 – 22 Blossom Street (2.3, 46), outside the walled city, in the early third century two large pits were dug into the main road that was found here, which would suggest that it had been decommissioned by this time.[82] What may have happened, therefore, was that, close to what is now the city gate, Micklegate Bar, a re-organisation of the approach to York involved moving the main road south-eastwards on to the top of a ridge of high ground running up to where Micklegate Bar stands. From here the road would have run to the river crossing. The reconstruction in 1.3 imagines the town south-west of the Ouse just after the diversion had occurred. This may have been connected with the construction of defences around the Roman town in that a gate on the site of Micklegate Bar would be far more imposing than one on the original road-line on lower lying ground to the north-west. It would, moreover, be surprising if, in the late eleventh century, Micklegate Bar had been built on a new site to give access through any earlier defences if there was a Roman gateway that could be refurbished. It therefore seems very likely that Micklegate Bar, which contains a lot of re-used Roman masonry, is a direct heir to a Roman gate as Bootham Bar is to the north-west gate of the fortress and many medieval town gates elsewhere in England are to their Roman forebears.

Town streets
Characteristic of the plans of most major Roman towns is a street grid that was usually set out on one single occasion or, at most, in just a few successive stages. There was presumably a fairly regular street grid in York, south-west of the Ouse, although there is, as yet, little clear evidence for it. However, where dated, the earliest surfaces of those streets that have been recorded appear to be consistently late second-century, although they were not necessarily exactly contemporary, suggesting an element of evolution in the plan rather than its setting out as a one-off episode.

A brief review of evidence for the streets may begin by suggesting that perpendicular to the main road from the south-west, a street ran south-eastwards towards what is now the Bishophill district of the city along the top of a Roman terrace described below. What was thought to be Roman road metalling was found in Trinity Lane in 1995 (2.3, 34). A pair of column bases found in sewer excavations in 1895/1901, near a medieval house, Jacob's Well (2.3, 31), may have supported the façade of a building on this street's frontage.[83]

Close to the riverside, at the Wellington Row site (2.3, 16), a street 8m wide was found at right angles to the main road (3.18,1). It had a short life before being moved a little to the north-east to accommodate the late second-century building described below. The width of the new street is not known as it lay largely outside the excavated area. Some 25m to the south-west of it, and on the same alignment, another street, whose full width was also not determined, was found at the 5 Rougier Street site (2.3, 18).[84] This street was composed initially of compacted gravel and was repaired on two occasions in the late second or early third centuries (3.14). Whether it continued south-eastwards beyond the main road is not known, but the street may have joined up, after a change of alignment, with a stretch roughly parallel to the river in the south-eastern part of the Roman town, excavated at 58 – 9 Skeldergate (2.3, 41).[85] The first surface of the latter, at least 3m wide but still surprisingly narrow, was composed largely of cobbles in clay. After a deliberate raising of the ground level a new surface, 2.5 – 3m wide, made of magnesian limestone blocks, was laid down, the material perhaps from the same source as that in the main road at Wellington Row. A third surface, 5m wide, was composed of hard compacted gravel and neatly cambered on each side. This surface could have been contemporary with the first street at Rougier Street (made of gravel) and part of a wide-reaching programme of work on the town's streets in the late second century. Ground level at 58 – 9 Skeldergate was then deliberately raised again by *c.* 0.30m before a succession of four later Roman street surfaces.

Finally, on the higher ground to the south, on Bishophill Junior (2.3, 39), a Roman street running north-east/south-west was excavated in 1961 – 2 in two small trenches.[86] There seems to have been only one phase composed of clay and cobble partly bedded on limestone slabs, the whole being 0.75m thick. Its width was uncertain but may have been as much as 9m.

3.14: 5 Rougier Street: surface of a late second-century street looking south-east (top), scale 1m. (© York Archaeological Trust)

Taking all the evidence together, the overall impression of the streets of Roman York is that although, of course, far better made than anything seen previously in the region, and afterwards for several hundred years, they were nothing like what we are used to today. They had fairly rough surfaces that were repaired on an *ad hoc* basis, although they may have been kept reasonably clean, at least until the later Roman period. However, quite apart from any pot-holes, streets were full of other hazards. As well as people, there would have been animals in the streets in a way that is almost unimaginable today. Farm animals were driven through them to slaughterhouse and market, horses were ridden by soldiers and wealthy private individuals, donkeys by the poor, and dogs ran around largely unchecked looking for scraps. As if the hazards of being knocked over, kicked or bitten were not enough, the ubiquity of the faeces from all these creatures would have created a distinctive and powerful odour. In the absence of adequate lighting, streets were always hazardous in poor light, a particular problem in winter as far north as York with as little as 8 hours of daylight around the time of the solstice. However, rather than walking any distance, well-born ladies like Julia Velva were probably carried around by their slaves in some form of covered litter, or palanquin – a *lectica*. On occasions, perhaps 'she raced through all quarters of the city', as women apparently did in fourth-century Rome.[87]

Water supply

The Romans were masters of hydrological engineering, especially moving water around by means of gravity. If we look at the cross-section of the Ouse river valley in 2.5, which is on the (original) line of the main approach road from the south-west and so probably more-or-less on the line of the water main found at Wellington Row, we can see that it could have worked as a large siphon. The high ground on the south-west side of the valley would probably have been at a level sufficiently above that on the north-east side such that adequate pressure could build up to move the water from a reservoir on the south-west side to, perhaps, the fortress baths on the other. The siphon principle was known in the Roman world as a means of taking water across valleys, although only used occasionally. In the west, a rather grander version than proposed here for York, incorporating a number of aqueducts, supplied Lyon (*Lugdunum*) in Gaul.[88] At York, a reservoir for a head of water would probably have been located somewhere in the Micklegate Bar area, about 800m to the south-west of Wellington Row. Such a reservoir would have been supplied by local springs as well as rainfall. At St Paul's Green, Holgate (1.1, 9; 2.4, 4), *c*. 90m west of the walled city, a wooden (elm) water pipe with a bore of *c*. 110mm, late second century in date, was found.[89] It was probably part of a network of pipes carrying spring water to the Roman town.

Julia Velva's York: 'the summit of sublunary grandeur' 95

As part of a system of water supply based on a principal main, there would have been subsidiary pipes that took water to bath houses, both public and private, and to street fountains. A fine example of a fountain, one of very few known in Roman Britain, was found during sewer excavations in Bishophill Junior in 1906, and we can now see that it stood alongside the street described above (2.3, 39; 3.15).[90] It existed as a large tank, 1m high and 1m square, constructed of

3.15: The street fountain, composed of magnesian limestone slabs, from Bishophill Junior. (© York Museums Trust)

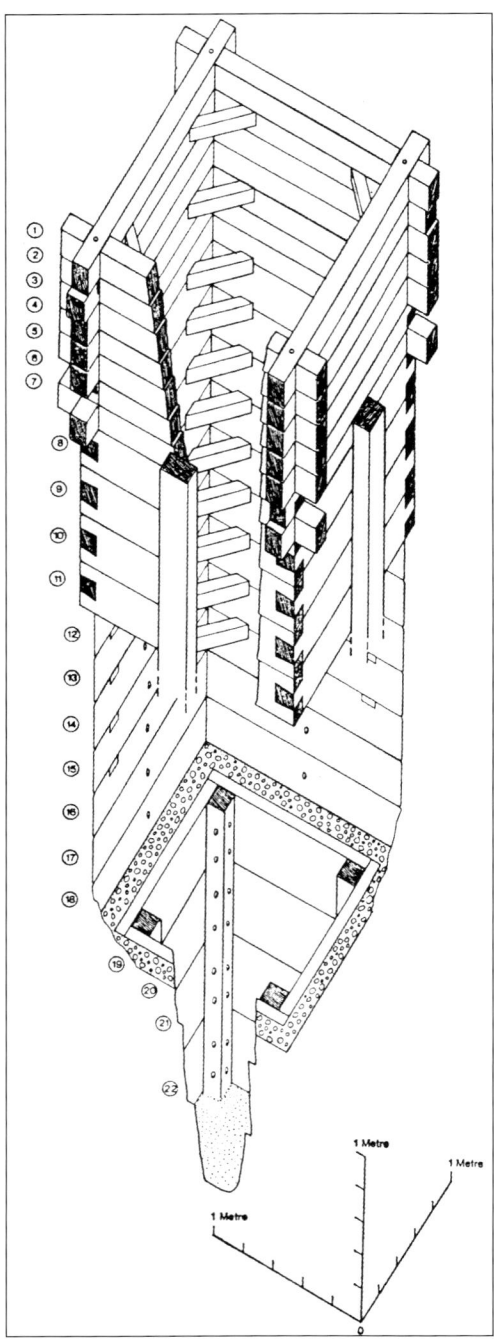

3.16: Isometric drawing of the timber-lined well at 58 – 9 Skeldergate, south-west of the Ouse. (© York Archaeological Trust)

magnesian limestone blocks bound together with iron straps. The back slab rose a further 220mm and was pierced by an inlet, originally housing a spout, which would have been connected to the water supply. The fountain would have been protected from the weather by a vaulted superstructure. There may well have been other street fountains in Roman York which, as can still be seen at Pompeii, would have provided focal points for individual neighbourhoods where local people might meet each other while drawing water.[91] However, piped water could not be relied on to supply all the community's needs and, as in the legionary fortress, there were also wells. One very fine timber-lined example, some 6m deep, was excavated at 58 – 9 Skeldergate – the 'Skeldergate well' (2.3, 41; 3.16). Its construction was dated by pottery to the late second to mid-third century with a radiocarbon-date range centred on c. 200.[92] The well eventually silted up and went out of use in the early fourth century.

It was once thought that lead in water derived from pipes was a major cause of ill health in the Roman world. At York, although water may have been transported in lead pipes (as well as wood), a study in 1975 of samples from seventy-seven individuals from the Trentholme Drive cemetery showed concentrations of lead in the skeletons were only a little higher than today and did not suggest any evidence of lead poisoning.[93]

The built environment
In addition to some elements of a street plan, evidence for many Roman buildings has been found south-west of the Ouse. However, except in the case of an example at Wellington Row (2.3, 16), we have no complete ground plans. Knowledge of

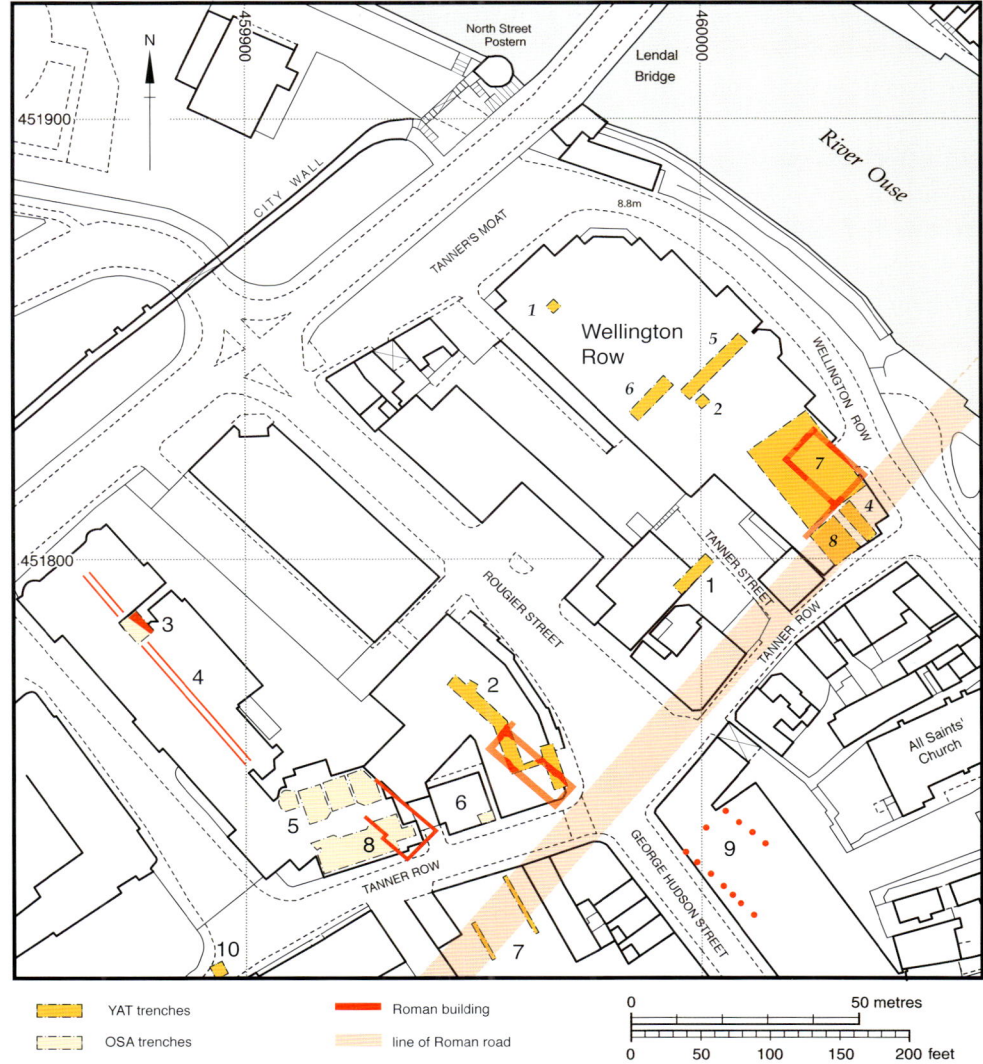

3.17: Plan of archaeological sites in the Rougier Street and Tanner Row area (date of discovery in brackets). For Wellington Row site (1987 – 90), top right, the individual trench numbers are in italics. 1, 5 Rougier Street (1981); 2, 24 – 30 Tanner Row (1983 – 4); 3, Grand Hotel, Trench 1 (2008 – 09); 4, Cobble-lined channel at railway offices (1901); 5, Grand Hotel, other trenches (2008 – 09); 6, 4 – 8 Rougier Street (2017); 7, 27 Tanner Row (1971); 8, Roman building at railway offices (1901); 9, column bases at the Co-op (1898); 10, 39 Tanner Row (1992). (Drawn by Lesley Collett, © York Archaeological Trust)

what the others, only recorded as fragments, were once part of is limited. Even the major public buildings, usually accurately located and well understood in the Roman towns of Britain, remain, more-or-less, unknown to us at York. Nevertheless, there are now enough building fragments to allow us to correlate them, primarily on the basis of construction materials and architectural features, with different zones within the settled areas such as to attempt an outline reconstruction of the Roman townscape. In particular, buildings in which millstone grit was used for construction were concentrated around the bridgehead south-west of the Ouse and, north-east of the Ouse, in an area 100m or so south-east of the south corner of the fortress. As this was the preferred material for large monumental structures in York, we probably have a good impression at least of where the public buildings were to be found.

A review of the evidence for the built environment will break down the Roman settlement south-west of the Ouse into a series of five separate zones as shown on 2.3. Site locations are shown on 2.3 and those in Zone 1 on 3.17 (but not usually referenced in text).

Zone 1: near the bridgehead

An exception to the fragmentary record for most of the buildings in Roman York was found at the Wellington Row site (2.3, 16). Unusually for York, not only was its complete plan revealed but its walls had, in places, survived later stone robbing to a height of more than 2m. Furthermore, as its interior had not been heavily disturbed by medieval pits, it was possible to trace the building's long and varied history in some detail (3.18).[94]

As originally constructed, the Wellington Row building measured about 15.5m x 10.5m (a ratio of length to width of 1.5: 1), and it lay end-on to the main road from the south-west (3.19). Its south-eastern end wall was founded on the edge of the limestone road surface described above, and the two must have been contemporary, i.e. early in the late Antonine period. The other building walls were founded on footings of clay and cobble supported by short timber piles. In contrast to the road surface, the walls were built throughout of oolitic rather than magnesian limestone. A doorway probably allowed entry directly from the road. Equidistant from the side walls at the south-east end of the building was a substantial pillar composed of three millstone grit blocks. This must have been the base for a roof support post and three other similar pillars had clearly been removed in medieval times as their foundation pits had survived. The roof itself was probably composed of thin sandstone slabs, which were found in abundance (3.34). As far as the floor was concerned, the south-eastern third of the building, divided from the rest by a partition, had a timber floor supported by joists. At the rear, against the south-west wall, was an oven made of clay, presumably for cooking

Julia Velva's York: 'the summit of sublunary grandeur'   99

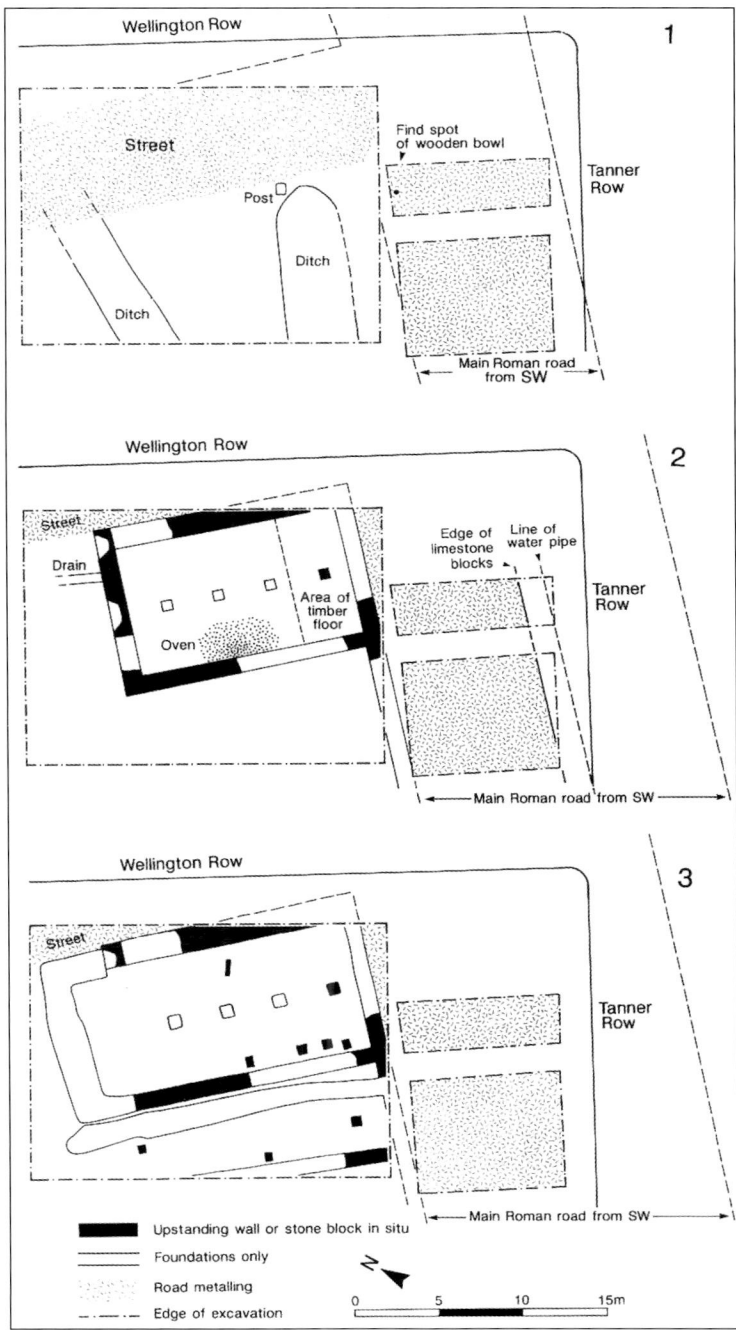

3.18: Wellington Row excavation: plans to show the sequence of (1) early street and Roman road from the south-west; (2) the stone building as originally constructed, and (3) extended after a fire with addition of other structures to the south-west.

3.19: Wellington Row: remains of the late second-century stone building, looking north-east, with stone roof support pillar (right), location of burnt floor joists (right), burnt material from a fire (centre), scale 2m.

and baking. Unfortunately, the function of this building remains unknown. But on the street frontage there may have been a shop. One possibility is that it served travellers, who had just crossed, or were about to cross, the river, with food prepared in the oven.

This oven seems likely to have been the source of a spark for a fire that swept through the building early in its life. Evidence of a fire of a similar, late second-century date was also found nearby at 5 Rougier Street (2.3, 18, see below). It is possible that the whole of the immediate area went up in flames, although sporadic fires were probably a constant hazard in York throughout the Roman period. At all events, damage to the Wellington Row building was considerable and although the debris was largely cleared away, some charred floor timbers and joists remained in the ground (3.20). Most striking of all, the walls had gone a bright pink colour due to the heat.

3.20: Wellington Row: south-east corner of the building, looking south-west, showing a heavily burnt timber and the roof support pillar (right).

After the fire the opportunity was taken in reconstruction to extend the building 2m to the north-west (3.18, 2). The upstanding wall of this extension did not survive, but a substantial structure was implied by a construction trench 1.5m deep and packed with clay and cobbles. Driven into its base were 200 timber piles, about 3m long, which were mostly oak logs but included some re-used timbers. It may be conjectured that a grand, even monumental, entrance to the building had been added, although why this was done remains unknown. At the same time, the floor in the building was levelled up with a thick layer of limestone rubble and mortar. Set on its surface were a number of stone blocks that probably supported a suspended timber floor. During reconstruction, several small pits were dug into the rubble and mortar, in three cases for the burial of pots and in a fourth for a glass bowl. One of the pots had been buried in a wooden box and was filled with crushed fish bones, possibly the remains of the fish sauce (*garum*) much loved by the Romans. The burial of vessels (also known in the fortress), whether with a recognisable content or not, was not uncommon in Roman buildings. Usually, it would seem, they served as votive offerings to the *genius loci* (spirit of the place) for the good fortune of the occupants. The later history of the Wellington Row building falls outside the scope of this book, but it continued in use until the late fourth century before collapse or demolition.

In a small (10m long) trench, up to 5m deep, at 5 Rougier Street, immediately to the south-west of the Wellington Row site (2.3, 18), there was further evidence for a very well-preserved, buried Roman townscape in this part of York and for its complex history.[95] The earliest (late second century) structural phase was represented first by two stone pillars each 1.25m high, one composed of two re-used gritstone column drums. Secondly, running across the trench at its north-east end was a row of massive millstone grit blocks, probably the base of a wall or a stylobate (base for columns) forming part of a building largely lying to the north-east. Identification of the pillars as supports for the raised floor of a granary may be supported by a thick overlying dump of burnt material composed largely of grain (see p 129), but also including charred timber, which probably resulted from the collapse of the building during a fire. After the fire the gritstone blocks were covered over by the street described above. South-west of it a new building

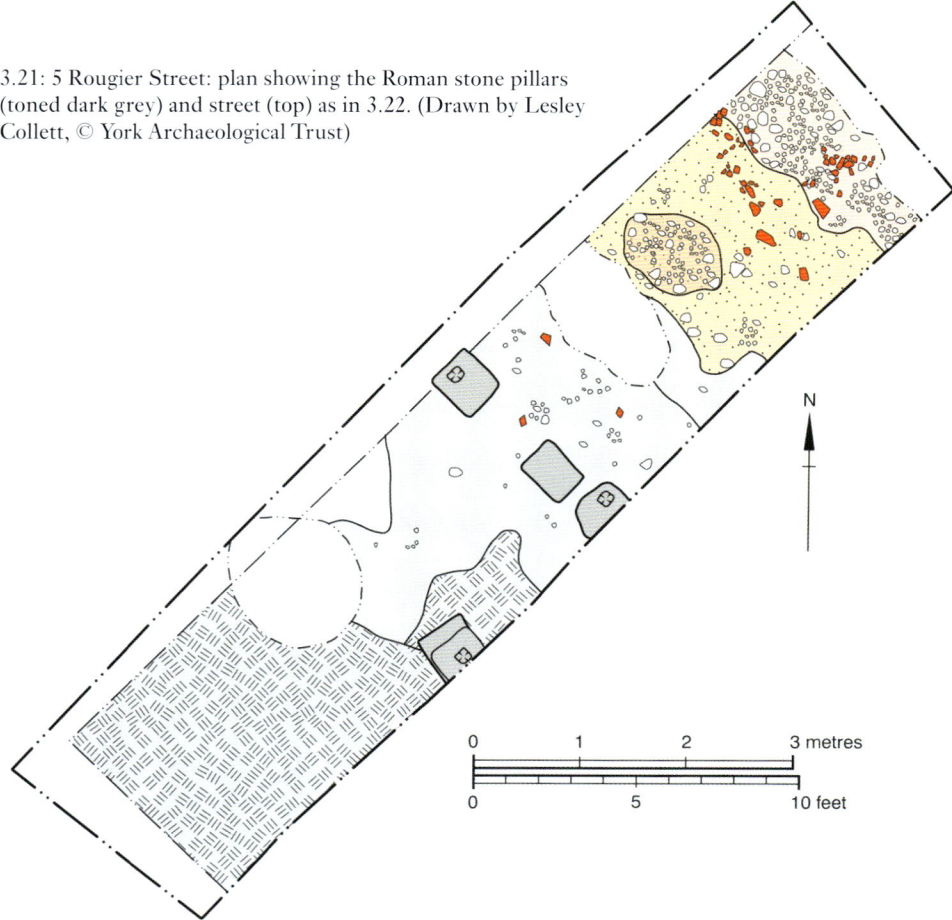

3.21: 5 Rougier Street: plan showing the Roman stone pillars (toned dark grey) and street (top) as in 3.22. (Drawn by Lesley Collett, © York Archaeological Trust)

3.22: 5 Rougier Street: millstone grit stone pillars, and another block in the centre, from a Roman structure, looking north-east. The 1m scale lies on a surface of the street running north-west/south-east (left to right).

was constructed with a group of pillars comprising large millstone grit blocks, although in such a small trench what they were part of could not be determined (3.21 – 22).

Also close to the main road from the south-west lay the site of 24 – 30 Tanner Row excavated in 1983 – 4 as five narrow but deep (up to 5m) trenches (2.3, 19; 3.23).[96] In this case it was the remains of timber rather than stone buildings that were found (3.24 – 26). The excavation examined a complex sequence, probably within part of a property on the north-west side of the main approach road from the south-west, beginning in the late Antonine period. An episode of ground preparation involved raising the level with layers of turf and clay to compensate for a gentle natural slope falling from north-west to south-east. On two level platforms thereby created were the remains of several buildings, but the two most substantial (1 succeeded by 5) were near the main road.

The south-eastern (front) wall of Building 1 was constructed of horizontal boards nailed onto posts driven into the ground. The north-east and north-west walls, also formed from boards, were supported by posts driven through beams laid flat on the ground. Within the building were horizontal timbers which had probably supported a plank floor, although no trace of this had survived. Immediately to the north-west of the building there was a large drain (Structure 5), lined with

3.23: 24 – 30 Tanner Row: view to the south-east showing machine clearance in progress prior to archaeological excavation. Rougier Street is on the left and Tanner Row crosses it from right to left. The main Roman approach road from the south-west was found in 1971 on the site of the building on the extreme right (2.3, 22 and 3.17, 7) next to the County Hotel (grey building). The road runs from there under the continuation of Tanner Row to the left. The building in the top left of the image is the Co-op, where column bases were found during construction in 1898 (2.3, 23 and 3.17, 9). (© York Archaeological Trust)

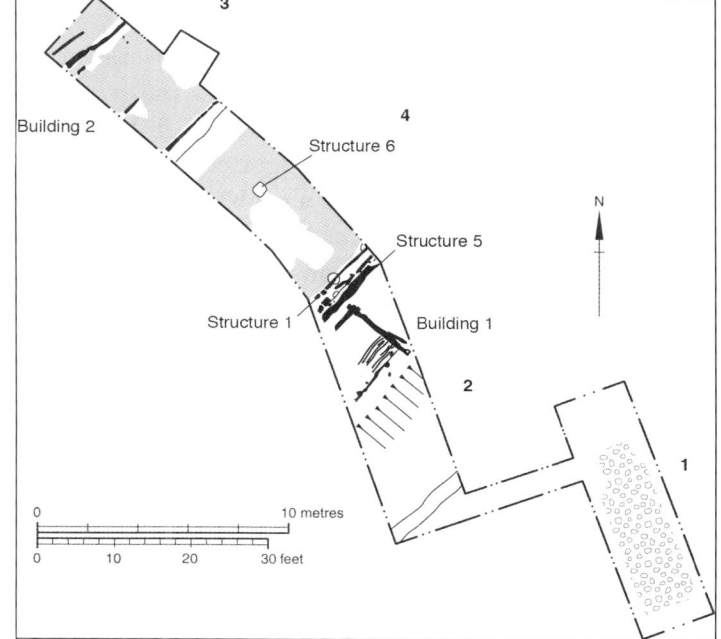

3.24: 24 – 30 Tanner Row: Building 1 looking south-west, the north-east wall runs diagonally left to right above the 1m scale. Timber-lined drain (Structure 5) is on the right. (© York Archaeological Trust)

3.25: 24 – 30 Tanner Row (Trenches 1-4): plan showing Buildings 1 and 2 and Structure 1 (a timber revetment between ground at different levels), 5 (a drain) and 6 (a well). (Drawn by Lesley Collett, © York Archaeological Trust)

3.26: 24 – 30 Tanner Row: Detail of the front (south-east) wall of Building 1 showing planking nailed to the internal face of the timber uprights. View north-west, scale 0.50m. (© York Archaeological Trust)

oak boards which had, at the end of its life, been used for the disposal of kitchen waste, in the form of abundant food remains, as well as human faeces, the latter represented by large quantities of the eggs of parasitic worms that live in the gut.[97] Unfortunately, the south-western limit of the building was not located so its size is uncertain. However, it was apparently only one room in depth and might have served as a single room shop or workshop from which goods were sold to passers-by. Beyond the drain was a pit or well (Structure 6) lined with boards. Building 2 survived only as timber sill beams resting on a base layer of clay and stones. They may have supported a shed at the rear of the property. At the south-eastern end of the site a cobbled surface was found, which must have been very close indeed to the road. It appears that horses or cattle were corralled here as the overlying deposit consisted largely of hay-rich dung, identified on the basis of surviving fibrous matter and presence of insect species known to live in stables.[98] Still in the late Antonine period, Building 1 was reconstructed (Building 5), again with horizontal boards nailed to posts. Part of the north-west (rear) wall of Building 5 was rather unusual in having boards nailed to both sides of the posts creating a form of cavity wall. The void between the boards was perhaps packed with some sort of insulation material. The well-preserved timbers in the principal buildings at 24 – 30 Tanner Row exhibit a wealth of evidence for the techniques of the Roman carpenter. There is a range of joints and mortises, and marks of the axe and adze are common.[99] Also visible are the marks of the saw, a woodworking tool known in the Roman period but not used subsequently in England until the twelfth century.

Deposits around Building 5 produced a great quantity of butchered cattle limb bones and scapulae, indicating that systematic, and fairly large-scale, carcass processing was being carried out in the vicinity.[100] The building may even have been a butcher's shop in which an iron meat cleaver found nearby had been used. In addition to the bones, the site produced abundant artefacts, many of which were associated with crafts, notably metal- and leatherworking (discussed in more detail in Chapter 6), providing some of the best evidence for Roman York as a manufacturing centre in the Julia Velva period.

By the beginning of third century, the ground had risen by 3m from its original level, testimony to the amount of activity in this part of the town in no more than about fifty to sixty years. In the mid-third century, a stone building was constructed above the remains of the timber buildings, although only the substantial clay and cobble foundations, supported on timber piles, had survived (see 3.17, 2). This was probably part of some larger public building and is, perhaps, a small piece of evidence for an architectural transformation of the town south-west of the Ouse after it had become a provincial capital.

Some 20m south-west of 24–30 Tanner Row, an area of c. 2,510m^2 was excavated to a depth of between 4.35m and 8.40m for construction of the LNER offices – now the Grand Hotel – in 1901 (2.3, 21).[101] Hastily recorded during the work was part of what must have been a monumental building with a wall of millstone grit blocks parallel to and c. 10m from the main road from the south-west. The wall survived c. 1.5m high and about a 3m length was observed. Other walls were noted suggesting a building at least 15m x 9m. Some hint of architectural splendour was provided by three column capitals, one of Corinthian type decorated with acanthus leaves.[102] In 2013, small-scale excavation below the floors of the hotel, largely at the south-east (Tanner Row) end, in advance of a hydrotherapy pool, showed that construction in 1901 had not been as destructive of archaeology as was feared.[103] However, although well-preserved sequences of Roman remains, indicating structures, were found, it was difficult to make much sense of them in small trenches. There was no evidence for any surviving walls similar to those found in 1901, although the trench for a substantial wall, running north-west/south-east, was found below the central part of the hotel (2.3, 20). There was no further evidence either for a 2m-wide 56m-long Roman cobble-lined water channel or drain found in 1901.

On the opposite side of the main Roman road from the south-west, on the site of the Co-op building (in George Hudson Street; 2.3, 23), a group of millstone grit column bases was found in 1898 at a depth of 2.60m.[104] There was a row of seven and another of four, suggesting two parallel colonnades 12m apart, more-or-less at right angles to the road. Although the record is inadequate, it appears that the distance between the columns (centre to centre) in each row was *c*. 2.75m (rather less than half the *c*. 6.2m between the columns, centre to centre, in the fortress headquarters basilica). The diameter of the bases was a substantial 0.91m, leading Gordon Home to reconstruct columns 9.75m high,[105] a little higher than those in the headquarters basilica, although Home probably made a bit of an overestimate. The distance between the colonnades is similar to the distance between those dividing up the space in the fortress basilica. However, at the Tanner Row (north-west) end, another base lay between the two, a hint perhaps of a building of a rather different sort. Also found hereabouts, in 1909, was an (incomplete) altar dedicated to the imperial numen and *genius* of *Eboracum*.[106] This is just the sort of dedication one might expect to find in the shrine of a public building, perhaps the town forum, a shrine that would have served as the focus for ceremonies sponsored by the civic authorities to appeal to the emperor, in his divine aspect and as *pater patriae* (father of the homeland), to look with favour on and protect the local population.

Originally, the word 'forum' in the Roman world meant a large open area for markets and assemblies, but it came to describe a range of buildings organised around a central courtyard. In Britain, the urban fora usually resemble a military headquarters with, on one side of the courtyard, a basilica including, to the rear, offices for civic administration and a shrine. There would also have been a space for the meetings of the *ordo*, a body that governed the town and dispensed justice. The *ordo* comprised 100 local men, known as decurions. They were drawn from local elite families, all Roman citizens, who fulfilled a wealth qualification based largely on property ownership. The decurions were expected to maintain the roads, drains, water supply and other infrastructure of the town, for which they used taxes collected from the local population. It was also expected that the decurions and other wealthy people would use their own resources to support their communities and by their generosity they would gain status and reputation. In addition to the useful stuff like drains, entertainments in the theatre and amphitheatre were provided and the temples were properly maintained.

The names of three York decurions are known from inscriptions, all of which should be dated after the promotion of the town to *colonia* status (i.e. after the early third century), as DEC COL (*decurio coloniae*) is included in the wording. On part of the tomb monument erected to his father-in-law, the camp prefect Antonius Gargilianus, found in the minster excavations, we have Claudius Florentinus.[107] The name of Flavius Bellator appears in the inscription on his stone sarcophagus in the railway station Roman cemetery (1.1).[108] His *cognomen*, Bellator, is thought to be a Latinised version of a native name that means 'warrior'. Bellator's skeleton still had a gold ring on one finger, indicating his membership of the equestrian order. The third named decurion, Marcus Aurelius Iraneus, is referred to on an incomplete Roman sarcophagus found re-used in a medieval cemetery on Fishergate, north-east of the Ouse.[109]

Either in the same *insula* as the building with the column bases, or in the next one to the south-east, a hint of another major building came to light in 1853 in a sewer trench west of the junction of George Hudson Street and Micklegate, opposite St Martin's Church (2.3, 28).[110] In addition to a course of large millstone grit blocks, there were fragments of column shafts and a moulded pedestal base for a column or statue.[111] These remains may have formed part of a temple of Mithras – a Mithraeum – as they were in much the same place in which the relief of the bull-slaying scene was found in 1747 (see p 219).

Zone 2: central

In many Roman towns, the forum was very close to the main public baths. At York, a few walls of what is likely to have been a bath house were found about 100m south-east of the suggested forum site. In 1989, excavations took place on the site of the former Queen's Hotel at 1 – 9 Micklegate (2.3, 29; 3.27). In a group of trenches, regrettably very limited in extent, substantial walls 2.2m thick, defining parts of three or four rooms of a late second- or early third-century building, were found. The walls stood to a height of *c.* 2m above their foundations but had been demolished to Roman ground floor level either at the end of the Roman period itself or some time afterwards. Most of what actually survived, therefore, formed the sides of a great under-floor hypocaust system occupying a space about 0.50m deep. The hot air passed through the walls between the rooms in great brick-lined

3.27: 1 – 9 Micklegate (former Queens Hotel): walls of early third-century building, probably a bath house (looking south-west, scale 2m), showing brick-lined arches (blocked in the fourth century) of the hypocaust system and the capping for a drain lower left. Original ground floor level was at the top of the walls.

3.28: Imaginative reconstruction of the interior of a Roman bath house by Sarah Hall Baqai.

arches – blocked in the late Roman period. Below the hypocaust the building foundations went down a further 1.5m into wet unstable ground, an indication of the likely massive size of the lost superstructure. This building did not follow the same alignments as most others south-west of the river but had probably been constructed to take advantage of fairly level ground on a terrace above the river as imagined in 1.3. Although only a small part of it was seen, we should nonetheless, I suggest, be thinking of a bath house suitable for a provincial capital, on the scale of, for example, the better-preserved and very extensive imperial baths at another capital, *Augusta Treverorum* (Trier) in Gallia Belgica (now Germany). The baths were one of the centres of social life in a Roman town where the likes of Aurelius Mercurialis not only met their friends but also received clients who came to them in search of assistance and favours. Many a deal was probably done in an intimate chat while the parties were naked in the steam room. Julia Velva and her cronies would also have enjoyed bathing, presumably at times when the men were elsewhere (3.28).

Zone 3: north-west

Evidence was found for another Roman bath house in the north-western part of the Roman town during construction of the old station in 1839 – 40 and again at the LNER wartime facility site in 1939.[112] Although the records made at the station are inadequate, it seems clear that a bath suite of five or more rooms was found, including two with cold plunges, set out in a linear arrangement *c.* 15m long. To the west of the suite was a small building with a tile drain under the floor, suggesting it too was baths-related. The drain was traced to the northeast for more than 100m. It was in the fabric of this latter building that the altar to Fortuna, dedicated by Sosia Juncina, had been re-used (2.23). As her husband is thought to have been a Sixth Legion legate in York in the mid-130s, the building, and those adjacent, probably belong to the later second century or an even later date. In 2012, excavations (a trench *c.* 40m x 10m) in advance of development of new council offices, more-or-less on the same site as the linear bath house, showed that some of what were probably its walls had surprisingly survived construction of the station.[113]

If we return to the 1839 – 40 discoveries, we find that about 76m to the northeast of the linear bath suite was a room (*c.* 11.25m x 9m) also part of the same building complex with, on its north-east side, a plunge pool with a lead pipe outlet. This was approached by two steps from the other part of the room, which was paved with sandstone flags. A furnace adjoined this room on its south-west side. South-west of the linear bath suite was yet another stone building (11.9m x 7.5m) with an apsidal north-west end. The floor, as described by Wellbeloved, suggests it was made of *opus signinum* – a form of Roman concrete made with crushed tile to make it waterproof – and so is also likely to be baths-related.

The relationship of the buildings found in 1839 – 40 to those found in 1939 is unfortunately not at all clear. The main building of 1939, with an apse at the southwest end, survived as the foundations and the lowest parts of walls that enclosed remains of a hypocaust in which there were a few tile *pilae* still standing on a stone-flagged base.[114] Although its north-eastern limit was not found, this building was a substantial *c.* 11m wide and at least 12.8m long. In the reconstruction drawing, I estimated a length of 22m based on a 2:1 ratio, length to width, and a height equivalent to the width of 11m (3.29). Appended to the north-west wall was a small room for a furnace that had supplied the hypocaust with hot air through a stone-lined duct. Immediately north-east of the apsed building there were fragmentary remains of other stone structures, but it was not possible to make much sense of them.

The 1939 building was interpreted by RCHME as a bath house *caldarium* which, it claimed, was the largest known in Roman Britain. Another possibility (as discussed above) is that this was a great hall forming part of the palace of the governor of Lower Britain, who was established in York following Caracalla's division of the province of *Britannia* into two. If this was indeed the case, then all the buildings in this area, including the baths, may have belonged to a palace complex. However, whatever their function, on the relatively high ground overlooking the Ouse, the 1939 building and others around it must have been an imposing presence in the urban landscape.

3.29: Reconstruction drawing of the apsed building found at the LNER wartime facility in 1939, looking north-east. The room for the furnace is in the centre.

Another indication of the association of this old station area with the military and imperial authorities may derive from the slab recording the construction of a temple of Serapis hereabouts by a legionary commander, probably in the 190s (see pp 217–18). The word '*templum*' in the inscription implies that we should envisage not just a building but one standing within a dedicated precinct that had been marked out following enunciation of appropriate sacred formulae by the augurs (official fortune-tellers) for religious purposes. Found at the same time as the slab, in 1770, was another apsed building, seen again in 1840, when a fourth-century mosaic was recovered on the site but, although possible, it is not entirely clear if this building was, in fact, related to the temple (2.3, 24).[115]

South-west of the apsed building, a Roman house of several rooms was found on Toft Green in 1853 (2.3, 25). It contained two fourth-century mosaics, but earlier floors were recorded, and the building's origins may well lie in the period of initial urban growth a hundred-or-so years earlier.[116]

Zone 4: south-west

This zone lies south-east of the main Roman road from the south-west and is bounded to the south-west by the medieval walls (possibly overlying Roman defences). Today this is the residential Bishophill district. Little of this zone has been explored archaeologically, the Roman buildings referred to below being largely on its periphery.

In 1837, remains of Roman buildings were apparently found while digging sewer trenches in Micklegate between Priory Street and Micklegate Bar. Some remains of buildings were also found nearby in 2016 in the cellar of 120 Micklegate.

Roman building fragments were observed in 1752 and 1946 in the north-western part of this zone.[117] In 1752, 'several altars' were also found, including that dedicated to the mother goddesses by the river pilot Mudenus (pp 85 and 214), perhaps from a roadside shrine (2.3, 30). In 1946, part of a room with walls of York's typical small limestone blocks, 1.75 high, was found 3.35m below modern level (2.3, 27). The column bases at Jacob's Well (2.3, 31) have already been mentioned. One of them is in the porch of Holy Trinity Priory church nearby. A probable Roman wall was found under the church choir and numerous Roman finds in the Yorkshire Museum collection come from the priory precinct. To the south-west of it, evaluation trenches at the former Kennings Garage, Micklegate, produced the south-east corner of a quite substantial building with foundations, nearly 1m wide, of cobbles and clay, dated to the late second to early third centuries (2.3, 33).[118]

About 70m south-west of the 1 – 9 Micklegate site (2.3, 29) some remains of another Roman bath house, perhaps in a private house, were found on Fetter Lane during sewer excavations in 1852 (2.3, 36).[119] There were walls four to five courses high defining parts of three rooms, including one with a cold plunge bath. In 1998, in small-scale excavations in the same area, an *opus signinum* floor, as often found in bath houses, was recorded in a sequence of building-related layers.[120] This same site also produced evidence for terracing of the steeply sloping ground in this area, which is known to extend away to the south-east (see below).

Whilst the function of the buildings so far described in this zone is not readily apparent, when we reach the south-eastern part of it (and Zone 5), we seem to be in an area dedicated to houses. As far as we can tell, from admittedly limited evidence, these were large buildings, at least in part in stone, and had several rooms, so that they were very different from the roundhouses in which many of the rural population continued to live. A roundhouse usually had no internal divisions so that life was lived communally. But in a typical Roman house, a measure of privacy was possible and social distinctions could be reinforced by controlling access to its various parts.

At the junction of St Martin's Lane and Trinity Lane, poorly preserved remains of a house with two or more rooms were found in 1947 and 1993 – 4 (2.3, 35).[121] A little to the south, excavations north of the church of St Mary Bishophill Junior in 1961 – 3 revealed part of a large spacious house, probably built in the late second century (2.3, 38; 3.30).[122] Well-constructed stone-lined drains were found below the floors of parts of three rooms divided up by stone walls (3.31). An apse had been added to the south-east side of the building, initially perhaps for some sort of feature like a statue, but after enlargement, probably to create the sort of *triclinium* for polite dining in Roman style represented on Julia Velva's tombstone. This side of the house faced south-east and so one can imagine the apse also being part of an elegant 'morning room' for the residents.

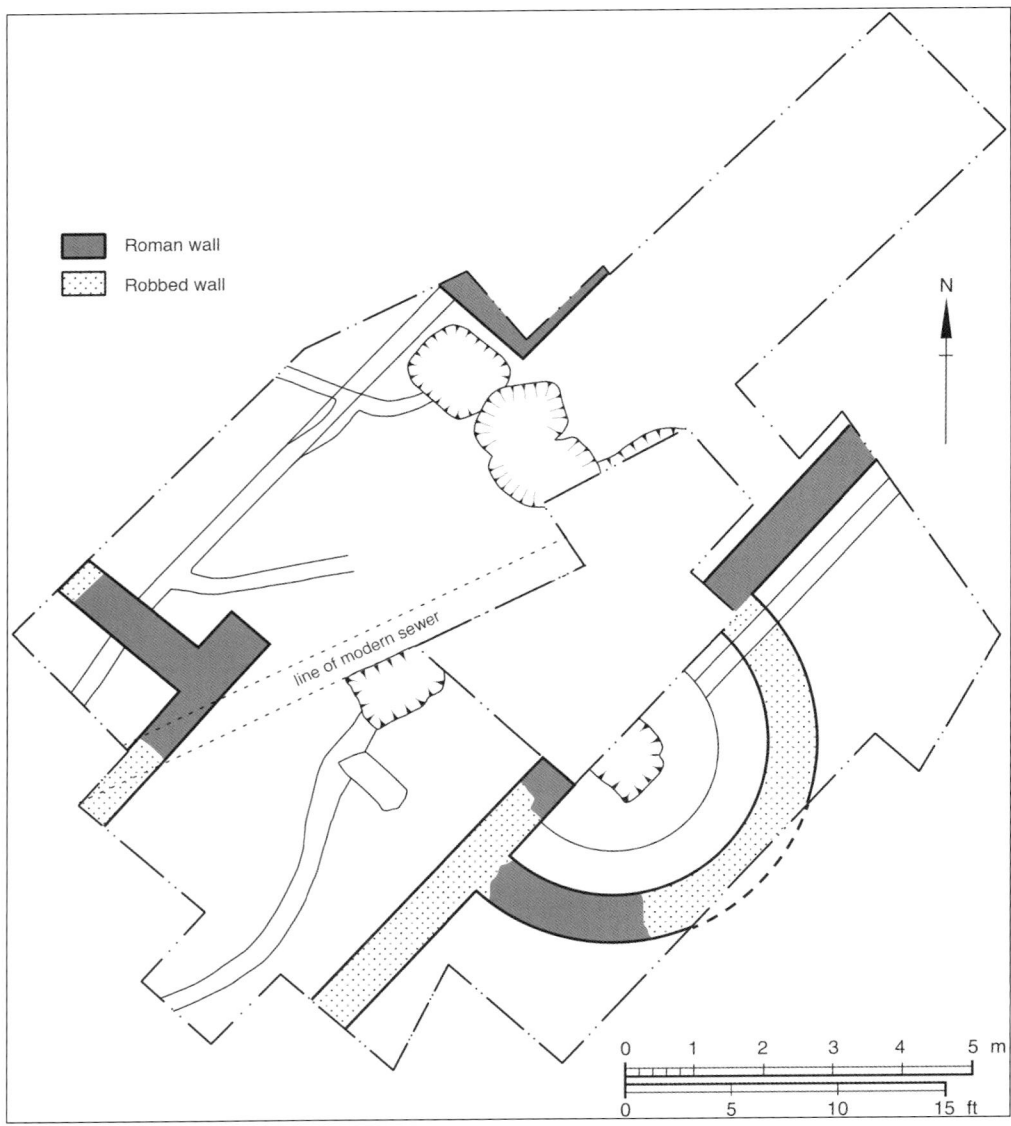

3.30: St Mary Bishophill Junior: plan of the Roman building found in 1961 – 3. There were two phases of the apse with the wall of the later outside that of the earlier. (Drawn by Lesley Collett, © York Archaeological Trust)

Finally, in two of three small trenches dug on Bishophill Junior in 1961 – 2 (2.3, 39), close to the street described above, fragmentary evidence was found for two more stone buildings of the late second to early third centuries.[123] The *opus signinum* floor of one of them was covered by the burnt material referred to in my anecdote about Sir Mortimer Wheeler (pp 65–6).

3.31: St Mary Bishophill Junior: detail of the Roman building showing a stone-lined drain running under one of the stone walls. Scale: 3 feet.

Zone 5: south-east

It would seem entirely appropriate that the Roman altar found somewhere in Bishophill Senior in 1638 should be dedicated, *inter alia*, to the 'gods of hospitality and home', as it may well have come from a small roadside shrine standing in the residential zone on the south-eastern edge of the Roman town.[124]

Either in the late second or early third century, a terrace for new buildings was created in this zone. This involved, firstly, levelling the land on the uphill side and, secondly, building up the land on the sharply sloping downhill (north-eastern) side by up to 2.8m, as shown in an excavation at 37 Bishophill Senior (2.3, 40).[125] A terrace retaining wall was found on Fetter Lane (2.3, 37) and it was also found, standing at least 2m high, in excavations on the site of the demolished church at St Mary Bishophill Senior (2.3, 42).[126] The south-eastern limits of the terrace are unknown, but it continued beyond the church site and, in all, may have been at least 300m long. Construction was clearly a massive undertaking, requiring the mobilisation of a considerable amount of labour to move many thousands of tons of material.

On the St Mary Bishophill Senior site, there was evidence for the beginning of occupation in the late second century. This took the form of a timber building on drystone foundations (*c.* 5.5m x 9m), which was associated with evidence for metalworking (see p 142).[127] At this site subsequently and at 37 Bishophill Senior, just to the north, late second- to early third-century stone houses were built on the terrace (3.32). Fragments of other buildings, represented by stone walls, have been found elsewhere in this zone, which were probably also parts of houses.

Unfortunately, nothing approaching a complete plan was recorded for either of the buildings on Bishophill Senior and the walls had been almost completely demolished. It was clear, nevertheless, that they had both been constructed largely from magnesian limestone on mortared stone foundations supported in places by timber piles. Whilst the evidence seems unpromising, there is, in fact, sufficient to allow a reconstruction drawing to be made as shown in 3.33. Although a good deal is uncertain, what is clear is that these were two large buildings, each one probably covering as much as 600m^2. They are not the average detached houses of modern times, but more along the lines of country mansions brought into town to accommodate large elite households.

The late second- to early third-century house at St Mary Bishophill Senior, which survived only as fragmentary foundations re-used for a fourth-century rebuilding, appears to have included a range (the south-eastern in 3.32) *c.* 25m x 7.5m, initially divided up into three (possibly four) rooms, the largest of which measured, internally, a fairly substantial *c.* 50m^2. This may have served for the reception of guests, clients, etc. There was probably a corridor at the

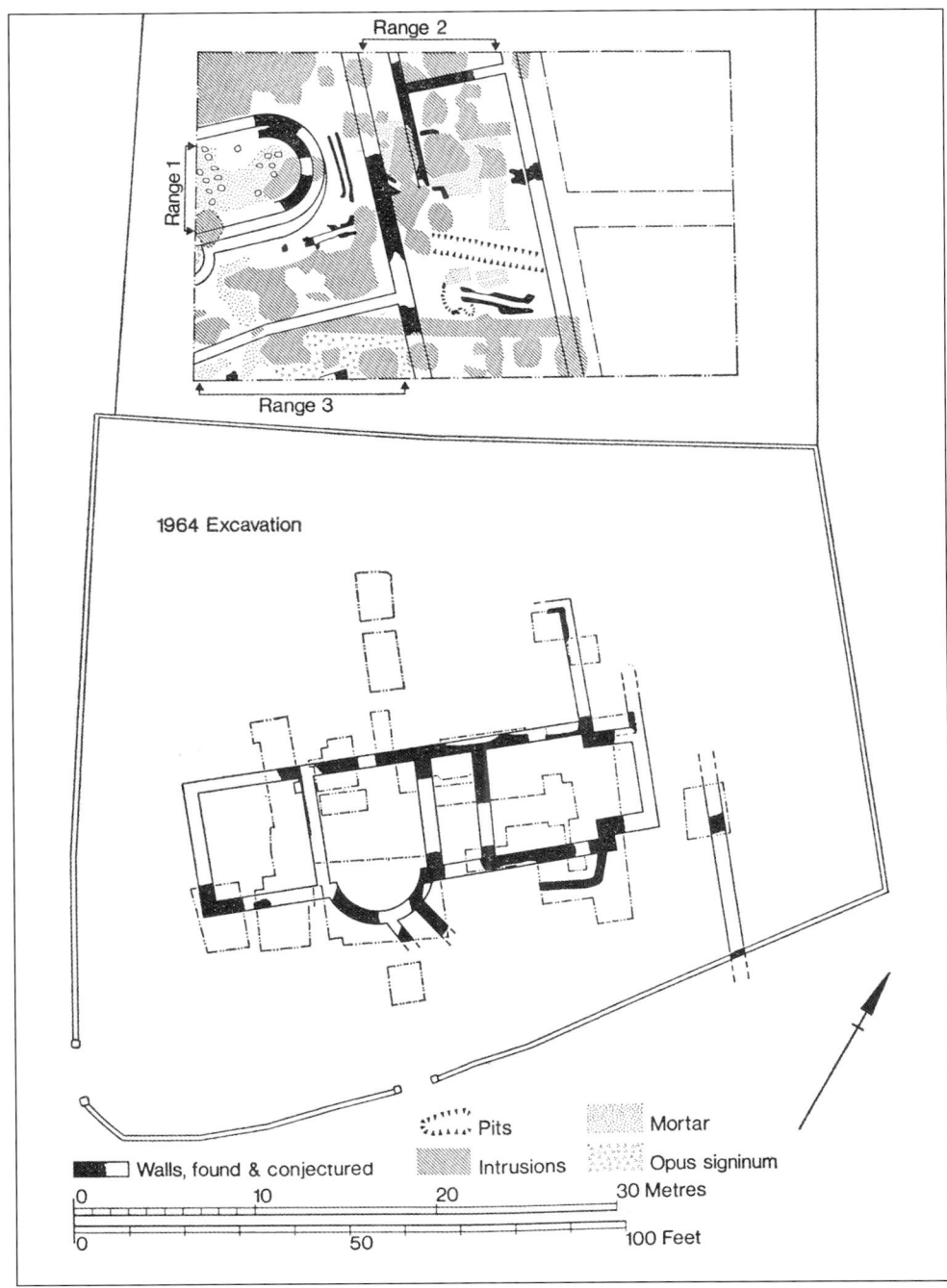

3.32: Plan of the Roman buildings found on Bishophill Senior at No 37 (top) and (fourth century on earlier walls) at the site of the church of St Mary Bishophill Senior. (© York Archaeological Trust)

3.33: Reconstruction drawing of Roman houses at 37 Bishophill Senior (left) and St Mary Bishophill Senior (right), looking south-east.

south-east end of this range leading to a north-western range of rooms, which may have been of similar size to the first. If so, then the width of the building was about 22m. In the centre, between the ranges, one can envisage a rather narrow courtyard.

As far as the house at 37 Bishophill Senior is concerned, the excavation probably revealed the south-eastern quarter, although the corner itself was not recorded. A north-eastern wing ('Range 2'), 9.2m wide, had a corridor that would have connected a series of rooms, although only two, possibly three, could be defined. Little of the south-eastern wing ('Range 3') was recorded, but it may also have had a corridor leading to other rooms. These two wings appear to have flanked a courtyard in which there was a building with an apse at its north-east end. Numerous timber piles up to 1m long, which gave stability to foundations over 1m wide, suggest this building was quite substantial. Within it there were some tile *pilae* of a hypocaust, indicating a heated room that may be interpreted as the *caldarium* of a private bath house. If this apsed building was on the central north-east/south-west axis of the house (as shown in 3.33), then the location of a north-west wing that closed off the courtyard can be predicted. It might seem a little inconvenient to have a bath house in the middle of the courtyard, rendering it rather useless for other activities, but it would have been a great asset to the residents and a mark of the owner's status. Most people in Roman York presumably had to go the public baths for a wash. A bath house here would probably have been connected to the water supply system that also fed the street fountain found nearby (see pp 95–6).

Numerous fragments indicate that both houses had painted plaster on their walls, although the original decorative schemes are hard to determine.[128] Material found in the north-eastern wing of the 37 Bishophill Senior house was interpreted as having three superimposed layers of painting, each with different designs – the owners clearly had the decorators in to freshen the place up from time to time. The uppermost layer was perhaps fourth-century. The earlier, second, layer had a predominantly vermilion background decorated with flower buds in dark red, grey and white. The earliest layer was decorated with bands of varying width in dark yellow, red, black and green. Patterns based primarily on coloured bands and stripes are typical of Roman Britain. One rarely finds the decorative sophistication of the provinces in the Mediterranean heartland. The pigments on the 37 Bishophill Senior plaster were made from the usual locally sourced minerals (see p 78), except that the vermilion in the second layer was red ochre mixed with cinnabar (mercuric sulphide), probably imported from Spain where, according to Pliny, it was found in the silver mines.[129] Other debris from the two houses included roofing material. Abundant ceramic tiles were found at St Mary Bishophill Senior, whilst sandstone slabs probably formed the roof at 37 Bishophill Senior (3.34). On the roofs of either house there could have been the sort of decorative roof finial, cum chimney, in the form of a tower with its doorway and windows, pictured in 3.35, which was

(*Right*) 3.35: Ceramic chimney and roof finial found in Bishophill in 1872, height: 175mm. (© York Museums Trust)

(*Below*) 3.34: A group of Roman sandstone slabs arranged as on a roof. Scale: 1 foot

found somewhere in Bishophill.¹³⁰ In the absence of hypocausts, the houses would have been heated by hearths – low platforms of stone or tiles set on the floors. In a traditional Roman home, they were consecrated to the *lares*, guardian spirits of the household, and considered sacred places. In addition to hearths there were probably stoves that could be moved around to where they were needed. It was not until the fourth century that a hypocaust appeared at St Mary Bishophill Senior. Fuel was usually firewood or peat.¹³¹

A matter that cannot be easily resolved is whether these houses had two (or more) storeys. Good evidence for upper storeys from Roman Britain as a whole is, unsurprisingly, sparse as walls rarely survive above the lower courses. However, the collapsed stone gable wall of a building found at Carsington (Derbyshire) was 0.60m thick, on foundations 0.80m deep, and had once stood *c*.10.50m high.¹³² This would have easily allowed the building to have two storeys with an attic. Taking this information into account, both wings of the house at St Mary Bishophill Senior and the north-eastern wing at 37 Bishophill Senior have been shown in 3.33 with two storeys in the reconstruction. If this is accurate, then we can, perhaps, suggest the size of the households living in them, the sorts of households over which Julia Velva and Aurelius Mercurialis probably presided. They would have been quite large by modern standards in Britain, including not only the master and mistress and their own children, but also other relatives and the slaves who cooked, cleaned and did other domestic tasks. In addition, there might have been freed slaves who continued to look to their former owners as their patrons. Although residents may have lived, and slept, in rather closer proximity than we might think normal in a middle-class home today, both the Bishophill houses could probably have accommodated fifteen or sixteen people. For much of the day the male head of household was probably absent, spending much of his time in public places where he met clients, attended to civic or private business, or enjoyed himself at the baths. The mistress was much more constrained in her freedom of movement, spending much of her time supervising, as circumstances demanded, the childcare and routine tasks, and involving herself in household-based crafts such as spinning and weaving.

In the clement weather for which York is famous, one can imagine that Bishophill residents enjoyed their gardens. There is little archaeological evidence for them, but it is possible that they were laid out on land below the terrace on the north-east (river) side of the houses. As far as plants are concerned, the well found on the nearby 58 – 9 Skeldergate site (2.3, 41) and the Bedern well on the fortress ramparts (2.2, 7) both produced clippings of box (*Buxus sempervirens*), presumably from hedges.¹³³ An evergreen, box looks good in a formal garden setting throughout the year and is pleasantly aromatic. There is little evidence for other garden plants, although rose seeds (*Rosa* sp.) occurred in the Bedern well and the opium poppy (*Papaver somniferum*; 5.1), seeds of which have been recorded in a number of Roman contexts in York, was probably considered decorative as well as having a use in food and medicine (p 171). Garden trees would have included well-established native species common in the city today including oak, beech, birch, rowan and willow.

Zone 6: south-west of the walled city
Roman urban development in the late second century was not confined within what may have been the walled area. Fragmentary remains of Roman buildings have been found outside what is now Micklegate Bar. They include what was possibly the paved corridor of a house at the junction of Queen Street and Blossom Street (found in 1826) (2.3, 44).[134] Immediately to the south-west, evidence for a complex sequence of structures was found at 14 – 20 Blossom Street in 1994 (2.3, 45).[135] Unfortunately, this site was mostly recorded in a hasty watching brief rather than a formal excavation. However, a very substantial wall foundation trench, filled with cobbles in clay, 1.60m wide and 1.20m deep, was found. The upstanding wall itself, probably as substantial as almost any Roman wall in York, had been completely demolished. There were two other slightly smaller wall foundations as well as some cobbled surfaces and other features. It was not possible to make much sense of what was seen, but there had clearly been at least one major stone building here on the approach to the Roman town.

At some distance from what has just been described, south-east of the medieval walls, on another artificial terrace, two rooms and parts of another, belonging to a large house built in stone in the late second or early third century, were found at Clementhorpe (1.1, 14).[136] As their house had been built on a north-south axis, the residents would have had agreeable views over the River Ouse to the east while enjoying the morning sun.

How can the evidence for the townscape and built environment south-west of the Ouse as experienced by Julia Velva, Aurelius Mercurialis and their contemporaries be summarised? Our knowledge is, of course, very limited, but there were possibly walled defences and there was probably a street grid of the usual orthogonal Roman type, although not all the streets had the same alignment. The town appears to have been structured, up to a point at least, into zones with different functions. Monumental buildings, probably largely, if not exclusively, public – i.e. the forum, baths and temples – appear to be concentrated in Zones 1 and 2, close to the main approach road from the south-west and on a narrow strip of fairly level ground close to the river. There may have been a distinct official enclave of some sort on the high ground overlooking the river (Zone 3). Residential areas may have been largely on the high ground in the north-western part (Zone 3) and to the south-east of the main approach road (Zones 4 and 5).

There is no reason to suppose the town was densely built-up except perhaps along the main streets, and there was probably a good deal of open space for gardens and allotments.

The town north-east of the Ouse

North-east of the Ouse the evidence for streets and buildings in the Roman period is even more fragmentary and difficult to understand than it is south-west of the river. However, it seems clear that much of the land around the legionary fortress was built-up by the end of the second or early third century. Most, if not all, of the stone buildings known are probably of this period. As discussed above, in origin land north-east of the river was probably occupied by a settlement under military control (the '*canabae*'), but by the early third century it is likely to have become part of the same self-governing community as the settlement ('town') south-west of the Ouse. What little is known about the built environment north-east of the Ouse may be described by working our way anti-clockwise around the fortress beginning at the south-west gate.

South-west and south of the fortress
Site locations are shown on 2.3.

Immediately outside the south-west gate the main road from the south-west, approaching from the river crossing, presumably a bridge by the late second century (p 89), met another road approaching from the north-west. By the late second century, the latter would continue to the south-east beyond the road junction as a riverside street. Surprisingly close to the junction, part of a substantial stone building was found in 1883 on the site of Lendal Post Office (2.3, 1).[137] It had walls 1.50m thick and surviving over 1m high. Some 200m south-east of this at 39 – 41 Coney Street (WH Smith's; 2.3, 4), the remains of the timber granary described above (p 60) were overlain by the river-side street, here composed of gravel with a stone gutter on its south-west (river side) edge.[138] This street was also seen in 1959 a little further to the south-east at 7 – 15 Spurriergate (2.3, 5), where it met another approaching from the north-east.[139] This was clearly a densely built-up area around the south corner of the fortress, as the remains of as many as five stone buildings have been found (in 1959 and 2000 to 2005) on this site, including one with a hypocaust, interpreted in RCHME's *Eburacum* as a part of a bath house, and another with an apsidal end.[140]

In the area around the corner of Spurriergate and Low Ousegate, the presence of monumental Roman structures, perhaps facing the river, is suggested by numerous large millstone grit blocks, some with eroded architectural features, built into the south-west end of the medieval church of St Michael Spurriergate (2.3, 7; 3.36). The continuation to the south-east of Spurriergate today is Nessgate. We now come to a ridge of raised ground between the Rivers Ouse and Foss where there are hints of a zone devoted to religious observance in the Roman period. In 1839, in advance of construction of 1 – 3 Nessgate (2.3, 9), at a depth of 2.4m to 3m below modern street level, Roman building remains found included an inscribed tablet, unfortunately incomplete but apparently referring to the restoration of a temple of Hercules by two men whose names are TITVS PERPET... (incomplete) and AETERNVS.[141] The word EBVR (*Eburacum*) in the inscription suggests they had official status in the community, perhaps as members of a college of priests. Another temple is hinted at by an (incomplete) inscribed tablet from the same site bearing a dedication to a local goddess, whose name begins IOV, combined with the numen of the emperors, probably Septimius Severus and his sons.[142] Found in the street Nessgate itself in 1928 was a column shaft, ornamented with stylised acanthus leaves (3.37).[143] Columns with similar ornamentation found elsewhere in the western empire formed part of freestanding Jupiter columns, which feature

(*Below left*) 3.36: Millstone grit blocks, which must come from major Roman buildings north-east of the Ouse, reused in the south-west wall of St Michael Spurriergate.

(*Below right*) 3.37: Millstone grit column (top broken), probably from a Jupiter column, carved with acanthus leaf pattern, found on the corner of High Ousegate and Nessgate (adjacent to 2.3, 9) (height 1m).

a statue of the god on the top wielding his thunderbolts, symbols of power to control the cosmos and everything within it.

A short distance to the north-east of Nessgate, during construction of 25 – 7 High Ousegate (2.3, 8) in 1902 – 3, at a depth of up to 3.2m, Roman structural remains included some fragmentary walls, including large blocks probably of millstone grit, two column capitals of Ionic form, and two column bases.[144] On the opposite (north-west) side of High Ousegate, in 1977, observations of Roman walls in a narrow passage between Nos 8 and 9 (2.3, 6) gave a hint of another large stone building.[145] To the north-west, on the corner of Parliament Street and Market Street (2.3, 3), now HSBC Bank, excavation for cellars in 1835 revealed a Roman wall and a stone-flagged floor as much as 4.9m below modern level. In 1971, a watching brief on the same site recorded further walls and produced an altar dedicated by Quintus Creperius Marcus, probably a soldier, to the *genius loci* (spirit of the place), perhaps from a shrine.[146] Shrines and temples jostled for space outside forts and fortresses, offering soldiers places where they could worship whom they chose, provided they also participated in the official cult ceremonies. Finally, on what was probably the eastern edge of the built-up area, the 16 – 22 Coppergate site (2.3, 10) appears to have remained marginal land sloping down to the River Foss, used largely for refuse tipping, until buildings were constructed here in the late Roman period. However, there was evidence here for the manufacture of glass in the early third century (discussed further below).

East and north-east of the fortress
Site locations shown on 1.1.

On the north-east side of the likely line of a Roman road approaching the fortress south-east gate we seem, once again, to be in marginal land. On a large site at Garden Place (in 1950; 1.1, 6), evidence for Roman structures included a depression or channel lined on one side with a 10m-long double row of timber piles, originally linked together by horizontal timbers. This was interpreted as an inlet for drawing up small boats on the north-west bank of the Roman River Foss, although it lies 80m to the north of its present course.[147] The base of a rectangular structure, 7m x 4.6m, comprising gritstone blocks, found nearby, was imaginatively reconstructed as a crane base in RCHME's *Eburacum*.[148] However, in view of more recent excavations in the area and the height (*c.* 3m) of the structures above likely contemporary river level, it seems they must have some other interpretation. Otherwise the land in this area was used for burials, as shown by excavation of a large site on Hungate in 2009 – 11 (1.1, 5). Further north, between the east corner of the fortress and the Foss, evidence has been found for legionary pottery and ceramic tile production (see p 138).[149] There is, as yet, little evidence for any settlement nearby until the late Roman period, when a house with a mosaic was built 60m from the fortress defences (21 – 33 Aldwark site).[150]

Land immediately north-east of the legionary fortress was, for the most part, not built-up either, although a tessellated pavement (from a building) was found in 1911 near the *porta decumana*. Further investigation in 2005 produced evidence of a timber structure.[151] Otherwise the area seems to have been open land in part dedicated to burials.

North-west of the fortress
North-west of the fortress there is little evidence for Roman settlement immediately outside the legionary fortress, although the area has not been extensively explored. Mention should be made, however, of some archaeological work, limited in scale, by G.F. Wilmott under the south-east aisle of St Mary's Abbey at the south-west end of the nave (it lies on a north-east/south-west line) in 1952 – 6 (1.1, 3). In a trench about 28m x 10.6m (but reduced in area by three substantial abbey walls), an early Roman timber structure (aligned north-west/south-east) was succeeded, on the same alignment, by walls of a substantial stone building, probably of the second century, itself succeeded by a Roman wall incorporating some stamped tiles of Emperor Severus Alexander (222 – 35).[152] It is difficult to make much sense of what was found except that it provides a hint that this was a significant built-up area in the second and third centuries. Nearby, in the north range of the abbey cloister, Wilmott found a very substantial Roman wall, 2.5m thick and surviving 0.60m high. It adopted a north-west/south-east alignment and was on the line of the south-west side of the legionary fortress *c*. 95m to the south-east. The significance of this wall is, unfortunately, uncertain but one possibility is that it was on the perimeter of an annexe to the fortress or even, perhaps, of an enclosure containing the elusive amphitheatre.[153]

Settlement beyond the core
Intermittent settlement evidence along the main Roman roads approaching York has been found in a number of places. South-west of the Ouse, *c*. 3.25km from the river crossing, at Dringhouses (2.4, 9), two structures with stone foundations, elongated in plan with their narrow ends facing the main road from the south-west, were found (on the site of the Starting Gate pub) in 2003. They are of a type, common in Romano-British roadside settlements, usually described as 'strip buildings', which often have a shop at the front and living quarters at the rear.[154] Dringhouses has also produced evidence for iron-working in the Roman period as well as a fine relief of a blacksmith with his tools, perhaps a tombstone or part of a shrine to the smith god Vulcan.[155] Between Dringhouses and the city, along the line of the main Roman road, there is other evidence, largely in the form of pits, ditches, surfaces and other features, rather than buildings, for sporadic late second-century and later settlement, as well as for burials.

North-east of the Ouse, there is similar evidence from roads approaching from the north-east and north-west, extending for at least a kilometre out from the fortress.

The hinterland: an enclosed landscape

In the hinterland of Roman York, beyond the main roads, there is evidence for the emergence of a new land management regime in the Antonine period. One aspect of this probably involved conversion of what had previously been simple paths into minor metalled roads. For example, in a back garden on the east side of the city, east of the Foss, at 2.4, 6, a cobble and limestone surface *c.* 4m wide was found laid over a low mound (*agger*) of clay.[156] This was probably a road approaching York from the high ground of the moraine to the east. South-west of the Ouse, on the west side of the city, at Holgate Cattle Dock (1.1, 9), a cobbled surface 4.1m wide and 0.5m thick was found, probably forming a minor road approaching York from the north-west.[157]

These two minor roads, and no doubt others like them, ran through areas of what had been open land that appears to have been divided up into small enclosures by means of ditches, probably to create fields or stock enclosures.[158] These Roman ditches have been found in many places around York, within about 3km from the city centre, as a result of archaeological evaluation in advance of development in previously unexplored suburban or rural areas. A little further out, at Heslington East (2.4, 7) east of the city, a new landscape of ditched enclosures, around a small farmstead, was created on the high ground of the moraine where a small farmstead would be built in the late Roman period.[159]

What the proliferation of ditches seems to suggest is a co-ordinated process of land management, perhaps controlled by the army, if still within a legionary *territorium*, or by a civilian authority that had taken on the army's responsibilities. In most cases, however, the enclosures seem to represent quite a brief episode in the landscape as most of the ditches do not seem to have been cleaned out on any regular basis but just left to silt up naturally. Other forms of boundary, perhaps hedges, which leave no trace in the ground, may have replaced them. In any event, the enclosure of land may have been part of a new agricultural regime, if only a temporary one, intended to produce the extra food required by a permanent military garrison and a growing civilian population at York in the late Antonine and Severan periods. The survival of the *territorium* may explain why York was not, like most other Roman towns in Britain, surrounded by estates centred on villas that were country houses in Roman style accompanied by farm buildings. Although there are villas in the wider region, there appear to be only one or two at all close to York, the nearest being at Wilstrop, *c.*12km west of the city on the River Nidd.[160]

Chapter 4

Producers and traders

Introduction

Whether in the streets of *Eboracum*, on the riverbanks or in the local fields and woodland, Julia Velva would have seen people at work even if she, herself, was a lady of leisure. As the Roman economy largely lacked the sources of energy we take for granted today, much of this work involved manual labour, labour which, moreover, used the simplest of tools and equipment. Most of the workers, whether free or slaves, would not have been working entirely to support themselves but were constrained to make a sufficient return on their endeavours to allow others to live without working. Today we find Roman elite attitudes to work rather shocking. We usually take the view that, of whatever description, work dignifies rather than demeans us. However, the ability to live a life of leisure (*'otium'*) was regarded in the Roman world as entirely appropriate for men of high social status, men who had every right to pursue their interests, intellectual or otherwise, and enjoy their pleasures exactly as they chose.

This chapter is primarily concerned with the archaeological evidence for economic activity (production and trade) in late Antonine and Severan York. However, this evidence should be seen against the background of some of the more important aspects of how the economy of the empire, as a whole, operated. One of these is the ownership of both land and the means of production, whether in agriculture or manufacturing or in the extraction from the ground of minerals, building stone and other resources. Unfortunately, we know little in any detail about patterns of ownership in Roman Britain as a whole, although we can infer that it was in relatively few hands.[1]

In the York area, the army was, in effect, a major landowner as far as any *territorium* it controlled is concerned, at least until it was, perhaps, handed over to the civilian authorities in the later Roman period. Civilian landowners, many of them likely to have been legionary veterans, probably had estates that included urban property as well as tracts of the countryside.[2] In both cases, these estates would have been worked by free tenants paying rent, as well as by slaves. Even if they did not care to manage their estates themselves, owners were happy enough to use agents to ensure good returns from exploitation of the human, agricultural and other resources of their land. Some men also invested in commercial ventures as well, men like Lucius Viducius Placidus (who paid for part of a temple in York, p 76) and Marcus Aurelius Lunaris (who dedicated the altar at Bordeaux, p 76). Both of them had York and Gallic connections and were probably involved in lucrative long-distance interprovincial trade. Alongside the great estate owners there may have been a free peasantry, who owned some land of their own, or a group of wage-earning urban artisans who owned their own premises. But we have no easy means of knowing how significant they were in terms of numbers or economic importance.

There would appear to have been a steady, if not continuous, increase in economic activity – production, trade and consumption – in the western Roman Empire in the imperial period at least until the mid-third century, an increase in gross domestic (or 'imperial') product we might call it, in modern terms. Unfortunately, we have few reliable statistics for the period and instead must rely largely on the archaeological evidence. However, some aspects of it seem clear enough to support our overall impression of growth. In rural areas, for example, we find the clearance of new land for settlement and cultivation, and more efficient approaches to farming;[3] evidence for the latter in the York hinterland may, perhaps, be seen in the new ditched enclosures described above (p 126). As far as production of manufactured goods is concerned, this also increased, much of it in the workshops of emerging towns like York which, by the late Antonine period, should be seen as an important engine of economic development in its region. It was the sort of place to which underemployed labour on rural estates moved voluntarily or was moved deliberately by estate owners to undertake work that yielded higher returns on investment than farming. Moreover, a town like York had a sufficiently large population, including some very wealthy consumers, which allowed for specialisation in production of certain 'luxury' goods, such as jewellery or cosmetics, which increased returns even further.

Whilst estate owners and their tenants alike might well have been motivated by a general desire to enrich themselves, another factor driving economic activity in the period up to *c*. 200 was, it has been suggested, the need to raise money for taxes, raised largely on land ownership, and, in the case of tenants, to meet rent charges.[4] However, as far as the York area is concerned, taxation did not have an entirely negative impact on those required to pay as the army based here itself benefitted from taxation raised in other parts of the empire. The money was sent to frontier areas like the north of Britain, thereby allowing troops to add to the level of local demand for the products of the farms and urban workshops as well as suppliers of commodities at a distance, sometimes quite a considerable distance, from York.

Agriculture in the York region

We should begin our survey of the economy of Roman York with local agriculture, as this was the most important source of the region's wealth for almost all its people. Roman York was a relatively small place surrounded, hemmed in even, by farmland, as the reconstruction in 1.3 is intended to show. Many, perhaps most, of its inhabitants may well have worked on the land, at least on a part-time basis. In addition, they probably produced their own food in gardens, backyards and on any other open land.

Our knowledge of the crops that were grown is good as a result of extensive deposit sampling on archaeological excavations in recent years. Most informative, specifically for the Julia Velva period, was the large deposit of burnt grain from 5 Rougier Street in the heart of the Roman town south-west of the Ouse (2.3, 18).[5] 88 per cent of it was spelt wheat (*Triticum spelta*), whilst the remainder was largely barley (*Hordeum vulgare*) as well some cultivated oats (*Avena sativa*). The associated weeds, represented by their seeds, were of taxa, which might be expected in the local fields, including corncockle (*Agrostemma githago*), wild radish (*Raphanus raphanistrum*) and black bindweed (*Fallopia convolvulus*).

Spelt wheat is rather different from the wheat we are familiar with today.[6] Not only did it stand higher in a field than modern wheat, which has been bred to suit the combine harvester, but it is also harder to thresh. However, the tough hull ('glume') around the grain protects it from insects and disease. Furthermore, spelt will tolerate a wide range of soil types, not just the light and well-drained, but also heavy clays, and it copes well with the cold. It is therefore suited to winter sowing. Spelt has good storage capabilities both in the deep pits, often used in the pre-Roman period, and in Roman granaries. Although it gives poorer yields per hectare than modern wheat, experimental farming at Butser Iron Age Farm in Hampshire suggests that about 1ha of spelt, grown in the traditional manner without weedkillers, would feed a family of eight for a year.[7]

The Rougier Street grain was, of course, the end-product of a very long process of cultivation requiring considerable labour on the part of those working the land. This began with ploughing the fields, usually in the autumn, to break up the ground and kill off the weeds (4.1).[8] The plough was usually drawn by cattle, rather than horses. The Roman plough is usually thought of as a simple tool – an ard as it was sometimes described – little changed from earlier times, with an iron-shod wooden share (blade) that was dragged through the ground but did not turn it over. However, during the Roman period, a rather more sophisticated plough was introduced to Britain, which had a coulter, set in front of the share, that cut through the earth. The iron parts of such a plough were found in York in Parliament Street near the fortress wall (2.3, 2; 4.2).[9]

4.1: Reconstruction drawing of a man ploughing with cattle – probably a familiar sight in the fields close to Roman York.

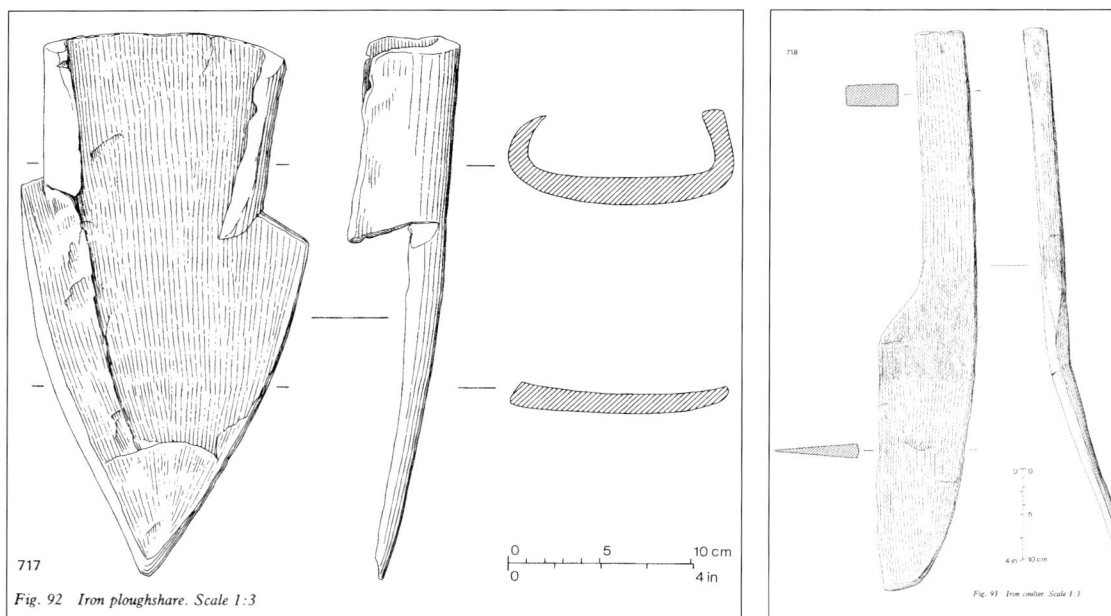

4.2: Drawings of an iron coulter (right) and a share from a plough, found in Parliament Street. (© York Archaeological Trust)

The cycle for spelt wheat began, after ploughing, with sowing in autumn/winter with a view to a harvest the following summer.[10] Harvest involved mobilising large numbers of people in a short period. Even soldiers might turn to, if need be, as shown in a scene on Trajan's column in Rome. Reaping was back-breaking work. The occurrence of seeds from low-growing plants and twining weeds in York's Roman grain samples indicates that the stalks ('culms') were cut fairly low down with the sickle, or simply uprooted.[11] Anything missed by the reapers would be collected by gleaners, who followed along behind them. The next stage, threshing, was intended to separate the ears (comprising numerous 'spikelets' containing the grain) from what would become straw, usually by beating the stalks on the ground with flails. Removing the grain from the ears was done by pounding them, but first they had to be dry enough to render the glumes suitably brittle. Drying might involve spreading the crop out on an enclosed floor surface or holding it over an open hearth. But an innovation of the second century AD, as far as the York region is concerned, was the dedicated grain-drying kiln.[12] Local examples were found at Heslington East. These kilns usually appear in the ground as a T-shaped flue, into which hot air was introduced from a hearth at the end of the longer arm. There would have been a hard surface above the flue on which the grain was laid. The kiln as a whole would have been protected by a small shed.[13] Drying would also prevent the grain germinating, thereby lessening the risk of it rotting during storage. An appreciable proportion of the Rougier Street grain had sprouted, showing germination had begun. Preventing this was not only important for food production but also for malting. During germination, enzymes in grain break down the starch it contains to form sugars used by a plant as it grows. In order to make use of these sugars – i.e. the malt – in brewing, or distilling, germination must be stopped.

The result of pounding was a pile of debris ('chaff') to be sorted. Coarser weed seeds and any remaining straw were removed by raking and hand-picking. What was left was winnowed, i.e. thrown in the air during a light breeze to remove the finer material, and then sieved to collect the grain, which could then be sent to the granary for storage. Some weed seeds might still survive in the grain, especially if they were the same size such as, unfortunately, those of corncockle, which are poisonous.

A Roman stone-built granary was designed, like the timber versions to keep the grain dry, at an even temperature and free of vermin. Typically, therefore, the building had thick walls, a heavy roof and a floor raised above the ground. However, whilst rats and mice might have been kept out, up to a point, by the raised floor, another hazard of grain storage less easy to prevent was infestation by weevils and other insect pests. They have been found, in some numbers, not only in the early

Roman granary on Coney Street (pp 60–1), but also in the 5 Rougier Street grain and in the Bedern well (2.2, 7).[14]

The final stage in processing grain for food was to grind it to make the meal which could be refined for flour. There is some evidence for mills in Roman Britain, largely in the form of the millstones, usually defined as stone discs with a diameter of more than 550mm to distinguish them from rotary querns (see below). Mills with wheels driven by water may have existed on both the Rivers Ouse and Foss. Others may have been powered by animals or humans, although there is no good evidence for them in York. In the absence of a mill, grain had to be ground with a quern. As it was hard to store meal for long before it went off, the grinding had to be done regularly, a routine daily task, presumably, for slaves attached to the army or to civilian households.

There were two types of quern known in Roman York. The first is the beehive quern, originally introduced during the Iron Age, which consisted of two stones: a circular base and a domed – hence the name – upper stone pierced in the centre to form a hopper into which a wooden rod was set. This fitted into a hole in the base stone such as to keep the two parts together (4.3). The side of the upper stone was also pierced either once for a wooden handle or twice for a pair of opposed handles. Grain was introduced through the hopper and ground between the stones by agitating or rotating the upper one – gradually the meal would emerge from between the stones and was then collected. Lower stones are often found set in the ground, suggesting the work involved squatting or kneeling – no doubt seen as a suitable posture for a slave.

An introduction of the Roman period, initially by the military, was the rotary, or disc, quern consisting of two flattish circular stones, pierced in the centre. Recent practice in remoter parts of Britain, for example, on St Kilda in the Hebrides, suggests the rotary quern was operated by a person seated on the ground. But it is also possible that in Roman times the quern was placed on some sort of table to make the work a little less arduous. Whilst beehive querns in the York area were usually made of millstone grit, rotary querns were often made of volcanic lava found in the Eiffel mountains of Germany. A number of roughouts for lava querns were found at Wellington Row (2.3, 16), which had probably been imported to York from the Rhineland for finishing to local specifications.[15] There have been various attempts at calculating the time and effort needed to produce meal using a rotary quern. Hilary Cool quotes a figure of 1.8kg per hour based on observation of its use in present day Algeria.[16]

Just as important as the arable fields around Roman York were the hay meadows, which provided fodder for animals, especially in winter. Seeds of bent grasses (*Agrostis* sp(p)) and foxtails (*Alopecurus* sp(p)), which both make good quality hay, were found in Roman deposits at 24 – 30 Tanner Row and in the Bedern well.[17]

4.3: Reconstruction drawing of a slave using a beehive quern but taking a break to stroke her dog.

Our understanding of animal husbandry, and of the preparation and consumption of meat, whether from cattle, sheep and goat, or pig, in the Roman period depends largely on the study of their bones from archaeological deposits. The relative numbers of bones of each animal can give some impression of their importance in local agricultural and dietary regimes. However, it must be borne in mind when converting numbers of bones to weight of meat that the carcase size of a cow is roughly equivalent to eleven sheep or six pigs.[18] A large assemblage (7,320) of bones of the three principal meat-yielding animals from mid-second to third-century contexts at 24 – 30 Tanner Row (2.3, 19) has been studied by T.P. O'Connor.[19] Of these, 69 per cent were cattle, 17 per cent sheep and 14 per cent pig, suggesting a diet dominated by beef. Other smaller assemblages of Roman animal bones from excavations at the minster library (in the fortress)[20] and at the former Starting Gate public house in the York suburb of Dringhouses (2.4, 9)[21] tell a similar story.

The farm animals one would have seen in the fields around Roman York had not, of course, been subject to the sort of the selective breeding of recent times, and so were usually smaller and more gracile than those we see around us today. Roman cattle from York and in the Yorkshire region stood, on average, 1.1m high at the withers.[22] Of a breed sometimes known as 'Celtic shorthorn', they were similar to the cattle of prehistoric times and to Dexter cattle, a 'rare breed' of today (4.4). There was some evidence at Tanner Row that larger animals with less tightly curved horn cores had been introduced to local stock, but they were

4.4: Dexter cattle of a similar size and conformation to Roman cattle.

still small by modern standards, weighing only 200kg to 250kg (a dairy cow today weighs at least 450kg). Age at death can be worked out from the extent of wear on an animal's teeth. The patterns in the data from Tanner Row differ markedly from those of today when, for example, beef cattle are usually killed before they reach 18 months. The majority of the Tanner Row cattle were slaughtered when mature or elderly (5 to 9 years). This is because they were multi-purpose animals raised for both meat and, in the case of cows, for milk. They were also used for ploughing and for pulling carts and wagons.

Roman sheep were a source of both wool and, if female, milk before their slaughter for consumption. The bones found at 24 – 30 Tanner Row suggest *c.* 40 per cent of sheep reached maturity between the ages of 3 and 6 years. There were also bones of young lambs, presumably killed not just for eating but to maximise the yield of the mothers' milk.[23] There is some variation in size (in twenty-four specimens). Height to withers ranged between 0.53m and 0.65m with a mean of 0.59m very similar to data for sheep in the region as a whole.[24] The smallest would have been like the modern rare breed Soay sheep, but a few others, perhaps introduced for breeding purposes, were taller and longer in the leg. Pigs had no other use but for their meat, blood and lard, and so they would usually be killed at their prime eating age of *c.* 2 years.

One gets a good impression of the range of butchery techniques practised in York from the Tanner Row bones. Rather than cutting the meat from a carcase with knives, as in the prehistoric period, large cleavers were used by skilled operatives to carve up the carcases into joints. In addition, there were numerous smashed-up cattle limbs. They are commonly found in Roman contexts in Britain and thought to be the residue of the systematic extraction of bone marrow, probably to make soup or glue. A number of cattle scapulae (shoulder blades) had been pierced, suggesting that they had been hung up to be smoked or steeped in brine, two means of preserving meat in an era before refrigeration. Roman York's butchers probably worked closely with other trades in the local economy as no part of an animal was wasted: hide, hair, hooves, horns, bones and blood all had a use, and there would have been a specialist able to make use of each product in some way.

Natural resources

In addition to the fruits of agriculture, Roman York required many other natural resources from the region to sustain itself. For one important example, a considerable quantity of timber would have been needed, initially by the army for construction in the early years of the legionary fortress. Although stone became more widely used as time went on, the demand for timber continued to place a heavy demand on available resources, in spite of there being a much greater extent of woodland in Roman times than today. It was no surprise, therefore, to find re-used timbers in the 24 – 30 Tanner Row buildings and in the piles for the building extension at Wellington Row. Whether in the legionary *territorium* or private estates elsewhere in the region, the woodland would have been actively managed to ensure adequate supply. At 24 – 30 Tanner Row the principal species in the structures found in the excavation was oak. There were also pieces of ash, used for stakes, hazel and willow, for wattles, and alder, elm and pine.[25] In addition to construction, a very important use of wood was fuel, whether for homes or the baths or for manufacturing processes, notably (as charcoal) for metalworking.

York's building stone was one of the most obvious aspects of the townscape to give it a distinctive character. However, because there is none to be found in and around York itself, stone had to be brought in from elsewhere.[26] Almost as soon as the Ninth Legion arrived, bringing with it the technology for heavy duty quarrying and the capacity for transporting bulky heavy materials, by water or over land, building stone was on its way into York. If we take them in the order of the geological sequence, beginning with the oldest, a description of the stone used in Roman York must begin with millstone grit, the coarse-grained sandstone used for monumental structures and for tombstones (including Julia Velva's) and sculptures. At its nearest to York, millstone grit occurs near Wetherby, *c*. 25km west of the city from where it was probably shipped down the River Wharfe to its confluence with the Ouse at Cawood, 12km south of York, and then back up, against the current, to York. Also of the Carboniferous period is a sandstone, often known as Elland flag, or in recent times as York stone, occurring as thin flat slabs. This was used largely as roofing and, at York, had largely replaced ceramic tiles by the third century (3.34). Quarries, as the place name Elland suggests, were located south of Bradford in West Yorkshire.

Of the two types of limestone known in Roman York, magnesian limestone of the Permian period, was the most commonly used in both the legionary fortresses and civilian settlements as it was, subsequently, in the medieval period for the walls, the minster, parish churches, etc. This is a very good stone for both building and sculpture as it does not have a distinct bedding plane and can be cut in any direction. Magnesian limestone is found west of York, and it is thought that there were Roman quarries in the Tadcaster area *c*. 16km away. Again, the Wharfe would have been used for transport.

Rather less common, and probably only used to supplement magnesian limestone for the great building programmes of the late Antonine and Severan periods, is oolitic limestone of the Jurassic period. This is not such a good building stone.

It has a marked bedding plane and usually occurs in flat slabs as was seen, for example, in the building at Wellington Row (p 98) and the baths at 1 – 9 Micklegate (p 109). Oolitic limestone is found in the Malton area, *c.* 26km north-east of York from where, if brought by water rather than in wagons, it would have had a circuitous route via the River Derwent to its confluence with the Ouse near Hemingbrough 25km south of York.

In addition to possessing the technology for stone quarrying, the Romans also knew what was required for extraction of metal ores by mining. These ores would, moreover, have been smelted on a much larger scale than hitherto in the region. Although a good deal of the iron, and other metals, used in Roman York were probably derived from recycling, as extraction and smelting were very costly in terms of fuel and personnel, this would not fully satisfy a demand that continued to rise as time went on. Sources of iron ore used to supply Roman York probably included both the Rosedale area in the North York Moors and north Lincolnshire. From the latter it could be transported via the Humber Estuary and the Ouse, although to save transport costs the ore was probably smelted and turned into bars at the mines before being transported to the smiths in York. Another source of iron lay in deposits that accumulated on the edges of lakes or marshes. This so-called 'bog ore' is known to have been exploited on a large scale locally in the late Iron Age, for example, in the valley of the River Foulness near Holme-on-Spalding Moor about 25km south-east of York.[27] Bog ore probably continued to be a source of iron in the Roman period.

Although iron had been widely used in the York region in pre-Roman times, lead apparently was not. However, we know that the Roman Army was mining lead ore (galena) in the Pennines as early as the late first century because of four lead ingots ('pigs') bearing imperial stamps found either near Pateley Bridge or further north on Hurst Moor near Reeth in Swaledale.[28] Each one bears the reigning emperor's name and examples are known of Domitian, Trajan and Hadrian. In addition, two of them also bear the stamp BRIG(ANTICVM), meaning from the territory of the Brigantes.

It is not clear where the copper used in Roman York was sourced. Although the metal occurs widely in Britain, it is not found in the immediate locality. Tin, alloyed with copper to make bronze, probably came all the way from mines in Cornwall, a source well-known long before the Roman period. Zinc, used to alloy with copper for brass, may also have come from the south-west of England. The source of the precious metals, gold and silver, was probably quite varied and, again, much of it was probably recycled. In addition, silver may have been produced as a by-product of lead mining whether in the Pennines or elsewhere. Gold was mined or panned in parts of Wales in Roman times.

Manufacturing

York in the Julia Velva period was a place where people made things. Not only the army, but members of the civilian population as well, made things here on a scale greater than ever before or indeed afterwards, until 700 years later in the Viking Age city. The most prominent archaeological evidence for manufacturing relates to pottery and metalwork, but there were many other crafts practiced in *Eboracum* as well. Certain areas, especially perhaps by the bridgehead south-west of the Ouse or east of the fortress, would have been suffused by smoke and fumes from workshops and kilns of one sort or another as well as being noisy with the sound of tools striking stone, metal and so forth, and of the cries of the workers.

As far as the Roman Army is concerned, it had, on its arrival in York, immediately faced problems of how to supply itself with a whole range of different commodities, not just food and raw materials. The York region was not one in which, as the Romans would have seen it, there were many native craftsmen possessing a high level of technological sophistication, except perhaps in some aspects of metalworking, and they were not able to supply manufactured goods, however simple, in large quantities. The army, therefore, had two options. Either make what they needed themselves or import it from elsewhere.

Whilst there may be no building stone at York itself there is clay, some of which was clearly suitable for making pottery vessels or ceramic tiles. Kilns (*figlinae*), operated under military supervision, are thought to have existed immediately east of the fortress, close to the bank of the River Foss where there was clay in an area which also had the advantage of being downwind of the fortress, so any noxious smoke would usually be carried away from it. The principal type of pottery is what is known to archaeologists as Ebor Ware, a distinctive wheel-made red earthenware.[29] The evidence for its production is debris in the form of kiln furniture and misfired vessels – 'wasters' – found at several adjacent sites (1.1, 4).[30] Most striking, in the upper 1.5m of a 16m-long trench in Peasholme Green, there were dumps of kiln waste of the Hadrianic to Antonine periods and, in larger quantities, of the early third century (4.5).

Although no kilns have yet been found, they would have been of the updraught type, a Roman innovation to the region, in which hot air was drawn from a stoking pit along a rising flue to the firing chamber where the vessels were stacked. It was possible to control the atmosphere within the chamber such that it was either oxidising, giving vessels a reddish colour, as is usually the case for Ebor Ware, or reducing, such that they were grey or black. This type of kiln was a great improvement on the simple bonfire, or clamp, kilns routinely used by native potters who, for the most part, only produced a limited range of jars suitable for cooking. The legionary kilns produced a range of vessel types including bowls, platters and flagons, as well as jars, for use in the kitchen and dining room (4.6).

4.5: Dump of Roman kiln debris found in a trench on Peasholme Green, scale 2m. (© MAP)

(*Above left*) 4.6: Jar in Ebor Ware. (YORYM H2357, © York Museums Trust)

(*Above right*) 4.7: Ebor Ware candle-holder. (YORYM H80, Yorkshire Museum)

Other distinctive vessels include candle holders (4.7), lamps and a form of cup known as a 'tazza' thought to have been used for drinking wine during cult rituals.

The first episode of Ebor Ware pottery production took place in the late first century, soon after the army arrived in York. There was then a break in the early second century before a Hadrianic episode, coinciding with the arrival of the Sixth Legion.[31] At about the same time, the production of vessels in a similar fabric to Ebor Ware took place at Appletree Farm, Heworth (2.4, 3) on the Tang Hall Beck, where two kilns were excavated in the late 1980s.[32] These, and others, may have been operated by a legionary veteran who had set up in business for himself after leaving the army. Mortaria, heavy bowls used for preparing food, were also produced here, some of which bear the stamp AGRIPPA, probably the veteran's name. His stamp has also been found on tiles.[33] A final episode of pottery production east of the fortress took place in the early third century, probably at the time of Septimius Severus's visit to York.

Other types of Roman pottery found in York may have been produced in local kilns. However, it seems unlikely that samian was made here, although a piece of a mould for figure-decorated bowls datable to the early second century was found at the railway station.[34] Samian, of rather poor quality, is known to have been briefly made in Britain at Colchester. No products of a York industry have yet been identified, although the occasional batch of vessels might have been made here as something of a novelty.

Tiles and bricks were, like pottery, produced in York by the Ninth Legion.[35] For the typical Roman roof there were two types of tile: the *tegula* and *imbrex*. The former is flat and rectangular with the sides turned over at 90°. The latter is semi-circular in cross-section and covered the junctions between the *tegulae*. Together they created the sort of roofscape imagined in 3.6. Production involved forming the tiles in damp clay and leaving them to dry 'leather-hard' in the open air before firing. One can imagine a fairly large area being dedicated to the drying process at times of production, an area that was probably not closely supervised to judge by the frequent occurrence of animal foot and hoof prints in the tiles. Under both the Ninth and Sixth Legions' regimes, tiles were routinely, if not always, stamped before firing.[36] There is a great range of stamps known from both legionary periods, although usually just with the unit's name and title (HISPANA or VICTRIX) in some abbreviated form. However, belonging to the early third century are Sixth Legion tiles with the stamps BRITANNICA or SEVERIANA. The former is thought to belong to Septimius Severus's stay in York, and the latter may do also, although it is normally thought to belong to the reign of Severus Alexander (222 – 35). A stamp including the title GORDIANA refers to Gordian III, who ruled 238 – 44.

The best archaeological evidence for metalworking in Roman York, in the form of abundant smithing slag, including the hammer scale that derives from welding, comes from deposits around the late Antonine timber buildings at 24 – 30 Tanner Row and probably derived from a smithy nearby, although not on the site itself.[37] There were probably many other smithies in Roman York and there is evidence for another on the terrace in the south-eastern part of the town at St Mary Bishophill Senior, where a hearth, iron fragments and slag were found.[38] Near to the north-east bank of the Ouse, on Sycamore Place, 0.80km west of the fortress (1.1, 2), an evaluation excavation in 2013 produced slag and other debris from Roman ironworking, evidence that this was a craft often kept at a distance from densely settled areas.[39] No smithing hearths are known from Roman York. They may have usually been in pits dug into the ground, although raised hearths, as shown in 4.8, which are known elsewhere in the Roman world may also have existed. In any event, a forge would have been regarded by outsiders as a mysterious sort of place, an impression enhanced by its being kept fairly dark so that the smith could see the colour of the hot metal, which would have been critical to his ability to assess its character and quality.

4.8: A blacksmithing scene showing Vulcan at work at a raised hearth, based on a Roman relief.

Most products of the Roman blacksmith were day-to-day items including craft tools, structural fittings, especially the nails that are so abundant on any Roman site, locks and keys and equipment such as bridle bits for horses. However, amongst the iron objects from Tanner Row was something more unusual: a sword, in origin a valuable item but one that may have been discarded for some reason before it could be recycled or repaired.[40] Its blade has a pattern-welded core that involved the forging together of strips of iron with a high and low carbon content. The two types each have slightly different visual properties, which could be enhanced by careful polishing. A sword like this was the acme of the smith's craft involving competence in the making of steel, i.e. iron with a carbon content of in excess of $c.0.5\%$.[41] Carbon was usually introduced into the iron by a process, 'carburisation', that involved heating it in charcoal over a prolonged period. The steel was then welded on to the sword, knife, etc., to make a sharp edge. Before it was fit for use, this edge had to be quenched and tempered – 'heat-treated' – to ensure it was hard but not brittle. That some Roman smiths were better at heat treatment than others is shown by the variable quality of their products as revealed by metallographic examination. Only three objects from Roman York itself, two knives and a shears blade, have been analysed, but they make the point.[42] One knife had no obvious steel cutting edge and was almost pure iron, and so was not a very effective implement. The other knife had a steel sheath wrapped around an iron core, but it had not been expertly heat-treated. The shears blade was much more competently made with a high carbon steel edge that had been expertly heat-treated before being welded onto the body of the blade.

Some of the lead mined in the Pennines was brought to York for further export, but some was worked here by specialist craftsmen (*plumbatores*). They would have made the water pipes, known from both the fortress and town, and boilers and tanks for the baths. Smaller lead items included lamps and lamp- and candleholders. Another popular lead product, of which there are numerous examples from York (see p 240), was the coffin or coffin lining. Lead was alloyed with tin to make pewter, which was made up into plates, bowls and other vessels.

The 24 – 30 Tanner Row site produced a number of iron tools, or fragments of tools, for various crafts (4.9), including a few suitable for non-ferrous metalworking.[43] The site also produced fragments of crucibles used for melting both copper alloys and gold. Alongside iron, copper alloy also seems to have been worked on or near the site at St Mary Bishophill Senior (2.3, 42), where a pit with two boxes containing scrap copper alloy were found. Presumably, the material had been carefully collected and buried for safekeeping with a view to recycling.[44]

Native craftsmen were skilled in working copper alloy, but metallographic analyses have shown that the metal, often recycled scrap, that was used in the Roman period in our region would have included alloys such as brass, notably in

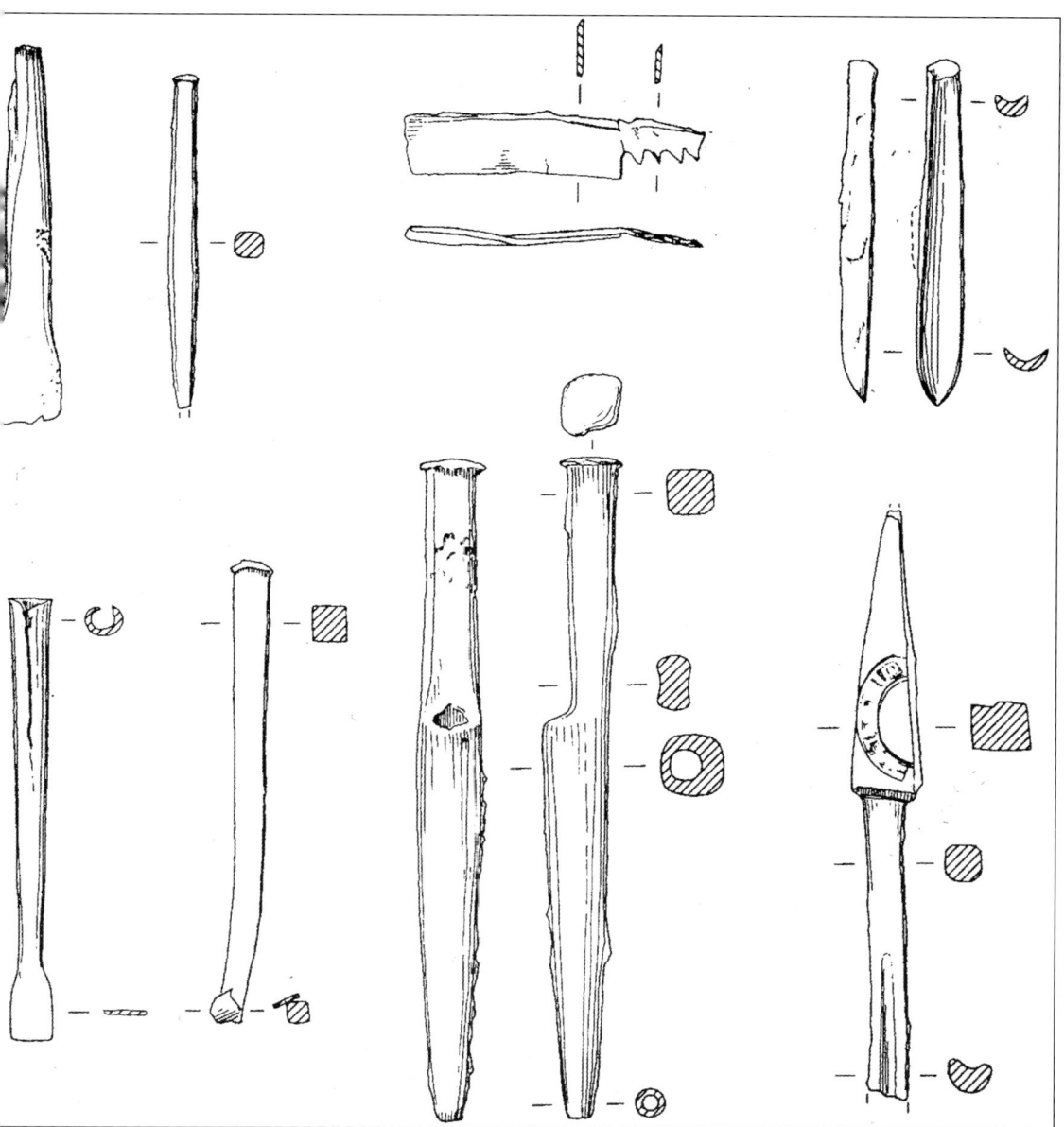

4.9: Iron tools (some incomplete) for metalworking and other crafts from 24 – 30 Tanner Row. (© York Archaeological Trust)

military fittings and armour.[45] Being composed of copper and zinc, manufacturing in brass would have posed difficulties for the native smiths because of their unfamiliarity with zinc, a highly volatile metal with a lower melting point than copper. Another alloy widely used by the Romans was gunmetal, usually a mixture of scrap bronze (copper and tin) and brass. We may assume that the products of the smiths working in copper alloys included the usual range of small items commonly found on Roman sites all over Britain, including jewellery, casket fittings, toilet equipment and small figurines. Manufacturing usually involved the lost-wax process that was already of considerable antiquity and is still in use today. A wax model of the intended item is placed in a clay mould. This is then heated so that the wax melts and is drained off to be replaced by the molten metal. Once cool, the mould can be broken open to remove the object, which can then be finished off manually with files, punches, etc. On occasions, a coating of tin, silver or even gilding was added.

Objects, usually jewellery (see pp 196–9), made entirely of silver or gold are fairly rare finds in York as they were carefully curated by their owners and anything that had become redundant was recycled. However, items in the precious metals are occasionally found where they could not have been recovered, such as the drains and sewers in the baths, or where there was some taboo on recovery, as in the case of burials (5.20).

Roman glass found in Britain, primarily in the form of vessels but also as windows and jewellery, was manufactured, for the most part, in Britain itself, northern France or the Rhineland.[46] For those pieces made in Britain, recycled material rather than newly produced glass was usually used. However, on the north-east bank of the Ouse, at 16 – 22 Coppergate, about 200m south-east of the fortress (2.3, 10), evidence was found for the production, in the early third century, of glass from its raw materials, making it the only site yet known in Roman Britain where this took place.[47] The evidence exists as fragments of unreacted silica (silicon dioxide) in a glassy matrix arising from the first stage of the process of making glass from sand and soda (sodium carbonate). There was also evidence for the process, more widely known in Britain, of melting down glass waste – 'cullet'. This latter took the form of some 3kg of pottery sherds derived from receptacles used for both colourless and green glass. Glass melting may have taken place here on quite a large scale. One product is thought to have been windowpanes. In addition, there were a few glass fragments derived from the use of a blowing iron to form vessels. In view of the site's location, the glassworks may have been under military control, although the windowpanes were probably destined for civilian as well as military buildings. Some fragments were found in the fortress in the first cohort barracks.[48] A hint that production of glass also took place south-west of the Ouse is provided by three glass workers' crucibles found in Toft Green near the old station site.[49]

If we now turn to manufacturing using organic materials, we find another craft clearly practiced in the 24 – 30 Tanner Row area was leatherworking. Leather, made from animal hides, was a durable and supple material suitable for many different uses in the Roman period. Its manufacture on a large scale, at least, was a major technological innovation brought to Britain by the Romans. The butchers of York would have supplied cattle hides, which were prepared for the leatherworkers by tanning, a process that requires an abundant water supply. And so it would be no surprise if it were to have been practiced near the river in Roman times – as it has in more recent times, hence the name of streets leading to the river: Tanner Row and Tanner's Moat. The material from 24 – 30 Tanner Row speaks primarily of the repair (rather than manufacture) of leather goods, taking the form of numerous shoe fragments and offcuts.[50] Of greatest interest, perhaps, was a complete panel and a number of other fragments from the sort of tents in which the Roman Army was accommodated when on campaign. Although fairly durable, they were exposed to considerable wear and tear. Repair and maintenance would probably have provided steady employment for a local workshop.

Unlike leatherworking, production of woollen and linen textiles has a long history going back well before the Romans arrived in Britain. Unfortunately, very little textile has survived from Roman York, except as impressions in the gypsum casts encasing human remains in some of the burials (see p 240). We can also infer a little about the preparation of wool and the weaving process locally from related artefacts. In the Yorkshire Museum's collection, there is a flat iron wool comb of Roman type from Kirby Knowle near Thirsk, the only one known from the north-east of England,[51] although similar combs were probably widely used in the York region for removing foreign matter from a fleece and aligning the fibres to make spinning easier. Spinning involved a distaff from which the unspun fibres were drawn onto a spindle. This latter had to be weighted with a spindle whorl, a pierced circular or domed object of which there are numerous Roman examples from York, largely made of stone or ceramic, although they also occur in jet and shale.[52] Representations of spinning in Roman art, often depictions of the fates (*Parcae*) (4.10), or descriptions in Roman literature, such as that of Arachne in Ovid's *Metamorphoses*, suggest spinning was largely women's work and a routine household task.[53]

Weaving also seems to have been a household task carried out by women. Arachne was turned into a spider by Minerva after a weaving contest at which other women were present. However, weaving may also have been undertaken by men in state-run workshops or factories, such as that recorded in southern Britain at Winchester in the late Roman period.[54] The usual loom for weaving cloth in both prehistoric and early Roman Britain was the vertical warp-weighted loom comprising two uprights joined together near the base by a cross-beam (4.11).[55] It also had a cylindrical upper beam at the top of the uprights that could be rotated to wind on the woven cloth. The warp (vertical) threads were weighted at the base to keep

(*Above left*) 4.10: Woman spinning, based on an original Roman depiction of Clotho, one of the three fates (*Parcae*) spinning the thread of life. (Drawn by Sarah Hall Baqai)

(*Above right*) 4.11: Reconstruction drawing of a vertical warp-weighted loom.

them in tension. The weft (horizontal) threads were beaten upwards as weaving proceeded to keep them tight together, perhaps using a wooden 'weaving sword' or a type of handled bone comb, of which several examples are known from the York region. Multiple heddle rods on a loom, as shown in 4.11, were used in the weaving of twill fabrics. Although the looms themselves have not survived, the roughly triangular weights, usually made of clay, are sometimes found. In Roman Gaul, there was also what is known as the two-beam vertical loom, which may have spread to Britain and displaced the warp-weighted loom in the latter part of the Roman period.[56] In addition, straps and belts were woven using small triangular tablets of bone or ivory pierced in such a way as to accommodate and manipulate the threads. An ivory example came from the centurion's quarters in the first cohort barracks where it was dropped, perhaps, by an army wife.[57]

In her study of textile impressions in the gypsum casts, Audrey Henshall identified woollen cloth of varying quality, but all fairly fine. It appeared to be in plain weave patterns and no twills were seen.[58] In the burial of a mother and baby, narrow strips of a red ribbed woollen cloth were thought to represent a selvage, or border, for a garment or shroud. The baby's body had been wrapped in fine linen. For making up clothing there are needles in bone and copper alloy, and shears made of iron in the Yorkshire Museum collections. But as far as what types and styles of dress people wore here in Roman times, we have to rely primarily on images on some of the altars and tombstones (see pp 187–90). These monuments are now, of course, devoid of any of their original colouring, but we know from analysis of dyes on surviving textile that clothing in Roman Britain was often brightly coloured. At 24 – 30 Tanner Row seeds of weld (*Reseda luteola*) were found. This is a plant from which a yellow dye was made.[59] No other remains of dye plants have been identified in Roman deposits at York, but a similar range was probably available as in later times including the sources of the primary colours: dyer's greenweed (yellow), madder (red) and woad (blue).

In addition to wool and linen, another fibre for which there was evidence in the form of seeds at Tanner Row was hemp (*Cannabis sativa* – not the strain used as a drug), which was used for making rope and sailcloth.[60]

Bone, another by-product of butchery, was worked up into a great variety of different objects in the Roman period. York has, for example, produced hundreds of bone pins used primarily for keeping women's hair tidy and for holding garments in place.[61] Most pins are fairly plain with a variety of simple head forms, but there are some that are elaborately carved. Some pin heads were covered in gold leaf and there are others made of jet.[62] Other common bone objects from York include spoons and the handles for knives and other tools (4.12).

Whilst bone pins were most common, they also exist in jet, which was very much a York speciality in the Roman period.[63] Jet is a mineral of the early Jurassic period, similar to coal, which is found on the east coast of England in the Whitby area. In Roman times, it was probably gathered on the beaches and then brought back to workshops in York. Jet's shiny black appearance made it attractive for a range of small objects. It may also have been prized for its supposed magical qualities perceived, perhaps, because it is electrostatic and when rubbed in the dark will be seen to throw off little sparks. In his *Natural History*, Pliny the Elder refers to jet's curative qualities. When boiled with wine it would cure toothache and, if combined with wax, eased the glandular swellings caused by scrofula, probably a form of tuberculosis.[64] Other jet-like materials occurring in the Yorkshire region,

4.12: Two Roman bone knife handles from York. (Yorkshire Museum; left YORYM 2012.319, length 80mm and YORYM 2012.320)

known to the Romans, include shale, which occurs in North Yorkshire, and cannel coal and durains from the coal measure sandstone of West Yorkshire.

Manufacturing of jet objects may have taken place just outside the town southwest of the Ouse in the railway station area where a number of workshop rejects and roughouts, including partly turned pieces representing pins and bead blanks, have been found.[65] A little manufacturing debris was also found at 24 – 30 Tanner Row, within the town, and there may, in fact, have been a number of jet workshops in Roman York. Production of jet objects required little specialist equipment except for a lathe operated by a treadle and a range of files, saws, drills and chisels. The principal products were items worn about the female person, including dress and hair pins, bracelets and rings. They seem to have been very popular in York, especially in the late Roman period. Particularly attractive to the discerning consumer, perhaps, were portrait medallions worn as pendants of which there are six from York.[66] Three depict Medusa (6.18 and see below) and the others a female bust (in cannel coal), a young couple and a family group of three, this last recalling portraiture of the Severan period. Other items in jet from York include dice, spindle whorls, decorative plaques and lids, and, particularly charming, two small model bears, pierced as pendants.[67]

Items made from lithic materials, i.e. stone of various types, in Roman York include querns (discussed above) and hones used for sharpening blades. Examples of the latter found in York are often made of Kentish ragstone and so imported from some distance, perhaps as roughouts that were then finished, like the lava querns, in York itself. Produced for a rather different market was sculpture in stone, whether in the round or in relief, which was the work of specialist masons. One of these men carved a set-square and hammer, his tools and perhaps his trademark, onto the side of Flavia Augustina's tombstone (4.13).[68] He and colleagues served

4.13: Mason's square and hammer incised on the side of Flavia Augustina's tombstone (see 5.8).

wealthy patrons, military and civilian, who wanted permanent works of art, such as statues, to express their status and wealth, whether displayed in public buildings or private houses or as funerary monuments (see pp 245–8).

In conclusion, whilst many of the crafts described here were practiced widely in Roman Britain, York, was also a centre for specialists, like goldsmiths, *plumbatores* and masons, who served a fairly limited market of wealthy consumers. These specialists made a distinctive contribution to the character of *Eboracum*, helping to set it apart from other places in the north of Britain. As far as the organisation of manufacturing is concerned, in some cases such as pottery and ceramic tiles, it involved workshops manned by full-time staff producing on an industrial scale. Other crafts using heat, including metalworking and glass-working, or using water in any quantity, such as dyeing or tanning, would also have been workshop-based. Crafts not requiring much in the way of equipment, such as bone- and jet-working and aspects of textile and clothing production, may have been primarily based in local households.

The services sector

The great range of Roman artefacts we have from York tends to draw our attention towards the manufacturing side of the local economy, but we should not forget there was also a services sector about which we can infer a good deal. Some services relied heavily on manufactured goods, providing an intermediate stage between producer and consumer. Others provided services based primarily on the special skills of the practitioners.

In the first category we may put one of most important pillars of the economy of Roman York: the building and construction trades. Originally they may have been largely the preserve of the army, but by the mid-second century there would have been skilled civilians able to undertake most of the tasks involved in construction of buildings in timber and stone as well as of the making of roads, water mains and drains. Masons, tilers, plasterers, painters and carpenters would have served the population of Roman York just as they serve the people of York today.

One cannot easily make a comprehensive list of service providers in my second category, but prominent amongst them were those involved with food and drink. Because of the cost of fuel and dangers of open fires, many people probably purchased cooked food from 'take away' outlets and bread, cakes, etc., from specialist bakers. For drink there would have been taverns – just as one can see today at Pompeii – where ale and wine, as well as meals, were available. Assuming that there was an amphitheatre, then we can include gladiators in our list of service providers as well as the acrobats, actors and musicians who no doubt performed in various venues around *Eboracum*.

Trade

In the streets of Roman York, whether in shops or temporary market stalls, people would have been able to purchase not only locally produced goods but also many that had travelled over considerable distances. By the end of the second century, York had become one of Britain's principal *entrepôts* for export, import and redistribution serving official, military and private consumers. One can imagine a steady stream of carts, beasts of burden and people on foot travelling to and fro on the roads around York laden with all sorts of different things from live animals to clothes to quern stones to jewellery and so on. On the riverbanks, one would have seen a great number of vessels of one sort or another, from sea-going ships to small rowing boats. In general terms, the character and volume of trade in a particular commodity would have been largely, if not entirely, dependent on its value in relation to the cost of its transportation. Heavy and bulky low value items, such as building stone, usually travelled only short distances, whilst rare and expensive commodities, such as wine, especially if easily transported, might travel over much longer ones.

Exports

There is little evidence for the commodities that were exported from York in Roman times and one must rely, up to a point, on making inferences from the evidence for Britain as a whole. Writing in either the late first century BC or early first century AD, the Greek geographer Strabo, in a well-known passage, described Britain as the source of grain, cattle, gold, silver and iron along with hides, slaves and dogs bred specifically for hunting.[69] Whilst there may have been little gold in the York region, we know that all the other things listed would have been readily available, but in particular, perhaps, grain and cattle given that York was surrounded by productive farmland. The granaries at South Shields (see p 72) may well have been, at least in part, supplied by ships sailing up the coast from York. In *Pro Restaurandis Scholis*, the Gallic panegyrist Eumenius, born in the mid-third century, referred to Britain's 'wealth in corn', and Ammianus Marcellinus tells us Britain was a source of grain for the Roman Army on the Rhineland in the mid-fourth century.[70]

We do not know about Strabo's iron, but it seems likely that lead was exported from York. A lead 'pig' found at Faxfleet, at the mouth of the River Foulness on the Humber Estuary, was stamped SOCIOR LVT BR EX ARG or 'product of the Lutudarensian partners: British lead from the lead-silver works' – *Lutudarum* is probably Carsington in Derbyshire.[71] Ten other lead pigs have been found near to Faxfleet at Brough on Humber and in the immediate area. What this evidence seems to suggest is that lead mined in the both the Yorkshire Dales and Derbyshire was exported via the Humber Estuary, having begun its journey in York.

The archaeological evidence for the distribution to the local region of goods manufactured in York is limited, but pottery falls into this category. Ebor Ware from the legion's kilns has been found in small quantities elsewhere, largely at fort sites such as Doncaster and Malton, although, perhaps because of its reddish colour, it was not particularly attractive to a civilian population whose pottery was traditionally dark coloured. Alternatively, there may have been little left over for general sale and distribution once the army's needs had been satisfied. Ceramic tiles produced in the legionary kilns were also sent to other forts. But they were probably intended for specific building projects, such as the Castleford fort bath house, which produced several stamped Ninth Legion tiles,[72] and were not made available to all-comers.

Another specialist York product was the millstone grit sarcophagus. In addition to examples in local cemeteries, quite a number have been recorded in the region including inscribed examples found at Hovingham (now lost) and Sutton under Whitestonecliffe, near Thirsk.[73] Many of the altars and sculptures from the region, whether made from millstone grit or magnesian limestone, are also likely to be the work of York masons. Finally, jet jewellery and other jet items from Roman Britain may often (but not always) have had a York origin. Furthermore, certain features in their decoration and form suggests many of the jet pieces found in Gaul and the Rhineland came from York or alternatively, perhaps, that raw material was exported to be worked by craftsmen originally from Britain.[74]

Imports

If the evidence for exports is a little scarce, imports show more clearly how Roman York was linked to a great range of trading networks. They appear to have been at their most extensive and wide-reaching between the mid-second and early third centuries. However, determining what commodities were involved, and therefore the likely volume and direction of trade, depends a good deal on our ability to identify their places of origin. Certain materials, such as stone or lead, can often be tracked to a very restricted range of sources. It may be possible to determine the source of certain foodstuffs because their production was only possible under particular environmental conditions that are geographically limited. For man-made items, one must look not only at the material of which they were composed but also at the style of manufacture, which may betray an origin in some particular place or region. Because so much of it survives, on account of both its durability and its widespread use, and because it can often be readily ascribed to a source on the basis of fabric, style, finish, etc., one of the principal forms of evidence for trade in the Roman period is pottery. It may, moreover, be taken, up to a point, to stand for trade in other commodities that have either not survived in the ground at all or only to a much lesser extent.

We can divide imports up into those that came in from the York region, roughly speaking the historic county of Yorkshire, those from elsewhere in Britain, and those from even further afield.

Regional imports

Throughout the Roman period, locally produced pottery in York was supplemented by the import of vessels from a variety of other sources. By the early third century, the most common component of all York's Roman pottery assemblages is what is known generically as 'grey ware'. Some may have been produced in York itself, but it largely came from various kiln sites in east Yorkshire.[75] Another fairly common regionally produced ware was what, on account of its shiny appearance, is known as black burnished ware ('BB1'), largely in the form of jars. In York it occurs as *c.* 5 per cent of Hadrianic to early Antonine assemblages and 10 per cent or more of late Antonine and some early third-century assemblages.[76] Black burnished ware may have come from kilns in Dorset, where it was originally produced, or locally from either Doncaster, 50km distant, or Malton, only 26km away.

For evidence of food imports to York from the region, our principal body of data comes from the waterlogged deposits on the 24 – 30 Tanner Row site (2.3, 19) in which organic materials were well-preserved. As we have already seen, this includes animal bone in some considerable quantity. Because evidence for complete, rather than partial, carcases was found, it would appear that beasts were brought live to York for slaughter. On occasions they apparently came from some distance, perhaps by boat as well as on the hoof. In matter interpreted as manure, there were seeds of plants that prefer a salt marsh environment which, it is suggested, came from the guts of cattle grazed on land downstream from York on the banks of the Humber Estuary.[77] Similar evidence was found in dung identified in the Bedern well on the fortress rampart (2.2, 7).[78]

The fish whose bones survived at Tanner Row and in the Bedern well were largely of fresh-water origin and probably caught locally, but there were also bones of herring likely to come from the Humber Estuary.[79] From the east coast of Yorkshire came edible crab represented by their carapace fragments.[80] A whale vertebra from a Roman deposit at Dringhouses was probably a one-off item brought from the coast as a curiosity rather than evidence for consumption of the meat.[81]

Small amounts of coal have been found in Roman deposits in York that probably originated in the Coal Measures east of Leeds where, in places, it can be dug up near the surface and does not require deep mines.[82] Coal was probably used largely for cremating the dead (see p 234) and for fires in a ritual context rather than for industry.

Imports from Britain beyond the York region

As far as commodities imported to Roman York from beyond the local region are concerned, the evidence is, once again, primarily pottery. A source that would become particularly important for York by the early third century was the Lower Nene Valley, around Peterborough, which produced distinctive colour-coated vessels (4.14).[83] Popular in the city's households were 'hunt cups', attractive beakers with relief models of stags, hares and hounds applied *en barbotine* to the surface, and 'folded' or 'indented' beakers often embellished with scale patterns. Other regional wares included Dales Ware – a hand-made, shell-tempered coarse pottery thought to have been produced in north Lincolnshire from *c.* 200 onwards.[84] It appears, in small quantities in York, on occasions as cremation urns as in the Trentholme Drive cemetery. So-called Dales Ware-type jars, which were wheel-made, came from somewhere in east Yorkshire in the third century.[85] There was also a new type of black burnished ware (BB2) occurring as dishes and jars, thought to come from kilns, perhaps as far away as Kent, or elsewhere in eastern England. This ware appeared principally in contexts of the period *c.* 140 to *c.* 250 and especially in those of *c.* 200 to *c.* 225.[86] Some mortaria were made locally in York but others were imported, most commonly from the well-known kilns at Mancetter and Hartshill in Warwickshire, but also from Lincolnshire kilns at South Carlton and Swanpool, and from the Nene Valley.[87]

That York was, on occasion at least, supplied with grain from elsewhere in Britain, or even the continent, rather than purely local sources, is suggested by the presence of alien weed seeds in the charred material from the burnt granary at 39 – 41 Coney Street.[88] However, this material is dated to the late first or early second century. One would think that by the late Antonine period the local farmland, which probably supplied the Rougier Street grain, was able to cope with the usual level of demand from soldiers and civilians alike, although southern British, or even continental, supplies might have been called on, if only for the army, when harvests were poor in the York region.

4.14: A hunt cup in Nene Valley Ware, height 85mm. (YORYM H160, © York Museums Trust)

Imports from the continent

In addition to local and British wares, a small but important contribution was made to the suite of Roman pottery found in York by vessels imported from the near continent. They came largely from Gaul, of which the most important, shipped here in large quantities, were made from samian ware. This had been imported, initially from sources in south Gaul (up to *c.* 100), largely found on sites in the fortress, but in the civilian settlements at York, especially south-west of the river, the principal sources were workshops in central and eastern Gaul from *c.* 120 until *c.* 230 (4.15).[89] Another feature of York's samian is that it derives from a greater number of workshops than is normal for places in Britain in general, and in its diversity compares well with other major centres in Roman Britain, such as London and Colchester. There are, moreover, a small number of vessels from factories that exported rarely to Britain, although they may have come in as personal possessions rather than formally traded goods.

Samian vessels include cups, jars, bowls, dishes, jugs and platters making up the tableware one would need for dining according to Roman customs. A selection was no doubt seen in the households of most social classes in York. Rarer samian

4.15: Late second-century samian jar (in form Déchelette 72), found in Bootham, York. (YORYM 2008.98, © York Museums Trust)

Producers and traders 155

4.16: Early third-century samian bowl (form Dr30), with chained captives in relief, found at the railway station, York. (YORYM H32, Yorkshire Museum)

vessel types from York include ink wells and mortaria, including ten unused examples of the latter from Wellington Row, perhaps the residue of a consignment unloaded on the riverside nearby. A great range of decorative motifs is found on York's samian vessels, which often includes humans and animals with a mythological or religious significance. A particularly striking bowl made at Rheinzabern in eastern Gaul is shown in 4.16. This was found at the railway station and probably came from a burial of the early third century.[90] It features a row of captives chained together at the neck. Although this is a theme found widely in Roman art, one wonders whether perhaps the original owner of the vessel was sufficiently educated to recall the 'Allegory of the Cave' in Plato's *Republic*,[91] a parable to illustrate the acquisition of knowledge in which we are invited to:

> *Imagine the condition of men living in a sort of underground chamber ... Here they have been since childhood chained by the leg and also by the neck so they cannot move and can see only what is in front of them.*

The late second- to mid-third-century pottery assemblage from York as a whole, and from sites south-west of the Ouse, like Wellington Row and 24 – 30 Tanner Row in particular, stand out in having not only an unusually high percentage (by sherd count) of samian, but also of other continental imports (up to 9 per cent). They include, from amongst the sherds at Wellington Row, two pieces of a rare green-glazed vessel, probably a sort of double-handled loving cup (4.17).[92] It is decorated *en barbotine*, with naked men surrounded by vines, one holding a wreath and another holding a bunch of grapes. This vessel was probably made in Lyon or Cologne. Other continental imports to York include colour-coated vessels from Cologne and the Lower Rhineland and small quantities of dark colour-coated beakers with a lustrous finish from the Moselle region (hence 'Moselkeramik') around Trier.[93] A few of these bear white-painted mottoes

4.17: Fragments of an imported green-glazed double-handled cup with, in relief, naked men surrounded by vines, from Wellington Row. (© York Archaeological Trust)

(hence 'motto beakers') such as DAMI(HI) – 'give it to me' – and NOLITE SITIRE – 'do not be thirsty'(4.18).[94]

Imported to York from the continent for their contents, rather than primarily for table or kitchen use, were amphorae – large thick-walled jars.[95] As is usual in Roman Britain, most commonly found in York are the Baetican olive oil amphorae, known as the 'Dressel 20' (after the classification system of the eponymous German scholar), which are globular in shape and were made on the banks of the River Guadalquivir and its tributaries in the south of Spain – the province of *Baetica*. Their average capacity was 60 to 65 litres.[96] Also shipped in these amphorae were whole olives, of which a number of stones were found at 24 – 30 Tanner Row, and the highly prized fish sauces *garum* and *liquamen*. The amphorae and their contents would have begun their

4.18: Late second-century or early third-century Rhenish Ware beaker with legend VIVATIS ('may you live well'). (YORYM H154, © York Museums Trust)

voyages to York from the river ports at Cordoba and Seville. By the early third century, olive oil was also brought to York in small quantities from North Africa in its own distinctive amphorae.[97]

Wine came to York largely from ports on the Mediterranean coast of Gaul, such as Marseilles, or from Bordeaux, on the Atlantic coast. The most common containers were flat-bottomed amphorae, a type known to archaeologists as 'Gauloise 4' made in the south of France, especially around the mouth of the River Rhone (4.19). The average capacity of these vessels was between 26 and 37 litres.[98] A more effective means of meeting a growing demand for wine in Roman York was probably to bring it in barrels, which might have a capacity of up to 900 litres. In the well at 58 – 9 Skeldergate (2.3, 41), a wooden bucket was found that had been made from silver fir.[99] This is not a local tree but indigenous to the mountains of central and southern Europe. It is possible, therefore, that the wood used to make the bucket had begun its life in a wine barrel from Gaul or the Rhineland. Also made from silver fir was a remarkable piece of board, thought to come originally from an item of furniture, perhaps a cupboard door, that was found re-used in a building wall at 24 – 30 Tanner Row (4.20).[100]

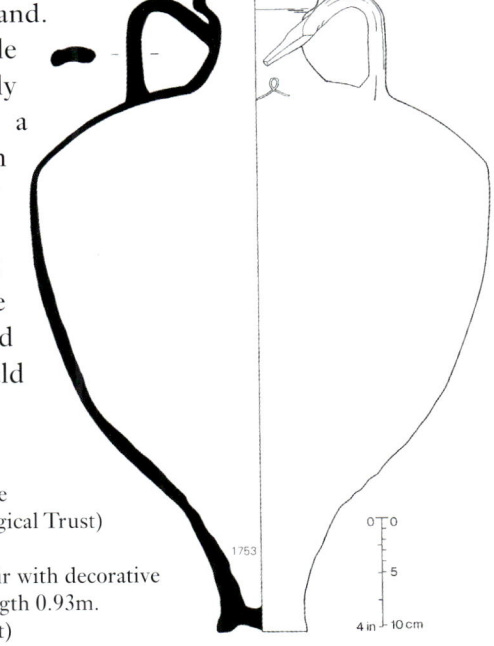

The principal period of glass import from the Rhineland appears to have been, as for pottery, the late second and early third centuries when, Donald

(*Right*) 4.19: Cross-section drawing of a Gallic wine amphora, found in Coppergate. (© York Archaeological Trust)

(*Below*) 4.20: 24 – 30 Tanner Row: board of silver fir with decorative treatment, probably part of a door or panelling, length 0.93m. (Photo by Steve Allen, © York Archaeological Trust)

Harden has commented '… examples of some of the best Rhineland glass of the period – the hey-day of the Cologne glass-houses – was reaching York in some quantity.'[101] They included vessels decorated with delicate facets and linear cutting (4.21). Fragments of hemispherical bowls, and cups and jugs with these features were found in the minster excavations.[102] Occasional imports from elsewhere include a fragment of a colourless beaker with fine deep facets, thought to come from Italy.[103] In some cases, glass vessels may have been imported for their contents, such as unguents or perfumes, rather than in their own right.

In addition to the olives that were imported from the continent, there is evidence, again primarily from 24 – 30 Tanner Row, for other exotica on the dinner tables in York. On occasions it seems that what one was washing down with one's wine was a species of edible dormouse, not the type (*Glis glis*) known to have been consumed in Rome itself, but a central or western European substitute (*Eliomys quercinus*).[104] This '*amuse bouche*' might have been followed up with grapes, black mulberries, figs and walnuts.[105] All of these can be grown today in sheltered places in England, but not as a viable commercial crop as far north as York, even allowing for summers a little warmer in Roman times. And so they are likely to have been continental imports.

In addition to food and drink, we also have imports that can be considered under the broad heading of 'works of art'. For example, small ceramic figurines were mass-produced in Gaul and distributed widely in Britain, largely during the second century (see 6.6).[106] They were primarily for use in shrines, whether in households, workshops or other locales. Rather more prestigious is the small white marble statuette of a male athlete (4.22).[107] In marble also from York is a small head of a statuette of Venus.[108] Both these items are likely to have come from Italy where the marble was readily available. Semi-precious gemstones, either ready engraved or

4.21: Third-century faceted glass bowl from the Rhineland, the base (a) and sides (b) are covered with geometrical patterns of grooves and facets, width 88mm. (YORYM HG210, © York Museums Trust)

as blanks for local engraving, were imported to Britain for use as settings for rings – 'intaglios' – of which there are numerous examples from York (see p 199).[109] They come in the usual range of stone type one finds in Roman Britain, including carnelian and jasper, forms of the silica-based mineral chalcedony, found in eastern Europe but also in other parts of the world known to the Romans, including India. Finally, under the heading of continental imports we may note again the use of cinnabar, a red pigment for wall paintings, and a cosmetic, which was probably imported from Spain (p 119).

Items from Roman York with an origin further afield than continental Europe are rare indeed. However, Donald Harden identified the rim sherd of a second-century glass vessel as part of a shallow bowl of Alexandrian origin.[110] From a source equally distant is a fragment of silk found in the sewer serving the fortress baths.[111] It may have been last used as toilet paper, but presumably represents an occasional consignment of the fabric from the near East, or even China, brought in to make into soft furnishings or clothes for the ladies of the local elite.

4.22: Statuette, probably of an athlete, in white marble, found at the old railway station, height 250mm. (YORYM 1998.22, © York Museums Trust)

When all the evidence for trade described above is drawn together, we can see that Roman York was able to reach out over networks that extended beyond the immediate region into many other parts of the empire. In doing so, not only the everyday requirements of sustenance, fuel and construction were satisfied, but also the exacting tastes of those same discerning and wealthy consumers who availed themselves of locally produced luxuries. York's power to do this was at its greatest extent in the late second and early third century, the Julia Velva period, thanks to the presence of a military and civilian elite larger here than almost anywhere else in Roman Britain except, in the latter respect, for London. However, to understand how this power was exerted we need to consider the means by which trade was conducted.

The conduct of trade

Arising from studies of trade, both in antiquity and in simple societies in more recent times, several means by which goods passed from hand to hand have been identified that are relevant to our understanding of Roman Britain. Some involved the use of money, but the majority did not. In a society in which relatively few people, other than soldiers and imperial officials, received an income paid to them even in part in money, other ways were found to establish the relative values of goods (and services) as a basis for trade.

As far as local trade in the basics for sustaining life are concerned, various forms of reciprocal arrangement would have prevailed.[112] For example, on rural estates or in urban households, food and shelter would be provided to workers, whether free or enslaved, in return for their labour. In other circumstances there was what might be best described as barter between the parties. This might have been the sort of simple one-off transaction in which a pottery vessel was exchanged for a pair of shoes. Alternatively, a transaction might have been conducted over a period of time during which, for example, one party might agree to help another harvest his crops in exchange for receiving a regular supply of eggs. Gift-giving, from the lavish openhanded generosity of the emperors to their clients down through all levels of society, may also be seen as a form of reciprocity in which individuals or communities cemented good relationships by the exchange of goods in which the giving process itself was seen to be as important as what was actually exchanged. One particular category of reciprocal gift was the dowry in which one family acknowledged another for accepting a daughter in marriage to one of its sons.

Another form of trade may be described under the heading of redistribution. In a pre-Roman context this might have involved, first of all, tribute rendered in kind, usually as agricultural products, to a tribal leader, such as Cartimandua. Some part of this would then have been redistributed to the leader's followers as a reward for, or in anticipation of, services provided by them as warriors, craft specialists, etc. Another form of redistribution, which clearly involved Cartimandua or her predecessors, is suggested by the presence in the Stanwick enclosure of samian, amphorae and Roman glass.[113] These items may be thought of as what archaeologists sometimes call 'prestige goods', valued by the recipient for their exclusivity and rarity. In this case, the donor would have been the Romans, who were seeking to ensure the loyalty of the Brigantian elite with gifts of tableware and wine. They in turn could then have redistributed them to their followers. After the conquest, one can envisage that similar patron and client relationships were maintained between the Romans and the native elites. This may account for some of the samian and amphorae found at rural sites in the York area.

Supply of the Roman Army did not just involve grain or other foodstuffs, of course, but many other commodities, some of which it could not, or chose not to, source in the immediate region in which it found itself. As far as the fortress at York is concerned, such things as fine tableware, in glass or ceramic, wine and olive oil, and lava quern stones were, as we have seen, brought in from the continent. Supply of these materials may, as a rule, have been the preserve of middle-men holding army contracts.[114] These contractors would have been involved in a version of what is often referred to as 'administered trade', i.e. trade not subject to the usual discipline of a competitive market. Contracts held perhaps by the likes of the *negotiator* Lucius Viducius Placidus and by Marcus Aurelius Lunaris, who set up the altar in Bordeaux (see p 76), probably accounted for a considerable proportion of the ships sailing up the Ouse to York. Whether purely civilian trading contacts were established between York and places far beyond the region seems less likely. The problem which parties some considerable distance apart faced in the ancient world was one of trust if they were not personally known to one another. A producer, for example, of glassware in Cologne, might be happy enough to fulfil an army contract, but would he wish to respond to an order from York when he did not know the customer and, more to the point, know how reliable he would be in paying the bill? However, our producer would be fairly sure of getting paid if he did business on a regular basis with an army contractor. Many of the more exotic items from Roman York, such as the olives, the cinnabar, or the marble sculpture, may well have come as part of consignments of goods intended primarily for the army or as a result of being passed from hand to hand over short distances between parties well-acquainted with one another.

To what extent payments in money formed part of the commercial environment Julia Velva was familiar with is hard to know. However, in light of the numerous Roman coins found in York, one can envisage that shops and local markets did operate on a cash basis, rather like York market does today, at least until the early third century, when small change became scarce. There may also have been money substitutes, items like the sweets or cigarettes one used to get as change in Italy in the 1960s when its coinage was in short supply. The benefit of money, in economic terms, was that it allowed a greater flexibility in settling transactions making those that would otherwise be cumbersome using barter much easier and quicker. The introduction of money was probably, therefore, a factor in increasing economic activity in the York region at least until the Severan period.

Money for cash transactions was initially introduced to York, and the north of Britain as a whole, by the Roman Army, but subsequently came in through trade. The imperial currency system included, first of all, a copper-based, low-value coinage that was used as small change for day-to-day transactions. There was also a precious metal coinage in which, in theory, a piece was worth its weight whether in silver or gold. This was used for paying the army, the biggest item in the imperial budget, and for collecting taxes, which is why the imperial authorities, although they had no economic policy in any sense in which we understand it today, were interested in the adequate circulation of the currency and in its value. In Roman Britain, although the supply of coinage, largely from mints in Gaul and Rome itself, in the first century and most of the second, did not fluctuate greatly, it is generally thought that there were usually insufficient coins in circulation to allow all or even a substantial proportion of transactions to be conducted using money.[115] Even in Roman York, many transactions were probably conducted on a non-monetary basis or using money substitutes.

The lack of small change became more serious after the beginning of the Severan era when the supply to Britain of bronze coinage dwindled rapidly. As far as the silver coinage (the denarius) is concerned, from the mid-second century onwards its weight and especially its fineness were increasingly manipulated to produce more coins from a given amount of silver. R. Duncan-Jones estimates that 120 denarii were minted from a pound (*c.* 322gm) of silver under Marcus Aurelius, 152 under Commodus, and by the end of the Severan period 226.[116] Under Emperor Caracalla a new coin, the antoninianus, was introduced, which was supposedly worth two denarii but in fact contained a good deal less than twice the silver content. Pressure on fineness continued after the fall of the Severi such that the denarius eventually contained minimal amounts of silver. By contrast to silver, gold coinage, although minted in much smaller quantities, maintained its fineness until Caracalla made a 10 per cent reduction.

The principal reason for imperial manipulation of the coinage was to pay an increasingly assertive army that was relied on more and more by emperors to stay in power. However, pay rises granted by Septimius Severus and Caracalla were probably not worth a great deal in real terms because of inflation. If a denarius, for example, was not regarded as worth its weight, then more would be demanded in any given transaction. In this situation, taxation involved increased exactions in kind, largely in the form of agricultural produce, which was passed directly to the army in *lieu* of payment. As well as regular army pay, emperors also committed themselves, from time to time, to other handouts, whether as one-off donations to the soldiers or as bribes and inducements to other parties for political reasons. A good example is the 'large sum' given to the *Maeatae* by Septimius Severus (see p 69). As a result of the increasing problems of matching the supply of bullion to demands on the treasury, the monetary system had more-or-less collapsed by the mid-third century. Very little silver coinage appears to have been supplied to the army in Britain under the later Severi and their immediate successors. It was not until after about the year 260 that the authorities in charge of what was then the breakaway Gallic empire in the western provinces made an attempt to revive and reform the coinage, which led to the minting of vast quantities of low value largely copper-based coins.[117]

One response to the shortage of officially minted coinage in York under the Severi and afterwards appears to have been local manufacture. In a sense this might be called forgery, but it may have been sanctioned by the authorities to make up the shortfall needed for transactions. These local coins were not struck in the usual manner but cast in a ceramic mould. At York, seven coin moulds for issues of Commodus and Septimius Severus were found at 21 – 33 Aldwark, just outside the fortress near the east corner.[118] Another group, of fifty moulds, was found in field ditches at an otherwise unremarkable archaeological site in Fulford, *c.* 3km south of the centre of York.[119] In both cases the moulds were probably for making coins earlier in date than those generally available at the time of the forgery, perhaps the mid-third century. By doing this, forgers might have been able to fool people into thinking the coins had a higher silver content than was actually the case.

In addition to coinage, another Roman introduction to Britain, which allowed for a more systematic approach to transactions and the reliable keeping of accounts, was a sophisticated system of weights and measures. Once again, the evidence comes largely from military sites and towns, such as York. In the Yorkshire Museum's collection, there are pieces of steelyard, a weighing device that consisted of a bar suspended on a hook and chain. Weights were moved along the bar to balance the item to be weighed, which was suspended on another hook at one end of it. There are also examples of the weights, including one in the form of the torso of a young man and another of a recumbent ram.[120] Small hand-held balances for weighing small items are also known.[121]

Conclusion

In the introduction to this chapter I noted the problem of quantifying economic growth in Roman Britain. Nonetheless, the archaeological evidence from Roman York would suggest that it participated in a period of apparent prosperity in the late Antonine and Severan periods. One can see that this occurred all over the western empire as witnessed, for example, by the expansion of towns and the increased output of pottery, metalwork and other material culture. To some extent the appearance of growth may have been simply due to a rising population, but increasing demand for goods and services, especially from urban populations, thriving interregional trade, a reasonably stable supply of money, as well as the stimulus of the tax system, probably led to some real growth in average *per capita* productivity and income. Serious obstacles to growth in the Roman economy remained, however, not least the inadequacy of sources of energy, other than manual labour, and the hazards of communication over any great distance. Any benefits from growth were, of course, not in any sense equally diffused through the population. In York it was probably only a small group of privileged families who were able to take advantage of profits generated by their estates and workshops and indulge in conspicuous consumption, whether of locally produced luxury goods or imported works of art, wine, silk and so forth. Amongst the lower orders, the fluctuations in the fortunes of agriculture would have meant the continuation of a regime of alternating feast and famine as old as human existence. When famine prevailed, conflict no doubt arose and there may have been occasions when as the renowned physician, Galen (mid-second century) writes: 'The city-dwellers, as was their practice, collected and stored enough corn for all the coming year immediately after the harvest. They carried off all the wheat, the barley, the beans and the lentils and left what remained to the countryfolk.'[122]

Chapter 5

Provincial society and daily life

The people of Roman York

We only know the names of about 120 people who lived for at least some of their lives in Roman York – Julia Velva and Aurelius Mercurialis are very much the exception to the almost complete anonymity of their fellow residents. Most of the evidence for names comes from inscriptions on funerary monuments and a little from inscriptions, including graffiti, on other items. About two-thirds of the names are male and the other third female, a division that neatly reflects the more prominent role men played in Roman society. Only eleven are, or in the absence of a stated age are probably, children of about 13 or younger. The vast majority of these named people would have belonged to the upper echelons of society. But in any event, 120 is a very small proportion indeed of the total population of Roman York over the 330 or so years of its existence. We only know about the rest from the archaeological evidence of what they wittingly, or otherwise, left behind and, of course, from their physical remains recovered from burials.

Population size

What was the size of Roman York's population? The short answer is that we do not know, although we can say that it would have varied a good deal over time. Initially, it was pretty much confined to the 5,000 or so men of the Ninth Legion plus their camp followers. However, a hundred years later, at the beginning of the late Antonine period, although the army was still here, the civilian population began to grow rapidly, as we can see in the expansion of the settled areas – and cemeteries – on both sides of the River Ouse. At the time of the visit of the emperor Septimius Severus in 208 – 11, and during the reigns of his immediate successors, the population of Roman York was probably as large as it ever would be.

One way of reckoning the size of a settlement's population is by estimating the number of burials, as Lauren McIntyre has done for Roman York.[1] She concludes that a maximum number, probably in the late second to early third century, including civilian and military, was between 10,000 and 14,500. However, our knowledge of the cemeteries remains incomplete and there is, moreover, no way of knowing whether the cemeteries only accommodated York people or if others were brought here for burial from the surrounding region. Another way of reckoning population is to assess the density of habitation. But, again, at York we do not really have adequate evidence for this or for knowing how much land was given over to public buildings and spaces as opposed to housing. However, if the area of about 20ha within the medieval walls south-west of the Ouse – excluding the south-easternmost part (p 89) – had on average the same density of population as Roman Pompeii for which one estimate is *c*.166 people per ha,[2] similar to many other pre-industrial cities, then we would have a population of up to about 3,300. To this can probably be added a small number of people living outside the walled area. The maximum area settled north-east of the Ouse may have been about 10 ha in extent. A grand total, therefore, of about 5,000 – 5,500 civilians can then be added to the army (if all were resident), giving a maximum population of perhaps 10,000 – 11,000 in the early third century. This is rather less than McIntyre's maximum. In any event, if the army is taken out of the equation, then we have a population that was not large by the standards of towns today, or even by those of the Roman world as a whole, but it was much larger than that of any other settlement in the north, except perhaps the *civitas* capital at Aldborough.

Society in Roman York

One's place in York society in Roman times (especially before Caracalla's *constitutio*) would have been determined primarily by whether one was born a citizen, had acquired citizenship (becoming a 'freedman' or 'freedwoman'), or was a non-citizen. Amongst the third group there was, of course, an important distinction between the free-born and the slaves. Matters of rank and status are discussed further below. But before the late Antonine period, local society at York itself would have been dominated by the legionaries, all of whom were Roman citizens. The surrounding area, by contrast, was occupied almost exclusively by an indigenous, non-citizen population in which society probably continued to be structured in the pre-Roman manner, with hereditary landowners and 'aristocrats' at the top of the heap.

From the beginning of the late Antonine period, as the numbers of civilians in York increased, society rapidly became more diverse than hitherto. There were, of course, as always, men and women of all ages, as well as children. But on a walk through the streets at the end of the second century one would probably have found oneself mixing with a pretty varied crowd in terms of social status, occupation, geographical origins and ethnic identity. However, the glue that held this society together, as it did all over the Roman world, was family loyalty and *clientela*, the traditional relationship between patrons and their clients based on the exchange of favours granted and services rendered. Whilst money and goods may have played their part in these relationships, so too, in an era without the sort of police force we are familiar with, did personal protection. One only has to glance at contemporary literature to get the clear impression that life in the Roman world was characterised by a degree of violence on a day-to-day basis far greater than we are used to today. It was essential, therefore, when under threat of harm to have a patron who could come to one's aid.

The balance of the sexes

In most human societies, numbers of males and females are, more-or-less, equal. Any great disparities are usually due to exceptional factors such as warfare or selective infanticide. As far as Roman York is concerned, the first (1968) major study of human remains, from the Trentholme Drive cemetery (late second- to early fourth-century, location on 1.1), suggested that the ratio of males to females was 4:1.[3] Re-examination of the skeletons in 2009 by Joseph Peck, using improved techniques, gave a ratio of 1.76:1 (104 sexable males and fifty-nine females).[4] In Lauren McIntyre's doctoral thesis, which recorded 464 sexable skeletons from Roman York (all periods), she reckoned the ratio was 1.88:1.[5] Her data are slightly biased, however, by the inclusion in the sample of burials from two sites on Driffield Terrace in the cemetery on The Mount (1.1, 13).[6] Of about eighty burials (largely late second- to early fourth-century) all were males (or probable males) (see also p 170). Nevertheless, there seems to be a preponderance of males in Roman York's cemeteries, the most obvious explanation being the large military component in the population. In view of the discovery of two military tombstones on Driffield Terrace, of Lucius Baebius Crescens and an unnamed centurion,[7] the men buried there were probably soldiers for the most part.

Age structure

Conventional wisdom has it that people in antiquity bred like rabbits and died like flies. This would imply a population, on average, much younger than our own. However, in the absence of detailed records of births and deaths, it is difficult to determine the age structure of an ancient population with any accuracy.[8] Some evidence can, nonetheless, be drawn, first of all, from burial data. As far as York is concerned, if we refer to the Trentholme Drive cemetery, Peck's study suggested that of 262 skeletons, he could age only fourteen that had not survived to be 10 years old or more.[9] However, it seems clear that neonates and infants are vastly underrepresented. Data from other Roman cemeteries in Britain where infants have been present give an impression of very high mortality – perhaps 40 per cent of live births failed to reach 18 months of age.[10] The absence of the youngest at Trentholme Drive, and in other Roman cemeteries in York, may be because their bones are very fragile and do not survive in the ground and/or because, sometimes, they are simply missed during excavation. Moreover, it was often the case that infants were not buried in formal cemeteries but in other places, often within the settled areas otherwise forbidden to the dead.

After 10 years of age, survival in the Roman period declines fairly sharply if not evenly. Peck reckoned only 15 per cent of the Trentholme Drive population lived to 50 or more. Taking all individuals (including infants and neonates) in her larger sample into account, McIntyre reckons that average life expectancy at birth in Roman York was 32.6 years, although it improved once adolescence was reached.[11] Peck detected a slightly higher mortality of females than males in his 20 to 34 years cohort (55.8% to 44.2%) at Trentholme Drive, which was probably due to fatalities when giving birth as a result of poor hygiene and a limited knowledge of obstetrics.

We can compare the burial data with that from funerary inscriptions from York and elsewhere in Roman Britain that give the age of the deceased. In general terms, the inscriptions confirm the pattern of mortality derived from burials, although they must be treated with some care. First of all, ages were not necessarily recorded accurately. In the absence of systematic record-keeping, one suspects there was a certain amount of rounding-up and down of ages to the nearest decade or half decade (e.g. 30 or 35), as in the case of Julia Velva (50) perhaps. Moreover, as Keith Hopkins has shown for the empire as a whole, funerary monuments did not commemorate a representative sample of the population, but for the most part the better off and privileged, who tended to live longer.[12] The newborn and the very young are not commemorated to nearly the same extent as adults. This is clearly the case at York. The youngest person to appear in an inscription (on her sarcophagus) is Simplicia Florentina, who died at the age of 10 months – she is also the youngest person to be commemorated in Roman Britain.[13] Next come the two children, both 1 year old (so not necessarily siblings), referred to on Flavia Augustina's tombstone (5.8).[14] Including these three, the average age at death of those commemorated on tombstones from York is 26.11 years (eighteen recorded) surprisingly, perhaps, rather lower than McIntyre's figure quoted above. In any event, Julia Velva at 50 had reached a pretty good age by Roman standards. In York only Antonius Gargilianus, the camp prefect, is recorded as older at death, at 56 years and 6 months,[15] although even he is eclipsed by Roman Britain's only known centenarian who benefitted from the salubrious south Wales environment at Caerleon.[16]

To conclude on the matter of age, one would have seen very few people in Roman York who in modern times would be considered old or even middle-aged. As in many developing countries today, *Eboracum* had an overwhelmingly young population. Moreover, many people in their 30s and 40s would probably have appeared much older than their modern contemporaries as a result of poor diet, health problems and a life of hard manual labour.

In light of an age structure very different from our own, it is not surprising that Roman attitudes to, and awareness of, age and ageing were also different. Few children would have known both sets of grandparents. Many children would have been orphans and only the fortunate would have been fostered by others, as in the case of Hyllus (named after one of Hercules' children) described as an ALVMNVS (foster child) on his tombstone from York.[17] As for the adults, many of them might have had several spouses, especially as women could be married as young as 12 years of age, often to men who were quite a bit older. One can imagine that Julia Velva, in light of her age, might have buried at least one husband before marrying, or associating in some unspecified way with, Aurelius Mercurialis, her heir. Grief at a premature death is, however, eternal and was just as heartfelt in Britain in the Roman period as in any other, especially in the case of young children such as Simplicia Florentina and Corellia Optata. The latter's *cognomen* means 'wished for' or 'welcome', but she died aged 13 years and was commemorated by her father, Quintus Corellius Fortis, in a very touching poem on her tombstone (5.6 and see below).

Physical condition and health

From the study of their skeletons, Lauren McIntyre concluded that the average height of an adult male in Roman York (165 examples) was 1.71m (5ft 6ins) and of an adult female (sixty-one examples) 1.59m (5ft 3in).[18] These figures are much the same as recorded elsewhere in Roman Britain. In addition to height, skeletons can provide information on some other aspects of a population's physical condition and general health, although not usually cause of death, which in many cases was probably due to incurable diseases. These would have included cholera, typhoid, influenza and various forms of plague such as the so-called 'plague of Galen' carried by soldiers returning to Rome from the east in *c.* 165. Evidence for infections is rarely seen on bones, although Anwen Caffell and Malin Holst concluded from their study of the Driffield Terrace skeletons that respiratory and lung conditions may have been quite common.[19]

Metabolic conditions (those related to nutrition in some way) detected on Roman skeletons from York include *cribra orbitalia* and porotic hyperostosis, represented in the pathology of the cranial vault by spongy or porous bone tissue. These conditions were probably due to poor nutrition in the early years. There was evidence, for example, on almost a third of the Driffield Terrace skulls.[20] Various forms of joint disease, particularly osteoarthritis, were also quite common in the people of Roman York occurring in 17.82% of the individuals studied by McIntyre.[21] A higher figure comes from the all-male group at Driffield Terrace, whereby 38.7% of individuals, of whom sufficient skeletal remains survived for analysis, had suffered from osteoarthritis in their spines and/or other joints.[22] Evidence for the disease often occurs on the lower spine, in the costovertebral joint, i.e. where the ribs join the spine, and in the hip joints. It is a result of, or exacerbated by, the stress arising from regular heavy lifting and other manual work. As far as feet are concerned, a study of the wear on leather shoe soles from 24 – 30 Tanner Row suggested many of them had been worn by individuals who were not only bow-legged and flat-footed but suffered from *hallux rigidus*, a progressively degenerative disorder of the joint at the base of the big toe.[23]

Evidence for trauma on York skeletons features the usual range of fractures of limb bones due to falls, trips, etc., that one would expect in any population. However, particularly striking in the Driffield Terrace skeletons was the way decapitation by execution had left very graphic traces of the implement employed in taking the men's lives, presumably a sword or an axe, on the upper vertebra. Also striking were the number of fractures of the cranium and other bones that suggested to Caffell and Holst that the men had been regularly involved in fighting.[24] Whether this was in the context of formal combat, as boxers or gladiators for example, or simply in the sort of drunken brawls that are common in and around any army garrison is, however, not clear.

Lauren McIntyre looked at teeth in the Roman York population and concluded that oral health was generally good by Romano-British standards, although there was widespread evidence for the usual range of conditions prevailing in the period. They include enamel hypoplasia (i.e. inadequate covering of enamel on the teeth), periodontal disease (inflammation of the gums), caries, abscesses and tooth loss.[25] As a postscript to modern research, we might note that back in 1924, Gordon Home had ascertained from a local dentist that Julia Fortunata (whose remains and sarcophagus are still in the Yorkshire Museum collection) had suffered from toothache but that her teeth were admirably regular and would have given her 'charm when she smiled'.[26]

Another health hazard in Roman times was infestation of the gut with parasitic worms. In the deposits at 24 – 30 Tanner Row and in the Bedern well there were numerous eggs of the human whipworm (*Trichuris*) and mawworm (*Ascaris*).[27] These parasites are passed on by contact with the faeces of infected individuals to be found, for example, on middens or in drains and sewers. Worms can cause acute stomach pain and compromise the benefits of nutrition even leading to death in some cases. Defecation in the open is not usually associated with the Romans but may in fact have been quite widespread. Flush latrines would have been available to both the military and civilian population in the bath houses, but otherwise there is little evidence of them in York, nor is there much evidence for the cess pits that were common in the medieval city.

Although knowledge of diseases and injuries, and how to treat them effectively, was limited compared to today, Roman York would have had professional doctors to provide advice to the sick and a range of remedies and medicines. Some were bogus, but others had real therapeutic value. Critical to medical practice were manuals detailing the uses of plant extracts and other naturally occurring substances. The best-known was, perhaps, *De Materia Medica* in five volumes by the Greek Pedanius Dioscorides (*c.* AD 40 – 90), although he worked largely in the eastern Mediterranean. Some of the plants he refers to did, nevertheless, grow in Britain. In the deposits at 24 – 30 Tanner Row there were seeds of henbane (*Hyoscyamus niger*) and deadly nightshade (*Bella donna*).[28] Both are highly toxic but can be judiciously prepared for medicinal purposes.[29] Henbane is used today in treatments for a variety of conditions including rheumatism and toothache. Deadly Nightshade can be used as a pain-reliever and an anti-inflammatory. From Roman deposits in York also there are seeds of opium poppy (*Papaver somniferum*), from which it is also possible to make a pain-reliever – as well as more harmful drugs (5.1). A range of ointments and salves would have been available for skin and eye conditions. A small slab of soapstone from York used for stamping cakes of such material is inscribed 'Julius Alexander's salve made from *diamisus* [probably copper pyrites] for irritations'.[30]

5.1: The opium poppy (*Papaver somniferum*).

There are numerous surgical instruments from Roman Britain, scalpels, forceps, cauteries, etc., although none has yet been recognised at York.[31] However, no matter how ill one was, surgery was not to be recommended as other than a last resort in the absence of an understanding of how infection spread and the need for hygiene during operations.

Ethnicity

Ethnicity in the study of antiquity may be regarded largely as a cultural phenomenon referring to aspects of shared identity within communities. From an archaeological point of view, ethnicity is usually defined by distinctive aspects of material culture, such as dress, types of jewellery, pottery vessels or weapons.[32] Less tangible factors related to identity, such as language and ideas about a common geographical and/or mythological origin, rely on the survival of relevant written sources. Ethnicity can also have a biological aspect. There are features in human genetic inheritance, such as stature, skull shape and colour of eyes, hair and skin, that may cluster in particular geographical locations.[33] Use of the term 'race' in relation to ethnicity in the past can be a little awkward given the conflicted and controversial meanings of the word in modern political discourse. However, terms such as 'racial affinity' or 'racial type' can be appropriate when considering certain human physical features (see below).

There can be no doubt that in respect of both cultural identity and genetic inheritance the Roman Empire was extremely heterogeneous. However, in respect of the former one might say that the social elite, whether in the army, imperial bureaucracy or leading families in the cities of the empire, can be considered a distinct ethnic group more-or-less regardless of their genetic inheritance.[34] They accepted a social structure that gave them a privileged position and shared in many aspects of a culture that legitimised the structure to be found, for example, in the use of Latin or Greek, in artistic and literary tastes, and in religious beliefs and practices. An important factor in the creation of homogeneity was the mobility arising from service in the army and government which, as we have seen in the careers of legionary legates in York (pp 64–5), took men and their families all over the empire. Below the elite level, amongst the provincial populations who by and large did not move around so much, one might expect to find communities defined to a rather greater extent by distinctive cultural traits as well as a shared genetic inheritance.

On the eve of the Roman conquest, the local population in the York area was probably descended largely from a native stock that went back many generations into the prehistoric period. The idea of a series of waves of immigration to Britain from the continent during the Iron Age is not now accepted in the way it once was.[35] However, the Roman conquest clearly brought many people to Britain from other parts of the world, not only as soldiers and administrators, but also as merchants, slaves, wives, partners, etc. The proportion of the residents of Roman Britain who were born, or who were first generation descendants of someone born, outside Britain may never have been particularly large, at least compared to the present day. However, in a few places, such as York or London, it was probably appreciably higher than the norm, especially at certain times such as, in York's case, during the visit of the emperor Septimius Severus and his court. This matter of ethnic identity can be approached both through the evidence from inscriptions, from items of material culture and through recent scientific research.

As far as York inscriptions are concerned, there are a few in which we find names thought to be characteristically British or Celtic.[36] They include the Velva of Julia Velva herself and Barita, the cognomen of Candida Barita, whose tombstone was found near to that of Julia Velva's.[37] Both women were members of the local elite, but they may well have been descended from native stock, although it is always possible that native names were given to the daughters of migrants, rather as daughters of recent migrants are sometimes given English names. A male name of native type was Bikkus scratched – unusually using 'k' instead of 'c' – onto a samian vessel.[38] Other names may indicate a family origin in Gaul or the Rhineland. For example, the *nomen* (family name) Simplicia, the daughter of Felicius Simplex, was fabricated from her father's *cognomen* (personal name) in a manner commonly found in both areas.[39]

When we look at the small number of funerary inscriptions in which a place of origin is stated we find most of the people named came from the western part of the empire. In the military, we have only Lucius Baebius Crescens from Augsburg (*Augusta Vindelicorum*),[40] now in Bavaria, but there are other migrants amongst the civilians. From *Gallia Belgica* we have Lucius Viducius Placidus from the territory of the *Veliocasses* around Rouen (*Rotomagus*), who we have already met as the *negotiator* who sponsored part of a temple in 221 (p 76). He may have fabricated his nomen Viducius from his father's *cognomen* (Viducus) in the Gallic manner on receiving citizenship, perhaps following Caracalla's extension of citizenship.[41] From another regional capital in Gaul, this time in *Gallia Lugdunensis*, we have Verecundius Diogenes from Bourges (*Avaricum Biturgum*).[42] Remarkably, we also have the sarcophagus of Diogenes' wife, Julia Fortunata, of the nice smile, who, the inscription tells us, had her home in Sardinia.[43] One wonders how and where the couple met.

We may have another Gaul, this time from *Gallia Narbonnensis*, in the centurion Sollius Julianus known from the graffito on a piece of leather (p 65), whose *nomen* is well attested in that province. From further afield was Nikomedes, a freedman of the emperor, who appears on a (lost) dedication to the holy goddess *Britannia*, presiding deity of the province. His name suggests he was Greek in origin.[44] Other Greek male *cognomina* known in York belong to Volusius Iraneus, Marcus Aurelius Iraneus and Valentinus Theodorianus.[45] The last, according to Gordon Home, had a 'skull of noble proportions'. He came from *Nomentum* (Mentana) in central Italy. Two Greek female *cognomina* we know of in York belong to (Emilia) Theodora, mother of Theodorianus, and Andronica, whose name was one of three inscribed on a lead ossuarium (container for cremated bones) (7.3 and see p 236).

Spotting the presence of ethnic groups in the Roman Empire on the basis of distinctive material culture can be quite difficult given the high degree of stylistic and formal homogeneity in many of its more common components. However, as far as identifying native British people in York is concerned, we should note a very particular type of bone spoon with a pierced bowl (5.2), examples of which are almost exclusively found in York itself (four) and the north-east of England, many of them from caves in the Yorkshire Dales.[46] The function of these spoons remains a mystery. It has been suggested that they served as forms of brooch or distaff although, given the cult practices thought to have taken place in the dark and silent atmosphere of the caves, they may have been some sort of implement used in associated rituals. In any event, these spoons may, in their small way, have operated as some sort of expression of regional or community identity, perhaps with pre-Roman origins.

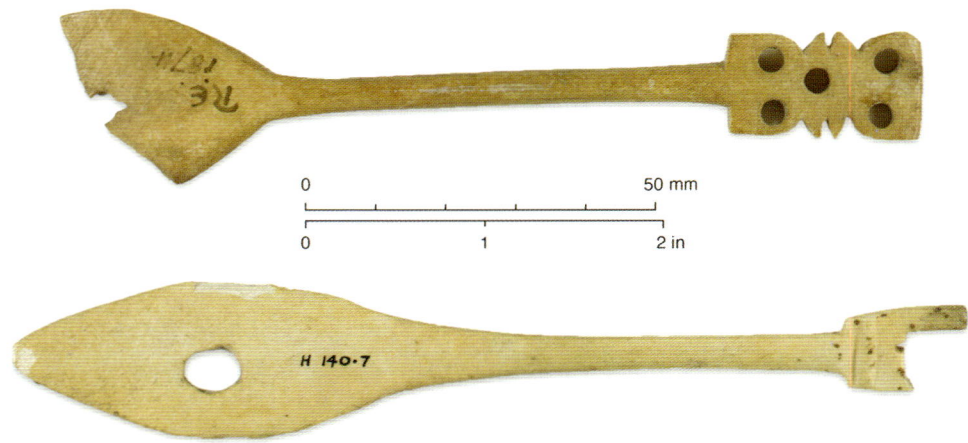

5.2: Pierced bone spoons from York, YORYM H140.3-2 unbroken head, length 115mm, and YORYM H140.7-1, complete bowl. (© York Museums Trust)

As for identifying immigrants from material culture, one might point to some of the York tombstones and sarcophagi, including Julia Velva's, which are thought to indicate Rhenish influence.[47] But whether this means that the craftsmen who made them came from somewhere like Cologne or Bonn is not known. It may simply be that ideas about design and style travelled with the army and were realised here by local men. Rhenish influence on pottery styles in the early third century has also been identified,[48] but perhaps of greater interest in the debate on immigrants are large Ebor Ware carinated (i.e. shaped like opposed keels in cross-section) bowls – 'casseroles' – of the early third century (5.3).[49] They are thought to have been made in York to suit the way Africans, perhaps in Severus's army, cooked their meals on braziers – ceramic vessels with lugs on the rim on which the cooking pot rested above the hot charcoal below.[50] It was more usual in Britain for cooking pots to be placed in the hot ashes of a hearth on the ground. As far as the casseroles are concerned, Michael Fulford has pointed out that no braziers have been found in York and similar bowls with sagging bases belong to a long tradition of potting in the western Mediterranean and not just north Africa.[51] Once again, we should probably be thinking about ideas rather than people travelling and the same may, perhaps, be said of York's head pots, also thought to have been made in an African tradition (see p 225).

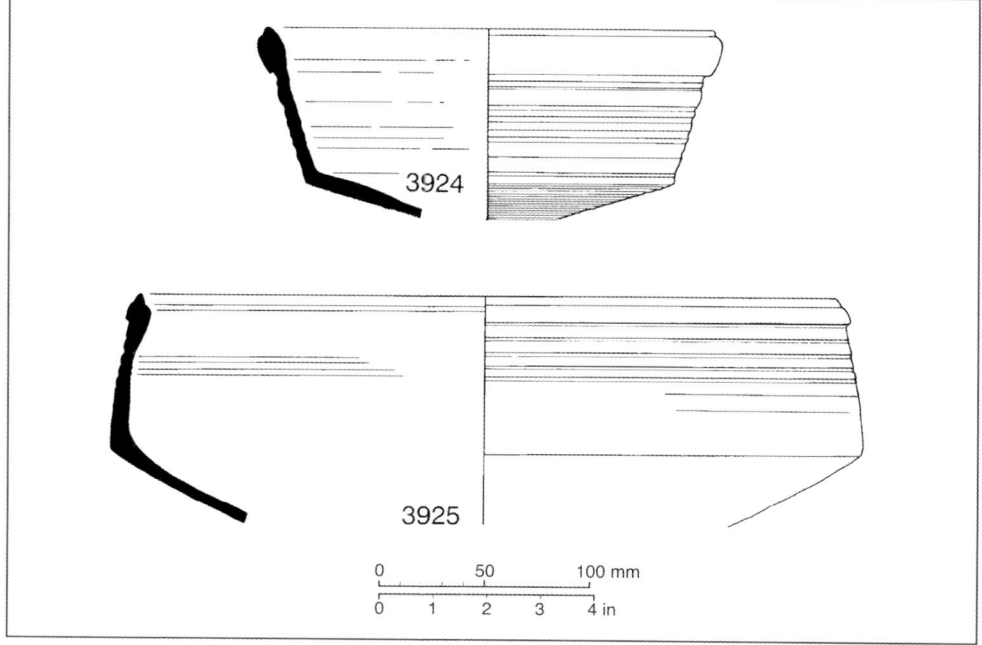

5.3: Cross-section drawings of early third-century 'casserole' dishes. (From Monaghan 1997, © York Archaeological Trust)

Scientific techniques and ethnicity

Whether or not we should be thinking about a group of North African potters in York or of soldiers from the same region eating their dinners in a manner one might have seen in Lepcis Magna, there is now evidence for people of North African heritage arising from the application of new scientific techniques to human remains. There are three of these that have been used in recent years: craniometrics, isotope analysis and genomics. As far as the first two are concerned, four recent studies have looked at the question of origins and racial type in Roman York based, in two cases, on both isotopes and craniometrics and, in the other two, on isotopes alone. In summary, they suggest an unusual measure of diversity in the population, although the different data sets do not present an entirely consistent picture.

The traditional approach to determining racial type in human skeletons was arthroscopy, based on an assessment of visible traits, primarily of the skull. This can, however, be highly subjective. The first published study of Romano-British material, based solely on the study of skulls including sixty-one specimens from the railway station cemetery at York, appeared in 1935.[52] Although the methodology and ideas about race that the study describes are hopelessly out of date, the study did at least suggest the Roman population of York was more mixed than that of other parts of Roman Britain because of the presence of the army. In 1968, Dr Roger Warwick returned to the subject with a study of cranial measurements in the Trentholme Drive report.[53] He found that the majority of the crania he examined resembled those of other inhabitants of Roman Britain. However, he identified some males who he thought might come from 'the eastern end of the Mediterranean'. Another seven were thought to be 'Scandinavians' or 'Gauls'. Several men were thought to have limb proportions close to those of negroid people and one skull with 'pronouncedly negroid characters' was found, although no other parts of the skeleton survived.

Crainiometrics is a rather more sophisticated technique of studying human remains, involving the creation of a set of cranial measurements for computer-based multivariate analysis that can give a quantified assessment of affinity between the subject group and one or more, usually modern, reference populations.

Isotope analysis looks at the form of selected chemical elements in the subject samples. Isotopes of an element may contain equal numbers of protons but different numbers of neutrons in their nuclei, and hence differ in relative atomic mass, although not in chemical properties. The critical isotopes for studying human remains in terms of their geographical origins are those of the elements oxygen (O_2) and strontium (Sr), which are collected from tooth enamel. Oxygen and strontium (an alkaline earth metal) form two independent isotopic systems reflecting local geology and climate. They are fixed in the biogenic phosphate of the enamel in the early years of life and the signature of those elements may betray the location of an individual at this time or at least eliminate where he/she was not. Oxygen isotopes in phosphates are derived primarily from ingested fluids and indirectly reflect the isotopic value of available drinking water. The isotope value of water in any location depends on a number of factors including the source of the water, its distance from the coast, and its latitude and altitude. Strontium isotopes are derived from both solid and liquid food, and directly relate to the geology of the area where the food was produced.

The first of the three studies referred to above, published in 2009, involved arthroscopy, craniometrics and isotope analysis of skeletons from the Trentholme Drive and the railway station cemeteries, with a further six isotopes from other York sites (Table 1).[54] Unfortunately, there is no close dating for the individual skeletons at either site, but they are probably, for the most part, from burials of the mid-second to early fourth century.

Table 1: Summary of sample of skulls used for analysis of racial affinity in 2009

Site	Arthroscopy	Craniometrics	Isotopes
Trentholme Drive	58: 42 male, 12 female, 4 unknown	44: 31 male, 10 female, 3 unknown	14: 12 male, 2 female
Railway Station	45: 20 male, 22 female, 3 unknown	41: 19 male, 19 female, 3 unknown	29: 9 male, 9 female, 11 unknown
Other York sites	–	–	6: 4 male, 2 female

The results of the study were complex and are hard to summarise. However, using the sort of basic distinctions one might find, for example, in modern diversity surveys, which ask whether one is 'white', 'black' or of 'mixed race', arthroscopy determined that 62 per cent of crania from Trentholme Drive were white whilst the others divided between black and mixed – a somewhat similar result to Warwick's study. By contrast, in the railway station sample 51 per cent were black or mixed, leading the researchers to wonder whether the data was skewed by a collection of human remains that had appeared unusual to the antiquarians of the 1870s.

The craniometric study gave broadly similar results to the arthroscopy. Data from 66 per cent of the sample from Trentholme Drive were within the parameters for modern western European populations, 23 per cent within those for African populations and 11 per cent within those for modern Egyptian populations. In the railway station sample, 53 per cent were within the parameters for modern western European populations whilst 32 per cent had African affinities, and 15 per cent had affinities with Germanic and central European populations. Of the six African reference populations that were used for comparison, greatest similarity was with African-American groups.

In the isotope analysis of the fifty crania sampled, there was a wide range of oxygen and strontium values, but the great majority were within the expected range for Britain – this presumably implies that those with alien craniometric characteristics were second generation immigrants. Standing out, however, was one sample from the railway station of a person who had, perhaps, grown up in a cooler climate or at higher altitude than would be usual in Britain – perhaps one of Warwick's 'Scandinavians'. For another three individuals (two from Trentholme Drive and one from the railway station), the data were consistent with origins in a warmer and more arid region than Britain. Differentiating between the remainder was difficult, but origins in different regions of Britain were thought to be indicated.

Although not strictly relevant to this book, in 2010 a one-off study was made of a late fourth-century female skeleton from York, dubbed 'Lady of the North'.[55] On the basis of craniometrics, she had greatest affinities with two reference populations of African-American females which, as in the case of the Trentholme Drive and railway station people, highlights that she was probably of mixed ancestry.

In 2011, the results of an isotope analysis of samples (all male) from Driffield Terrace were published.[56] Eighteen samples of dental enamel were taken for the study of origins. When the oxygen and strontium data were considered together, only five samples were thought to be entirely consistent with a childhood in the York locality. Of the others, one was thought likely to have had an Alpine origin and another to have begun life in a Mediterranean region, possibly in North Africa.

Another isotope study, which included samples from York, looked at the data for lead from 200 Roman burials from thirty-three sites in Britain.[57] This posed the question, firstly, of how lead pollution was reflected in the skeletons of people who suffered from it. Secondly, it asked when did the lead isotope content of the bones of ancient peoples cease to reflect their geographic origin and, as a result of mobility, start reflecting the 'culturally mediated' pollution of their environment, for example by drinking water conveyed in lead pipes? The aim was to establish if immigrants to Roman Britain could be identified on the basis of differential exposure to lead. The study picked out four individuals from Driffield Terrace who were thought to have a non-British origin – their high lead isotope signature is thought to be consistent with an origin in parts of the Mediterranean basin or Near East.

A different approach to the study of race and origins is taken by genomics, the study of genomes in living or, in the case of archaeological material, deceased organisms. A pioneering study of seven samples from Driffield Terrace in York (along with one Iron Age and one Anglo-Saxon) appeared in 2016.[58] The analyses used samples from the petrous bone in the ear, which offers the best location in the body for survival of DNA. They aimed to determine the entire sequence of DNA, or composition of the atoms that make up the DNA, and the chemical bonds between the DNA atoms. Out of the seven samples from Driffield Terrace, six were thought to represent individuals whose DNA corresponded to sub-lineages most frequent in western Europe. However, one stood out with DNA corresponding to a modern distribution centred on the Middle East but also present in the Caucasus mountains, the Balkans and Italy.[59] An isotope analysis of this individual's tooth enamel appeared to confirm a likely Middle East origin. As far as the other six are concerned, their DNA was thought to be closest to what would be found in a modern Welsh population, presumably indicating that they were of native British or Celtic genetic inheritance. The study went on to suggest that these men would have had brown eyes and brown or black hair except for one, who would have had blue eyes and blond hair.

The techniques outlined here are in the fairly early stages of development, but it is already clear that they have a lot to offer for the study of ancient populations in general and the population of Roman York in particular. As is hinted at by the funerary inscriptions, it was clearly varied in terms of place of birth and racial affinity. At present it is not possible to detect change, or its possible causes, in either respect over the course of the Roman period. To do this will require further sampling from well-dated burials. However, in general terms, the diversity at York would partly, at least, have been due to its being a military base where soldiers from all over the empire came to serve, some bringing families, even if by the third century recruitment was probably largely local. Some of these recruits may, however, have been sons or grandsons of migrants.

Rank and status

At the beginning of the imperial period, Roman citizens formed a small group relative to the population of the empire as a whole. They were inhabitants of Rome itself and of Roman colonies, deliberately planted settlements, largely in Italy, from which the soldiers of the legions were drawn. The benefits of citizenship were, in theory at least, considerable. Citizens, it has been said, received protection from the law whilst everyone else was subject to the law. Hence St Paul, when arrested in Jerusalem, avoided a scourging by telling the authorities that not only was he a Roman citizen but that, moreover, he had been born a citizen and was not a freed slave.[60] Freedmen and freedwomen were looked down on by citizens by birth. What were perceived as their social pretensions are memorably mocked in the *Satyricon* by the mid-first-century author Petronius. For example, he describes a banquet at the home of his 'hero' Trimalchio, portrayed as vulgar, boorish and ostentatious who, for example, at one point is 'carried in to the sound of orchestra music and set down on a pile of tightly stuffed cushions'.[61]

At the head of the citizen body were the so-called 'orders' (*ordines*), the senators, and just below them the equestrians or 'Roman knights' (*equites*) – in ancient times cavalrymen in the citizen army. A man would qualify to become a member of one or the other by possessing a certain level of wealth, whether tied up in property or held as cash. Reserved for each order there was a range of career options in government and the military. For a senator this usually began with an appointment as a praetor, a civilian magistrate, who administered justice in the city of Rome.[62] Subsequently, he might see service with the legions, initially as a tribune and, in due course, a legate before becoming the governor of a province like Britain (see p 30). The time he stayed in a province might have been brief, but while in post he was master of all he surveyed.

In the empire of the second century, citizenship became more widespread. Slaves of citizens became citizens themselves when receiving their freedom. Non-citizen men recruited into the army's auxiliary units from the conquered provinces received their citizenship on discharge. However, a legal distinction arose that divided citizens into two classes: the *honestiores* (the 'more honest ones') and the *humiliores* (the 'more humble ones'). To the first belonged the elite families in the governing class of the empire, the senators and equestrians who also numbered amongst their ranks some of the men who held, or had held, municipal office in towns outside Rome – and their families and descendants. More or less all other citizens belonged to the second class including, presumably, our Julia Velva and Aurelius Mercurialis. Distinctions in law were made between the two classes. For example, in respect of penalties following wrongdoing, so that for more serious crimes the *honestiores* were spared the more gruesome methods of despatch, such as crucifixion, and allowed execution with a sword or axe – a great comfort to them no doubt.[63]

A member of the *honestiores* we know of by name from York is Aelia Severa (5.4).[64] The inscription on her stone sarcophagus begins with the dedication to her as HONEST(A)E FEMIN(A)E (dative case). In the second line of the inscription we are told she had been the wife of Caecilius Rufus, who had predeceased her. The next line gives us her age as 27 years, 9 months and 4 days. On the last line we are told the sarcophagus is the work of Caecilius Musicus, a freed slave – LIBERTVS. In very compressed form, what we have here is an 'everyday story of Roman folk'. Presumably what had happened was that a slave

5.4: Sarcophagus of Aelia Severa, a lady of the upper echelons of society, the *honestiores* (length 2.24m). She was formerly the wife of Caecilius Rufus and lived 27 years, 9 months and 4 days. The sarcophagus was set in place by Caecilius Musicus, freedman. Found re-used for a male burial in 1859 in Dalton Terrace.

called Musicus – perhaps the household musician – had been given his freedom by his master Caecilius Rufus, perhaps after saving up to buy it. On receiving so called 'manumission', usually available to slaves after the age of 30, Musicus assumed, as was usual, his master's family name – hence Caecilius Musicus. He remained under the authority of his former master, now his patron, and would have been expected to perform various duties for him, including organising his burial and funeral. By freeing plenty of slaves, a man was assured of a good funeral. Aelia Severa, Musicus's former mistress, then died and Caecilius Musicus inherited the family fortune from which he was able to afford a fine inscribed sarcophagus for Severa, which was placed in the family mausoleum. This was probably somewhere on The Mount where the sarcophagus was found in 1859, although not apparently with the lady herself inside it. Violation of tombs was regarded as a criminal offence, but their re-use was, nonetheless, a common occurrence in the Roman world.[65] The only other freedman we know of by name from York is the Nikomedes we have already noted as a probable Greek. But he was no provincial, having apparently served an emperor, possibly Septimius Severus, before receiving his freedom.

It has been calculated that about 10 per cent of the population of the Roman Empire were slaves.[66] Some had very hard lives working in the mines or on landed estates. Others, like Musicus who worked in elite households, may have had a better time of it, and then there were slaves of the emperor who, like Nikomedes, were in a relatively privileged position and sometimes trusted to undertake sensitive business where a free man was not. Wherever they served, however, slaves could be treated with appalling cruelty, apparently as much by their mistresses as their masters if the satirist Juvenal (*c.* 55 – 140) is to be believed. He comments that a wife who suspected female slaves were sleeping with her husband, 'hired a torturer on a yearly salary' to keep them in line.[67] A rare insight into the maltreatment of a slave in York may be provided by one of the burials at Driffield Terrace. There were two male skeletons in one of the graves, both had been decapitated, but one of them had heavy iron rings around his ankles (5.5).[68] They had been worn during life and, although not shackles as such, would have been extremely awkward and probably painful. One can only think that they were some sort of punishment. Another example of the same treatment comes from a Roman slave cemetery at Himera, Sicily.[69] Brutal though owners could be, treatment of slaves did get better in the second century under the influence of the Stoic philosophers, such as Seneca, who believed that all human beings, regardless of their social status, were to some degree equal and entitled to compassionate and humane treatment.[70] One would hope that any slaves in Julia Velva's household benefitted from the spread of these ideas.

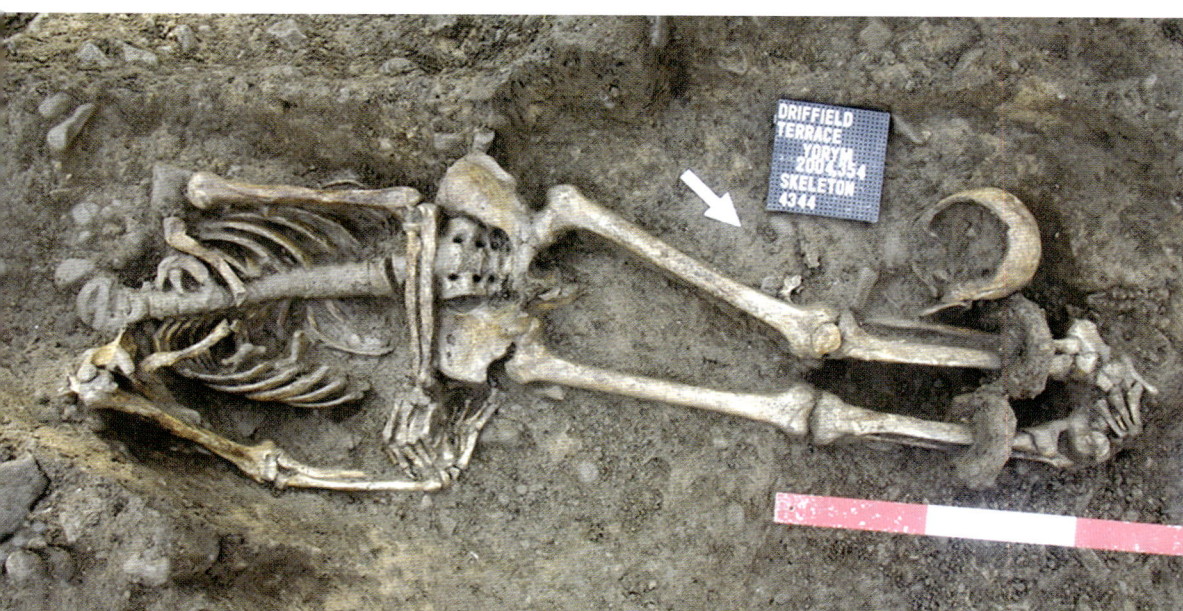

5.5: Skeleton of an executed male with iron rings around his ankles, from 1 – 3 Driffield Terrace, scale 0.30m and 0.20m. (© York Archaeological Trust)

The status of women

It is perhaps ironic, as Moses Finley noted, that the most famous woman in Roman history is probably Queen Cleopatra, lover of both Julius Caesar and the Roman general Antony, who was herself an Egyptian.[71] She comes to our notice, of course, because she wielded political power and influence in a way quite alien to Rome. Women, such as Aelia Severa, or Julia Velva, at the elite level of Roman York society, might appear to have been privileged compared to those lower down the social scale, but they were, nevertheless, constrained in their ability to act independently. At the head of a Roman family was the senior male, *pater familias*, who had total control over his wife and family and their slaves. Even after the death of her husband, or if she was unmarried, the death of her father, a woman had to have a legal guardian, usually another male family member. There were restrictions on her ability to control family affairs to own property, adopt a child and exercise legal control over her children, for example regarding their marriage.

A female child was deemed old enough to marry as early as 12 years, and the marriage would usually be arranged for her. Wives in the Roman world were expected to be agreeable, good humoured, interested in their husbands' affairs and obedient – 'very dutiful' as Julia Velva is called in an example of a formula popular by the third century.[72] They were expected to produce children, especially sons, to carry on the dynasty. Family size must have varied a good deal, but if a first child was born in its mother's teens then, if she remained healthy, there was a chance that she might have emulated the likes of my great grandmother who produced nine children in an eighteen-year period in the mid-nineteenth century. Flavia Augustina (p 188) may have been such a woman, as her tombstone records her death at 39 years along with one, if not two, infant sons. Exemplary (and exhausted) though Augustina may have been, however, any conduct considered by a woman's husband to be immoral might lead to a beating or even death, if her family agreed. In some households, the women, especially the slaves perhaps, were probably subjected to violence and sexual assault, without much hindrance, on a regular basis.

In the lower social orders, whether free or slave, life for women was probably rather different in that they were expected to work alongside their menfolk in the fields, markets or workshops, although we hear little about them in contemporary literature. A few women stepped outside the boundaries of respectable society, adopting such occupations as acrobats, dancers and concubines. However, while it was always possible for a capable and intelligent woman to gain considerable influence over her husband, as the empress Julia Domna is said to have had over Septimius Severus, she was never able, in whatever station of life, to have the sort of real freedom of action that comes as a matter of course today. She lived in a prison without bars.

Whether a wife in reality lived up to epithets such as 'very dutiful' or not, a man liked to present her as exemplary as he would feel it reflected well on him as a husband. The images of women on tombstones were intended to show them to advantage, with a man's wealth and status speaking through their fashionable clothes and hairstyles. Although there are only a few of these images from York, it is perhaps significant that they all appear to date to the later second or early third centuries. As Roman York's population grew rapidly at that time and became more diverse, the desire to assert status and express social aspiration may have stimulated patterns of behaviour and consumption, including those concerned with commemoration of the dead, more assertive and diverse than was the norm in Roman Britain. One can well imagine that attention-seeking by the socially ambitious reached a climax of unbridled proportions during the three brief years of the visit of Emperor Septimius Severus in 208 – 11.

How to make an impression in Julia Velva's York

There will always be many different ways in which people seek to make themselves appear in some way distinct from, if not superior to, others around them. We shall look at two of these as they relate to Roman York: first of all, educational attainment, and, secondly, personal appearance.

Education: literacy and numeracy

A formal education in the Roman world was given almost exclusively to boys of the social elite, usually within a domestic setting. It was considered preferable that a father should himself teach his sons the basics of the 'three Rs' and, equally important, the responsibilities of a good citizen to his family and to the gods. In addition, a man might hire private tutors or send his sons to a school, although there was no formal training for teachers. Only a few privileged youths would go on to a specialist study of public speaking, law and politics, the subjects necessary for the exercise of senior roles in government and administration. Nonetheless, basic literacy and numeracy were quite widespread in Rome itself and in the larger urban centres of the Mediterranean world. In the *Satyricon*, the freedman Giton comments on his education:

> *I didn't learn geometry and literary criticism and useless nonsense like that. I learned how to read the letters on public inscriptions. I learned how to divide things into hundreds and work out percentages, and I know weights, measures and currency.*[73]

Girls, at whatever social level, usually had little formal education, although in the elite they presumably acquired some competence in reading and writing.

A few, no doubt, like Sempronia, described by the historian Sallust (86 – 35 BC), studied Greek and Roman literature and could also play the lyre.[74]

The surviving documentation associated with the army such as, for example, the Vindolanda writing tablets,[75] brings home to us very forcibly that the Roman Army was one of bureaucrats as much as warriors whose skills in literacy and numeracy were put to the service of almost obsessive record-keeping. We often hear about the army as a ruthless killing machine. But the reason why Rome was able to hold on to a vast empire for so long may have had less to do with its soldiers' martial skills than with their ability to keep accounts of supplies, troop strengths and movements, and to send out instructions and requests based on this information. The Roman pen, one might say, was as mighty, if not mightier, than the Roman sword. In a civilian context, there was also record-keeping, for example relating to taxation and legal matters. As we can still see in some parts of the world today, if most of a population is illiterate, it can be easily controlled and subjugated by a governing class whose members can read and write and do sums. Some capability in respect of literacy and numeracy was, therefore, related to the exercise of power, and ways might be found to display this as a sign of superior status.[76] This was the intention perhaps of showing men holding scrolls on tombstones as, for example, Aurelius Mercurialis on Julia Velva's tombstone does. Even just a simple inkwell prominently placed on a person's table might make the point about its owner's ability to write.[77] York has produced a few Roman inkwells, including two samian examples from the minster excavations (in the fortress), presumably used by soldiers.[78]

Unfortunately, York has produced no examples of Roman writing tablets, but the 'wax type' was clearly widely used here. It existed as a flat rectangle of wood with one face hollowed out to make a reservoir for the wax on which one wrote with a metal stylus pointed at one end and widened out at the other to create an eraser.[79] Tablets were usually paired and, on completion of the message, were bound together. The knot was covered with sealing wax and might be stamped by the sender using the intaglio on his/her ring (see p 199). The seal was sometimes protected by a small box made of copper alloy. There are several examples from York including two from 9 Blake Street, presumably soldiers' property as one is decorated with a helmeted bust and the other with an eagle.[80]

On occasions there were clearly people in York who acquired more than a basic grasp of written Latin as we can see, for example, in the poetic epitaph offered on the tombstone to his daughter, Corellia Optata, by Q Corellius Fortis (5.6).[81] In translation it reads:

> *Oh mysterious spirits who dwell in Pluto's Acherusian realms and whom the meagre ashes and the shade, empty semblance of the body, seek, following the brief light of life; father of an innocent daughter, I, a pitiable victim of unfair hope, bewail her final end.*

5.6: The (incomplete) tombstone of Corellia Optata, who died aged 13 years. Found in Scarcroft Road in 1861. Her ashes were in the glass bottle in 5.24. Height 0.90m, width 0.61m. (Yorkshire Museum)

This is an original work, or it has not been copied from any recorded source, although whether it was by Fortis himself is not known. In any event, one would like to think that it was composed in York itself by someone who had a knowledge of formal poetic metre and classical sources including, perhaps, Virgil's *Aeneid*, or even Plato's *Phaedo*, from which the phrase 'Pluto's Acherusian realm' (i.e. referring to the River Acheron in the underworld) may have been drawn.[82]

Local people in the countryside around York would have spoken a Celtic language, but this was not written and so has left little trace except in a few place and river names, including both 'Foss' and 'Ouse'.[83] However, in York itself there were probably many people, whether locals or migrants, who could speak Latin but not write it with any facility. As a result writing, whether in the home, office or on monumental inscriptions in the mason's yard, depended heavily on the use of specialists who, as we see on most inscriptions from Britain created in a military milieu, including York, were usually pretty competent in grammar and spelling.[84] As for the mass of the population, some slight competence is suggested by graffiti scratched onto pottery sherds, tiles and other objects. They often take the form of names, although whether, for example, CANDIDA scratched on the bottom of a samian bowl from Blossom Street was the work of the woman herself or a male parent, partner or perhaps admirer is not clear.[85]

As far as numeracy is concerned, we know from the evidence of the plans of the fortress and buildings within it that the legion had specialist surveyors with sophisticated numeracy skills, men who could measure distances and angles accurately and make calculations using arithmetical techniques such as those based on Pythagoras's theorem. More generally in York there were probably quite a few, like Giton, male and female, who had sufficient competence with numbers to allow them to conduct business effectively. We may infer a modest ability to record quantities, weights, etc., at an everyday level from numbers scratched as graffiti

5.7: Roof tile with XX (20) scored into it (from Bishophill Junior).

on pots, tiles and other objects (5.7). However, the majority of the population of York and its region was probably unable to grapple with Roman numerals and were limited to such counting and simple arithmetic as could be done in the head or using an abacus.

Dress

Just as members of the elite, at least, might lose no opportunity to show off their learning, so they might also wish to show themselves to advantage in their personal appearance. In the Roman world 'clothes made the man'. Barbarians, almost by definition, went about inadequately dressed – or naked, witness the captives on the samian bowl described above (4.16). In contrast, clothing worn by the Romans usually appears to observe two basic rules, both practical for hot countries. First, that one should not expose more naked flesh than was necessary and, second, that clothes should not be too tight. The rules also spoke of the Roman ideal of strict moral rectitude. Those who failed to observe the rules because their occupations, for example as acrobats, athletes, gladiators and the like, required an element of nudity to allow free movement of their limbs, but they were not usually people of good social standing or reputation. Having said this, images of their gods and goddesses often show us that the erotic possibilities of clothing were not ignored by the Romans – although difficult to render in the millstone grit of Yorkshire as opposed to the marble of Italy.

As far as knowing what people wore in Roman York itself, we are largely reliant on just a few images, almost exclusively on tombstones or altars. However, these images probably belong, for the most part, to the late second or early third centuries and so, happily for this book, give us attire in the Julia Velva period. Even so, it is not always easy to understand exactly what the images show, and so it is not surprising, perhaps, that one finds some divergence both of opinion and the use of terminology amongst experts who have studied the subject. In general terms, however, we seem to see a preference for the sort of clothing one would have found in much of the western empire. One gets the impression that clothing played a part in expressing a shared identity and that there was no premium on any sort of novelty.

By the late second century, men in Roman York probably wore a toga rarely, if ever. Instead, both men and boys usually wore what is sometimes referred to as a 'Gallic coat', a simple woollen tunic, woven in one piece on the loom, which had short wide sleeves and fell in deep vertical folds to the knees.[86] It was sometimes worn without a belt, as shown by Aurelius Mercurialis (on Julia Velva's tombstone) and, under their cloaks, by the males on Flavia Augustina's tombstone (5.8).[87] Otherwise, the tunic was worn with a belt or girdle usually hidden from view by an overfold. On occasions, men in certain occupations involving heavy manual labour wore an 'exomis', a short tunic that left one shoulder bare.[88] This can be seen on a smith, perhaps intended to be Vulcan, the smith god, depicted on a relief from Dringhouses near York.[89] Other workmen might simply wear a loin cloth, as shown on 4.8. Although soldiers might wear breeches to the knees and leggings below the knees in cold weather, trousers were frowned on by the Romans as they were worn by people they regarded as barbarous. However, the Persians did wear trousers and so it was acceptable for Mithras, as a Persian god, to be shown wearing them (6.13).

5.8: Tombstone of Flavia Augustina, who died aged 39 years, 7 months and 11 days, and her children, who lived 1 year, 3 days and 1 year, 9 months and 5 days. The stone was set-up by Gaius Aeresius Saenus, veteran of the Sixth Legion. All wear cloaks over their tunics. The adults each carry a scroll and the boys a ball. Found in 1859, re-used as the lid for the coffin of Aelia Severa (5.4). Height 1.72m. (Yorkshire Museum)

Over the tunic men might wear a hooded cape (*birrus*), fastened down the front with toggles, which usually came to the knees. Alternatively, they wore some form of cloak. What was known as a *paenula* is worn by the unnamed centurion whose tombstone was found on The Mount.[90] This was made from a roughly circular piece of cloth with a hole in the centre that went over the wearer's head. A man might also wear a *sagum*, a cloak held in place by a brooch on the right shoulder as shown, for example, by a man and a boy on an incomplete tombstone from York.[91] As well as cloaks men, like Aurelius Mercurialis, had heavy woollen scarves or mantles at their disposal.

Images of women from York, such as Flavia Augustina, usually show them wearing a long-sleeved tunic without a belt, again sometimes known as a Gallic coat, which reached to their ankles to ensure modesty.[92] Although not seen at York, a woman shown on a tombstone from South Shields appears to wear a shift of some sort (probably linen) under her tunic, and this may have been general practice.[93] Rather different attire, perhaps less common in Roman Britain but more so in the Mediterranean world, is worn by Julia Brica on her tombstone (5.9).[94] She is the model for the women sketched in 5.10. Brica wears a long tunic or gown with wide sleeves that reaches down to her feet, over which she wears a shorter tunic, reaching to mid-thigh, which is gathered and tied with a cord under her breasts. Young girls wore similar clothes to adults. The unlucky Sempronia Martina, aged 6, is dressed like Brica her mother. The girl on Aelia Aeliana's tombstone also appears to wear a short tunic with short sleeves over a longer one covering her feet (5.11).[95]

5.9: Tombstone of Julia Brica, aged 31, and her daughter Sempronia Martina, aged 6, set-up by Sempronius Martinus. Julia Brica holds an urn and her daughter a bird. Found in 1892 on The Mount. Height 1.78m. (Yorkshire Museum)

(*Above left*) 5.10: Reconstruction drawing of women with hair and dress styles of the early third century.

(*Above right*) 5.11: Tombstone (incomplete) of Aelia Aeliana with her husband (height 0.95m). He has his arm around her, and they recline on a couch. She holds a cup in her left hand. On the floor is a costrel for wine and there is food on a three-legged table. A girl, probably a servant, stands in front of the couch. (Yorkshire Museum)

Over their tunics both women and girls, like Flavia Augustina and her daughter, might wear a cloak that fell to the knees but could be left open at the front to show the tunic underneath. Also popular was the mantle (*palla*), a large square or rectangular piece of cloth.[96] Julia Brica wears it with one end drawn down over her left shoulder, it would then have been wrapped around her back before being passed across the front of her body where the other end is held in her left hand. Alternatively, a mantle could be worn over the shoulders like a voluminous scarf. This may be what we see on a rather worn image of a woman shown in 5.12. When participating in religious rituals, the mantle would be worn to cover the head. In whichever way it was worn, a mantle restricted a woman's ability to use her hands as she had to hold it in place. For example, Julia Brica could have used her right hand easily enough but her left, even without the urn it is supporting, would have been fairly useless. However, the restriction on the hands was not necessarily considered an impediment as it made an important point about an elite woman's status as someone who did no work and, moreover, had a slave to dress her and do her hair – an *ornatrix* – and, in the absence of pockets and handbags, others to carry her possessions.

Before the Roman period, the people of Britain seem to have gone barefoot most of the time, there being very little archaeological evidence for shoes, and many of them, especially children, probably continued to do so after the conquest. Roman soldiers and most town-dwellers would, however, have been adequately shod. Shoes are not shown in any detail on York's tombstones and so we must rely on archaeological finds for further information about them. York itself has produced relatively few Roman shoes compared, for example, to the fort at Vindolanda, where several hundred have been found. Nevertheless, for the Julia Velva period we have the leatherwork from 24 – 30 Tanner Row, comprised largely of discarded soles,[97] as well as one or two pieces from other sites. There are also Roman shoes from other sites in Britain, including, in Yorkshire, Catterick (*Cataractonium*), so we have a fairly good idea of what would have been worn in York.

5.12: Incomplete relief in magnesian limestone of a female figure (probably part of a tombstone) found in the city wall south-west of the Ouse, height 0.85m, width 0.90m. (Courtesy of Margaret Rogers)

The *caliga*, which we might think of as the classic Roman shoe, with its thick nailed sole, bound to the foot by straps across the instep and around the bottom part of the leg, the 'gladiator sandal' as we might call its pastiche imitations today, had gone out of fashion by the late second century. Instead people were wearing a type of shoe in which the edge (lasting margin) of the upper part ('upper') was sandwiched between the sole and an insole and the three pieces were stitched together along that edge.[98] Sole and insole were nailed together and the domed heads of the 'hobnails' gave the shoes extra durability. Uppers were usually fastened to the foot by straps integral to them, as can be seen on York examples from the Skeldergate well (5.13).[99] On occasions, the upper may have come up over the ankle, making the shoe more of a boot. This may be what Aurelius Mercurialis and the male figures on Flavia Augustina's tombstone are wearing. In other types of shoe, the upper and sole were simply stitched together, without an insole, and there were no nails. Sometimes these shoes were closed over the toe, but there were also open-toed versions ('sandals'), such as an example from Tanner Row, probably worn by a woman, which has a sole bearing stamped decoration and a maker's mark (5.14). People also wore versions of the *carbatina*, a shoe made from a single piece of leather, folded and stitched to fit snugly around the foot and then held onto it with laces or thongs. Whether socks were generally worn is not known, although they are referred to on one of the Vindolanda tablets.[100]

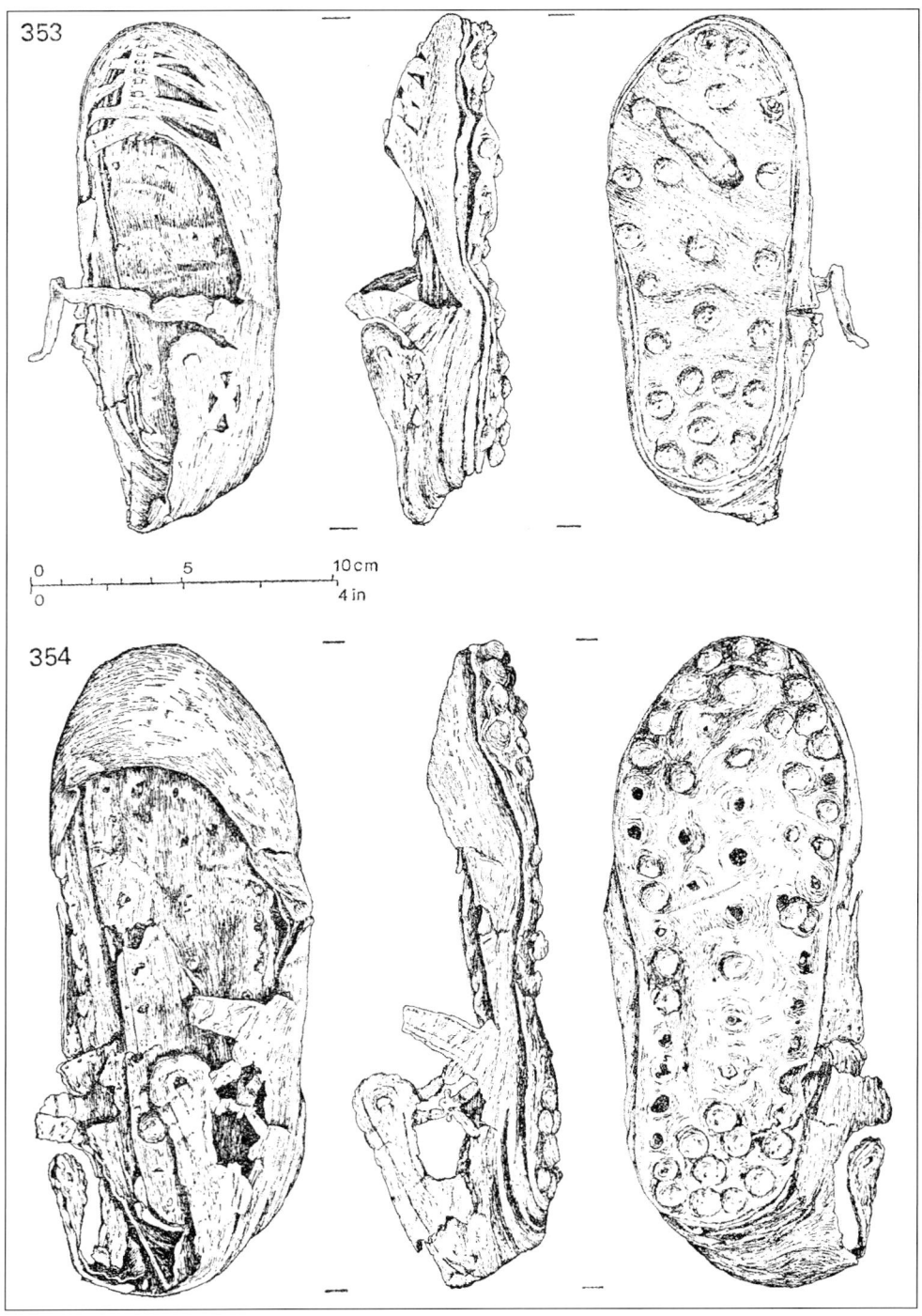

5.13: Shoes from the Roman well at 58 – 9 Skeldergate. (© York Archaeological Trust)

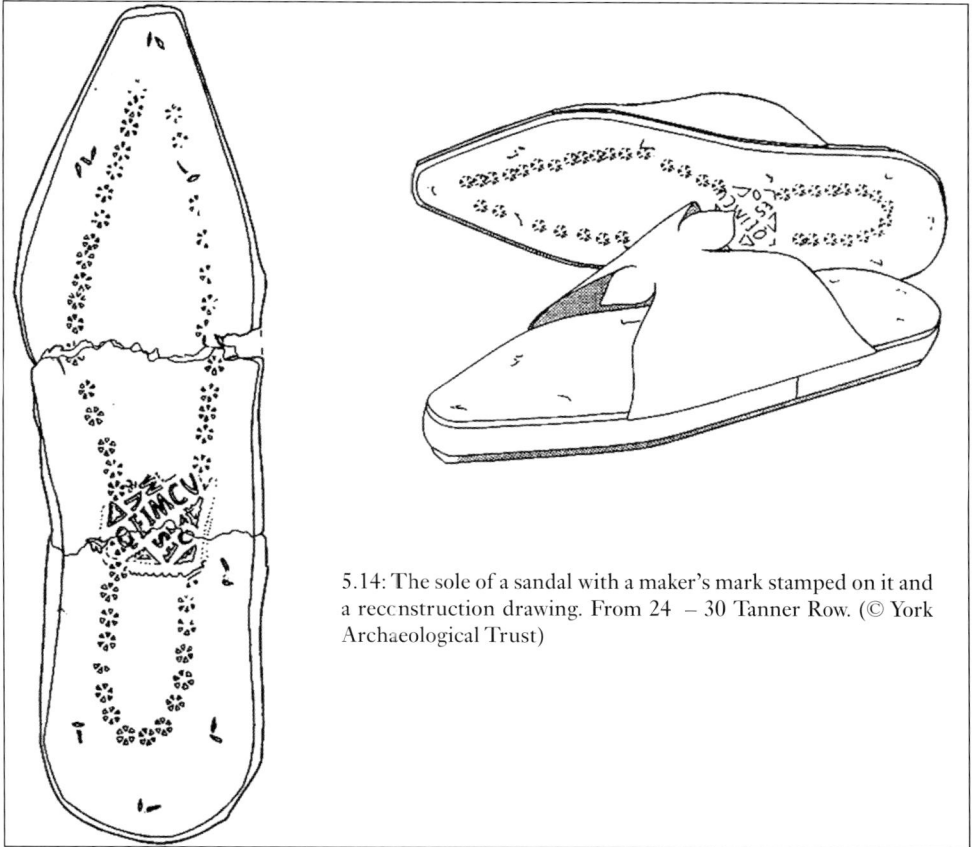

5.14: The sole of a sandal with a maker's mark stamped on it and a reconstruction drawing. From 24 – 30 Tanner Row. (© York Archaeological Trust)

Hairstyles

The Romans thought of barbarians as having wild unkempt hair and, in the case of males, scruffy beards and moustaches. However, for the Romans themselves, hair whether on the head or in the case of men on the face also, provided another arena in which they were able to display an awareness of current fashions and norms of appearance. As in the case of clothing, an important lead was provided by members of the imperial court who appeared on coins, statues and in other images.

Male hair in the early empire was worn characteristically short with a fringe and the face was clean-shaven. In the early second century, Hadrian affected a short beard in his desire to present himself as a philosopher and intellectual, a sort of latter-day Plato (whose busts show him bearded). For the rest of the second century, and much of the third, emperors and, therefore, other men wore beards and moustaches of various sorts. In images of males an absence of beard, as in the case of the servant on Julia Velva's tombstone, usually indicated youth or immaturity (1.10). By contrast, Aurelius Mercurialis has prominent and distinctive

(*Above*) 5.15: Male head with beard and moustache from the tombstone of Aelia Aeliana. (Yorkshire Museum)

(*Below*) 5.16: Reconstruction drawing of the head of Aelia Aeliana to show details of her hairstyle.

facial hair (1.8). Another fine beard is worn by the man, presumably her husband, accompanying Aelia Aeliana on her tombstone (5.15).

York is famous for a surviving swatch of female hair preserved in a lead coffin found at the railway station, but as two associated jet pins suggest a fourth-century date, it does not bear directly on our story here.[101] However, there are other things more relevant to be said about the hair of York's Roman women. After the Roman conquest native British women may have continued, as they had before, to wear their hair either loose or in plaits. The latter is suggested by a woman of the native Cornovii people depicted on a tombstone from the Yorkshire fort at Ilkley.[102] Roman women are not usually portrayed with their hair loose. This was considered immoral, although it was acceptable if one was in distress, for example at the death of a loved one. By the late Antonine period, as seen for example in coin portraits of empresses such as Faustina junior, wife of Marcus Aurelius, and Lucilla, wife of Lucius Verus, the hair of women in the Roman elite was waved and drawn away from a central parting before it covered the ears and was plaited into a neat bun at the back of the head.[103] A similar style remained in fashion for early third century empresses, including Julia Domna whose hair is usually shown very tightly waved (3.1).[104] Her elaborately plaited and coiled buns or chignons may have been made bulkier with artificial hair. If a woman's hair was not naturally curly or wavy, it could be artificially waved with crimping irons. Versions of prevailing imperial styles can be seen on the heads of Julia Velva (1.6) and Aelia Aeliana, and the girls alongside them, on their York tombstones (5.11), although as far as Aelia Aeliana is concerned, what we may be seeing in stone is so complex as to be more likely the depiction of a wig rather than her real hair (5.16). For a woman to keep any sort of elaborate hairstyle in place she would have required pins (see p 147). There are large numbers from York, mostly in bone and copper alloy but also in jet, which would perhaps have looked particularly good on blondes and red heads.[105]

Cosmetics

Ovid writes at the beginning of *Cosmetics for Ladies*:[106]

> *Learn, girls, the methods that improve complexions,*
> *The means by which your looks you may defend.*

In what the poet goes on to say, and elsewhere, one finds a somewhat equivocal attitude in Roman literature to the use of cosmetics by women – all written by men, of course.[107] On the one hand a woman was expected to make herself presentable and pleasing to men. On the other, she was not expected to use artifice for immoral purposes. No doubt women, and some men, in Roman York did use cosmetics, although archaeological evidence is limited for the most part to a number of small glass phials (*unguentaria*) used for perfumes and unguents, many found in burials.[108] In addition, an unusual item found in the railway station cemetery, probably from a burial, is a small copper alloy vessel in the form of the bust of an infant, which has been referred to as a 'balsamarium' (5.17).[109] Balsam can refer to aromatic resin from a number of sources including the Terebinth tree, which produced what is described in the bible as the 'balm of Gilead'.[110] The vessel has links at the top for attachment to a chain by which the owner would have carried it,

5.17: Copper alloy balsamarium, or incense container, in the form of an infant bust. In the centre of the head is a hinged lid (500mm x 500mm). (YORYM H2407-74, © York Museums Trust)

perhaps around the neck. Presumably this owner was a woman, although the use of balsam by a man is mentioned, disapprovingly, by the poet Martial.[111]

Face make-up was prepared on small tablets like one in slate inscribed with the name CANDIDVS, perhaps a supplier of the raw materials, probably from a burial (in the railway station cemetery).[112] A pale complexion was considered desirable in Roman times for women of high social status, showing they were not constrained to become weather-beaten by working in the open air. There were various forms of foundation used to give the complexion the preferred colour tone and to cover blemishes arising from diseases like smallpox. One of these was white lead, or carbonate of lead. Unfortunately, this was poisonous and so potentially damaging to health, as was mercury-based cinnabar used for rouge. Less hazardous to those wishing to improve the appearance of their hair were various vegetable dyes such as the juice of elderberries (*Sambucus nigra*).[113] These were found in some quantity at 24 – 30 Tanner Row, although probably representing food remains.

Jewellery

Women like Julia Velva would probably have owned at least one jewellery casket. The remains of a few examples were found in burials at the railway station. One of these had been a wooden box with copper alloy bindings and a lock, which contained a silver ring, a mirror handle, three dress-fasteners, two plain and one enamelled, and two plate brooches, one lozenge-shaped and one designed as a flower, as well as six glass vessels.[114] Another, described by RCHME's *Eburacum* as a 'trinket box', was similar and contained four jet bracelets, and two glass phials for perfume.[115] In addition to these two, many other Roman burials in York have produced jewellery which was often, if not always, worn by the deceased at the time of interment.

As far as adornment of the female head is concerned, there is, amongst a small number of Roman earrings from York, a pair in gold from a burial on Blossom Street (1.1).[116] Single gold earrings include one shown on 5.20, found in the sewer serving the fortress baths, but lost, no doubt to her great chagrin, by a lady bather.[117] A pair of silver earrings, probably from a burial, was found near Holgate Bridge.[118] Although not known before the Roman period, after the conquest, women in Britain soon took to wearing necklaces. There are numerous beads from York in bone, glass and jet, and a few of amber, which probably come from necklaces.[119] They may be disc shaped, cylindrical, globular or, in the case of some jet beads, fashioned in such a way as to interlock as a sinuous rope. Complete necklaces (without the string) have occasionally been found in York burials, including a group of seven from an early third-century female inhumation found in Walmgate, east of the River Foss.[120] Two were strung with jet beads, one also

Provincial society and daily life 197

with a jet pendant medallion of Medusa, another three with bone beads and two with glass beads. The necklaces of bone beads and one of those with glass beads had been worn low on the chest, whilst the others had fitted more closely around the throat. Part of what may be a necklace made from a gold chain and a gold pendant, perhaps from a necklace, are shown on 5.20.[121]

Brooches known from pre-Roman times in the York region are of the simple safety-pin type (*fibula*), made of either iron or copper alloy. With the Roman conquest, a number of new types of *fibulae* were introduced, usually made in copper alloy but occasionally in precious metals.[122] Amongst the more common types found in York and its region is the dragonesque brooch that was current in the late first and second centuries. It is S-shaped with a stylised head at one end and a tail at the other. There is often enamel in the eyes and in panels on the dragon's body. Also well-known in York in the same time period were various types of brooches shaped like a bow with a pin hinged at one end and a catch at the other.[123] Julia Velva would have been more familiar with a late second- to early third-century type known, because of the shape of the bow, as a knee brooch, of which there are a few examples from York.[124]

There is also a range of Roman brooches from York that exist as decorative plates with the pin and catch attached to the back. The plates include examples in the form of various animals and birds, such as the crow shown in 5.18.[125] This may have been worn as an emblem of Apollo, to whom the crow was sacred. By the end of the second century, brooch-wearing seems to have declined dramatically amongst the people of Roman Britain and was largely confined to men in the military and bureaucracy, who used them to fasten their cloaks.[126]

Also known in pre-Roman times and remaining very much in fashion for women throughout the Roman period, were bracelets and armlets (or arm rings).[127] Those from York occur in bone, ivory, copper alloy, silver, glass and jet. In burials they sometimes occur as multiples. In the railway station cemetery, a female had been buried with two of copper alloy on each arm.[128] The most common bracelets exist as simple continuous bands, but quite common in copper alloy is a type simply made of lengths of wire, usually closed by overlapping the ends. Alternatively, two or more pieces of wire were twisted together to create the appearance of a rope or cable. A hook and eye formed a catch. An unusual example found in a late second-century burial in Bishophill is made of gold and silver wire twisted together (5.19).[129] Some of the jet bracelets from York were made from a single piece decorated using the 'chip-carved' technique. Others were made from beads, sometimes, like those used in necklaces, neatly interlocking with one another.[130]

Finger rings were introduced to Britain by the Romans and became very popular with both men and women. York has produced a large number, including examples in gold. There are seven in the Yorkshire Museum collection of which three are

198 *Julia Velva, A Roman Lady from York*

(*Above left*) 5.18: Copper alloy plate brooch in the form of a crow, length 30mm. (YORYM H193c, © York Museums Trust)

(*Above right*) 5.19: Bracelet found in a late second-century burial in Bishophill made of gold and silver wire twisted together, diameter 40mm. (YORYM2012_502, © York Museums Trust)

5.20: Gold jewellery from York. Top row: finger rings. Bottom row: (left to right) pin with a circular head, pendant fitting from a necklace, earring and a chain, possibly from a necklace (the two in the centre from the Church Street sewer). (© York Museums Trust)

shown in 5.20.¹³¹ Others occur in silver, copper alloy, iron and jet. Burials show that on occasion rings were worn in multiples. For example, in a burial at Royal York Hotel (1.1, 8) three silver rings were found on a male skeleton's left hand.¹³²

Many Roman rings have gems, known as intaglios, set in the bezel, which were made from glass or a variety of semi-precious stones (5.21). Intaglios are usually engraved and there is quite a wide range of subjects depicted on the York examples, including the deities Bonus Eventus ('good outcome'), Ceres, Diana, Fortuna, Mars, Minerva (5.22), Roma and Selene (the Greek moon goddess). Others depict Ajax seizing Cassandra at the altar of Athene, a crescent moon and stars, a satyr, a stag, a stork and a cupid.¹³³ More unusual is a depiction of Jupiter conflated with the Egyptian god Ammon, shown as a bearded and horned head.¹³⁴ A distinctive design would have served to identify the sender of letters, packets, etc., if the ring was used to stamp the wax that sealed them up before they went in the mail.

5.21: Drawings of intaglios from the fortress baths sewer in Church Street. Key: 1, Mars; 2, Fortuna; 3, Aequitas (equity); 4, Moon and stars; 5, Maenad – participant in the cult of Bacchus; 6, Cupid on a hippocamp with a dolphin behind. (By Sheena Howarth, © York Archaeological Trust)

5.22: Carnelian intaglio of Minerva from 24 – 30 Tanner Row, width 7mm. (© York Archaeological Trust)

Food and drink in Roman York

For the majority of the population of Roman York, food and drink was primarily a means of sustaining life. However, for members of the elite, what was on offer at their tables would have been, on occasions at least, another means of displaying their superior social status through an ability to summon exotic delicacies from far and wide. Perhaps the sort of extravagant Roman banquet of legend hosted, for example, by the odious Trimalchio in the *Satyricon*, with its wild boar stuffed with live thrushes,[135] was served up on special occasions by senior army officers or the governor of Lower Britain.

For our Julia Velva period, the archaeological evidence for food in Roman York relates primarily to the dietary staples that were consumed on a daily basis, although there are also traces of food consumed more for pleasure and, perhaps, to impress guests. We have already noted that the burnt grain from 5 Rougier Street (p 129) was largely composed of spelt wheat as well as some barley. Both cereals would have been made into a range of foodstuffs, not only bread but also porridge and other dishes.[136] As spelt contains gluten it can be made into risen loaves. The yeast for leavening the dough was probably a by-product of brewing. Alternatively, York's Roman bakers may have made loaves in the sourdough technique, which uses dough leavened with naturally occurring lactobacilli and yeast. Rye (*Secale cereale*) can be made into sourdough bread, and there was a small amount of rye in the early Roman burnt grain from Coney Street (p 61), presumably used either for bread or distilling. Barley, also used for animal feed, lacks gluten, so it would have been used to make griddle cakes, or 'bannocks', by mixing the dough with buttermilk or water and baking over a hearth (oats can also be used).[137]

As far as meat is concerned, the bones recovered from 24 – 30 Tanner Row, and other sites in York (p 133), show that beef was consumed to a much greater extent than lamb and mutton or bacon, pork and ham. However, there are few bones of calves to suggest consumption of veal. Much of the beef, as it came from elderly animals, was probably quite tough and so was probably stewed rather than roasted. Other meat in the Roman diet in York was provided, if only in a small way, by domestic fowl and geese. But there is hardly any evidence for consumption of wild animals. Just a few bones of red deer, hare and wild birds have been found. Most of the fish eaten would have come out of the Rivers Ouse and Foss. At both Tanner Row and in the Bedern well, there were bones of carp, eel, pike, salmon and smelt.[138]

Remains of the vegetables that accompanied meat and fish do not survive well in the ground. However, there was evidence of broad beans (*Vicia faba*) and lentils (*Lens culinaris*) at 24 – 30 Tanner Row.[139] Evidence was better both here and in the Bedern well for a range of fruits surviving as pips (apples) or stones (plums, sloes and cherries), whose trees were probably cultivated in local orchards.[140]

In addition, there were the seeds of wild fruits, including blackberries and elderberries, gathered in the local hedgerows. Hazel nuts would also have been gathered locally and formed an important addition to a healthy diet.[141] The walnuts, olives (surviving as stones) and the grapes and figs (as seeds) are, as suggested above (p 156), most likely to have been imported from the continent. Other seeds came from plants that were probably used for seasoning food.[142] They include opium poppy (*Papaver somniferum;* 5.1) and the herbs coriander (*Coriandrum sativum*), dill (*Anethum graveolens*) and summer savory (*Satureja hortensis*).

Cereal grain was not only a food staple but was also used in brewing ale (not beer, which contains hops used for preserving and flavouring). References in the Vindolanda writing tablets suggest that ale was consumed in some quantity by the Roman Army in Britain and no doubt civilians enjoyed it too.[143] In a world where the water was often contaminated, it would have been safer to drink ale – as the water was boiled during brewing – although the Romans may not have known this. Because ale goes off quite quickly, brewing would have been a daily task in the households and taverns of York and the army may have had its own specialist brewers (*cervesarii*). Also popular was wine, for which the evidence is the amphorae and perhaps barrels as already discussed (p 156). Evidence for the cultivation of vines in the Roman period has been found in Britain,[144] but wine came largely from Gaul and the Rhineland and occasionally from Italy. The Vindolanda tablets refer to different types of wine and they are also discussed by Pliny the Elder.[145] The problem for York's consumers and connoisseurs was that their wine had to travel over long distances in rather variable conditions on board ship, so there was a danger of it going off. In any event, the wine that did arrive here was probably, for the most part, not from fine vintages but a rather bitter drink that had to be sweetened with honey and watered down to become palatable.

Whether milk was drunk in Roman York is not known, although as tuberculosis can spread from cattle to humans in unpasteurised milk, it would have been better to convert it to butter or cheese. As in the case of polluted water, the Romans may not have been aware of the danger. There are a few examples from York of what are thought to be cheese presses – ceramic bowls with a perforated base.[146] There are also a few examples of tettines (5.23), equivalent to the baby's bottle of today, but whether they were filled with animals' milk or milk expressed from Mum is not known.[147]

Food in Roman Britain was usually cooked in ceramic vessels set into the hot ashes of a ground level hearth or in a cauldron suspended over the hearth. However, in large houses, like those on Bishophill, there may have been kitchens with the sort of stone or brick-built structure better known in Mediterranean provinces. This had a fuel store below a waist-level surface with holes for the hot ashes, over which the cooking pots were placed, sometimes using a small gridiron. A kitchen

5.23: A tettine, a pottery vessel for feeding babies and infants. (Yorkshire Museum)

would also have had tables for working on and shelves and cupboards for storage. In addition, large ceramic jars – *ollae* and *dolia* – and glass jars and bottles were used for storage. Water was probably heated up in metal vessels. Although there may have been sacks of flour brought in from a mill, a kitchen would also have had its querns (described above) for grinding grain on a day-to-day basis. Keeping food from going off was a challenge and, as there were in England before refrigerators, there was probably a cupboard or small larder with a cold slab of stone for meat and dairy items. Regardless of how food was cooked, a Roman kitchen must often have been a rather smoky place. But this may at least have had the merit of deterring flies in warmer months.

The lower social orders, as well as children of all classes, sat at a table for their main meals whilst the elite, when dining formally as we see on Julia Velva and Aelia Aeliana's tombstones, reclined on couches to consume food brought to them by their slaves (see 8.1). Diners usually had a knife, but other implements were rarely used, although small forks are known in the Roman period and may have been used for certain special delicacies like snails.[148] There were also spoons, of which there are a number from York, made in silver, copper alloy or bone, but they have small shallow bowls and so were not really suitable for porridge or soup.[149] Types of ceramic vessel suitable for food – bowls, cups, platters, etc. – are common in York's pottery assemblage, occurring primarily in the wares described in Chapter 6. For drink, there were beakers that were filled from flagons and, more rarely, casks like that shown under the couch on Aelia Aeliana's tombstone (5.11). If they had no dining implements or tableware, folk may have used a piece of bread or the equivalent of a pizza to serve as a form of plate, as described in Book 7 of the *Aeneid*:

> *they set on the grass, instead of tables and plates for food, some meal cakes, and on this flooring provided by Ceres they piled fruits of the countryside … they were forced because they were still hungry and there was nothing else to eat to turn to the thin cereal platters, boldly snap them in their fingers and jaws, and bite this round-crust of destiny …*

Wealthier households could usually afford vessels for the kitchen and table in glass and metal. There is a large assemblage of glass vessels in the Yorkshire Museum collection and numerous fragments come from excavations. Those in the museum come largely from burials but are usually designed to be containers for food and drink.[150] Either colourless or pale green, they include bottles of various sizes with bodies of a square, hexagonal, rectangular or octagonal cross-section shape (5.24). Glass drinking vessels in the early to mid-second century were cups and beakers of carinated or cylindrical form, some decorated with bands of lines incised with a wheel. There were also bowls and some large jars with lids. Cups in the Julia Velva period, and later in the third century, were again cylindrical and might be decorated with abraded or incised designs, such as the attractive fragment shown in 5.25.[151] More rarely in York there were vessels bearing painted designs.[152]

5.24: Glass bottle from the grave of Corellia Optata. (YORYM HG53, © York Museums Trust)

5.25: Drawing of a fragment of a glass bowl from 37 Bishophill Senior. Below the rim is part of an inscription in wheel-abraded letters, below which a figure with curly hair stands to the left of fluted column holding a cymbal or small shield in his left hand. Estimated width of bowl: 144mm. (By Sheena Howarth, © York Archaeological Trust)

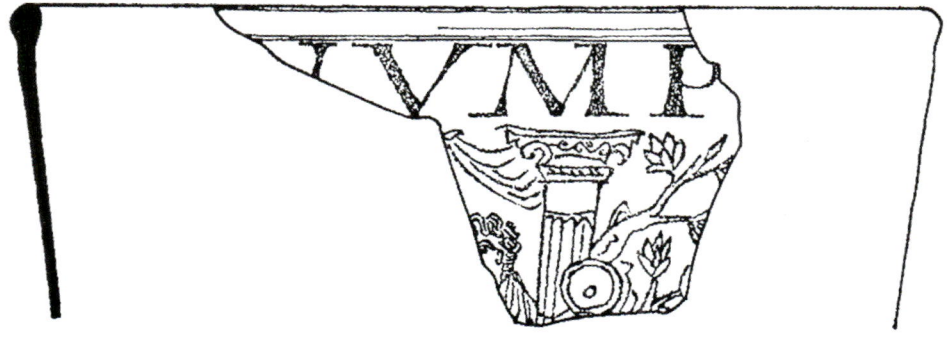

After a meal, the debris had to be disposed of. One imagines that this was when the household dogs got their chance to eat. Roman deposits in York and elsewhere have produced numerous dog bones and there are also a few dog burials in which a faithful friend was carefully laid to rest. The evidence is that, in addition to the large 'hunting dogs' for which Britain was famous, according to Strabo (p 150), there were smaller animals of poodle- or terrier-size perhaps as much pets as working dogs. For example, found in the Bedern well was a dog, whose bones suggest 'a short-legged', 'short-muzzled' type, 250mm (about 10 inches) to the shoulder.[153] Pets or not, one task a dog (there were no cats) would have been expected to tackle was killing the rats and mice that also had an interest in food waste. Their bones show that Roman York's rats were the black variety (*rattus rattus*), not their brown cousins (*rattus norwegicus*) we know so well today (5.26).[154] Food waste not claimed by the dogs was presumably deposited with other refuse in middens, where it could be consumed by pigs and other scavengers.

For those not occupied with taking out the refuse and washing-up, time after meals might be agreeably spent in various forms of entertainment. Unfortunately, music and dancing have left little trace in the archaeology of Roman York, but for board games such as *ludus latrunculorum*, similar to draughts, or *ludus duodecim scriptorum*, approximating to our backgammon, there are dice, largely in bone[155] but also jet,[156] and counters in ceramic, glass and bone.[157] In military circles at least, these games were no doubt accompanied by enthusiastic gambling, during which the gods were regularly appealed to for assistance.

5.26: Drawing of black rats.

Chapter 6

Religious belief and practice

Introduction
There is a sense in which this is the most important chapter in the book because if one really wants to understand what it was like to live in Roman times and what people thought about beyond the day-to-day routine, one has to be familiar with their religious beliefs and practices in all their great and wonderful variety.

It is difficult to know to what extent native religions persisted in the immediate York area after the Roman conquest, as they have left little evidence behind. However, the opposite is the case for those introduced by the Romans. Native people could not help being aware of the temples that probably dominated the street scene and the deities whose images were everywhere, as statues and reliefs or on smaller items such as figurines coins, samian pottery, intaglios, etc. For anyone who aspired to embrace Roman elite culture, like Julia Velva and Aurelius Mercurialis, one would imagine, observance of traditional religious rituals that bound the citizen to the Roman gods was of fundamental importance. They would, no doubt, have been thoroughly familiar with the narratives, or myths as we would call them, inhabited by the deities who crowded into their world. Religion for the people of the Roman Empire was a dominant force in their experience of life in a way that is, perhaps, hard for us to appreciate today. In the west, at least, we are largely undaunted by the uncertainties of existence, such as disease, famine and severe weather events, which were hard to cope with in antiquity and from which, it was thought, only the gods could provide protection. Our own intellectual discourse is pervaded by the rationalist view that all truth has its origins in human thought unaided by divine or supernatural agency and is conveyed to us through the experience of the senses. For the Romans, however, whilst there may have been scepticism amongst some philosophers about the power of the gods and their interest in human affairs, atheism was not really an option.

The derivation of the English word 'religion' is the Latin '*religio*', which refers to the traditional honours paid to the Roman gods. Any Roman male who aspired to make a name for himself in society would have been keen to display *religio* and was judged by the extent to which he did it in the appropriate manner. The Oxford English Dictionary (OED) has a rather broader definition of religion as, firstly, a 'particular system of faith and worship' and, secondly, as 'human recognition of superhuman controlling power and especially of a personal god or gods entitled to obedience and worship …' In other words, one might think of the religious person as one who has an awareness of a presence, or influence, if not always a 'controlling power', which is exercised on human affairs by a source that is unseen and intangible, yet can make itself felt in a manner that appears very real. To the person with faith the source of this presence must at least be acknowledged in some way if not propitiated and appealed to for assistance. As far as gods are concerned, by no means all religions have them in the sense that they are traditionally understood in Europe. Nor do all religions (including those of the native Britons) conceive of the gods in a human form. However, the Romans, like the Greeks, accepted the existence of gods who looked like their adherents and worshippers.

The gods we think of as being typically Roman inhabited a pantheon adopted largely from Greek and oriental traditions many centuries before the imperial period. They are described and alluded to in a great range of texts and inscriptions and they are depicted in works of art. A small but important example of an inscription from York taking us back to Greece in a fairly direct manner can be found on one of the two small copper alloy plaques from the old station (see p 75) that refers to Oceanus and Tethys (6.1).[1] This is an allusion to the 'Pelasgian' creation myth named after the first man, Pelasgus, who sprang from the soil of Arcadia in the Peloponnese. This begins with Euronyme, the goddess of all things, who rose naked from chaos and divided the sea and sky. She created the seven planetary powers with a titan and titaness, gigantic superhumans, controlling each of them. Oceanus and Tethys took charge of Aphrodite (Roman Venus), the goddess of love. Styx, the daughter of Oceanus and Tethys, dwelt at the entrance of the underworld, giving her name to its river. The children of Styx assisted Zeus (Roman Jupiter) in the revolt of the planets against the titans, which led to Zeus swallowing them up and destroying them for ever.

There were also religious ideas known in Roman York that did not have their cultural and geographical origins in the eastern Mediterranean. Some of these emerged out of the indigenous religions of Britain itself. Others were imported by the military and other migrants. However, varied though Roman religion may have been, an idea that was more-or-less universally accepted was what we might call 'animism', which attributes a living soul (*anima*), and thus a spirit or spark of the divine, to all natural phenomena, not just human beings and animals, birds, trees and so forth, but also things that we would think of as inanimate, such as mountains and rivers. A common dedication is simply 'to the spirit of the place' – *genio loci* (dative case in Latin) – as seen, for example on the altar in Parliament Street, York (p 124),[2] and another wishing happiness (*feliciter*) *genio loci* on a tablet from Coney Street outside the south-west defences of the fortress.[3] In addition (they did move after all), the seven planets of what was believed to be a geocentric (i.e. earth- rather than sun-centred) cosmos were thought of as animate and they represented important deities in the classical pantheon. In order of their distance from the earth they were Saturn, the farthest away, Jupiter, Mars, Sol (the sun), often associated with Apollo, Venus, Mercury and Luna (the moon), often associated with Diana.

6.1: Silvered copper alloy ansate plaques pierced for suspension, with inscriptions in punched dots: (lower) 'To the gods of the governor's residence, Scribonius Demetrius' (76mm x 50mm); (upper) 'To Ocean and Tethys, Demetrius' (50mm x 25mm). (YORYM H4.1-2, Yorkshire Museum)

Throughout the year there were religious festivals in the Roman world, often associated, as amongst the native Britons, with critical points in the agricultural and pastoral year. These were occasions when the attention and favour of the appropriate gods were sought by means of the correct execution of ritual acts and behaviour. Some form of ritual might be integrated into almost any aspect of life from the laying out of a legionary fortress (see p 32) to the burial of the dead, and at its heart one would have usually found a contract or bargain with the gods. This would have involved a request for assistance, favour or support backed up with the sacrificial offer of a living creature or creatures (but not a human being). An exchange of this sort had had a long history before the Romans got to York. For example, Livy (59 BC – AD 17) describes the traditional sacrifice of a bull, a sheep and a pig in about 550 BC on the Campus Martius in Rome by way of a request for its purification and the banishing of evil spirits following the quinquennial census.[4]

Sacrifice is often depicted in Roman art as in, for example, the relief on which 6.2 is based, but may also be alluded to on sacred objects, simply by depiction of the implements involved. For example an axe and knife are carved on an altar from Dunnington, a village 6km east of York.[5] Once the sacrificial animals had

6.2: Reconstruction drawing of a sacrifice scene adapted from an original Roman relief.

been ceremonially slaughtered, the entrails, especially the liver, were examined by a *haruspex*, a specialist with the power to foresee the future, and thus to judge whether the omens were favourable for, for example, a military campaign, beginning the harvest, etc. This sort of public prediction was considered perfectly respectable and of quite a different order from the private and informal advice dispensed by astrologers, fortune-tellers and soothsayers, popular with the Romans but disapproved of by the more conservative elements in society.[6] The ceremony ended with the more edible parts of the animals being eaten at a feast. The whole process of sacrifice is concisely described by Ovid in a passage on the Trojan War in *Metamorphoses*:[7]

> *there came a feast day on which Achilles … was propitiating Pallas with the sacrifice of a cow. When he had placed its entrails on the blazing altar and the aroma, dear to the gods, rose up to heaven, a portion of the meat was reserved for the sacred rites, and the rest was distributed to the tables.*

Having received divine favour and had their request granted, a group, or an individual, might express thanks with an altar or statue dedicated to the god in question, usually inscribed with one of several traditional formulae. For example, the base of a statue dedicated to Fortuna survives from York, on which the inscription concludes with METROBIANVS M L V S = MERITO LIBENS VOTUM SOLVENS, 'Metrobianus gave this gift deservedly fulfilling his vow'.[8]

Most Roman altars found in Britain adopt a similar form, which has very ancient origins. They are stone blocks, usually standing *c.* 0.30m – 1.50m high, with a plinth at the base and a cornice at the head (6.3). On the top there is a dished area, the *foculus* ('small hearth'), where materials, such as pinecones, or entrails (as in the passage from Ovid), were burnt, which were thought to give off an aroma that would attract the gods' attention. In addition, libations of wine were poured over the *foculus* as another form of votive offering. The *foculus* is often flanked by what are intended to represent bundles of rods, the *fasces*, a traditional symbol of authority in the Roman world – and origin of our word 'fascist'. In the shaft between the base and cornice, one or more faces usually bear an inscribed dedication and sometimes relief decoration as well. For example, a jug and pan (*patera*) on the altar *genio loci* from Parliament Street (p 124) represents the equipment traditionally involved in libation. Typically, an inscription, usually in a highly standardised format, will give the name of the god (or gods) to whom the dedication was made, the name and status of the person making it, and some version of a formula to say it is in fulfilment of a vow of gratitude, like that quoted above. In Britain it was soldiers in particular who were accustomed to addressing the gods with the sort of public statement an altar represents, and they had the means to pay for it. We know of fourteen named people who dedicated altars in York, of whom only the legate's wife, Sosia Juncina, was female (pp 61–2). In the five cases where their status is known, all the men have military connections, except for the imperial freedman Nikomedes.[9]

On occasions, wealthy people might go even further than setting up an altar and pay for, or contribute towards, the construction of a temple. This is what is recorded on the tablet from York set up

6.3: Altar dedicated to Arciacus and the imperial numen by a centurion, Vitalis, found in 1846 at St Denys Church (height 0.60m).

by the merchant Lucius Viducius Placidus (see p 76). The motivation for such a gift was partly to demonstrate piety, one of the admired virtues in the Roman world, and approved of by the gods, and partly to advertise the donor's wealth and status as an open-handed public benefactor.

In pre-Roman times the Britons worshipped their gods in the open air, by watery places, groves of trees and the like in the manner of the Germanic tribespeople described by Tacitus,[10] and presumably continued to do so. The Romans, however, preferred dedicated structures. As far as Britain was concerned, the principal type of temple, often described as 'Romano-Celtic', had a central cell, usually thought to have been a low tower where the god 'lived' and its sacred paraphernalia was kept, which was surrounded on all sides by a covered walkway. Much rarer in Britain was the 'classical' temple of which the best-known example is probably that dedicated to Sulis Minerva at Bath (*Aquae Sulis*). In this type, the cell, approached by a flight of steps, had a grand façade with columns supporting a gabled pediment elaborately decorated in relief. A Roman temple, of whatever type, usually stood within a sacred precinct ('*temenos*') and the ceremonies themselves were traditionally performed outside, in front of the building. There are no certain remains of temple buildings, Romano-Celtic, classical or any other type, known from York, although their presence is clearly indicated by some of the sculpture and inscriptions. In addition, a curious piece of evidence that may indicate the existence of classical-type temples here is a handle made from a sheep's tibia found at 24 – 30 Tanner Row, which was carved with several simple images (6.4). They include not only two figures and a dog but also the facades of what appear to be two buildings with gabled roofs held up by columns, with simply rendered bases and capitals, which may, perhaps, represent temples. There are also likely to have been small roadside shrines in York, like those still surviving at Pompeii,[11] where daily religious observance took place. Although not necessarily found in their original positions,

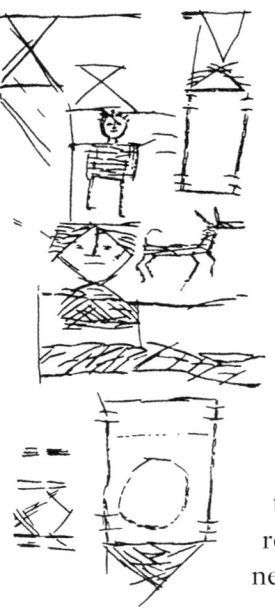

6.4: Sheep tibia with incised representations of human figure, dog and building facades from 24 – 30 Tanner Row, length 120mm. (© York Archaeological Trust)

many of the altars from York have been found close to the main Roman roads where they may have been set-up in such shrines.

Traditional Roman religious ceremonies were conducted not by full-time professional priests but by senior male members of a community who had assumed sacred duties, perhaps as part of a dedicated group, or 'college' (*collegium*). In an important town they might be known as *seviri augustales*, and we know of two from York, Verecundius Diogenes and Marcus Aurelius Lunaris (p 74). There is a sense in which their authority derived directly from the emperor himself, the *pontifex maximus* (chief priest) as he is referred to on inscriptions such as the Trajanic tablet from King's Square.[12] In the forts and fortresses around the empire the emperor's religious role devolved to his senior officers. At York this was the legate. He would have organised ceremonies on a regular basis according to the official calendar of festivals.[13] This responsibility was a critically important part of his job for, as Seneca remarks: '*primum militiae vinculum est religio*' ('the first link in the chain of military service is religion').[14] Worship of the emperor was also a feature of Roman religious practice. Integrating people of many different cultural and religious traditions into a large empire and encouraging them to accept the legitimacy of the emperor as their ruler was always going to be a problem for the Roman authorities. However, one way of doing it was to include deceased and deified emperors amongst the Roman gods, which a citizen was expected to honour. Also considered to have a divine aspect was the numen (spirit) of the living ruler and his close family members. The imperial numen is referred to on several inscriptions from York. One of the duties of the local *seviri augustales* was to manage and promote the cult of the emperor and honour him on his birthday and at other public festivals.

Roman deities in York

As far as the gods and goddesses of the classical pantheon are concerned, York has produced epigraphic references, sculpture and other material culture showing that most of the better known were worshipped here. All three of the principal protective deities of the Roman state Jupiter, Juno and Minerva, the so-called Capitoline Triad, named for their temples on the Capitoline Hill in Rome, no doubt featured prominently in official ceremonies. Jupiter would have been a particularly prominent presence in York if, as seems likely, a column dedicated to him stood somewhere in the Nessgate area north-east of the Ouse (pp 123–4). In addition, with the usual formula 'best and greatest' (IOM – IVPITER OPTIMVS MAXIMVS), the god is coupled with the 'gods of hospitality' and the household *penates*, on the altar from Bishophill Senior dedicated by Aelius Marcianus, the prefect of an auxiliary unit.[15] Minerva appears on an intaglio from 24 – 30 Tanner Row (5.22).

6.5: Millstone grit statue of the god Mars, height 1.78m. (© York Museums Trust)

The other planetary deities are represented, first of all, by Mars, of whom there is a life-sized statue in millstone grit that greets visitors to the Yorkshire Museum galleries (6.5).[16] He is depicted in Greek rather than Roman armour, thereby making a connection to his Greek equivalent god, Ares. A spectroscopic study of the sculpture found some traces of surviving paint, which suggest he was originally, at least in part, gilded. York has also produced two altars dedicated to Mars,[17] a god not just of war but also of agriculture equally fundamental to the wellbeing of humanity. An intaglio depicting Mars appears as 5.21, 1.

Ares loved and was loved by Aphrodite, the goddess of love and beauty, whom the Romans equated with Venus. A small female head in marble thought to be from a statuette of Venus comes from Toft Green, in the Roman town south-west of the Ouse.[18] A ceramic figurine from 24 – 30 Tanner Row represents Venus Anadyomene – 'rising from the sea' (6.6) – who had probably originally stood in a small domestic shrine.[19] Her right hand is supposed to be wringing out her hair on her emergence from the water, although her coiffure is otherwise tidily arranged in a style of the mid-second century. As she was made in Gaul, one should probably call her a Celtic Venus, not so much the classical goddess of love but a domestic fertility goddess who draws our attention to her (wet) hair as a symbol of female sexuality.[20]

There is a small rather crude relief in millstone grit, probably from York, of Mercury standing behind an altar, holding his special staff, the *caduceus*, in his left hand.[21] In his right hand is a purse symbolising the god's role as protector of those engaged in commerce. To the right of the altar is a cockerel and to the left a stag, the god's two totemic animals. Mercury's patronage of commerce may explain why it was near to the south-west bank of the Ouse, at the 5 Rougier Street excavation (2.3, 18), that a small incomplete relief was found on which one sees the feet of the god above a fine cockerel. The bird carries a pair of bags tied across his back that contain messages delivered by Mercury in his role as the Roman version of the Greek Hermes (6.7).[22]

A deity, probably well-known in Roman York, who by his parentage occupied the boundary between men and gods, was Bacchus, the Roman version of the

6.6: Pipe clay figurine of Venus Anadyomene, from 24 – 30 Tanner Row. Her hair has a top knot similar to that seen on goddesses of the Antonine period, such as the 'Capitoline Venus' in Rome, a copy of a Greek original, height 180mm. (© York Archaeological Trust)

6.7: Incomplete relief of a cockerel with bags across his back, probably representing Mercury, whose feet can be seen above, along with the cloven hooves of a ram or stag. Found at 5 Rougier Street in 1981. Height 110mm, width 100mm. (© York Archaeological Trust)

Greek Dionysus. He was the youthful and beautiful, if effeminate, god of wine – hence the meaning of his name as 'noisy' or 'riotous'. Bacchus was the son of Zeus (Roman Jupiter) and the mortal Semele, daughter of King Cadmus of Thebes. Jealousy caused Zeus's consort Hera (Juno) to drive the adult Bacchus mad, and he is then thought to have wandered the world teaching the cultivation of the vine, regarded by Greeks and Romans alike as one of the critical benefits of civilisation. Bacchus is sometimes seen accompanied on his travels by the bacchantes, or maenads, unruly drunken women holding the thyrsus, a staff entwined with ivy and headed with a pinecone. A stone head of a curly haired and clean-shaven youth from York is thought to represent Bacchus, probably on account of his slightly languid even bleary eyes suggesting intoxication (6.8).[23] A jasper intaglio from the fortress baths sewer depicts a maenad in profile wearing a fawn's skin (*nebris*), symbol of Bacchus, over her shoulders (5.21, 5).[24] Another son of Zeus, also out of a mortal, Alcmene, Queen of Thebes, was Heracles, the Roman Hercules.

6.8: Head in millstone grit, thought to be from a statue of the god Bacchus (height 190mm, width 180mm, Yorkshire Museum)

He evidently had a temple on the northeast bank of the Ouse at York from which an incomplete inscribed tablet has survived (p 123).[25]

A very characteristic form of Roman religious practice was to create deities who were allegorical representations of various qualities and virtues. They include Fortuna, goddess of good fortune and luck. The altar dedicated to her by Sosia Juncina in the baths at the old station and the statue dedicated by Metrobianus for the good health of Auspicata and Simplicia have already been mentioned. Fortuna appears on another of the intaglios from the fortress baths sewer (5.21, 2). Appropriate to a military context, she wears the helmet of Minerva and eagle wing of Victory as well as holding an ear of corn and the rudder with which she steers the fate of humanity.[26] Dedications to Fortuna were common in Roman bath houses, not only because the patrons played games of chance there but also, it seems, because they felt particularly vulnerable to evil spirits while performing their ablutions naked.

The Romans frequently took on the gods of conquered or neighbouring peoples and made them their own. Consequently, the alien deity's name would appear in inscriptions in a Latin version and, often for the first time, in a human form in works of art. A good example is provided by the mother goddesses – *Deae Matres* – who originated as fertility spirits in Gaul.[27] They were probably brought to Britain by Roman soldiers who often made dedications to the deities of the places in which they had formerly served. There are four altars dedicated to the mother goddesses from York.[28] One (uninscribed), now rather weathered, depicts them as a threesome. This is common in Celtic religious expression serving to emphasise the power of the deity (6.9).[29] The goddesses are seated in characteristic pose with their right hands across their chests and their left hands in their laps. On the two flanking faces of the altar are cloaked male figures and on the back are a pig and a jar (the latter to collect the blood) representing sacrifice. Dedications to the *matres* in Britain are often linked to particular localities and we can see this on the York altar dedicated by Marcus Minucius Mudenus, the river pilot, to the mother goddesses of Africa, Italy and Gaul.[30]

Religious belief and practice 215

6.9: Heavily weathered altar in millstone grit dedicated to the *Matres*, who appear in triplicate on the front. A pig and a jar on the rear represent sacrifice, height 0.54mm. (From Wellbeloved 1842)

Whilst the *Matres* represent the female aspect of fertility in a sacred context, the male aspect is frequently represented by the phallic symbol, which has its roots in native as well as Roman religion.[31] It was also considered apotropaic, meaning it had the power to counter the evil eye and turn aside bad luck. In Britain as a whole, phallic carvings are most commonly found on military sites. York has produced one carved in the round, 0.66m high, with a curious conical tip, probably from a funerary monument, and three in relief that were originally built into the fortress wall near the west corner (Multangular Tower).[32]

Besides the *Matres*, other deities known at York thought to be Gallic in origin include Sucellus and Toutatis, both referred to in inscriptions on silver rings. In Gaul, the former is often represented with a hammer and is thought to have had some role in protecting the fertility of crops and vines.[33] Toutatis (much loved by the cartoon character Asterix the Gaul) appears in the abbreviated form 'TOT' on a ring found at the railway station, probably in a burial (6.10). He is linked to Mars in Gaul and may himself have been a war god.[34]

A god from Germany rather than Gaul is Veteris, who was probably brought to Britain by men who had served in the Rhineland. Known also as Huitris or Vitris, he is well-known on Hadrian's Wall but there is a York altar dedicated by one Primulus whose status is unknown but possibly an army veteran.[35] Closer to home, Romanised native British deities from York include Arciacus, of whom an

6.10: Silver ring inscribed TOT, meaning the god Toutatis, found at the railway station in 1875. (Yorkshire Museum)

altar was found east of the Foss at St Denys Church, Walmgate (1.1, 7; 6.3).³⁶ The inscription is the only known reference to the god, so he is very local indeed. The dedicator, a centurion, links Arciacus with the imperial numen, making this a good example of the way the presiding deity of a place in the provinces was put under the emperor's protection. Another York example appears on the relief from Nessgate that links a British goddess with the numen of multiple emperors, probably Septimius Severus and his sons (p 123).

A striking aspect of religion in Roman York, found in only a few other places in Britain, is the cult of alien deities of eastern origin who would have been brought here by soldiers, officials, merchants and other travellers. In their various ways these deities seem to have fulfilled spiritual needs that were not fully satisfied by traditional cults. One of the earliest to appear in the west, with a temple dedicated to her in Rome in 191 BC, was Cybele, *Magna Mater* (the great mother), who originated in Asia Minor.³⁷ Her ceremonies were noisy and raucous, but by the mid-second century she was sufficiently respectable to appear on the coins of the empresses Sabina and Fausta and, subsequently, of the emperor Commodus. Cybele was, in essence, a fertility goddess and one of the ways her sacrificial demands were met was by the ritual self-castration of her priests and acolytes, the so-called '*galli*', at an annual spring festival. This was done in imitation of Attis, Cybele's consort, who had gone mad and castrated himself in remorse for abandoning his vow of chastity by having sexual relations with a nymph, a sort of B-list female goddess. Attis was symbolised by violets, which his blood had caused to grow, and by pinecones, representing the pine tree into which he was transformed by Cybele. It is as symbols of eternal life and of Attis as a protector of the dead that we should see the pinecones on Julia Velva's tombstone. Also from York are several large pinecone finials, three on block bases, which were probably part of tomb monuments.³⁸ In addition, there is a striking relief of Attis, found on The Mount, which must also come from a tomb monument (6.11).³⁹ The god rests his head on his left hand in an attitude of mourning and wears the distinctive Phrygian cap (also worn by Mithras, see below), originally derived from the legend of King Midas of Phrygia – in Asia Minor. Midas had given the prize in a music contest to a mortal, Marsyas, not to the god Apollo. In revenge, Apollo gave the king an ass's ears, which he had to then conceal under the special cap.

6.11: Relief in millstone grit of the god Attis, showing him in Phrygian dress resting his head on his left hand in mourning and holding a shepherd's crook (height 1.06m). Found on The Mount in 1927. (Yorkshire Museum)

Besides Cybele, the goddess Isis also appears on the emperor Commodus's coins. She was of Egyptian origin and her cult arrived in Rome at the end of the Republican period before spreading to the north-western provinces.⁴⁰ In due course, Isis crossed the Channel to London where it is thought she had a temple, an *Iseum*. Isis's male consort was Osiris, a god of fertility and the afterlife, who was associated with another known as Apis, represented by a sacred bull, whom the Greeks in Egypt converted into a god, Serapis, in human form. The myth of Isis and Osiris/ Serapis concerns his death at the hands of the evil Set, or Seth, who was in turn slain by Harpokrates, their son. The goddess then restored her consort to life. Some indication of the elaborate ceremonies associated with the cult of Isis may be found in a description by the second-century author Apuleius (*c.* 124 – *c.* 170) in his fable *The Golden Ass*, of a procession in her honour at Corinth.⁴¹ This begins by describing the women, clearly playing a prominent role, who 'resplendent in their white robes, happily carrying different kinds of emblems, and decked in spring flowers, strewed the ground with blooms, drawn from their breasts, along the path that the holy company trod …' Such processions may well have been an integral part of worship of the goddess in Julia Velva's York. Apuleius mentions Serapis only briefly, but the god seems to have had a semi-independent existence and, like Isis herself, had a role in curing the sick and representing the hope of rebirth after death, especially in military circles.⁴² Isis was, perhaps, seen as a bit 'girly' by soldiers, but construction of a temple of Serapis, a *Serapeum*, in York is

6.12: Tablet in millstone grit inscribed with notice of the construction of a temple dedicated to the god Serapis by Claudius Hieronymianus, legate of the Sixth Legion, 0.91m x 0.64m. (Yorkshire Museum)

commemorated by the tablet from Toft Green, near the old station (see p 112), dedicated by the legionary legate Claudius Hieronymianus who may himself have been an Egyptian in origin (6.12).[43]

The emperor Septimius Severus was another avid follower of Serapis, whom he would probably have first encountered in his birthplace, Lepcis Magna, and he erected a huge *Serapeum* in Rome.[44] His son Caracalla was a votary too. The god appears on his coins and he dedicated to Serapis the weapon with which killed his brother Geta.[45] Another intriguing piece of evidence for the cult at York is a small bronze model of the sacred bull Apis, with the rays of the sun shining from his head.[46] Quite how it reached its find spot on Hob Moor, open land 2km south-west of the city centre, remains a mystery.

The cult of Mithras

The question, or 'mystery', of how human life could be prolonged into eternity, which attracted the followers of Isis and Serapis, also attracted those of Mithras, a sun god of Persian origin whose cult became widely known in the north-western provinces from about the beginning of the second century AD.

Religious belief and practice 219

In York we have two sculptures that suggest the presence of Mithraists in the community, probably made up largely of soldiers and veterans. Unlike the cult of Isis, women were excluded. One of these sculptures (found in Micklegate, see p 109) is a version of the relief that was displayed prominently in all Mithraic temples showing the tauroctony – bull-slaying – claimed to depict the origin of all creation (6.13).[47] Unfortunately, the relief from York, in soft magnesian limestone,

6.13: Relief (incomplete) in magnesian limestone, showing the god Mithras slaying the bull of life (0.68m x 0.56m). Below are figures probably undergoing some of the rites involved in transition between the seven grades of initiation. Found in Micklegate in 1747. (Yorkshire Museum)

220   *Julia Velva, A Roman Lady from York*

is incomplete and badly worn. The semi-circular arc of the heavens above the figures is largely missing. However, it can be reconstructed from what survives to show that the right-hand edge, as well as the top, of the stone has been cut away, although all the expected features (just about) survive (6.14). Visible in the centre is Mithras himself in Persian dress, wearing a tunic, tight-fitting trousers and

6.14: Reconstruction drawing of the relief of Mithras, suggesting aspects of its original appearance.

Phrygian cap, in characteristic pose astride the bull of life. The god's left knee is driven into the bull's throat whilst his cloak billows out behind him, representing energy and vigour. Perched on his cloak is the raven that brought Mithras the sun's instruction to slay the bull. With his right hand, Mithras plunges the knife into the bull's neck to release the blood of life. The dog and what appear to be two intertwined snakes drink the blood, thereby symbolising the act of creation. These two creatures were probably chosen for Mithraic reliefs because of their role in healing. Dog saliva was known to be a strong antiseptic and snakes were thought to lead human beings to where healing plants would be found.

Still surviving to the right and left, respectively, of Mithras are the so-called 'bearers', Cautes and Cautopates. The former holds a torch upwards, symbolising the rising sun, and the latter holds a torch downwards, symbolising the setting sun. Mithras between them is, of course, the midday sun. In addition, or alternatively, the bearers represent the equinoxes and Mithras the summer solstice.[48] The bearers can also be taken to symbolise the forces of good and evil between which, it was believed, a continual battle raged for control of the cosmos. A bust at the top of the relief on the left wearing a rather crude radiate crown may represent the sun, but this is not certain. He is not obviously balanced by the moon to the right as one would expect. As on some other tauroctony tablets, the sun and moon may, in fact, have been depicted above the bull-slaying scene in a part now lost. The faces of the pair of busts in the upper right of the relief are missing, although that to the left appears to have worn a crown with short projections that may represent the sun's rays or the points of a star. In the latter case the pair may, perhaps, represent the Dioscuri, Castor and Pollux, the heavenly twins. They would be appropriate companions of Mithras as the summer solstice usually falls on the last, or next to last, day of the sun's transit of Gemini, the twins (20 – 21 June).

Whilst Mithraism offered its adherents the promise of acquiring the secret knowledge that would guarantee eternal life, its followers were, for their part, expected to commit themselves to the cult for their lifetime during which they would attempt to pass through the seven grades of membership. Each grade was associated with one of the planets and eventually one reached the status of *pater*, father, under the aegis of Saturn. Access to each grade required the candidate to submit to an initiation ritual of some sort. The enigmatic and misshapen figures at the base of the York relief probably represent an initiate being accompanied by the god through three of these rituals. On the left we see Mithras – recognisable by the stubby cloak at his back – touching the initiate on the forehead to grant him the lowest grade of soldier. The next scene may be a fire, crudely rendered, in which the god accompanies the initiate into the grade of lion. Finally, on the right the pair mount a horse-drawn chariot in which they will ride across the sky signifying achievement of the grade of Heliodromos ('runner of the sun'), the second highest.

Being restricted to initiates, rather than all comers, like traditional cults, Mithraic ceremonies took place in an enclosed space and not in the open air. Since the bull-slaying is thought to have taken place in a cave, temples, *mithraea*, were constructed in subterranean locations, or at least in windowless buildings, both to imitate the cave and create a dark and mysterious environment. The best surviving examples in Britain are in London and at Carrawburgh fort on Hadrian's Wall. At the centre of the temple rituals was a shared meal eaten off a bull's skin.

The other Mithraic sculpture from York was found on the north-western edge of the town south-west of the Ouse (2.3, 11) and so it was at some distance from the bull-slaying relief.[49] There may, therefore, have been a second *mithraeum* in the old station area, perhaps associated with the governor's palace (see p 75). The statue is dedicated to Arimanius by Volusius Iraneus, perhaps, considering his *cognomen*, of Greek origin (6.15). Arimanius, the 'Lord of the Aeon', the current phase in the life of the cosmos, is the spirit of evil in Mithraic myth, who had to be placated by every soul who aspired to eternal life. He appears as a male figure, now decapitated, winged and naked except for a fringed loin cloth tied with a knotted snake symbolising the annual journey of the sun in the ecliptic, its passage through the constellations during the year. In his right hand the figure once had a sceptre representing lordship and dominion, and in his left is a pair of keys, the keys to heaven. The missing head probably had a ghastly leonine aspect, comparable to one surviving on a similar relief from Rome,[50] which symbolised the devouring power of time.

Also from York, rather humbler evidence for the cult of Mithras may be represented by a small bronze bull head,[51] but of particular interest are two (incomplete) antefixes each bearing a relief that appears to be the head of the god wearing his

6.15: Statue in millstone grit dedicated by Volusius Irenaeus to the evil god Arimanius. The figure has lost its head but survives as a winged male who is naked, except for a loin cloth tied with a knotted snake. He carries a pair of keys, height 0.61m. (Yorkshire Museum)

Phrygian cap (6.16).[52] One comes from 16 – 22 Coppergate, outside the fortress (2.3, 10), and the other from Interval Tower NE6, near the east corner of the fortress. Originally, they may both have adorned the roofs of barrack blocks serving as symbols of the god's protection of the soldiers.

In its ambitious theology, claims of universal cosmic significance, demands on its initiates and promises of eternal life arising from secret knowledge, Mithraism clearly bears some similarity to Christianity but without the ethical maturity, or social inclusiveness, of the latter. However, in simply placing itself alongside other religious beliefs and practices, Mithraism was not in any sense a threat to the established religious or political order. Christianity, however, rejected all other religious ideas, including the cult of the emperor, as divine. It was, therefore, seen by the Roman authorities as a threat to the links between citizenship, traditional forms of piety and the sacred quality of imperial power. Christianity does not form a significant part of our story being much more a feature of the religion of Roman York (and Britain) in the fourth century. Julia Velva and her circle were probably completely unaware of the Gospels, although they may have heard of, and wondered at, the first recorded martyrdom of a Christian in Britain, that of St Alban who met his end in *c*. 209. However, Christians may have passed through York from time to time from as early as the late first century. The second legate of the Ninth Legion, Gaius Caristanius Fronto, from Antioch, was married to a woman who could have been a Christian, as she was the daughter, or sister, of a man, L Sergius Paullus, who had been governor of Cyprus in AD 46 – 7 when encountered and apparently converted by St Paul.[53]

6.16: Ceramic antefix from excavations at Interval Tower NE6, showing the head of Mithras in relief. (Yorkshire Museum)

Religion and death

Whilst cults like those of Isis/Serapis and Mithras laid particular emphasis on promises of rebirth after death, the fate of the deceased in the hereafter was a matter of general interest in the Roman world. The ideas of native British people are a little obscure, but there does seem to have been a belief that the dead, or at least those belonging to the warrior elite, would travel to another world. This was one where equipment from life on earth would be required, hence the examples of late prehistoric burials accompanied by amphorae and other vessels suitable for future feasts.[54] Traditional Roman religious beliefs of the pre-imperial era seem somewhat vague about the afterlife, but by the reign of Emperor Augustus, ideas of Greek origin about the immortality of the soul, as described, for example, in Plato's *Phaedo*, had been adopted in some circles.[55] This is apparent from the account to be found in Book 6 of Virgil's *Aeneid*. Following an appropriate sacrifice supervised by the Cumaean Sibyl, Aeneas, in search of his father, headed for the realm ruled by Hades, also known euphemistically, so as not to offend him, as Pluto – 'giver of wealth'. Aeneas's journey involves crossing the River Styx ferried by the 'dreaded Charon'. Although not specifically mentioned in the *Aeneid*, it was widely thought that the dead had to pay Charon to gain access to the underworld. This idea may be represented by the coins found occasionally in the mouth or hand of skeletons in York's Roman burials. Guarding the underworld was Cerberus, the three-headed dog. Once he had been passed, the deceased reached the Fields of Memory. A belief in the judgement of the dead is evident in the destiny for some in the 'Land of Joy' and the 'Fortunate Woods' where there are the 'Homes of the Blessed'. However, as Ovid remarks on the same subject: 'others again are subjected to punishment each according to his crime.'[56]

Plato, like Pythagoras before him, not only considered that the soul was immortal but also that following death of the body, it would migrate to another in a process known as metempsychosis. Whether or not this idea was fully accepted by the Romans – indeed it was firmly rejected by Pliny the Elder[57] – by the Augustan era the souls or spirits of the departed, often referred to as the Manes (or *divi parentes*), were considered to survive in some form and to have a particular divine quality. Recognition of this is found in the dedication *Dis Manibus*, usually abbreviated to DM, in funerary inscriptions as can be seen in many York examples. Ideas of where the Manes dwelt after burial seem rather vague. Options included the grave itself or somewhere underground in Mother Earth nearby.[58] Another was the ascent of the soul into the heavens. Seven circular motifs, three either side and one in the centre, carved around the head of Flavia Augustina's tombstone, probably invoke the seven planetary deities (5.8).[59] A reference to this idea may also be found on an intaglio from the fortress sewer, which is engraved with a crescent moon, itself symbolic of eternal life, surrounded by six stars (the other planets) (5.21, 4).[60]

Alternatively, there were the 'Isles of the Blessed' across the ocean to which, if one had lived a good life, one might be transported on the back of friendly sea creatures. This idea is alluded to on Aelia Aeliana's tombstone, which features a pair of dolphins and stylised waves above the dining scene (5.11). Another of the intaglios from the sewer depicts cupid seated on a hippocamp (part horse, part fish), behind which is a dolphin (5.21, 6).[61] We might also note what is thought to be a Triton, a son of Poseidon (Neptune), part man, part sea creature, who appears on what is probably a funerary relief found near the north-west gate of the fortress (now Bootham Bar).⁶² He holds a form of trumpet, known as a conch, with which to calm the sea for the passage of the dead.

It seems to have been commonly believed in much of the Roman world that, at the time of burial, or shortly afterwards, the journey of the dead to the next world, wherever it was, had begun. It was incumbent, therefore, on friends and relatives to progress this satisfactorily to a happy outcome. One way of doing this was the sort of funerary banquet (*silicernium*) we see represented on the tombstones of Julia Velva, Aelia Aeliana and Candida Barita from York. The initial send-off might be followed up on special days in the calendar when ceremonies to worship the spirits of the ancestors were conducted at the grave-side. They included the *Parentalia*, 13 – 21 February, and the *Lemuria* on 9 – 13 May, when food and drink were brought to the grave to share with the deceased. A reference to this may be a basket of fruit carved in relief on Decimina's tombstone from York.⁶³

Whilst the traditional Roman rites may have been observed by some in York, we do not know how widely people of native British origin accepted these customs of commemoration or interaction with the dead. However, throughout the community it is likely that every aspect of death, from the end of life to the interment, and in a few cases the raising of a monument, would have had its accompanying rituals, although they are, of course, largely lost to us as they have left little trace in the ground. There are nonetheless examples of artefacts accompanying burials in addition to the coins already referred to, for which some ritual funerary purpose can be suggested. Pottery vessels are the most common. They include the head pots characteristic of the Severan era in York, and thought to have been made to represent members of the imperial house, which have been found used occasionally as cremation urns in York burials, both in the Trentholme Drive and Fishergate cemeteries (6.17).⁶⁴ As they were considered semi-divine beings, the use of a pot representing, for example, Julia Domna or Caracalla for

6.17: Pot in the shape of a female head, thought to be Empress Julia Domna. (© York Museums Trust)

a cremation was, perhaps, an attempt to invoke some special protection for the dead. The urns apart, vessels in burials are usually found empty, although they may once have contained food and drink for the sustenance of the deceased on his or her journey to the next world and/or for offering to any other spirits they might encounter on the way. Where some vessel content is found in York, it is most commonly the bones of what had once been a fowl. Of the Julia Velva period, examples come from Blossom Street and Driffield Terrace in the cemeteries south-west of the Roman town.[65] A cockerel was, according to Pliny the Elder, responsible for omens, favourable or otherwise, for the dead, and its entrails were deemed highly acceptable by the gods.[66] The hen eggs found in a beaker in a burial at Trentholme Drive may have symbolised rebirth – the eternal cycle of the chicken and the egg.[67]

Potential danger from evil spirits on the journey to the afterlife may be the context for a jet pendant from the Walmgate burial described above (pp 196–7), which depicts the face of Medusa. Two similar examples from York may also be from burials (6.18).[68] In a fit of jealousy, Athena changed Medusa into a Gorgon with serpents for hair, huge teeth and a protruding tongue. Athena then caused the hero, and son of Zeus, Perseus to cut Medusa's head off with a sickle and as he carried it around, its repulsive face turned all who gazed upon it into stone, petrified with fright. Images of Medusa were displayed to avert bad luck and the evil eye.

6.18: Jet pendant with the head of Medusa, height 38mm. (© York Archaeological Trust)

Aspects of the iconography of the tomb monuments from York not already mentioned include, on the memorial tablet of Eglecta[69] and the sarcophagus of Julia Victorina[70] depictions, in relief, of cupids, or so-called '*amorini*', representing Cupid (Greek Eros), son of Venus and Roman god of love (3.10). Cupid is usually shown winged and naked, often with a bow and arrows, although on the sarcophagus the two figures each have a light shield (*pelta*) and a spear. Cupid in a funerary context is probably an allusion to his relationship with Psyche (one meaning of the Greek word is 'soul'), a princess whose beauty excited the jealousy of Venus. The story is told in its fullest form in *The*

Golden Ass by Apuleius, probably written in or after the 160s and so contemporary literature of the Julia Velva period.[71] On behalf of his mother, Cupid was supposed to inspire Psyche with love for the most contemptible of men, but instead Cupid fell for her himself and took her to a place where he could visit her at night. Psyche's sisters, also jealous of her, tried to make her believe she was embracing a monster in the dark. In an attempt to verify this, Psyche held a lamp over Cupid while he was asleep and found him the most handsome of men. With a drop of hot oil from the lamp, she accidentally awakened the god and he fled. Psyche wandered about looking for her lost love and eventually came to Venus who treated her as a slave, but Psyche was assisted by Cupid who still loved her. Eventually Psyche overcame Venus's jealousy. She became immortal and was united with Cupid for ever. This story can be interpreted as representing the journey of a human soul, especially of a female soul, which was purified by passions and misfortunes and thereby prepared for true and pure happiness in the afterlife.

Other funerary art from York has a rather less pleasant flavour. Representations of the devouring power of death include two stone lions from the railway station cemetery and two others found at the minster, but originally perhaps from tombs.[72] There is also a particularly striking sphinx of Greek type from The Mount cemetery (6.19).[73] This was possibly one of a group on an elaborate tomb monument. She is a naked, crouched figure with prominent breasts, eagle's wings and a serpent's tail. In Greek myth, the sphinx appeared outside Thebes, where she asked every passer-by the answer to the riddle: 'what speaks, and walks on two, three and four legs, but is strongest on two?' The answer is a human being, but those who could not solve the riddle were devoured on the spot. Oedipus managed to get the right answer and was acclaimed King of Thebes, although the rest of his life did not go so well.

6.19: Greek sphinx in millstone grit conceived as a nude crouched female with wings and a long tail, found in 1852 on The Mount, 0.68m x 1.37m x 0.51m. (Yorkshire Museum)

Chapter 7

Cemeteries and burials

The locations of the cemeteries of Roman York are shown on 1.1.

Introduction: the cities of the dead

After looking at how people in Roman York believed that the spirits or souls of the dead were conveyed to the afterlife, however it was conceived, and commended to those gods who might have jurisdiction over it, we should go on to look at wider issues related to death and burial. Julia Velva was, of course, only one of many thousands of former residents of *Eboracum* who was laid to rest in the cemeteries that formed such an extensive and prominent feature of the townscape.

The cemeteries of Roman York were located, for the most part, as one would expect in any major Roman settlement, along the principal approach roads. The Twelve Tables, the foundation of Roman law, by the imperial period already of considerable antiquity, which defined the rights and duties of the citizen, forbade burial from impinging on any space occupied by the living community. The 'cities of the dead' and the 'cities of the living' were kept apart, partly for fear by the latter of the spread of any disease to which the dead had succumbed, and partly for fear of defilement by evil spirits that might hasten their own death.

Our knowledge of the Roman cemeteries of York is incomplete and imperfect because of the circumstances in which many of them were discovered. Large parts were disturbed in the nineteenth century for suburban development, especially south-west of the city, and by the old and present railway stations in 1839 – 40 and 1874 – 77 respectively. Recording of burials and recovery of artefacts and, less often, the human remains (usually only the skulls were kept), did take place, notably by Charles Wellbeloved, at the old station, and James Raine at the present station, but always on an *ad hoc* basis. There was nothing in the way of systematic excavation and so information on, for example, the exact location and date of any particular burial and any relationship of the burials in space and time one to another is very patchy. There is an account of the cemeteries (as understood in 1962) in RCHME's *Eburacum*, skilfully extracted from a great variety of sources. However, those sources could profitably be re-examined, and the dating of the pottery and other finds needs revision in light of almost sixty years of further research.

The first excavation in York of a Roman cemetery to anything like modern standards, and still the largest in scale, took place on Trentholme Drive in the 1950s.[1] Some 342 inhumations (i.e. bodies buried unburnt) and up to fifty cremation burials dated between the late second century and early fourth century were recorded. In 1984, Professor Rick Jones (of Bradford University) reviewed the evidence for the York cemeteries. But he had to rely largely on RCHME's *Eburacum* and the Trentholme Drive report.[2] Since 1984, there have been several important excavations in the cemeteries, especially south-west of the Ouse, and records made of single burials or small groups all over the York area that allow us to revise our knowledge of the cemeteries and of burial practice quite considerably. For this book I compiled a database of 106 cremation burials and 857 inhumations with information (of variable quality) drawn from RCHME's *Eburacum* and more recent site reports. Because of the problems of dating many of them, it is difficult in the following discussion of burials to stick entirely to the period with which this book is primarily concerned (between the mid-second and mid-third centuries), and so it must, to some extent, consider the evidence for the whole of the Roman era.

Although the data is often inadequate, it is apparent nevertheless, that cemetery development during the Roman period in York was a complex process. It remains unclear when and where the principal cemeteries were established in the first place and how they then expanded over time. One can be fairly confident, however, that they did not simply expand further and further out from the legionary fortress or from the main civilian settlements as time went on. One suspects that, firstly, the use of land for burials was related in some way to overall patterns of land ownership and, secondly, that whereabouts in the cemeteries any particular interment was made depended on factors such as the residence, social status and occupational group of the deceased. The cemeteries of Roman York had probably reached their maximum extent by the early third century. Subsequent burials seem to have been largely fitted into cemeteries that already existed.

The cemeteries of Roman York
North-east of the River Ouse and north-west of the legionary fortress, what appear to be separate burial areas may, in fact, be part of a more-or-less uninterrupted cemetery zone extending for up to 1km along the lines of the two principal Roman approach roads. Some of the earliest burials at least may have been made close to the legionary fortress as a late first- or early second-century

Roman cremation was found (on the site of the art gallery) just outside the north-west gate.[3] Further out, a small group of second-century cremation burials was found at the junction of Burton Stone Lane and Clifton.[4] Otherwise, burials north-west of the fortress all come either from between the two Roman roads or close to the banks of the River Ouse. There are discrete zones around what are now The Avenue, the grounds of St Peter's School (formerly Clifton Fields), and St Mary's and Bootham Terrace.[5] Besides those from Burton Stone Lane, there are other cremation burials from the cemetery north-west of the fortress as well as many inhumations. Examples of both derive from the whole of the Roman period.

The zone north and north-east of the legionary fortress, in an arc between the modern streets of Bootham and Clifton and the River Foss, which appears to be largely devoid of Roman settlement, has relatively few recorded burials except for quite an extensive zone of scattered burials, all inhumations, immediately outside the fortress north-east gate.[6] South-east of the fortress scattered burials have been recorded in a cemetery of which a part was excavated by YAT on the Hungate site in 2009 – 11.[7] This produced eleven cremation burials of the mid-late second century and 111 inhumations of the mid-third to fourth century. Further south, 400m south-east of the fortress, in Castle Yard, a number of burials, probably of the early third century, have been found, including those in the stone sarcophagi of the centurion Aurelius Super (3.11) and of a centurion's wife, Julia Victorina (3.10).[8]

East of the Foss and *c.* 1.5km north-east of the fortress, what RCHME's *Eburacum* refers to in each case as a 'small cremation cemetery' was found at Heworth Green and, 300m south of it, in Heworth.[9] The evidence is, in fact, for very small groups of burials which, given their distance from the fortress, probably belonged to small local settlements rather than to Roman York itself. The same can also be said of another small group at Appletree Farm, Heworth (2.4, 3), on the Roman road approaching from the north-east, *c.* 3.5km from the fortress north-east gate.[10]

Also, east of the Foss, scattered burials have been found on Walmgate, which is close to the line of the Roman approach road from Brough on Humber. About 1.5km south-east of the fortress, some twenty or so burials as well as artefacts, largely pottery vessels, which may come from other burials, have been found either in the late nineteenth century or in 2000 – 02, on each side of Fishergate probably on the line of a Roman road approaching York from the south.[11] Most of the known burials are early Roman cremations. In addition, the incomplete Roman sarcophagus of a decurion was found re-used in the nearby medieval cemetery of the Gilbertine Priory, which is unlikely to have travelled far from where it was originally buried.[12]

South-west of the Ouse, a distinction was made in RCHME's *Eburacum* between the railway station cemetery and the cemetery south-west of the Roman town, although they were probably more-or-less contiguous. The railway station cemetery may be divided into two parts. The first and smaller part, at the site of the old station, lay within what would become the Roman town (within the medieval city walls; see p 62).[13] About sixteen burials are recorded in RCHME's *Eburacum*, both cremations and inhumations. The second and more substantial part of the railway station cemetery lies outside, largely west, of the walled city.[14] The east coast mainline, the old York to Scarborough railway line of 1845, the current railway station, and Leeman Road, including the short tunnel under the railway known as 'Marble Arch', have all altered the topography as it was in Roman times to a considerable extent. However, there was originally a low plateau of raised ground overlooking the Ouse to the north-east and extending north-westwards as far as Holgate Beck (2.4). Burials have been found in the south-eastern part of this plateau up to a point *c*. 400m from the city walls (as far as the National Railway Museum). The burials recovered in the railway station cemetery in the 1870s include both cremations and inhumations and appear to date from the late first century to the early to mid-fourth century. In 1999 – 2000, more inhumation burials in the same cemetery were recorded at what was then the Royal York Hotel close to the edge of the plateau before it dips away to the river (1.1, 8).[15]

The cemetery south-west of the Roman town (on Blossom Street and The Mount, including Mount Vale and Holgate Road), extends for *c*. 1.5km from the medieval walls.[16] The spine of the cemetery was formed by the main Roman road from the south-west, which reaches a high point on The Mount close to the site of Julia Velva's tombstone (1.1, 12; 2.4, 5; 7.1). An area where burial appears to have been particularly dense lies on the high ground, now occupied by The Mount School and Dalton Terrace, which extends west as far as Holgate. Amongst the more recent (2004 – 5) excavations in the south-western cemetery were two on Driffield Terrace (at Nos 1 – 3 and 6), which produced about eighty burials, all males, most of whom had been decapitated (see p 170).[17] Of these, about fifty-five were late second to early third century whilst the remainder were mid- to late third century/early fourth. Burials found on the opposite side of the street in The Mount School in 1987 included four more decapitated males.[18] One can envisage a zone in The Mount cemetery dedicated to the burial of execution victims, many of them perhaps soldiers, who met their end on a prominent site on the roadside. Public executions no doubt attracted large crowds of onlookers, as they did in eighteenth- and nineteenth-century York. Other recent excavations of note in the south-western cemetery, which have produced inhumations, took place at 35 – 41 Blossom Street (1.1, 10) and nearby at Moss Street, and on The Mount at Mill Mount (2004 – 5) and 89 The Mount (2008).[19] The limit of the

7.1: Imaginative illustration of the cemetery south-west of the Roman town looking north-eastwards from The Mount.

cemetery south-west of the town lay on Trentholme Drive where the excavations took place in the 1950s. More recently (2017), excavations at the nearby Newington Hotel on Mount Vale produced another seventy-five inhumations.[20] The cemetery, as a whole, had both cremation and inhumation burials and they represent the whole Roman period up to the mid-fourth century.

Also south-west of the Ouse, but south-east of the Roman town, a group of burials lay close to the site of the Norman motte at Baile Hill, within the medieval walled town. This group is represented primarily by four tombs constructed of roof tiles (7.6). They may have been at the north-western limit of another cemetery that extended uninterrupted southwards (across the line of the medieval city walls) on raised ground overlooking the Ouse as far as Clementhorpe.[21]

In peripheral areas south-west of the Ouse, scattered Roman burials have been found which, like those at Heworth north-east of the Ouse, were probably those of people living in small satellite settlements. About 1.25km south-west of Trentholme Drive, a few burials have been found in the York suburb of Dringhouses[22] and another small group was found a little to the west of here at Nunthorpe.[23]

This brief account places the dead of Roman York in various different zones around the settled areas, usually grouped in large cemeteries but also in discrete smaller groups or even isolated as single burials. In summary, the preferred locations appear to have been adjacent to the principal roads for obvious reasons of enabling both easy access and, for some families or groups at least, opportunities for the display of funerary monuments, and also close to the rivers, perhaps for the same reasons. In addition, there seems to have been a preference for areas of relatively elevated ground, especially perhaps for the burials of higher status individuals.

Burial practice in Roman York

There is evidence for a considerable diversity in Roman burial practice at York over and above a simple division into cremation and inhumation. This must, to some extent, be the result both of changes in fashions and preferences over time and also of the different traditions to which members of a socially heterogeneous population adhered. Unfortunately, we do not know whether Julia Velva was cremated or buried unburnt and her mortal remains are unlikely to be still surviving in the ground. The only tombstone from York found with the related remains, cremated, was that of Corellia Optata (see below).

In the late prehistoric period, burial of the dead appears, as in many other parts of England, to have been the exception rather than the rule in the York region.[24] Where burials do occur, and they are rare, they are usually inhumations in which the body was laid out in the crouched position. What may have been preferred was some form of excarnation, exposure of the corpse of the deceased to the elements followed, perhaps, by dispersal of any mortal remains in the landscape. The arrival of the Romans north of the Humber would, therefore, by introducing burial in the ground as the norm, have led to a marked change in how the dead were treated in the region, although prehistoric practices probably continued, especially in areas remote from immediate Roman impact. That inhumation in the native manner was still practiced in the York area is shown by the late first- or early second-century burials of an adult and infant, both in the crouched position, at Dringhouses.[25] In addition, inhumations, apparently early in a sequence of burials, found in 1867 – 8 near the York-Scarborough railway line (i.e. northern part of the railway station Roman cemetery), were in the crouched position. At the time they were thought to be 'British'.[26]

Cremation

In the Roman world as a whole, cremation of the dead, except for infants who had not yet cut their first teeth, was the prevailing mode of preparing them for burial in the first and much of the second century AD – the *mos Romanus* as it is called by Tacitus.[27] However, cremation was gradually being replaced by inhumation of the body unburnt by the mid-second century. This may, at least in part, be due to the influence of ideas about the soul's survival in the afterlife imported from Greece.[28] Inhumation may have been preferred by the imperial house, although, as Cassius Dio tells us, Septimius Severus was cremated following his death in York in 211.[29] However, this could have been done to allow the emperor's remains to be more easily transported back to Rome than if they had been a corpse. Caracalla, murdered in Rome in 215, was also cremated, but this was probably because his body had to be quickly removed for burial to avoid the risk of it being publicly mutilated.

At York, some evidence for the cremation process was provided by the discovery (in 1952) of what was interpreted as the site of an *ustrina*, or crematorium, on the corner of Trentholme Drive and Mount Vale, i.e. close to the main Roman approach road from the south-west.[30] Burnt debris up to 0.40m thick was found spread over a radius of about 10m. It consisted of charred wood, fragments of burnt human and animal bone, coal and coal ash, iron nails, pot sherds, pieces of glass and fragments of iron and copper alloy objects. Any structures from which this material derived may have been sited closer to the road, although they would not have been anything permanent – just temporary pyres (*rogi*) composed of timber and other flammable materials. The artefacts in the debris were interpreted as parting gifts placed with the bodies by the mourners before the pyres were lit – just as Cassius Dio describes happened at Septimius Severus's cremation. Being close to the roadside, the pyres must have made a rather grim sight for travellers to say nothing of the nuisance caused by the noxious smoke emitted from them. A use of the crematorium in the mid- to late second century is suggested since the latest of four coins found in the debris is dated to 177 – 8.

Except for a few excavated in recent times, details of most of the cremation burials from Roman York are rather sparse. In the pre-modern era, priority was placed on recovering the pottery and other artefacts rather than the cremated bone itself or any other organic materials, such as flowers or herbs, of which traces might have survived. However, it seems clear that part of the funerary ritual usually involved separating the cremated bone of the deceased from the pyre debris before its removal to the place of burial. How efficiently this separation was done seems to have varied. In ten of the cremation burial pits at Trentholme Drive, there was burnt material containing fragmentary artefacts, probably collected with the bone

7.2: Fishergate House: early Roman cremation burial with cremation urn (left), flagon and, between them, a glass unguent vessel. (© FAS Heritage)

of the deceased at the pyre site. All five in a group of cremation burials found in the Fishergate cemetery (7.2), four late first-/early second-century and one a little later, contained some burnt material in the form of animal and bird bones, pottery sherds, nails and a melted glass unguent jar.[31] The extent to which the human bone itself was collected for burial also seems to have varied. Three cremation burials at 1–3 Driffield Terrace produced 723g, 1,237g and 1,300g of burnt bone, whereas a weight of 1,600–2,000g is considered normal for a cremated human body today. This phenomenon of short weight in Roman cremations is, however, well documented elsewhere in Britain and finds no ready explanation, although it is possible that some part of the remains was given a form of disposal that did not involve burial.

For transportation from the crematorium and then burial, the burnt remains were usually placed in a vessel of some sort. At Trentholme Drive, and elsewhere in York, ceramic jars, no different from cooking pots, were usually used as cremation urns. Occasionally, there was some sort of lid or stopper for the urn. A cremation found at the top of The Mount was in an urn sealed up with lead and then inverted on a flat stone in the burial pit.[32] Sometimes ceramic vessels other than the standard jar might be used. They include a wine amphora, found in a burial on land now part of The Mount School.[33] The amphora had been cut in two for the insertion of the cremated remains, probably in a bag, before the break was sealed up. This is a very unusual burial as Roman amphorae are otherwise known only (and in small numbers) in burials in the south-east of England.

York has produced two examples of glass vessels used for cremated remains, one of which was a cylindrical green bottle, originally sealed with lead, containing the remains of Corellia Optata, found with her tombstone in The Mount cemetery in 1861 (5.6; 5.24).[34] The other vessel, a jar with a lid, was found somewhere on Clifton in 1871.[35] Also known from York are a few lead vessels, or 'ossuaria', containing cremated remains, including one from the railway station cemetery with an inscribed dedication to Ulpia Felicissima, aged 8 years, by her parents Felix and Andronica (7.3).[36] Boxes and bags may have been used to contain cremation burials on occasions, but do not survive in the ground. For example, at Driffield Terrace the pit shown under excavation in 7.4 had no evidence for a container for the burnt bone, burnt fragments of an Ebor Ware flagon and a samian bowl and other charred debris.[37] However, the small pit was typical in form and dimension of what was usually used for cremation burials in being just sufficiently large for the contents. An exception in terms of size is a cremation burial, found in Dringhouses, in which the burnt bone and pyre debris were interred in a large cist constructed of ceramic tiles bearing Ninth Legion stamps, which suggest an early date.[38]

(*Above left*) 7.3: Drawing of a lead ossuarium dedicated to Ulpia Felicissima, who lived for 8 years and 11 months, by Ulpius Felix and Andronica, her parents. Height: 0.31m. (After Benson, 1911)

(*Above right*) 7.4: Cremation burial (probably late second-century) accompanied by sherds of broken and burnt pottery vessels under excavation at 1 – 3 Driffield Terrace. (© York Archaeological Trust)

Inhumation

That inhumation of the body unburnt is a more frequently recorded form of Roman burial than cremation in York reflects the sharp increase in population after the mid-second century when this custom was gradually becoming more popular throughout the Roman world. Nonetheless, cremation continued to be practised until the end of the fourth century. The reasons for the replacement of cremation with inhumation in the Roman world are complex and related to changes in ideas about burial and its rituals, in actions, processes and utterances, which are not easily understood. However, one can envisage that almost every aspect of the treatment of the dead would have drawn on well-established traditions to ensure that their polluting power to draw the living after them was negated and that they were safely transferred to the next world. Any particular rationale for the rituals involved may have been long lost, but the community would have demanded that they were properly executed and in their execution shared values were reinforced and reassurance was given to those suffering from loss of a loved one. What we see with the growing popularity of inhumation is an unusual example of a major change in one aspect of the ritual around death. This presumably occurred because, even if only gradually, that part of the ritual involving cremation was no longer regarded as appropriate for the treatment of the dead or for the reassurance of the living.

It may simply be that inhumation came to be regarded as a gentler, more respectful way of laying the deceased to rest than cremation,[39] but another way of looking at the change may, perhaps, be found by considering the religious context. Not only did the Roman practice of inhumation have its origins in the eastern empire, but from the same source there came ideas that offered people a more intimate relationship with the divine and a firmer promise of eternal life than they had had in traditional religion. The York evidence has already been cited for the death and rebirth cults of Mithras and Serapis. Alongside a desire for a new relationship with the divine should we, perhaps, see a desire for a closer relationship with the spirits of the dead that would allow them to have a greater presence in the community of the living? Cremation may have released the soul from the shackles of the body, but it more-or-less completely removed the body itself from the world, whereas inhumation kept the dead in their community in a form from which rebirth and a renewed intimacy might appear more feasible.

The graves for Roman inhumation burials at York were usually simple bath-shaped pits just large enough to contain the remains of the deceased. However, there are examples of graves dug deeper than was strictly necessary for the body and any coffin or grave goods. None is known at Trentholme Drive or other more recently excavated cemeteries. But it was 2m from ground level to the top of a barrel-vaulted tomb built of tiles in the railway station cemetery.[40] A remarkable survival in this grave was the auburn hair in 'ringlets' belonging to a female who was interred in a gypsum-filled wooden coffin. A grave at Peasholme Green, in which there was a lead coffin, was 2.13m deep, whilst a grave at Clifton Fields, found in 1702, was apparently dug as much as 3m deep below the then ground level.[41] These unusually deep graves are known elsewhere in Roman Britain and may be some sort of expression of the status of the deceased, whose heirs could afford the extra effort to ensure he or she was put well on the way to Mother Earth and the next world.

At the other end of the spectrum were what Raine describes in the railway station cemetery as 'two *putei* or pits used for the burial of slaves or people of mean repute', which were 3m to 4m deep, 5m to 6m wide, and 10m long.[42] Whether they had been 'of mean repute', whatever that might mean, or not, the deceased had apparently been treated with little respect. Raine reports that the corpses had been dumped in large numbers with only a thin layer of earth between each one. One would like to know a lot more about these unusual features, but they sound like the '*puticoli*' described by the poet Horace (65 – 8 BC) in the common burial ground for the poor at Rome,[43] although at York they might instead represent hasty burial of victims of an epidemic of disease.

Many, if not most, inhumations were probably buried in coffins, of which the simplest type was made of wood held together with iron nails (7.5). These were usually ignored by the early antiquaries, but more recent discoveries have shown they were indeed common. A variant on the standard wooden coffin was the sort of chamber found in a grave near Holgate railway bridge, in which the sides were lined with oak planks, 1m to 1.2m long, driven into the ground, to which horizontal

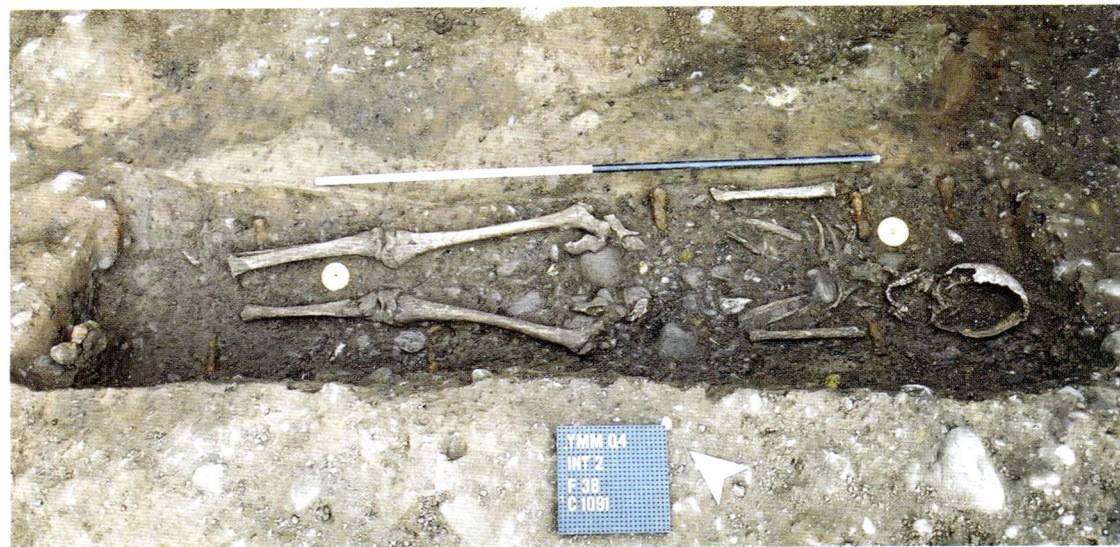

7.5: Child inhumation burial from The Mount cemetery (Mill Mount 2004), with iron nails from the wooden coffin surviving. Scale 1m. (© FAS Heritage)

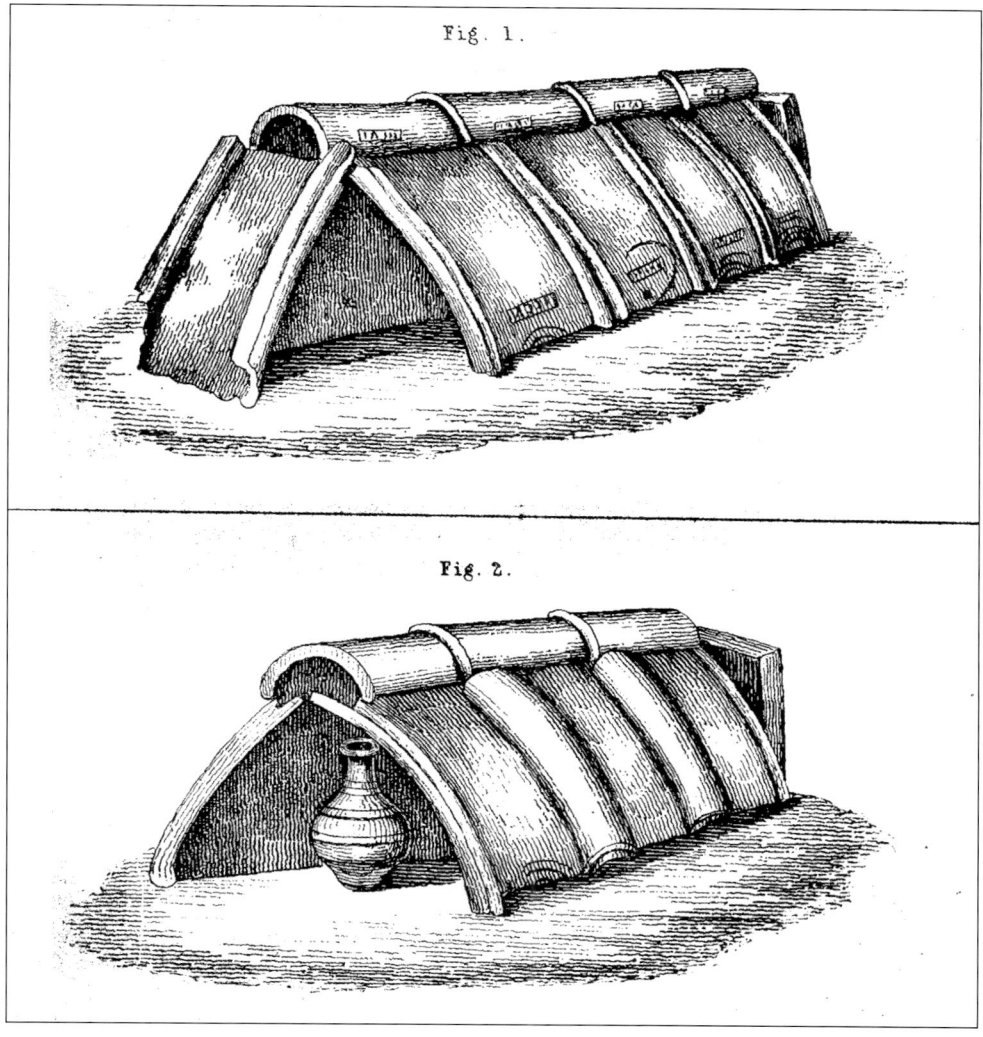

7.6: Tile cists from Roman cemeteries in York. (After Wellbeloved, 1842)

oak boards had been attached. Boards were also laid at the top and base of the grave.[44] Another form of tomb structure is suggested by the record of a pit lined with stone slabs in the railway station cemetery.[45] Also recorded in this cemetery were communal grave pits divided up with upright slabs.[46] Cists for inhumation burials made from roof tiles are well-known in York (fourteen examples), occurring in all the main cemetery zones (7.6). They usually existed as a sort of tent-like structure that covered the deceased and any grave goods. Tile stamps of the Sixth Legion in eight cases suggests the custom of cist-burial was largely current during the mid-second to early third centuries. Similar cists are rarely found in Roman

Britain except on other military and urban sites. More substantial than these cist-burials was a brick-built tomb (for a wooden coffin) found at the old station that had a flagged floor and walls 0.60m high to the springing of a vaulted roof.[47]

Recorded more often than wooden coffins before recent times were those made of lead and stone – sometimes referred to as 'sarcophagi' – of which about thirty-five and 100 (nine inscribed), respectively, have been found in York. In the burial with the famous hair in the railway station cemetery, both types were combined. A lead coffin, or perhaps more accurately a lining, was found inside a stone coffin – hence good preservation conditions in a sealed environment.[48] There are also examples of lead coffins with a wood lining, e.g. from Peasholme Green and the old station,[49] and of wooden coffins with a lead lining, e.g. at Clifton Fields and in the railway station cemetery.[50] There are more stone and lead coffins from York than from anywhere else in Roman Britain (apart from two other Yorkshire examples, there are only three other inscribed stone coffins from the whole province). This is partly because there was a ready supply both of suitable stone, millstone grit, and of lead, which passed through York on its way from the Pennines to the continent. Equally important, however, Roman York had people from the sort of social and cultural *milieu*, common elsewhere in the Roman world but less so in Britain, in which burial in a stone or lead coffin was a preferred means of burying the dead, people who were, at the same time, wealthy enough to be able to afford one.

Stone coffins (which on average weigh about 2 tons) were usually simple oblong blocks that had been hollowed out, probably at the quarry, before transportation to York. There is sometimes a hole in the base that allowed fluid arising from decay of the corpse to escape. Their heavy lids typically resemble low-pitched house roofs. Find spots of both stone and lead coffins in the York area are fairly well scattered, although a large number of them were found at the (present) railway station: thirty-seven stone and fourteen lead examples. Stone coffins have also been found in the immediate hinterland such as, for example, at Naburn and Nunthorpe, south of York (1.1; 2.4), and Appletree Farm to the east, which also produced a lead coffin (2.4, 3).[51] These were probably used for members of the elite who chose to be buried on their rural estates rather than in the town cemetery.

In both the stone and lead coffins, and in the tile cists, one often finds a deposit of gypsum, a white hydrated form of calcium sulphate, commonly known as Plaster of Paris (7.7). In a few cases gypsum completely encased the deceased, although there is usually much less and sometimes merely a token amount covering of the body. There are more than forty burials with at least some gypsum in them known from York, and others from its hinterland. Where the body is completely encased, it has sometimes been thought that this represented some sort of embalming exercise. In turn, this led to a suggestion that it was a specifically Christian attempt

7.7: Millstone grit sarcophagus from The Mount cemetery (Mill Mount 2004), showing the layer of gypsum over the human remains. (© FAS Heritage)

to preserve the body uncorrupted for judgement day. However, it is now clear that gypsum occurs in burials made long before there was any Christian community in York, the first being late second- or early third-century, such as, for example, that of an adolescent from The Mount cemetery (Mill Mount 2004).[52] The significance of gypsum for the Romans may have arisen from the fact that, when it is mixed with water to make a paste, there is an exothermic reaction causing the solution to heat up to $c.150°C$ as it sets. After setting hard, the material cools down. This process may have been seen as mysterious and in some way symbolic of the consumption and purification of the dead before their passage to the next world.

Organisation of the cemeteries

As far as the internal organisation of the cemeteries of Roman York is concerned, there is little archaeological evidence for the discrete plots enclosed by ditches, walls, etc., that have been found elsewhere in Britain. However, in the railway station cemetery it is reported that graves were arranged in 'walks' with markers in the form of small blocks of sandstone, about 0.60m long, and occasionally heaps of cobbles, at the head or foot of the grave.[53] In addition, somewhere in the railway station cemetery there was apparently a zone dedicated solely to cremation burials with what appeared to be straight boundary dividing it from an area of inhumations that had perhaps been maintained by a hedge or fence.[54]

We have little information on the alignment of graves from cemetery zones disturbed before recent times. However, where the information is available, the overwhelming majority of graves of all periods (including those that are undatable) are aligned north-west/south-east, east-west or north-east/south-west, although there is no clear pattern for which end of the grave the head of the deceased was placed. Graves aligned north-south are very unusual. To some extent, grave alignment may be due to the influence of the main Roman approach roads in proximity to the cemeteries in that they provided prominent topographical features in relation to which ordered plots could be easily laid out. However, we may also be seeing the influence of the sun's passage through the heavens as one end of so many graves lies somewhere between the points on the horizon at which the sun rises at the summer and winter solstices (furthest points to north-east and south-east). Digging a grave to align with the rising sun may have been seen as having some symbolic significance in respect of the eternal cycle of life and death. Circular features carved on several of the York tombstones, including that of the foster child Hyllus (7.8), are very similar to a spoked wheel but probably represent the sun.[55] A wheel-like sun symbol had a long history in Britain and in the wider Celtic world going back before the Roman period.[56]

As far as the extent of intercutting of graves is concerned, which would in turn tell us something further about the extent of grave markers, we again have little information except for sites excavated recently where practice seems to have varied. In the south-western cemetery at 1 – 3 Driffield Terrace, Trentholme Drive and the adjacent site at Newington Hotel, largely in use in the second and third centuries, there seems to be have been little compunction about digging a new grave into an earlier one within perhaps quite a short period of time (7.9).

Cemeteries and burials 243

7.8: Sun symbol at the head of the tombstone of Hyllus, the foster child. (Yorkshire Museum)

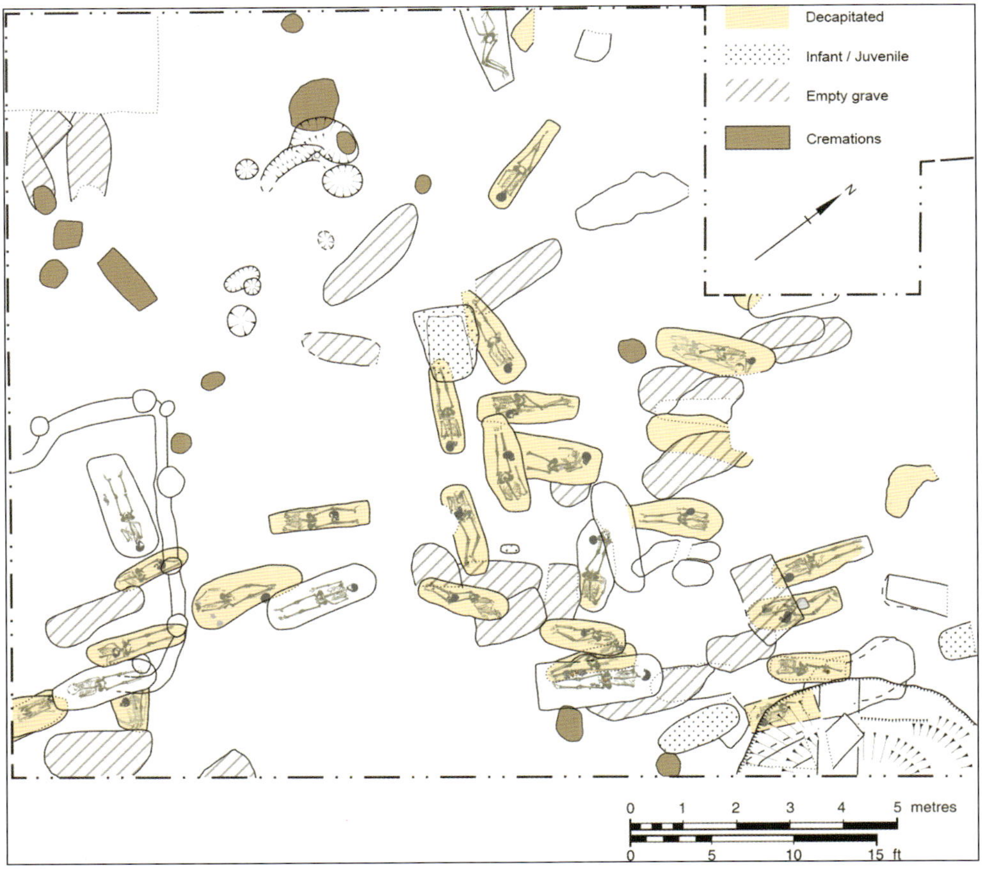

7.9: Plan of the Roman burials at 1 – 3 Driffield Terrace. (© York Archaeological Trust)

Presumably there were no clear markers that would have alerted grave-diggers to previous interments. Elsewhere, greater discipline seems to have been exercised involving regular rows of burials and minimal intercutting, perhaps because of the sort of markers noted above in the railway station cemetery. Regularity of alignment and absence of intercutting became the norm in the late Roman period, as at 35 – 41 Blossom Street or Hungate.[57]

Within the grave it is most common to find the body laid out supine with the arms either by the sides or with one or both arms across the waist. There are very few examples in York's Roman cemeteries of bodies laid out, like the early examples at Dringhouses, in a crouched position, although a few others have their legs 'flexed' (i.e. slightly bent) which may have been a nod towards the pre-Roman tradition. Bodies buried prone are rare. They may be the result of genuine mistakes, but they were perhaps of individuals who were criminals or outcasts or for some reason had to be prevented from rising from the grave to haunt the living.[58] Nevertheless, in whatever way they were laid out, the evidence usually suggests that care had been exercised to ensure the body of the deceased was treated with decency and respect. This was even the case at Driffield Terrace, in spite of many burials taking place here after execution. On being brought for burial from the site of execution, the heads were usually placed by the feet or between the knees, although occasionally they were in the correct anatomical position (7.10), but there is no suggestion of any mutilation of the deceased.

It is a moot point as to whether the dead of Roman York were usually or only rarely buried clothed, because no items of clothing have survived except as impressions in some of the gypsum casts. However, it is quite common to find the nails from footwear in graves suggesting either that the deceased were wearing their shoes or had them

7.10: 1 – 3 Driffield Terrace: burial of a decapitated male whose skull has been placed between his knees. (© York Archaeological Trust)

Cemeteries and burials 245

to hand for their journey to the next world. The existence of burials in which jewellery items, such as earrings, bracelets or necklaces (discussed on pp 196–9), were recorded as worn by the deceased would suggest that they were also clothed.

Funerary monuments

The most common type of tomb visible above ground was probably the sort of simple barrel-vaulted brick structure containing a stone coffin (with skeleton intact) that still survives below the ground floor at 104 The Mount (found in 1807) (1.1, 11; 7.11).[59] It would have stood immediately to the south-east of the main Roman approach road from the south-west, just below the top of The Mount. Another similar vaulted structure, with a lead coffin within, was found on the opposite side of the Roman road in 1769.[60] The remains of what was probably another, of the second quarter of the third century, surviving only as a square foundation, was found in the excavations at 35 – 41 Blossom Street close to the road, but nearer to town (1.1, 10).[61] These tombs may originally have displayed memorial tablets that have since disappeared.

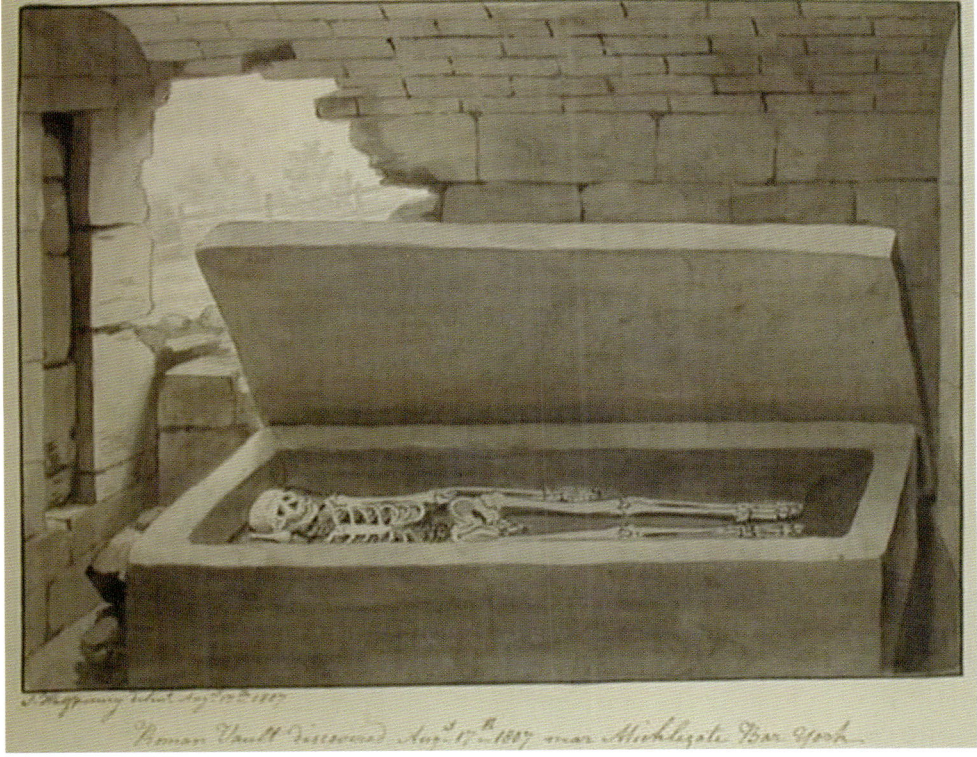

7.11: 'Roman vault discovered 17 August 1807 near Micklegate Bar' [at 104 The Mount], by Joseph Halfpenny. (R243, © York Museums Trust)

A small number of burials were dignified by a more substantial monument. On occasions, stone coffins, especially those bearing an inscription, presumably intended for public inspection, would have been placed above ground in a mausoleum, a small 'house' with internal niches of which many examples are known elsewhere in the Roman world. Another type of monument may be suggested by a large (1.14m x 0.74m x 0.28m) millstone grit slab with an inscription commemorating the centurion Titus Flavius Flavinus, found in Rawcliffe Lane north-west of the city (1.1, 1).[62] One can envisage that, located near one of the main approach roads from the north-west, it was set into the sort of tower-like monument standing in similar prominent locations elsewhere in the empire such as, for example, the so-called 'Tower of Scipio' outside Tarragona in Spain. Other tomb monuments of some architectural pretension would seem to be implied by various pieces of Roman sculpture from York (some described above, p 227) including the Greek sphinx from The Mount and the lions from the railway station cemetery and the minster.

There are thirty Roman tombstones from York, some, like Julia Velva's more-or-less complete, others less so, and some surviving only as fragments. They exist (or existed) as monolithic slabs standing up to about 1.80m high, almost all of millstone grit. In addition, there are five inscribed tablets that would have been set into other sorts of monument. These tombstones and tablets, like the inscribed sarcophagi, probably all (except for two early Roman examples) date to the late second or early third century. We can be fairly sure about this because of the style of lettering and use of words in the inscriptions and, where present, the character of relief decoration, including the dress and coiffure of any figures.

Of the surviving names of the deceased on Roman York's funerary monuments (tombstones, tablets and coffins) to which one can add the inscribed lead ossuarium, the majority are female (twenty). Of these we are told that three were wives, another three were both wives and mothers, one was just a mother, and six were daughters. Of the males we are told that one was a husband, one was a father, one was a father-in-law, five were sons, and one was a foster child. Information on occupational status is provided for nine, of which five were military and four civilians, the latter as either a decurion (three) or a *sevir augustalis* (one).

There are sixteen monuments for which we know the name of the dedicator and there are two names (parents of the deceased) on the lead ossuarium. Two dedicators (both male), including Aurelius Mercurialis on Julia Velva's tombstone, refer to themselves solely as heirs, and we can assume Caecilius Musicus was Aelia Severa's heir. All the others are family members. Of the four women, two identify themselves as mother and heir, one as a mother, and one as a wife. On the male side four are fathers, five husbands and fathers, and one a son-in-law. Three dedicators also give their status as soldiers of some sort, one as decurion, and Caecilius Musicus was a freedman. Although the York sample is small, patterns of dedication correspond to those found empire-wide with an emphasis on the nuclear family between whom feelings of affection and sense of duty (also ties of inheritance) were strongest rather than more distant kin or other members of an extended household.[63] The husband/wife split corresponds to the imperial pattern as a whole in which husband to wife dedications were more common than wife to husband.[64]

Inscribed tomb monuments kept the name and identity of the deceased in the memory of the living and provided a focus for devotions by their family and associates. They were also intended to express and advertise the status of that family and its prominent role in local society to the world at large. It is in this context that we may consider, for example, the tombstone of Flavia Augustina and her two infant children set up by her husband, a veteran of the Sixth Legion (5.8).[65] Augustina died aged 39 years, 7 months and 11 days, and the children were both under 2 years old – perhaps all three were victims of an epidemic. The tombstone depicts four persons, two adults and two children, but these children are not infants. They appear to be about 11 or 12 years old. For all we know there were other children in the family surviving and others were no doubt anticipated, as and when Augustina's husband Aeresius Saenus married again or adopted children. With this tombstone he is not only mourning his wife and the two infants, but he is also making a statement about his dynasty which, he wishes to assure us, will continue into the future and remain a force to be reckoned with. The sponsors of tombstones might also emphasise their status by the way the deceased is presented to the world in the sort of scene in relief on Julia Velva's tombstone. Their hairstyles and dress place the women, in particular, in the mainstream of Roman fashion as espoused by the imperial house. Depictions, however, of the dining rooms in their houses and of their furniture and other material possessions, were also important components of the message the tombstones might convey about the good and happy lives led by privileged members of the community.

The distribution of York's Roman tombstones and inscribed sarcophagi is, to some extent, a product of the pattern of suburban building development in York since about 1800. But nonetheless, where their original site can be determined, it seems that they were usually set up in prominent positions adjacent to the Roman approach roads and often on high ground where, perhaps, elite families or other high status groups, such as the military, had their private burial grounds. Julia Velva's tombstone and that of Candida Barita, found on the same spot near the top of The Mount, are good cases in point (1.1, 12; 2.4, 5).

Although it is likely that many of York's tombstones have been lost, they were probably not numerous in the first place and were very much the exception rather than the rule as monuments to the dead. This was partly because they were expensive bespoke items that were beyond the pocket of most families except the wealthiest. However, they were probably rare also because only certain families or groups in Roman York wished, or thought it appropriate, to have a tombstone to commemorate their dead in the first place. The sponsors may have come originally from parts of the empire where a tombstone was a more generally accepted mode of commemoration than it was in Britain. Alternatively, they were, like Aurelius Mercurialis perhaps, people who wished to advertise their family's social advancement to the citizen body. Aurelius Super's wife may have gone to the expense of an inscribed sarcophagus for the same reason (3.11). Caecilius Musicus, responsible for the sarcophagus of Aelia Severa (5.4), had, as a former slave, even more reason to be proud of his new position in society. After Caracalla's *Constitutio* of 212, being a Roman citizen became a less important mark of social status and this may be one reason for the declining popularity of funerary monuments.[66]

Grave goods

Whilst above ground monuments made for clear and visible distinctions between the last resting places of the deceased in Roman York, there were also distinctions, if only visible at the time of interment, in the grave goods, objects deliberately deposited alongside the bodies. Today we rarely place any objects in our burials (other than a coffin) believing that there is a measure of equality in death that should be respected. However, in Roman Britain people did not necessarily subscribe to that view and might choose objects to 'furnish' a grave and assist the dead in their passage to the next world whilst, at the same time, making a statement of some sort about themselves as part of the burial ritual.

As dating York's Roman graves closely is often difficult, so too is it also difficult to assess chronological patterns in the extent of the deposition of grave goods. However, whilst graves were furnished throughout the Roman period, of those that are datable most appear to be second- to early third-century. There appear to be differences between cemetery zones, probably used over much the same time period, that are difficult to interpret and must, in part, be due to the circumstances of recovery. For example, there is a large collection of grave goods that was recovered in the nineteenth and early twentieth century from the railway station, but the antiquaries of the time were largely interested in collecting artefacts rather than studying the burials as a whole, and so what proportion of them had grave goods is far from clear. Nevertheless, there probably is a real distinction to be drawn between the railway station cemetery and some of the others, especially Trentholme Drive. For example, jewellery was often found in burials at the railway station but is hardly known at Trentholme Drive. In general terms, there is quite a wide range of grave goods from Roman York's burials, although there are few that could be called at all richly furnished.

In my database there are few cremations with grave goods. At Trentholme Drive, only three (out of about fifty) cremation burials had another pot alongside the urn. Elsewhere, only a few were a little more generously furnished. For example, found on The Mount, a late second-century cremation burial in a jar had a beaker placed in the neck and was accompanied by two smaller beakers.[67] At Blue Bridge Lane, one of the cremation burials had an urn accompanied by two (one burnt) glass unguent bottles. Another had, besides the urn, a flagon and a (burnt) glass unguent bottle. Examples of other sorts of artefacts in cremation burials are almost unknown, although an urn found at the old station was accompanied by a coin (undated).[68]

About 20 per cent of inhumations in my database had artefacts deliberately buried in the grave, including items that were worn on the body. But this figure is probably too high as many unfurnished burials were ignored by the early antiquaries. The most common type of grave good – as in the case of cremations – is a pottery vessel, usually a jar, although the beaker was also popular. There are also a few examples of flagons. Several burials from Trentholme Drive have these. Whilst a single vessel is usual, there are a few examples of multiples. For example, a late second-century burial from Driffield Terrace was accompanied by three small beakers and a fourth that was broken (7.12). A mid-third-century burial from the railway station cemetery had three beakers.[69] Rather rarer than burials

7.12: Burial (4113) with three small Nene Valley pottery jars and a broken grey ware beaker at 1 – 3 Driffield Terrace. Scale: 0.30m and 0.20m. (© York Archaeological Trust)

with pottery vessels are those with glass vessels, but there are examples from the railway station cemetery including a burial in a lead coffin accompanied by four glass flasks.[70] The purpose and significance of these accessory vessels have been discussed in the previous chapter and need not be repeated here except to note that they could have contained actual food and drink, which has not survived, or were just a symbolic representation of sustenance for the deceased.

Jewellery worn by the deceased has been discussed above but is also found in graves unworn alongside the body, although notionally, perhaps, intended for wear in the next world. Unusual items used as grave furnishing for females in Roman York's inhumations include the ivory handles for a fan of which no remains survived, although perhaps made of silk, found in the railway station cemetery.[71] A small copper alloy perfume box with an inlaid and enamelled lid was found with a burial outside Monk Bar.[72] Another likely grave good is the balsamarium in the shape of an infant bust described above (p 195). A few of York's people, at least, were going to arrive in the next world smelling sweet.

Chapter 8

A Roman lady from York

The Roman period in York's history is, of course, very distant from us in time and the remains of it that we have, although apparently abundant, are, in fact, only fragments of a far greater whole. It is from these fragments, however, that archaeologists attempt to reconstruct the appearance of the place and find out who lived there and what their lives were like. In words and pictures, I have tried to give the reader some of my own ideas about these matters.

I have described the development of the legionary fortress from a base for conquest of the north to the seat of a permanent garrison, and that of the civilian settlement from one dependent on the army to an independent self-governing community, in effect a town, with the status of a provincial capital. I have suggested that it was in about the year 160 that the *canabae* around the fortress were supplemented by a new settlement south-west of the River Ouse. It seems clear that, subsequently, the size of the civilian population in all parts of Roman York rose rapidly. Although most people in the region, as a whole, remained working on the land, as they had from time immemorial, some of them probably became inhabitants of the new town. That townsfolk also came from other parts of the world is strikingly suggested by the scientific examination of the human remains.

A cosmopolitan atmosphere, also implied by a few of the funerary monuments (p 173–4), prevailed in the late Antonine to Severan periods when the legionary fortress was further dignified with new buildings to add to those of the reign of Trajan, although the principal focus of new construction in York was the town. Befitting a place that would attain the highest rank as a provincial capital, we find evidence for some grand public buildings and fine houses. Whether there were also town defences unfortunately remains uncertain, but in any event, one gets an impression that in its built environment and infrastructure York, if on a smaller scale, could hold its head up alongside London and other provincial capitals without too much of an inferiority complex.

It was in this same period that *Eboracum's* economy flourished to a greater extent, in both manufacturing and trade, than it had previously or would in the later Roman period. As far as trade is concerned, this is when the quantity of imports was at its greatest and the range of sources at its most diverse. We see this most clearly, perhaps, in the pottery (pp 154–6), which may stand, up to a point, for other commodities that have not survived. But there is also evidence from other artefacts and the remains of food. Links with Gaul and the Rhineland were particularly strong, but other commodities, not only olive oil and pots but the likes of cinnabar, semi-precious stones, glass vessels and silk arrived, if by circuitous routes rather than directly, from Italy, North Africa, the near east and even perhaps, in the case of the silk, from China. Imported goods satisfied the demands and tastes of sophisticated and wealthy consumers, whether soldiers, officials or private individuals, whose wealth would have derived largely from land ownership. Imported also were ideas about art, literature, religion and natural philosophy. The work of leading thinkers of the classical canon such as Pythagoras and Plato was probably well-known at least to a privileged few.

There are certainly aspects of Roman York that set it apart from most other Roman places in Britain, but in other ways it was not so radically different. Urban development and rising prosperity occurred all over the western empire in the second century and is manifested in the archaeological record in much the same way as it is in York. This takes us back to Edward Gibbon in the late eighteenth century, who wrote about the happiness and prosperity of the world under the first two Antonine emperors (p 64). Although I would not want to defend every aspect of the imperial approach to government, there is, nonetheless, I suggest a reason to cut those emperors and the early Severi some slack because of their success in maintaining peace.

As far as Britain is concerned, we do hear of episodes of conflict on the northern frontier in the second half of the second century and early in the third. There may have been others unreported in what are, after all, very limited sources, but on the frontier is where they stayed. We can be pretty certain that hostile hordes did not, as Ian Richmond once supposed, get as far as York and tear down the legionary fortress defences. As we can see only too well in our own time, peace brings prosperity and all sorts of other benefits, whereas war is destructive, impedes economic progress, constrains cultural development, forces people from their homes, brings psychopathic and sadistic elements in society to the fore, and falsely dignifies their values and achievements as heroic. Unfortunately for the people of the Roman Empire, after the death of Severus Alexander in 235, war with external enemies and internal strife between claimants to the imperial crown is what was visited on them to an ever-increasing degree. In 233, hostile Germanic tribespeople, the Alamanni and Franks, crossed the Rhine. We hear of further Germanic attacks in 253 – 8 and 275 – 6. Meanwhile in the Balkans, in Moesia Inferior (Bulgaria), the Romans were defeated by the Goths and Scythians in 251 at the Battle of Abritus and Emperor Decius was killed. In the east, the Romans faced the rising power of the Sassanid Persian empire, leading to a defeat in 253 and again in 260 when Emperor Valerian was captured. Some of what are probably the consequences of these conflicts for civilian life, even in parts of the empire some distance away, like Britain, can be readily seen in the archaeological record. At York, population decline is suggested by fewer burials, the settled area begins to contract, the ditches defining the field systems around it are allowed to silt up, there is little evidence for new construction, trade with the empire overseas dries up and, for perhaps a thirty-year period, little new currency arrives. Opportunities for York folk to avail themselves of the riches the Roman Empire had to offer would never be quite as good again after the first twenty to thirty years of the third century.

When one looks at the changed political and military circumstances in which the Roman Empire found itself by the mid-third century, one is drawn to conclude that Julia Velva was fortunate in living her fifty (or about fifty) years when she did. For her descendants, times would be a good deal more uncertain if not dangerous. Moreover, she was also fortunate in living as long as fifty years at a time when average life expectancy was a good deal less. A long life can be in one's genes, but a good diet and healthy lifestyle helps. By being a member of the elite, Julia Velva would probably have eaten well even when poor harvests and murrains caused many to starve. Roman women did not usually seek to stay healthy by going to a gym, although a few may have exercised at the baths. However, Julia Velva presumably had the time to take agreeable walks in her garden or on her country estate if she wished. When in town I would think it quite likely she lived in the Bishophill area, where good evidence for fine houses has been found (pp 116–20). Here she would have had the benefit of clean air away from the noxious fumes of the smiths and tanners down by the river bridge, and could avail herself of clean water from wells or street fountains.

Besides taking a walk now and then, how did a woman of Roman York like Julia Velva spend her time? Because she probably had slaves to wait on her, she never had to do the cooking, shopping or washing, and she could call on plenty of assistance both with her toilette and with any children. She may have done a bit of spinning and needlework, but was unlikely to have been under much constraint to treat either task as other than a hobby. Socialising with friends at the baths or around the dinner table probably featured a good deal in her life, especially if her husband was a man of consequence who wished to entertain on any scale (8.1). In view of her lifespan, Julia Velva may well have derived amusement and pleasure from more than one husband in her life. One would like to think so. In turn she may

8.1: An artist's impression of a Roman banquet by Wayne Laughlin. (© Gloucester City Council)

have given pleasure herself with a beautiful face, an elegant figure, or because, like the goddess Venus, as described by Virgil, she gave off 'a scent of heaven breathed from the divine hair of her head'.[1] Then again, she may have beguiled with her conversation or accomplishments as a dancer or musician. Whether Julia Velva was able to read with any facility or not we cannot know, of course. But the works of many Roman authors were surely readily available to her and would have given her a pleasant and stimulating occupation if of an intellectual turn of mind as well as providing subjects for discussion at those dinner parties.

Of course, Julia Velva may, in fact, have been tone deaf, illiterate and a bit of an air head. But whether she was brainy or dim, would we think she was good company and nice to know? One would like to think that, on the one hand, this proto-Yorkshire woman had many of the good qualities of her descendants in being friendly, good-humoured, kind, practical and plain-speaking. On the other hand, as a member of a small elite, surrounded by much larger numbers of the lower orders, and very jealous of her status, she may have been arrogant and narrow-minded. As she grew older and outlived her friends, and perhaps became arthritic and sickly, she may have become embittered by loneliness. We shall never know the truth, but I am grateful to Julia Velva, and to Aurelius Mercurialis who set up her tombstone, for giving me a starting point for so many stories about Roman York. May God rest their souls.

In the Roman world, visiting the burial places of one's ancestors was considered a sacred duty and, as I have already mentioned, there were special occasions in the year when the living gathered to acknowledge and pay respect to them. Failure to do this was considered a serious breach of trust and risked the return of the dead as ghosts to bring bad luck to the living and even their sudden demise. For people like Julia Velva and Aurelius Mercurialis, whose tombstone suggests a particular pride in their family's place in local society, the fear of an end to their dynasty with no one to care for its graves must surely have weighed heavily on their minds. Yet dynasties do come to an end and there came a time when the tombstone stood ignored and unvisited by the roadside, the graves around it untended by any grieving relatives. Fortunately, however, instead of meeting the fate of many other Roman tombstones in York in being defaced by vandals or iconoclasts or being taken away to repair a building or simply smashed up for hardcore, the stone just fell over, face-down, on to the ground and lay there under the turf until found again in 1922. We can now, in a sense, resume where the last of Julia Velva's line downed tools and, in the Yorkshire Museum, once more pay due respect to a remarkable reminder of a very special period in York's history.

Notes

Abbreviations
YORYM precedes catalogue numbers for items in the Yorkshire Museum collections

RCHME's *Eburacum* = Volume 1 of the RCHME Inventory of the Monuments of the City of York (1962). Burials are referred to by page reference, paragraph and number

YAJ — *Yorkshire Archaeological Journal*
YPSR — *Yorkshire Philosophical Society Annual Report*
YPS Comms — *Yorkshire Philosophical Society Communications* (bound with YPSR but different pagination)

Translations
Quotations from or references to original sources are based on the following translations.

Historia Augusta. Trans. Birley, A. 1976. *Lives of the Later Caesars* (Penguin Classics)

Ammianus Marcellinus. *The Later Roman Empire*: Hamilton, W. (trans.) and Wallace-Hadrill A. (introduction) 1986 (Penguin Classics)

Apuleius. *The Golden Ass:* trans. with introduction, Walsh, P.G. 1994 (Oxford World's Classics)

Cassius Dio. *Roman History* IX: trans. Cary, E. 1982 (Loeb Classical Library)

Juvenal. *The Sixteen Satires*: trans. Green, P. 1974 (Penguin Classics)

Livy. *The Early History of Rome*: de Selincourt, A. (trans.) and Ogilvie, R.M. (introduction) 1960/1971 (Penguin Classics)

Martial. *Epigrams*: trans. Michie, J. 1978 (Penguin Classics)

Ovid. *Metamorphoses*: trans. with introduction, Innes, M.M. 1955 (Penguin Classics)

Ovid. Cosmetics for ladies, in *The Love Poems*: trans. Melville, A.D. 1990 (Oxford World's Classics)

Petronius. *The Satyricon*, trans. Sullivan, J.P. 1986 (Penguin Classics)

Plato. *Phaedo: The Last Days of Socrates*, trans. Tredennick, H. 1954 (Penguin Classics)

Plato. *The Republic*: trans. Cornford, F.M. 1941 (Oxford University Press)

Pliny. *Natural History*: trans. with introduction, Healy, J.F. 1991 (Penguin Classics)

Tacitus. The *Agricola* and The *Germania*: trans. with introduction, Mattingly, H., revised Handford, S.A. 1970 (Penguin Classics)

Tacitus. *Annals of Imperial Rome*: trans. with introduction, Grant, M. 1959 (Penguin Classics)

Tacitus. *Histories*: trans. Wellesley, K. 1964 (Penguin Classics)

Thucydides. *The Peloponnesian War*: trans. with introduction, Warner, R. 1954 (Penguin Classics)

Virgil. *Aeneid*: trans. Jackson Knight, W.F. 1956 (Penguin Classics)

Vitruvius. *On Architecture*: trans. Granger, F. 1931 (Loeb Classical Library)

Chapter 1

1. RIB I, *688*; RCHME's *Eburacum*, 124, *82*; Tufi 1983, 27–8, *42*; Mattern 1989, 727, 799–800
2. Raine 1922
3. Buckland 1988, 239–49
4. RCHME's *Eburacum* 132, *124*
5. Hatt 1986, 391–4
6. RIB I, *682*; RCHME's *Eburacum*, 121, *71*
7. Wild 1968, 194
8. Hatt 1986, 394–7; Mattern 1989, 721
9. Birley 1979, 122
10. Inventory nos 575 (stylus tablet) and 1220 (ink tablet); Birley 1993, 26; 2002, 38
11. The works of Cassius Dio and Herodian and *The Augustan History* are discussed by Birley 1988, 203–06
12. Rivet and Smith 1979, 103–47; Jones and Mattingly 1990, 16–23
13. Rivet and Smith 1979, 150–80; Jones and Mattingly 1990, 23–9
14. Miller 1925; 1928
15. e.g. Kenward and Williams 1979; Hall *et al.* 1980; Kenward *et al.* 1986; Hall and Kenward 1990
16. Planning Policy Guidance Note 16 (Department of the Environment 1990); National Planning Policy Framework (Department of Communities and Local Government 2018)

Chapter 2

1. Atkinson 2003, 11
2. Atkinson 2003, 13
3. Gaunt and Buckland 2003, 21
4. Roskams and Neal 2020
5. Hall and Kenward 1990, 413–4
6. Dormor 2003, 79
7. Howard and Macklin 2003
8. VCHY, 473
9. VCHY, 475
10. Ottaway 2011, 225 (at 38 Piccadilly)
11. Kenward *et al.* 1986, 265
12. Hall *et al.* 1980, 105–11
13. Hall and Kenward 1990, 386–7
14. HAR–1416–8
15. Greig 1979
16. Rivet and Smith 1979, 355–7; Fellows-Jensen 1998
17. *Annals* XII, 32 and 40
18. *Annals* XIV, 37
19. *Histories* III, 45
20. Wacher 1969, 76–81
21. Good introductions to armour and weaponry of the imperial period can be found in Bishop and Coulston 1993 and Feugère 2002
22. Campbell 1984, 77
23. e.g. Cool *et al.* 1995, 1532–33 (one bolt and two balls); Evans 2000, 27–8 (group of balls); YORYM 2011.249–250 (bolts)
24. Fragments of scale armour and mail in Cool *et al.* 1995, 1531–2. An open work hinge and hook for *lorica segmentata* from Miller's 1925 excavations (YORYM 2002.203–4). Fragments of *lorica segmentata* from the minster library in Rogers 2016
25. Campbell 1978, 154
26. RIB I, *685*; RCHME's *Eburacum*, 122, *77*; Tufi 1983, 24–5, *39*; Mattern 1989, 796–7; Tomlin 2018, 231–2
27. RCHME's *Eburacum*, 128, *95*; Tufi 1983, 38–9, *57*
28. Frere 1980
29. RIB I, *673*; RCHME's *Eburacum*, 122, *75*
30. *Agricola*, 17
31. Boon 1972; Knight 2003
32. Mason 2012, 50
33. Pitts and St Joseph 1985, 207–13

34. *de munitionibus castrorum*; Johnson 1983, 27–30
35. Ovid, *Metamorphoses* XI
36. Adam 1989, 10–11
37. RIB I, *2145*
38. Ottaway 1996, 202–6; 1997a
39. RCHME's *Eburacum*, 37
40. RCHME's *Eburacum*, 37; Wenham 1962, 572–3
41. RCHME's *Eburacum*, 37
42. Ottaway 1997b
43. RCHME's *Eburacum*, 37–8; Wenham 1958
44. Ottaway 1996, 205–6
45. Miller 1925, 183
46. Ottaway 1996, 154
47. Ottaway 1996, 187–9
48. Wenham 1962, 557–9; Sumpter and Coll 1977, 68–70
49. Adam 1989, 76–8
50. McComish 2012, 89
51. Wheeler 1964, 12–13
52. Phillips 1995, 33–7
53. Blagg 1995
54. Vitruvius III, 3; Blagg 1995; Phillips 1995, 50
55. Phillips 1995, 50 and 53–4
56. RIB III, *3027*
57. Phillips 1995, 45, 54, 61
58. *Historia Augusta*, Severus, 6
59. Le Bohec 1994, 241–3
60. Phillips 1995, 152–7
61. Allen 1998, 37–8; Charlesworth 1976, 15–16
62. Roman Bath pub: RCHME's *Eburacum*, 42–3; Corder 1933. Church Street: Whitwell 1976. 12–18 Swinegate: Pearson 1990; Monaghan 1997, 1059–64
63. Buckland 1976a, 36
64. Buckland 1976b, 13–4
65. Martial *Epigrams* XII, 48, 7
66. Monaghan 1997, 1059–64
67. Bidwell 1979, 41, note 12
68. RCHME's *Eburacum*, 38
69. Buckland 1976b, 17–18
70. RCHME's *Eburacum*, 44–5. Dean's Park: Miller 1928, 90–4. SW3: Wenham 1962, 553–5. SW5: Sumpter and Coll 1977, 72–3

71. Near Multangular Tower: Miller 1925, 182; RCHME's *Eburacum*, 43. SW3: Wenham 1962, 569–70
72. Ottaway 1996, 198–9
73. Miller 1925, 187; RCHME's *Eburacum*, 35–7
74. North-west gate: RCHME's *Eburacum*, 25; Brinklow 1996. South-east gate: RCHME's *Eburacum*, 35; Stockwell and Marwood 1996
75. RIB I, *665*; RCHME's *Eburacum,* 111, *1*
76. RCHME's *Eburacum*, 12; Ottaway 1996, 247–9
77. RCHME's *Eburacum*, 10–11
78. Radley 1972; Hall *et al.* 1996
79. Dean's Park: RCHME's *Eburacum*, 29. King's Square: Stead 1968; Wenham 1968a
80. RCHME's *Eburacum*, 13; Stead 1958
81. *Natural History* III, 66–7
82. Wellbeloved 1842; RCHME's *Eburacum,* 112, *7*
83. RCHME's *Eburacum*, 12–13; Wenham 1965a; Sumpter and Coll 1977; Ottaway 1996, 247–9
84. RCHME's *Eburacum*, 28
85. SW6: RCHME's *Eburacum*, 22–5. SW5: Wenham 1965a; Coll 1977
86. Ward-Perkins 1981, 174–5
87. Pearson 2002, 65–6
88. Miller 1928, 94–5
89. Ramm 1956
90. Wenham 1961
91. Ottaway 1996, 286–7
92. Hunter-Mann 2009
93. Butler 1972, 62–3
94. Caerleon: Boon 1972, 37–9. Chester: le Quesne 1999, 145; Mason 2012, 139
95. RCHME's *Eburacum* 135, *149*
96. Boon 1972, 89–101; Knight 2003, 31–3
97. Mason 2012, 113–5
98. Wellbeloved 1842; RCHME's *Eburacum*, 132, *127*; Tufi 1983, 49–50, *79*
99. RCHME's *Eburacum*, 1–3; Brinklow 1986a
100. Wenham 1957; 1965b
101. Ottaway 2004, 49–51, 93–4
102. Wenham 1967, 52–6
103. Addyman 1984; Horne 2003
104. Jones 1988; 1990
105. Roskams and Neal 2020, 32-6
106. Mason 1988

107. Margary 1973, 401–3, Roads 72b and 729; Ramm 1976a
108. Margary 1973, 417–8, Road 280
109. Cruse and Heslop 2013
110. Monaghan 1997, 837–50
111. Published coin lists include: Wade 1957; Wade and Kent 1968; Casey 1978; 1995
112. Reece 2002, Chapter 1
113. Hall 1997, 344; Robertson 2000, Catalogue No 57
114. Hall 1986
115. Kenward 1979, 69
116. RCHME's *Eburacum*, 59
117. Ottaway 2011, 192–3
118. Mason 1988, 185
119. RCHME's *Eburacum*, 54; Robinson 2013a
120. RIB I, *644*; RCHME's *Eburacum*,116, *33*; Birley 2005, 250–1; Tomlin 2018, 197–8
121. RCHME's *Eburacum*, 55–6
122. Perrin 1975
123. RCHME's *Eburacum*, 80–1
124. Russell 2018
125. Bogaers and Haalebos 1979, 39–41; Tomlin 2018, 78–9
126. Bootham Stray: RCHME's *Eburacum*, 47. Huntington: Johnson 2005
127. RIB III, *3364*
128. The most recent account of Aldborough is by Millett and Ferraby 2016
129. Wells 1992, 253–4
130. *Aeneid* I
131. Birley 2005, 246–52
132. Hassall and Tomlin 1987; RIB II.4: *2445.16*; Hare Hill: RIB III, *3454*
133. RIB I, *1322*
134. Hodgson 1995; Bidwell and Hodgson 2009, 19–22
135. RIB I, *1389*

Chapter 3

1. *Historia Augusta*, Marcus Antoninus, 8.7
2. Dio LXXI, 16, 2; RIB I, *583*, *595*
3. Dio LXXII, 8
4. RIB I, *740*
5. Birley 1988, 138–9: *Historia Augusta*, Severus, 17.3-4
6. Dio LXXVI, 15, 1–2
7. Campbell 1978, 160–2

8. Dio LXXV, 5, 4
9. RCHME's *Eburacum*, xxxii
10. Birley 1988, 172
11. Herodian III, 14, 3–10
12. Herodian III, 14, 1; Cassius Dio LXXVI, 11, 1
13. *Historia Augusta*, Severus, 22.1-7
14. Dio LXXVII, 16, 5
15. Birley 1988, 175
16. Herodian III, 14, 3
17. Birley 1988, 175.
18. Bishop and Coulston 1993, 126–35
19. Ottaway 2016
20. RIB I, *1143*
21. Hodgson 2009, 63–7
22. RIB II, 4, 148
23. Dio LXXVII, 15, 3–4
24. *Historia Augusta*, Severus, 22.1-7
25. Dio LXXVIII, 9
26. Steer 1958, 108; Biró 1975, 31
27. *J. Roman Stud.* 11, 101
28. RIB I, *674, 678*; RCHME's *Eburacum*,130,*105*; 131,*110*; RIB III, *3203*
29. Hirschfeld and Zangemeister 1899, no 3162
30. Bidwell 2006
31. RIB I, *662–3*; RCHME's *Eburacum*, 133, *142*
32. Birley 1966, 731–2
33. RIB III, *3193*
34. RIB III, *3195*
35. Tomlin 2018, 307
36. Ottaway 1996, 174–7
37. Hall 1997, 328–31
38. RCHME's *Eburacum*, 38
39. RCHME's *Eburacum*, 43
40. Phillips 1995
41. Weatherhead 1995
42. Wetzel 1980, 12
43. Davygate/Little Stonegate: Wenham 1962; Evans 2000. Aldwark, Bedern: Ottaway 1996, 147–9, 155–9, 211–2. Minster Library: Garner-Lahire 2016
44. Low Petergate: Wenham 1972. 9 Blake Street: Hall 1997
45. Hall 1997, 344; Robertson 2000, Catalogue No 57

46. Kershaw 1997
47. Miller 1928, 61–9; RCHME's *Eburacum*, 29–31
48. Hall 1996
49. Ottaway 1996, 237–41
50. Ottaway 1996, 293
51. Kenward *et al.* 1986
52. Birley 2005, 265
53. RIB III, *3201*
54. RIB III, *3202*; RCHME's *Eburacum*, 130, *107*; Tomlin 2018, 215
55. RIB I, *675*; RCHME's *Eburacum*, 124, *78*
56. RCHME's *Eburacum*, 133, *143*
57. RIB I, *670*; RCHME's *Eburacum*, 128–30, *104*
58. RIB I, *640*; RCHME's *Eburacum*, 118, *40*
59. RIB I, *671*; RCHME's *Eburacum*, 121, *72*; Tufi 1983, 31, *46*
60. RIB I, *690*; RCHME's *Eburacum*, 130, *108*
61. RIB I, *653*; RCHME's *Eburacum*, 116, *36*
62. RIB I, *679*; RCHME's *Eburacum*, 126, *88*
63. RIB I, *685*; RCHME's *Eburacum*, 122–4, *77*
64. Monaghan 1997, 864
65. *Peloponnesian War*, 7, Chapter 7
66. Mason 1988, 189
67. Mócsy 1974; Poczy 1980, 255–6
68. Plutarch, *Parallel Lives of Noble Greeks and Romans*: *Life of Romulus*, 11
69. e.g. RCHME's *Eburacum*, fig. 37
70. Wheeler 1954, 107
71. Wellbeloved 1842, 47–8; RCHME's *Eburacum*, 49
72. *YPSR* 1874, 9; RCHME's *Eburacum*, 49
73. *YAJ* 35, 80; RCHME's *Eburacum*, 49
74. RCHME's *Eburacum*, 107
75. Addyman 1976, 7
76. *YPSR* 1893, 3; RCHME's *Eburacum*, 3
77. Wacher 1995, 308
78. Esmonde Cleary 1994, 267
79. RCHME's *Eburacum*, 51–2
80. Ottaway and Marwood in prep. (near 138 Micklegate)
81. Hinchliffe and Ottaway in prep.
82. Wenham 1965b, 541–2
83. Jacob's Well: RCHME's *Eburacum*, 52. Trinity Lane: Esmonde Cleary 1996, 411
84. Ottaway in prep.

85. Donaghey 1978a, 5–14
86. Wenham and Ottaway in prep.
87. Ammianus Marcellinus XIV, 6, 16
88. Pelletier 1982, 117–8
89. Ottaway 2011, 333
90. RCHME's *Eburacum*, 51
91. Lawrence 2007, 45–50
92. Donaghey 1978a, 14–29
93. Mackie *et al.* 1975
94. Ottaway 2004, 94–7
95. Ottaway in prep.
96. Pearson in prep.
97. Hall and Kenward 1990, 343
98. Hall and Kenward 1990, 350
99. Allen and Kenward in prep.
100. O'Connor 1988, 82–4, 117
101. *YPSR* 1901; RCHME's *Eburacum*, 53
102. RCHME's *Eburacum*, 112
103. Robinson 2013b
104. Benson 1911, fig. 20; RCHME's *Eburacum*, 53
105. Home 1924, 149
106. RCHME's *Eburacum*, 116, *35*
107. RIB III, *3201*
108. RIB I, *674*, RCHME's *Eburacum*, 130, *105*
109. RIB III, *3203*
110. RCHME's *Eburacum*, 52–3
111. RCHME's *Eburacum*, 113
112. Wellbeloved 1842, 70–3; RCHME's *Eburacum*, 54–7; Perrin 1975
113. Robinson 2013a
114. RCHME's *Eburacum*, 55
115. RCHME's *Eburacum*, 53–4
116. RCHME's *Eburacum*, 57–8
117. RCHME's *Eburacum*, 52
118. Tyler 2000
119. RCHME's *Eburacum*, 52
120. Pearson and Dickson 2000
121. RCHME's *Eburacum*, 52; Ottaway *et al.* in prep.
122. Ottaway and Wenham in prep.
123. Ottaway and Wenham in prep.

124. RIB I, *649*; RCHME's *Eburacum*, 114–5, *29*; Tufi 1983, 3–4, *6*; Cooley 2018, 226–30
125. Carver and Sumpter 1978
126. Ramm 1976b, 36–7
127. Ramm 1976b, 38–9; Biek 1976
128. Donaghey 1978b
129. *Natural History* XXXIII, 40
130. YORYM 2010.246
131. Hall and Kenward 1990, 413–4
132. Ling 1992
133. Hall *et al.* 1980, 128–9; Kenward *et al.* 1986, 263; Lodwick 2017, 139–44
134. RCHME's *Eburacum*, 53
135. Ottaway 2011, 275–90
136. Brinklow and Donaghey 1986
137. RCHME's *Eburacum*, 61
138. Hall 1986
139. RCHME's *Eburacum*, 59–61
140. MAP 2005a
141. RIB I, *648*; RCHME's *Eburacum*, 119, *53*
142. RIB I, *656*; RCHME's *Eburacum*, 119, *52*
143. RCHME's *Eburacum*, 112, *9*; Tufi 1983, 71. *121*
144. *YPSR* 1902; RCHME's *Eburacum*, 112–3, *11–12*
145. Brinklow 1986b
146. RCHME's *Eburacum*, 61; Hall and Hinchliffe 1986; RIB III, *3194*
147. RCHME's *Eburacum*, 64; Richardson 1959; Hunter-Mann 2007
148. RCHME's *Eburacum*, fig.53
149. RCHME's *Eburacum*, 65; Hargrove 1818, Vol. 2, Part 2, 346–7; King 1975; Swan and McBride 2002, 190–2
150. Magilton 1986
151. RCHME's *Eburacum*, 65; OSA 2005
152. Wilmott 1952–3; 1953–4; Gentil 1988
153. RCHME's *Eburacum*, 45–7
154. Ottaway 2011, 349–53; McComish 2006a
155. RCHME's *Eburacum*,128, *96;* Tufi 1983, 37–8, *56*
156. Ottaway 2011, 258–9 (on Belle Vue Street)
157. Ottaway 2011, 330
158. Ottaway 2011, 370–3
159. Roskams and Neal 2020, 36-7
160. Lawton 2002–03

Chapter 4

1. Erdkamp 2012, 257
2. Garnsey and Saller 1987, 49
3. O'Connor and van der Veen 1998
4. Hopkins 1980
5. Hall and Kenward 1990, 410–1
6. O'Connor and van der Veen 1998, 130
7. Reynolds 1979, 61–3
8. Hillman 1981, 146; Wilkinson and Stevens 2003, 187–9
9. Tweddle 1986, 195–7
10. Wilkinson and Stevens 2003, 190–200
11. Hillman 1981, 148–9; Wilkinson and Stevens 2003, fig. 62.
12. Ottaway 2013, 195–6
13. Reynolds and Langley 1979
14. 5 Rougier Street: Hall and Kenward 1990, 411–2. Bedern well: Kenward *et al.* 1986, 256
15. Information from John Cruse
16. Cool 2006, 71
17. Stamp 1955, 101; Kenward *et al.* 1986, 248; Hall and Kenward 1990, 307, 400
18. Maltby 2010, 109
19. O'Connor 1988
20. Jaques 2016
21. Palaeoecology Research Services 2006
22. O'Connor 1988, 92–7; Ottaway 2013, table 2
23. O'Connor 1988, 97–9
24. Ottaway 2013, table 3
25. Allen and Kenward in prep.
26. Buckland 1988
27. Halkon and Millett 1999, 75–81
28. RIB II, 1, *2404.61–4*
29. Perrin 1981, 58–61; 1990, 265–6; Monaghan 1993, 705–10; 1997, 869–82; Swan 1994, 1; 2002, 39
30. RCHME's *Eburacum*, 65; Hargrove 1818, Vol. 2, Part 2, 346–7; King 1975; Swan and McBride 2002, 192–5
31. Swan 2002, 47–52
32. Lawton 1992–3; Monaghan 1997, 870–1; Swan and McBride 2002, 194
33. RIB II, 5: *2489.2–3*
34. *YPSR* 1874; RCHME's *Eburacum*, 63; YORYM: H22–3
35. McComish 2012, 57–9
36. RIB II, 4

37. Cool 2002, 1–2
38. Ramm 1976b, 39; Biek 1976
39. Antoni and Johnson 2013
40. YORYM 1984.32.2355
41. Tylecote 1986, 145
42. Wiemer 1993
43. Hooley 1988; Cool 2002, 2
44. Ramm 1976b, 39
45. Dungworth 2002
46. Cool *et al.* 1995, 1560
47. Cool *et al.* 1999; Price 2002, 88–9
48. Price 1995, 346
49. YORYM 2010.393, 1–3
50. Hooley 1988–9
51. Note by Ottaway, May 1999, in the Yorkshire Museum. For the type Wild 2002, 5–6
52. Allason-Jones 1996, 47
53. *Metamorphoses*, VI; Wild 2002, 8–9
54. *Notitia Dignitatum* 11, 60
55. Wild 1976, 171–2; 2002, 10–12
56. Wild 1976, 172; 2002, 11; Walton Rogers 2001, 160–1
57. Walton 1995; Wild 2002, 11–12
58. Henshall 1962
59. Hall and Kenward 1990, 303, 326
60. Hall and Kenward 1990, 302, 330; Wild 2002, 7
61. e.g. Wenham 1965b, 547; MacGregor 1976, 12–13; MacGregor 1978, 35; Cool *et al.* 1995, 1543, 1603, and many in Yorkshire Museum collection
62. Allason-Jones 1996, 44–5, *275–80*
63. Allason-Jones 1996
64. *Natural History*, XXXVI
65. RCHME's *Eburacum*, 63, 143; Allason-Jones 1996, 12–13
66. Allason-Jones 1996, 24–5; Parker 2016
67. RCHME's *Eburacum*, 142; McComish 2006b, sf31
68. RIB I, *685*; RCHME's *Eburacum*, 122, *77*
69. Strabo IV, 5, 2
70. Ammianus Marcellinus XVIII, 2
71. Sitch 1989; 1990
72. Betts 1998, 231
73. RIB I, *720*; RIB III, *3209*
74. Todd 1992; Allason-Jones 1996, 14

75. Monaghan 1997, 900–1
76. Monaghan 1997, 891–2
77. Hall and Kenward 1990, 387
78. Kenward *et al.* 1986, 264
79. O'Connor 1988, 115–6
80. Hall and Kenward 1990, 407–8
81. Palaeoecology Research Services 2006
82. Edwards 1965; 1968
83. Perrin 1990, 267; Perrin 1995, 324; Monaghan 1997, 893–6
84. Monaghan 1997, 897–8
85. Monaghan 1997, 898–9
86. Perrin 1995, 330; Monaghan 1997, 892–3
87. Hartley 1995; Monaghan 1997, 930–43
88. Williams 1979, 62
89. On samian from York: Hartley and Dickinson 1990; Dickinson and Hartley 1971; 1993; Simpson 1995; Dickinson 1997
90. YORYM H32; Joanna Bird pers. comm.
91. *Republic* VII, 514
92. Monaghan 1997, 882
93. Perrin 1995, 330; Monaghan 1997, 890–1, 896–7
94. RCHME's *Eburacum*, 135; RIB II, 2, *2498.6–7, 14, 16, 18, 29*
95. Monaghan 1993, 721; Perrin 1981, 61; Williams 1990; 1995; 1997
96. Cool 2006, 19
97. Williams and Carreras 1995
98. Cool 2006, 19
99. MacGregor 1978, 47
100. Allen in prep.
101. Harden 1962, 137
102. Price 1995, 348–9
103. Harden 1962, 136; YORYM: HG205.3
104. O'Connor 1988, 108–10
105. Hall and Kenward 1990, 407
106. Jenkins 1978
107. RCHME's *Eburacum*, 120, *60*; Tufi 1983, 67, *108*
108. RCHME's *Eburacum*, 120, *62*; Tufi 1983, 6–7, *12*
109. Henig 1974; 1976; 1995
110. Harden 1962; YORYM: HG218
111. Hedges 1976
112. Greene 1990, 46; Morley 2012, 310
113. Willis 2016; Price 2016

114. Morley 2012, 310
115. Walker 1988, 304; Reece 2002, 115
116. Duncan-Jones 1994, 228
117. Reece 2002, 46
118. Magilton 1986, 39–40
119. MAP 2005b and R. Brickstock pers comm.
120. Steelyard pieces: YORYM 2007.6268–9; weights (young man): YORYM 2001.12496 and ram: YORYM 2003.264
121. Cool *et al.* 1995, 1550–2
122. Quoted in Brown 1971, 12

Chapter 5
1. McIntyre 2015
2. Storey 1997
3. Warwick 1968, 147
4. Peck 2009, 105
5. McIntyre 2013, 137
6. Ottaway 2005; Hunter-Mann 2006; Caffell and Holst 2012
7. RIB I, *671*; RCHME's *Eburacum*, 121, *72* and (centurion) RCHME's *Eburacum*, 128, *95*
8. Scheidel 2001
9. Peck 2009, 103
10. e.g. for Roman Winchester: Ottaway and Rees 2012, 349
11. McIntyre 2013, 157–9
12. Hopkins 1966
13. RIB I, *690*; RCHME's *Eburacum*, 130, *108*
14. RIB I, *685*; RCHME's *Eburacum*, 122, *77*
15. RIB III, *3201*
16. RIB I, *363*
17. RIB I, *681*; RCHME's *Eburacum*, 124, *79*
18. McIntyre 2013, 137
19. Caffell and Holst 2012, 80–3
20. Caffell and Holst 2012, 52–3; McIntyre 2013, 236–7
21. McIntyre 2013, 207–10
22. Caffell and Holst 2012, 90
23. Hooley 1988–9
24. Caffell and Holst 2012, 53–60, 99
25. McIntyre 2013, 179–92
26. RIB I, *687*; RCHME's *Eburacum*, 130, *106*; Home 1924, 171
27. Kenward *et al.* 1986, 252; Hall and Kenward 1990, 343, 394

28. Hall and Kenward 1990, 395
29. Cruse 2004, 63–4
30. RCHME's *Eburacum*, 134, *147*; RIB II, 4, *2446.1*
31. Cruse 2004, 159–63
32. Eckardt 2014, 25
33. Eckardt *et al.* 2010, 111
34. Wells 1992, 238
35. Cunliffe 2005, 582
36. Birley 1979, 121–2
37. RIB I, *689*; RCHME's *Eburacum*, 124–6, *84*; Tufi 1983, 28–9, *43*
38. RIB II, 7, *2501.101*
39. RIB I, *690*; RCHME's *Eburacum*, 130, *108*; Tomlin 2018, 216–7
40. RIB I, *671*; RCHME's *Eburacum*, 121–2, *72*
41. Tomlin 2018, 307
42. RIB I, *678*; RCHME's *Eburacum*, 131, *110;* Rollason 1998, 114
43. RIB I, *687*; RCHME's *Eburacum*, 130, *106*
44. RIB I, *643*; RCHME's *Eburacum*, 120, *57*
45. RIB I, *641*; *677*; RIB III, 3203; RCHME's *Eburacum*,120, *58*; 130, *109*
46. YORYM: H140.2, 3, 5, 7; Collinge 1935; King 1974; Eckardt 2014, 134–40
47. Mattern 1989, 721–2, 726
48. Swan and McBride 2002
49. Perrin 1981, 59; Swan 1994, 3–4; Monaghan 1997, 872, 999–1000
50. Croom 1997–8
51. Fulford 2010
52. Buxton 1935
53. Warwick 1968
54. Leach *et al.* 2009; Eckardt *et al.* 2010, 111
55. Leach *et al.* 2010
56. Müldner *et al.* 2011
57. Montgomery *et al.* 2010
58. Martiniano *et al.* 2016
59. 1–3 Driffield Terrace (Sample 26) Burial 4200
60. Acts 22.22–29
61. *Satyricon* XV, 32
62. Birley 2005, 3–14
63. Wells 1992, 214
64. RIB I, *683*; RCHME's *Eburacum*,128, *103*
65. Toynbee 1971, 76
66. Scheidel 2012, 92
67. Juvenal, *Satire* 6

68. 1–3 Driffield Terrace, Burial 4352
69. De Angelis 2012, 178
70. Long 2003, 205–06
71. Finley 1972, 124
72. Carroll 2006, 196
73. *Satyricon* XV, 58.7
74. Sallust, *The Catiline Conspiracy*, 25
75. Bowman 1994; Birley 2002
76. Eckardt 2014, 177
77. Eckardt 2014, 193–204
78. Simpson 1995, 272
79. e.g. Cool *et al*. 1995, 1548; others in Yorkshire Museum collection: YORYM: H2437.2; H2441.4; H2437; 2007.6215–6/6220–1; 1980.54.425; 2007.6200–1; 2012.421
80. Cool *et al*. 1995, 1548–9. Also from York: YORYM: H2440.12, 2002.226, 2007.6240.1, described by Andrews 2012
81. RIB I, *684*; RCHME's *Eburacum*, 122, *73;* Kruschwitz 2015, 53
82. Virgil, *Aeneid* VI; Plato, *Phaedo* 112D–114A
83. Ekwall 1960
84. Raybould 1999, 14
85. Wenham 1965b, 548, fig. 5, *7*; RIB II, 7, *2501.117*
86. Wild 1968, 168–9; 2002, 23
87. RIB I, *685*; RCHME's *Eburacum*, 122–4, *77*; Croom 2002, 33–4
88. Croom 2002, 39
89. RCHME's *Eburacum*, 128, *96*; Tufi 1983, 37–8, *56*
90. RCHME's *Eburacum*, 128, *95;* Tufi 1983, 38–9, *57*
91. RCHME's *Eburacum*, 126, *85*; Tufi 1983, 36–7, *55*
92. RIB I, *685*; RCHME's *Eburacum*, 122–4, *77*; Wild 1968, 194
93. Wild 1968, 198
94. RIB I, *686*; RCHME's *Eburacum*, 124, *80*; Mattern 1989, 795
95. RIB I, *682*; RCHME's *Eburacum*, 121, *71;* Tufi 1983, 25–6, *40*; Mattern 1989, 797–8
96. Croom 2002, 89–90
97. Hooley 1988–9
98. MacConnoran 1986, 218
99. MacGregor 1978, fig. 28, *353–4*
100. Bowman 1994, 139–40, *346*
101. RCHME's *Eburacum*, 83, d i
102. RIB I, *639*; Tufi 1983, 57, *98*
103. Croom 2002, 100–03

104. Croom 2002, 103–04; Levick 2007, 3; Baharal 1992
105. Allason-Jones 1996, 60
106. *Medicamina Faciei Feminae*, lines 1–2
107. Stewart 2007
108. Harden 1962, 136–7
109. Alcock 1977
110. Jeremiah 8.22
111. *Epigrams* III, 63
112. RCHME's *Eburacum*, 134, *146*
113. Stewart 2007, 45
114. RCHME's *Eburacum*, 82, c vi
115. RCHME's *Eburacum*, 84, e vi
116. YORYM 1971.319.3; Wenham 1960, 315; RCHME's *Eburacum*, 94, k x
117. MacGregor 1976, 10–11; YORYM 1972.22.6091
118. RCHME's *Eburacum*, 100–01, m xxi
119. e.g. MacGregor 1976, 10; Cool *et al.* 1995, 1544–6; Allason-Jones 1996, 26–9
120. RCHME's *Eburacum*, 70, c i; Allason-Jones 1996, 20–1
121. Pendant: MacGregor 1978, 11, *71*; YORYM: 1972.22.6093
122. Johns 1996, Chapter 7
123. e.g. Cool 1993; Butcher 1995; Rogers 2016
124. e.g. YORYM 2007.6013.11 and 2007.6266; Cool *et al.* 1995, 1622, *6532*
125. RCHME's *Eburacum*, pl. 34. YORYM: H31, a and c; H139a and c; H2426
126. Mackreth 2011, 237–8
127. Johns 1996, 108–24
128. RCHME's *Eburacum*, 84, e iii
129. YORYM: H67; RCHME's *Eburacum*, 107, a i
130. Allason-Jones 1996, 31
131. (left to right) YORYM 2011.185–6 and 2007.3059
132. Rutledge 2000, 3
133. Henig 1974; 1976; 1995
134. Henig 1974, *352*
135. *Satyricon* XV, 40
136. Cool 2006, 70–5
137. Cool 2006, 78
138. Kenward *et al.* 1986, 254; Hall and Kenward 1990, 409
139. Hall and Kenward 1990, 407, table 129A
140. Kenward *et al.* 1986, 262; Hall and Kenward 1990, 409
141. Kenward *et al.* 1986
142. Hall and Kenward 1990, 399

143. Birley 2002, 92, 129–30
144. Brown and Meadows 2000
145. Birley 2002, 135; Pliny *Natural History* XIV
146. Monaghan 1997, 1022
147. e.g. RCHME's *Eburacum* 90–1; YORYM: H1049, and H2076
148. Sherlock 2007
149. e.g. Yorkshire Museum collections include two of silver (YORYM 2002.223, 2013.1096) and one of pewter (YORYM 2012.883). In copper alloy: MacGregor 1976, 20
150. Harden 1962; Cool *et al.* 1995, 1559–88
151. Charlesworth 1976
152. Cool 2008
153. Kenward *et al.* 1986, 254
154. O'Connor 1988, 105
155. e.g. bone: Cool 1995, 1556, fig. 731, *6419*
156. Allason-Jones 1996, 49, *314*
157. MacGregor 1978, 33; Cool 1995, 1553–6

Chapter 6
1. RIB I, *662–3*; RCHME's *Eburacum* 133, *142*
2. Hall and Hinchliffe 1986; RIB III, *3194*
3. RIB I, *647*; RCHME's *Eburacum*, 119, *51*
4. Livy, *The Early History of Rome*, I, 43
5. Tufi 1983, 21, *35*
6. Beard *et al.* 1998, 232
7. *Metamorphoses* XII
8. RIB I, *645*; RCHME's *Eburacum*, 119–20, *56*
9. RIB I, 643; RCHME's *Eburacum*, 120, *57*
10. *Germania*, 9
11. Lawrence 2007, 41–5
12. RIB I, *665*; RCHME's *Eburacum*, 111, *1*
13. Beard *et al.* 1998, 324–5
14. *Epistles* 95, 35
15. RIB I, *649*; RCHME's *Eburacum*, 114–5, *29*
16. RCHME's *Eburacum*, 120, *59*; Tufi 1983, 5–6, *10*
17. RIB I, *650–1*; RCHME's *Eburacum*, 115–6, *30–1*
18. RCHME's *Eburacum*, 120, *62*
19. YORYM 1983.32.2275
20. Green 1986, 94
21. RCHME's *Eburacum*, 121, *68*; Tufi 1983, 4, *7*

22. Hassall and Tomlin 1983, 337
23. Tufi 1983, 67, *110*
24. Henig 1976, *14*
25. RIB I, *648*; RCHME's *Eburacum*, 119, *53*
26. Henig 1976, *11*
27. Green 1986, 78–85
28. RIB I, *652–4*; RCHME's *Eburacum*, 116–8, *36–8, 42*; Tufi 1983, 15–6, *26*
29. RCHME's *Eburacum*, 118, *42*
30. RIB I, *653*; RCHME's *Eburacum*, 116, *36*
31. Henig 1984, 185–6; Parker 2017
32. RCHME's *Eburacum*, 114, *18a–c* (in relief); 132, *133g* (finial); Tufi 1983, 71–2, *123–4*
33. RCHME's *Eburacum*, 133, *140*; Green 1986, 97
34. RCHME's *Eburacum*, 133, *141*; Green 1986, 111
35. RIB I, *660*; RCHME's *Eburacum*, 118, *39*
36. RIB I, *640*; RCHME's *Eburacum*, 118, *40*; Tufi 1983, 14, *24*
37. Turcan 1996, 37
38. RCHME's *Eburacum* 132, *133*; Tufi 1983, 54–5, *88–92*; from 16–22 Coppergate: Hall *et al.* 2011, 216
39. RCHME's *Eburacum*, 132, *124*
40. Turcan 1996, 99–104
41. *Golden Ass* XI, 9–10
42. Witt 1971, 189
43. RIB I, *658*; RCHME's *Eburacum*, 119, *54*; Tufi 1983, 11, *21*
44. Birley 1988, 35
45. Witt 1971, 238
46. YORYM 2001.12527
47. RCHME's *Eburacum*, 120–1, *67*; Tufi 1983, 12–13, *23;* Turcan 1996, 223–6
48. Barton 1994, 202
49. RIB I, *641*; RCHME's *Eburacum*, 120, *58*; Tufi 1983, 11–12, *22*
50. Turcan 1996, pl. 27
51. YORYM 2011.360
52. McComish 2012, 135–7, fig. 15 (16–22 Coppergate); YORYM1977.55 (NE6)
53. Acts 13.12; Levick 1967, 112; Birley 2005, 239–40
54. Green 1986, 103
55. Toynbee 1971, 37
56. *Metamorphoses* IV
57. *Natural History* VII, 188
58. Toynbee 1971, 37
59. RIB I, *685*; RCHME's *Eburacum*, 122–4, *77*

60. Henig 1976, *13*
61. Henig 1976, *15*
62. RCHME's *Eburacum*, 132, *126*; Tufi 1983, 50, *80*
63. RIB I, *692*; RCHME's *Eburacum*, 122, *74*
64. Swan 1994, 15–21; Swan and Monaghan 1993; Monaghan 1997, 914–21;
65. 35–41 Blossom Street Burial 2263 (female). 1–3 Driffield Terrace Burials 4140 and 4162 (male)
66. *Natural History* X, 49
67. Wenham 1968b, Burial 211
68. Allason–Jones 1996, 24–5; Parker 2016
69. RIB I, *695*; RCHME's *Eburacum*, 122, *76*
70. RIB III, *3202*; RCHME's *Eburacum*, 130, *107*
71. Walsh 1999, xx
72. RCHME's *Eburacum*, 131, *123*; Tufi 1983, 53, *85–6*; Henig 1984, 199; Blagg 1995, 241–2
73. RCHME's *Eburacum*, 131, *120*; Tufi 1983, 50–1, *81*

Chapter 7

1. Wenham 1968b
2. Jones 1984
3. RCHME's *Eburacum*, 72, a
4. RCHME's *Eburacum*, 73–6
5. RCHME's *Eburacum*, 72–5
6. RCHME's *Eburacum*, 71; Ottaway 2011, 193–4
7. RCHME's *Eburacum*, 71; Kendall 2010; Connelly 2011
8. Ramm 1958; RCHME's *Eburacum*, 67–9
9. RCHME's *Eburacum*, 70–1
10. Wenham 1967
11. RCHME's *Eburacum*, 69; Spall and Toop 2005a
12. RIB III, *3203*
13. RCHME's *Eburacum*, 80–1
14. RCHME's *Eburacum*, 81–91
15. A summary in Rutledge 2000, but otherwise no report
16. RCHME's *Eburacum*, 92–101
17. 1–3 Driffield Terrace: Ottaway 2005. 6 Driffield Terrace: Hunter–Mann 2006. Human remains from both sites: Caffell and Holst 2012
18. Ottaway 2011, 319
19. 35–41 Blossom Street (31 burials): Ottaway 2011, 291–308. Moss Street (4): Toop 2008. Mill Mount (19): Spall and Toop 2005b; FAS 2006. 89 The Mount (8) no report

20. Savine 2017
21. RCHME's *Eburacum*, 107–8; Ottaway 2011, 267
22. RCHME's *Eburacum*, 107; Ottaway 2011, 351–5
23. RCHME's *Eburacum*, 108
24. Ottaway 2013, 90–2
25. Ottaway 2011, 351–2
26. RCHME's *Eburacum*, 85, f vi
27. *Annals* XVI, 6
28. Morris 1992, 53
29. Dio LXXVII, 15; Rollason 1998, 109 (for translation)
30. Wenham 1968b, 21–6
31. Spall and Toop 2005
32. RCHME's *Eburacum*, 98, m iv
33. RCHME's *Eburacum*, 100, m xvii
34. Harden 1962, 136; YORYM: HG53
35. *YPSR* 1947–8, fig. 3.8; RCHME's *Eburacum*, 75–6, f; Harden 1962, 136–7; YORYM 1948.3.1
36. RIB I, *691*; RCHME's *Eburacum*, 134, *145*
37. 1–3 Driffield Terrace: Burial 4084
38. RCHME's *Eburacum*, 107, q i
39. Toynbee 1971, 40
40. RCHME's *Eburacum*, 81, b vi
41. RCHME's *Eburacum*, 71, d iii and 74, d
42. *YPS Comms* 1876, 6; RCHME's *Eburacum*, 79
43. Horace, *Satires* I, 8, 10
44. RCHME's *Eburacum*, 100, m xx
45. RCHME's *Eburacum*, 84, d xiii
46. RCHME's *Eburacum*, 81, b viii
47. RCHME's *Eburacum*, 80, a viii
48. RCHME's *Eburacum*, 83, d i
49. RCHME's *Eburacum*, 71, d iii and 80, a i
50. RCHME's *Eburacum*, 74, d and 85, f i
51. Naburn: Ottaway 2011, 260. Nunthorpe: RCHME's *Eburacum*, 108, c. Appletree Farm: Wenham 1967, 50–2
52. Spall and Toop 2005b, Burial 15
53. *YPS Comms* 1876; RCHME's *Eburacum*, 85
54. *YPS Comms* 1876; RCHME's *Eburacum*, 79
55. RIB I, 681, RCHME's *Eburacum*, 124, *79*
56. Green 1986, 39–40
57. Ottaway 2011, 297–308; Connelly 2011

58. Philpott 1991, 75
59. RCHME's *Eburacum*, 95–6, l i
60. RCHME's *Eburacum*, 97, m i
61. Ottaway 2011, 299–301
62. RIB I, *675*; RCHME's *Eburacum*, 124, *78*
63. Saller and Shaw 1984, 145
64. Morris 1992, 160
65. RIB I, *685*; RCHME's *Eburacum*, 77; Tomlin 2018, 231–2
66. Morris 1992, 168
67. RCHME's *Eburacum*, 97, l xi
68. RCHME's *Eburacum*, 80, a iv
69. RCHME's *Eburacum*, 86, f xiv
70. RCHME's *Eburacum*, 81, b ii
71. RCHME's *Eburacum*, 82, c ix
72. Wellbeloved 1842, 131, pl. XVII, fig. 1; RCHME's *Eburacum*, 71, e i

Chapter 8
1. Virgil, *Aeneid* I

Bibliography

Abbreviations

Archaeol. York	Archaeology of York–the York Archaeological Trust publication series The web publications are available on www.yorkarchaeology.co.uk
Interim	Bulletin of the York Archaeological Trust
OSA	On Site Archaeology
RIB	*Roman Inscriptions of Britain* (Vols I–III)
YAJ	*Yorkshire Archaeological Journal*
YAT	York Archaeological Trust
YPS	Yorkshire Philosophical Society
YPSR	Yorkshire Philosophical Society Annual Report
YPS Comms	Yorkshire Philosophical Society Communications

Adam, J-P. 1989. *La Construction Romaine* (2nd edn)

Addyman, P.V. 1976. *Excavations in York, 1973–74, Second Interim Report*

Addyman, P.V. 1984. York in its archaeological setting, in Addyman and Black 1984, 7–21

Addyman, P.V. and Black, V.E. (eds) 1984. *Archaeological Papers from York Presented to M.W. Barley*

Alcock, J.P. 1977. A balsamarium in the Yorkshire Museum, York, *YAJ* **49**, 35–7

Allason-Jones, L. 1996. *Roman Jet in the Yorkshire Museum*

Allen, D. 1998. *Roman Glass in Britain*, Shire Archaeology **76**

Allen, S.J. and Kenward, K. in prep. Structural timbers, in Ottaway *et al.* in prep.

Allen, S.J. in prep. The board of silver fir from 24–30 Tanner Row, in Ottaway *et al.* in prep.

Andrews, C. 2012. *Roman Seal-boxes in Britain*, Brit. Archaeol. Rep. Brit. Ser. **567**

Antoni, B. and Johnson, M. 2013. *Former Bowling Green, Sycamore Place, York*, YAT Rep. **2013/14**

Atkinson, K. 2003. Glacial history, in Butlin 2003, 10–13

Baharal, D. 1992. The portraits of Julia Domna for the years 193–211 and the dynastic propaganda of L Septimius Severus, *Latomus* **51**, 110–8

Barton, T. 1994. *Ancient Astrology*

Beard, M., North, J. and Price, S. 1998. *Religions of Rome* (2 vols)

Benson, G. 1911. *An Account of the City and County of the City of York, Vol.1* (reprinted 1968)

Betts, I.M. 1998. The Roman tile, in H.E.M. Cool and C. Philo (eds), *Roman Castleford: Excavations 1974–85, Vol. 1, The Small Finds,* Yorkshire Archaeol. **4**, 225–32

Bidwell, P. 1979. *The Legionary Bath House and Basilica and Forum at Exeter.* Exeter Archaeol. Rep. **1**

Bidwell, P. 2006, Constantius and Constantine at York, in E. Hartley, J. Hawkes, M. Henig and F. Mee (eds) *Constantine the Great: York's Roman Emperor*, 31–40

Bidwell, P.T. and Hodgson, N. 2009. *The Roman Army in Northern England*

Biek, L. 1976. The metalworking residues, in Ramm 1976b, 68

Birley, A.R. 1979. *The People of Roman Britain*

Birley, A.R. 1988. *The African Emperor: Septimius Severus* (updated edn)

Birley, A.R. 1993. Review of the texts, in E.R. and A. Birley, *The Early Wooden Forts,* Vindolanda Res. Rep. New Ser. **2**, 18–72

Birley, A.R. 2002. *Garrison Life at Vindolanda: A Band of Brothers*

Birley, A.R. 2005. *The Roman Government of Britain*

Birley, E. 1966. The Roman inscriptions of York, *YAJ* **41**, 726–34

Biró, M. 1975. The Inscriptions of Roman Britain, *Acta Archaeologica Academiae Scientiarum Hungaricae* **27**, 13–58

Bishop, M.C. and Coulston, J.C.N. 1993 *Roman Military Equipment from the Punic Wars to the Fall of Rome*

Blagg, T.F.C. 1995. Roman architectural and sculptured stonework, in Phillips and Heywood 1995, 223–45

Bogaers, J.E. and Haalebos, J.K. 1979. *Noviomagus: auf den Spuren der Römer in Nijmegen*

Boon, G.C. 1972. *Isca: The Roman Legionary Fortress at Caerleon, Mon.*

Bowman, A.K. 1994. *Life and Letters on the Roman Frontier*

Brinklow, D.A. 1986a. Main roads serving Roman York, in Brinklow *et al.* 1986, 84–101

Brinklow, D.A. 1986b. Roman remains from High Ousegate, in Brinklow *et al.* 1986, 21–4

Brinklow, D.A. 1996. An observation of the fortress wall at Bootham Bar, in Ottaway 1996, 273–8

Brinklow, D.A. and Donaghey, S. 1986. A Roman building in Clementhorpe, in Brinklow *et al.* 1986, 54–73

Brinklow, D., Hall, R.A., Magilton, J.R. and Donaghey, S. 1986. *Coney Street, Aldwark and Clementhorpe, Minor Sites and Roman Roads*, Archaeol. York **6/1**

Brown, A.G. and Meadows, I. 2000. Roman vineyards in Britain: finds from the Nene Valley and new research, *Antiquity* **74**, 491–2

Brown, P. 1971. *The World of Late Antiquity*

Buckland, P.C. 1976a. Geological and archaeological notes on the rocks used in the construction of the sewer, in Whitwell 1976, 32–7

Buckland, P.C. 1976b. *The Environmental Evidence from the Church Street Roman Sewer System*, Archaeol. York **14/1**

Buckland, P.C. 1988. The stones of York: building materials in Roman Yorkshire, in Price and Wilson 1988, 237–87

Butcher, S.A. 1995. Roman brooches, in Phillips and Heywood 1995, 391–3

Butler, R.M. 1972. The excavations of 1970 and 1971, in Radley 1972, 59–64

Butlin, R.A. (ed.) 2003. *Historical Atlas of North Yorkshire*,

Buxton, L.H.D. 1935. The racial affinities of the Romano-Britons, *J. Roman Stud.* **25**, 35–50

Caffell, A. and Holst, M. 2012. *Osteological Analysis: 3 and 6 Driffield Terrace*, York Osteoarchaeology Rep.

Campbell, B. 1978. The marriage of soldiers under the empire, *J. Roman Stud.* **68**, 153–66

Campbell, B. 1984. *Ballistaria* in first to mid-third century Britain, *Britannia* **15**, 75–84

Carroll, M. 2006. *Spirits of the Dead. Roman Funerary Commemoration in Western Europe*

Carver, M.O.H., Donaghey, S. and Sumpter, A.B. 1978. *Riverside Structures and a Well in Bishophill*, Archaeol. York **4/1**

Carver, M.O.H. and Sumpter, A.B. 1978. Buildings in Bishophill, in Carver *et al.* 1978, 29–40

Casey, P.J. 1978. Coins, in MacGregor 1978, 41–7

Casey, P.J. 1995. Roman coins, in Phillips and Heywood 1995, 394–413

Charlesworth, D. 1976. Glass vessels, in MacGregor 1976, 15–18

Charlesworth, D. 1978. Glass vessels, in MacGregor 1978, 54–7

Coll, S. 1977. Excavation of the defensive ditches, in Sumpter and Coll 1977, 61–4

Collinge, W. 1935. On some spoon-shaped fibulae in the Yorkshire Museum and elsewhere, Proc. YPS, (1935) 1–4

Connelly, P. 2011. Hungate: the final year, *Yorkshire Archaeol. Today* **20**, 1–6

Cool, H.E.M. 1993. Comments in N.S.H. Rogers 1993, *Anglian and Other Finds from Fishergate*, Archaeol. York **17/9**, 1357

Cool, H.E.M. 2002. Craft and industry in Roman York, in Wilson and Price 2002, 13–20

Cool, H.E.M. 2006. *Eating and Drinking in Roman Britain*
Cool, H.E.M. 2008. The Roman glass, in Toop 2008, 35–8
Cool, H.E.M., Lloyd-Morgan, G. and Hooley, A.D. 1995. *Finds from the Fortress*, Archaeol. York **17/10**
Cool, H.E.M., Jackson, C.M. and Monaghan. J. 1999. Glass-making and the Sixth Legion at York, *Britannia* **30**, 147–62
Cooley, A. 2018. Monumental Latin inscriptions from Roman Britain in the Ashmolean Museum Collection, *Britannia* **49**, 225–49
Corder, P. 1933. Roman bath discovered in 1930–31 during the reconstruction of the Mail Coach Inn, St Sampson's Square, *Yorkshire Architectural and York Archaeological Soc. Proc.* 1 (1933)
Croom, A. 1997–8. Experiments in Roman military cooking methods, *The Arbeia Journal* **6–7**, 37–47
Croom, A. 2002. *Roman Clothing and Fashion* (paperback edn)
Cruse, A. 2004. *Roman Medicine*
Cruse, J. and Heslop, D.H. 2013. Querns, millstones and other stone artefacts, in L. Martin, J. Richardson and I. Roberts, *Iron Age and Roman Settlements at Wattle Syke*, Yorkshire Archaeol. **11**, 165–83
Cunliffe, B. 2005. *Iron Age Communities in Britain* (4th edn)
De Angelis, F. 2012. *Archaeology in Sicily 2006–2010*, Soc. Prom. Hellenic Stud. Rep. **58**, 123–95
Dickinson, B.M. 1997. Samian, in Monaghan 1997, 943–6
Dickinson, B.M. and Hartley, K.F. 1971. The evidence of potters' stamps on samian ware and on mortaria for the trading connections of Roman York, in R.M. Butler (ed.) *Soldier and Civilian in Roman Yorkshire*, 127–42
Dickinson, B.M. and Hartley, B.R. 1993. Samian ware, in Monaghan 1993, 722–5
Donaghey, S. 1978a. Riverside structures and a well in Skeldergate, in Carver *et al.* 1978, 4–29
Donaghey, S. 1978b. Painted wall-plaster, in Carver *et al.* 1978, 44–6
Dormor, I. 2003. Medieval forests and parks, in Butlin 2003, 78–82
Drake, F. 1736. *Eboracum or the History and Antiquities of the City of York*
Duncan-Jones, R. 1994. *Money and Government in the Roman Empire*
Dungworth, D. 2002. Copper alloys in Roman Yorkshire, in Wilson and Price 2002, 95–9
RCHME's *Eburacum* 1962. Royal Commission on Historical Monuments for England: An Inventory of the Historic Monuments in the City of York: 1. *Eburacum, Roman York*
Eckardt, H. 2014. *Objects and Identities*
Eckardt, H. (ed.) 2010. *Roman Diasporas: Archaeological Approaches to Mobility and Diversity in the Roman Empire*. J. Roman Archaeol. Suppl. Ser. **78**

Eckardt, H., Chenery, C., Leach, S., Lewis, M., Müldner, G. and Nimmo, E. 2010. A long way from home: diaspora communities in Roman Britain. in Eckardt 2010, 104–30

Edwards, A.H. 1965. Report on pieces of coal found in Trench 23, in Wenham 1965b

Edwards, A.H. 1968. A sample of coal from the cremation area, in Wenham 1968b, 102–3

Ekwall, E. 1960. *The Concise Dictionary of English Place names* (4th edn)

Erdkamp, P. 2012. Urbanism, in Scheidel 2012, 241–65

Esmonde-Cleary, A.S. 1994. 'England' in Roman Britain in 1993, *Britannia* **25**, 261–91

Esmonde-Cleary, A.S., 1996. 'England' in Roman Britain in 1995, *Britannia* **27**, 405–38

Evans, D.T. 2000. The former primitive Methodist chapel, 3 Little Stonegate, *Interim* **23.2**, 24–8

FAS (Field Archaeology Services) 2006. *Mill Mount, The Mount, York: Archaeological Watching Brief*

Fellows-Jensen, G. 1998. The origins and development of the name York, in Rollason 1998, 226–37

Feugère, M. 2002. *Weapons of the Romans* (English trans.)

Finley, M.I. 1972. The silent women of Rome, in M.I. Finley 1972, *Aspects of Antiquity: Discoveries and Controversies* (second Pelican edn)

Frere, S.S. 1980. Hyginus and the first cohort, *Britannia* **11**, 51–60

Fulford, M. 2010. Roman Britain: immigration and material culture, in Eckardt 2010, 67–78

Garner-Lahire, J. 2016. *Excavations at the Minster Library, York 1997*, Brit. Archaeol. Rep. Brit. Ser. **622**

Garnsey, P. and Saller, R. 1987. *The Roman Empire: Economy, Society and Culture*

Gaunt, G.D. and Buckland, P.C. 2003. The geological background to Yorkshire's archaeology, in T. Manby, S. Moorhouse and P. Ottaway (eds) 2003. *The Archaeology of Yorkshire: An Assessment at the Beginning of the 21st Century*, Yorkshire Archaeol. Soc. Occ, Pap. **3**, 17–23

Gentil, P. 1988. *G.F. Wilmot's Excavation at St Mary's Abbey, York*, unpublished B.A. dissertation, Dept of Archaeology, York University

Green, M. 1986. *The Gods of the Celts*

Greene, K. 1990. *The Archaeology of the Roman Economy*

Greig, J.R.A. 1979. Pollen from the lower silts, in Kenward and Williams 1979, 52

Halkon, P. and Millett, M. (eds) 1999. *Rural Settlement and Industry: Studies in the Iron Age and Roman Archaeology of Lowland East Yorkshire*, Yorkshire Archaeol. Rep. **4**

Hall, A.R., Kenward, H.K. and Williams, D. 1980. *Environmental Evidence from Roman Deposits in Skeldergate*, Archaeol. York **14/3**

Hall, A.R. and Kenward, H.K. 1990. *Environmental Evidence from the* Colonia: *Tanner Row and Rougier Street*, Archaeol. York **14/6**

Hall, R.A. 1986. Roman warehouses and other riverside structures in Coney Street, in Brinklow *et al.* 1986, 5–20

Hall, R.A. 1996. An observation of the fortress wall in Parliament Street, in Ottaway 1996, 227–31

Hall, R.A. 1997. *Excavations in the* Praetentura: *9 Blake Street,* Archaeol. York **3/4**

Hall, R.A. and Hinchliffe, J. 1986. A watching brief at 11–13 Parliament Street in 1971, in Brinklow *et al.* 1986, 25–8

Hall, R.A., Ottaway, P. and Davison, B. 1996. B.K. Davison's investigations of York's defences between the Multangular and Anglian towers, 1970, in Ottaway 1996, 256–73

Hall, R.A., Evans, D.T. and Ottaway, P. 2011. 16–22 Coppergate, in Ottaway 2011, 199–221

Harden, D.B. 1962. Glass in Roman York, in RCHME's *Eburacum*, 136–41

Hargrove, W. 1818. *History and Description of the Ancient City of York* (2 Vols)

Hartley, B.R. and Dickinson, B. 1990. Samian ware, in Perrin 1990, 264–5

Hartley, K. 1995. Mortaria, in Phillips and Heywood 1995, 304–23

Haselgrove, C. (ed.) 2016. *Cartimandua's Capital: The Late Iron Age Royal Site at Stanwick, North Yorkshire, Fieldwork and Analysis 1981–2011*

Hassall, M.W.C. and Tomlin, R.S.O. 1983. Roman Britain in 1982, II, Inscriptions, *Britannia* **14**, 336–56

Hassall, M.W.C. and Tomlin, R.S.O. 1987. Roman Britain in 1986, II, Inscriptions, *Britannia* **18**, 361–77

Hatt, J-J. 1986. *La Tombe Gallo-Romaine* (reprint of original edn, 1951)

Hedges, J. 1976. Textile, in MacGregor 1976, 14–15

Henig, M. 1974. *A Corpus of Roman Engraved Gemstones from British Sites*, Brit. Archaeol. Rep. Brit. Ser. **8**

Henig, M. 1976. Intagli, in MacGregor 1976, 6–10

Henig, M. 1984. *Religion in Roman Britain*

Henig, M. 1995. Roman intaglios, in Philips and Heywood 1995, 372–3

Henshall, A.S. 1962. Clothes in burials with gypsum, in RCHME's *Eburacum*, 108–09

Hillman, G. 1981. Reconstructing crop husbandry practices from charred remains of crops, in R. Mercer (ed.) *Farming Production in British Prehistory*, 123–62

Hinchliffe, J, and Ottaway, P. in prep. Excavations at 27 Tanner Row, in Ottaway *et al.* in prep.

Hirschfeld, O. and Zangemeister, K. (eds) 1899. *Inscriptiones Trium Galliarum et Germanicarum Latinae*, Corpus Inscriptionum Latinarum **13.1** (Berlin)

Hodgson, N. 1995. Were there two Antonine occupations of Scotland? *Britannia* **26**, 29–49

Hodgson, N. 2009. *Hadrian's Wall 1999–2009: A Summary of Excavation and Research*

Home, G. 1924. *Roman York*

Hooley, A.D. 1988. General points from an accident of fortune, *Interim* **13.1**, 15–24

Hooley, A.D. 1988–9. Roman leatherwork from the General Accident site, York and Catterick, North Yorkshire, *Yorkshire Archaeol. Soc. Roman Antiquities Section Bull.* **6**, 16–26

Hopkins, K. 1966. On the probable age structure of the Roman population, *Population Stud.* **220**, 245–64

Hopkins, K. 1980. Taxes and trade in the Roman Empire, *J. Roman Stud.* **70**, 101–25

Horne, P.D. 2003. Case Study 2: Rural settlement in Roman North Yorkshire, an aerial view, in Butlin 2003, 58–61

Howard, A.J. and Macklin, M.G. 2003. The rivers, in Butlin 2003, 14–17

Hunter-Mann, K. 2006. *An Unusual Cemetery at The Mount, York*, Archaeol. York Web Publ. **6**

Hunter-Mann, K. 2007. Excavations in Hungate 1950–51: what did they really find? *Yorkshire Archaeol. Today* **12**, 15–18

Hunter-Mann, K. 2009. New light on the Roman fortress defences, *Yorkshire Archaeol. Today* **17**, 1–4

Jaques, D. 2016. Vertebrate remains, in Garner-Lahire 2016, 71–3

Jenkins, F. 1978. Pipeclay figurines, in MacGregor 1978, 35–7

Johns, C. 1996. *The Jewellery of Roman Britain: Celtic and Classical Traditions*

Johnson, A. 1983. *Roman Forts*

Johnson, M. 2005. *A Roman Site and Prehistoric Camp at Monk's Cross, York*, Archaeol. York Web Publ. **4**

Jones, B. and Mattingly, D. 1990. *An Atlas of Roman Britain*

Jones, R.F.J. 1984. The cemeteries of Roman York, in Addyman and Black 1984, 34–42

Jones, R.F.J. 1988. The hinterland of Roman York, in Price and Wilson 1988, 161–70

Jones, R.F.J. 1990. Natives and the Roman Army: three model relationships, in H. Vetters, and M. Kandler, *Akten des 14 Internationalen Limeskongress 1986 in Carnuntum*, 99–110

Kendall, T. 2010. Jet and glass and rocks 'n' bones: Hungate Block H in 2010, *Yorkshire Archaeol. Today* **19**, 5–11

Kenward, H.K. 1979. The insect remains, in Kenward and Williams 1979, 62-78

Kenward, H.K. and Williams, D. 1979. *Biological Evidence from the Roman Warehouses in Coney Street*, Archaeol. York **14/2**

Kenward, H.K., Hall, A.R. and Jones, A.K.G. 1986. *Environmental Evidence from a Roman Well and Anglian Pits in the Legionary Fortress*, Archaeol. York **14/5**

Kershaw, A. 1997. Painted plaster from 9 Blake Street, in Hall 1997, 372–6

King, A. 1974. A review of archaeological work in the caves of north-west England, in A.C. Waltham and M.M. Sweeting (eds) *The Limestone Caves of North-west England*, 182–200

King, E. 1975. Roman kiln material from the Borthwick Institute, Peasholme Green: a report for the York Excavation Group, in P.V. Addyman, Excavations in York 1972–3, First Interim Report. *Antiq. J.* **54**, 213–7

Knight, J.K. 2003. *Caerleon Roman Fortress* (3rd edn)

Kruschwitz, P. 2015. *Undying Voices: The Poetry of Roman Britain*

Lawrence, R. 2007. *Roman Pompeii, Space and Society* (2nd edn)

Lawton, I.G. 1992–3. Apple Tree Farm 1987–1992: an Ebor Ware kiln site, *Yorkshire Archaeol. Soc. Roman Antiquities Section Bull.* **10**, 4–8

Lawton, I.G. 2002–3. Wilstrop Hall, Green Hammerton: a Roman villa site, *Yorkshire Archaeol. Soc. Roman Antiquities Section Bull.* **19**, 6–8

Leach, S., Lewis, M.E., Chenery, C., Müldner, G.H. and Eckhardt, H. 2009. Migration and diversity in Roman Britain: a multidisciplinary approach to immigrants in Roman York, England, *American J Physical Anthropology*, **140 (3)**, 546–61

Leach, S., Eckhardt, H., Chenery, C., Müldner, G.H. and Lewis, M.E. 2010. 'Lady of the north': migration, ethnicity and identity in Roman Britain, *Antiquity* **84**, 131–45

Le Bohec, Y. 1994. *The Imperial Roman Army* (English trans.)

Le Quesne, C. 1999. *Excavations at Chester. The Roman and Later Defences, Part 1. Investigations 1978–90*, Chester Archaeol. Excavation and Survey Rep. **11**

Levick, B. 1967. *Roman Colonies in Southern Asia Minor*

Levick, B. 2007. *Julia Domna: Syrian Empress*

Ling, R. 1992. A collapsed building facade at Carsington, Derbyshire, *Britannia* **23**, 233–6

Lodwick, L.A. 2017. Evergreen plants in Roman Britain and beyond: movement, meaning and materiality, *Britannia* **48**, 135–73

Long, A.A. 2003. Roman philosophy, in D. Sedley (ed.) *The Cambridge Companion to Greek and Roman Philosophy*, 184–210

MacConnoran, P. 1986. Footwear, in L. Miller, J. Schofield and M. Rhodes, *The Roman Quay at St Magnus House, London*, London and Middlesex Archaeol. Soc. Spec. Pap. **8**, 218–26

Mackie, A., Townshend, A., and Waldron, H. A. 1975. Lead concentrations in bones from Roman York. *J. Archaeol. Sci.* **2 (3)**, 235–7

Mackreth, D.F. 2011. *Brooches in Iron Age and Roman Britain*

MacGregor, A. 1976. *Finds from a Roman Sewer and an Adjacent Building in Church Street*, Archaeol. York **17/1**

MacGregor, A. 1978. *Roman Finds from Skeldergate and Bishophill*, Archaeol. York **17/2**

Magilton, J.R. 1986. A Roman building and Roman roads in Aldwark, in Brinklow et al. 1986, 32–47

Maltby, M. 2010. *Feeding a Roman Town*

MAP, 2005a. *7–15 Spurriergate, York, Archaeological Assessment Report*

MAP, 2005b. *St Oswald's School, Fulford, York, North Yorkshire, Archaeological Assessment Report*

Margary, I.D. 1973. *Roman Roads in Britain* (3rd edn)

Martiniano, R. and 21 others 2016. Genomic signals of migration and continuity in Britain before the Anglo-Saxons, Nature Communications, *DOI: 10/1038/ ncomms 10326*

Mason, D.J.P. 1988. *Prata Legionis* in Britain, *Britannia* **19**, 163–90

Mason, D.J.P. 2012. *Roman Chester: Fortress at the Edge of the World* (paperback edn)

Mattern, M. 1989. Die reliefverzierten Römischen Grabstelen der Provinz Britannia, Themen und Typen, *Kölner Jahrbuch für Vor- und Frühgeschichte* **22**, 707–801

McComish, J. 2006a. *Roman Occupation at the Site of the Former Starting Gate Public House 42–50 Tadcaster Road, Dringhouses, York*, Archaeology of York Web Publication **8**

McComish, J. 2006b. *Land at the Junction of Dixon Lane and George Street, Archaeological Excavation Assessment Report*, YAT Rep. **2006.53** and Archaeology of York Web Publication **9**

McComish, J.M. 2012. *An Analysis of Roman Ceramic Building Material from York and its Immediate Environs*, unpubl. MA, University of York

McIntyre, L. 2013. *Demography, Diet and State of Health in Roman York*, unpubl. PhD Dept of Archaeology, University of Sheffield

McIntyre, L. 2015. Reconstructing population size in a Roman *colonia*; the case of *Eboracum*, *J. Roman Archaeol.* **28**, 413–29

Miller, S. 1925. Roman York: excavations of 1925, *J. Roman Stud.* **15**, 176–94

Miller, S. 1928. Roman York: excavations of 1926–27, *J. Roman Stud.* **18**, 61–99

Milllett, M. and Ferraby, R. 2016. *Aldborough Roman Town* (English Heritage Guidebook)

Mócsy, A. 1974. *The Provinces of the Roman Empire: Pannonia and Upper Moesia*

Monaghan, J. 1993. *Roman Pottery from the Fortress: 9 Blake Street*, Archaeol. York **16/7**

Monaghan, J. 1997. *Roman Pottery from York*, Archaeol. York **16/8**

Montgomery, J., Evans, J., Chenery, S., Pashley, V. and Killgrove, K. 2010. 'Gleaming white and deadly': using lead to track human exposure and geographic origins in the Roman period in Britain, in Eckardt 2010, 199–226

Morley, N. 2012. A forum on trade: 14E, in Scheidel 2012, 309–17

Morris, I. 1992. *Death Ritual and Social Structure in Classical Antiquity*

Müldner, G., Chenery, C. and Eckardt, H. 2011. The 'headless Romans': multi-isotope investigations of an unusual burial ground from Roman Britain. *J. Archaeol. Sci.* **38 (2)**, 280–90

O'Connor, T.P. 1988. *Bones from the General Accident Site, Tanner Row*, Archaeol. York **15/2**

O'Connor, T.P. and van der Veen, M. 1998. *The Expansion of Agricultural Production in Late Iron Age and Roman Britain*

OSA 2005. *18–20 St Maurice's Road*, **OSA05EV04**

Ottaway, P. 1996. *Excavations and Observations on and Adjacent to the Defences 1971–90*, Archaeol. York **3/3**

Ottaway, P. 1997a. The legionary fortress plan, in Hall 1997, 389–93

Ottaway, P. 1997b. The sewer trenches in Low Petergate, *Interim* **22.3**, 15–23

Ottaway, P. 2004. *Roman York* (2nd edn)

Ottaway, P. 2005. *1–3 Driffield Terrace, York: Assessment Report on an Archaeological Excavation*, YAT Field Rep. **1213**

Ottaway, P. 2011. *Archaeology in the Environs of Roman York: Excavations 1976 – 2005*, Archaeol. York **6/2**

Ottaway, P. 2013. *Roman Yorkshire: People, Culture, Landscape*

Ottaway, P. 2016. Ferrous metalwork, in Garner-Lahire 2016, 63–5

Ottaway, P. in prep. 5 Rougier Street, in Ottaway *et al.* in prep.

Ottaway, P. and Rees, H. 2012. The cemeteries of Roman Winchester, in P. Ottaway, K.E. Qualmann, H. Rees and G.D. Scobie 2012, *The Roman Cemeteries and Suburbs of Winchester: Excavations 1971–86*, 340–70

Ottaway, P., Antoni, A. and Marwood, R. in prep. A watching brief at 12 St Martin's Lane, in Ottaway *et al.* in prep.

Ottaway, P. and Marwood, R. in prep. A watching brief near No 138 Micklegate, in Ottaway *et al.* in prep.

Ottaway, P., Pearson, N. and Wenham, L.P. in prep. *Roman York: Excavations South-West of The Ouse (1961–1993) at 5 Rougier Street, 24–30 Tanner Row and Sites in Bishophill*, Archaeol. York **4/2**

Palaeoecology Research Services 2006. The animal bones in McComish 2006a

Parker, A. 2016. Staring at death, the jet *gorgoneia* of Roman Britain, in S. Hoss and A. Whitmore (eds), *Small Finds and Ancient Social Practices in the North-West Provinces of the Roman Empire*, 98–113

Parker, A. 2017. Protecting the troops? Phallic carvings in the north of Roman Britain, in A. Parker (ed.) Ad Vallum: *Papers on the Roman Army and Frontiers in Celebration of Dr Brian Dobson*, Brit. Archaeol. Rep. Brit. Ser. **631**, 117–30

Pearson, A. 2002. *The Roman Shore Forts*

Pearson, N. 1990. Swinegate excavation, *Interim*, Spring 1990, 2–10

Pearson, N. in prep. 24–30 Tanner Row, in Ottaway *et al.* in prep.

Pearson, N. and Dickson, A. 2000. *Fetter Lane Electricity Sub-Station, York, Report on an Archaeological Evaluation and Watching Brief*, **OSA98EV07**

Peck, J.J. 2009. *The Biological Impact of Culture Contact: a Bioarchaeological Study of Roman Colonialism in Britain*, unpubl. PhD thesis, Ohio State University

Pelletier, A. 1982. *L'Urbanisme Romain Sous L'Empire*

Perrin, J.R. 1975. *A Study of the Roman Pottery from an Excavation of the Roman Civil Baths, York in 1939, Air Raid Control Centre Site*, unpubl. M.Litt diss., Univ. Newcastle

Perrin, J.R. 1981. *Roman pottery from the Colonia: Skeldergate and Bishophill*, Archaeol. York **16/1**

Perrin, J.R. 1990. *Roman Pottery from the Colonia 2: General Accident and Rougier Street*, Archaeol. York **16/2**

Perrin, J.R. 1995. Roman coarse pottery in Phillips and Heywood 1995, 324–45

Phillips, A.D. 1995. The excavations, in Phillips and Heywood 1995, 33–176

Phillips, A.D. and Heywood, B. 1995. *Excavations at York Minster, Vol. 1: From Roman Fortress to Norman Cathedral*

Philpott, R. 1991. *Burial Practices in Roman Britain: A Survey of Grave Treatment and Furnishing AD 43–410*, Brit. Archaeol. Rep. Brit. Ser. **219**

Pitts, L.F. and St Joseph, J.K. 1985. *Inchtuthil: The Roman Legionary Fortress*, Britannia Monogr. **6**

Póczy, K. 1980. Pannonian cities, in A. Lengyel and G.T.B. Radan, *The Archaeology of Roman Pannonia*, 239–74

Price, J. 1995. Roman glass, in Phillips and Heywood 1995, 346–71

Price, J. 2002. Broken bottles and quartz-sand: glass production in Yorkshire and the north in the Roman period, in Wilson and Price 2002, 81–93

Price, J. 2016. Roman glass and obsidian vessels, in Haselgrove 2016, 262–7

Price, J. and Wilson, P. R. (eds) 1988. *Recent Research in Roman Yorkshire*, Brit. Arch. Reports, Brit. Ser. **193**

Radley, J. 1972. Excavations in the defences of the City of York: an early medieval stone tower and the successive earth ramparts, *YAJ* **44**, 38–64

Raine, A. 1922. Two new Roman memorial stones, *YPSR* 1922, 61

Ramm, H.G. 1956. Roman York: excavations of 1955, *J. Roman Stud.* **46**, 76–90

Ramm, H.G. 1958. Roman burials from Castle Yard, York, *YAJ* **39**, 400–18

Ramm, H.G. 1976a. The Roman roads west of Tadcaster, *York Historian* **1**, 3–12

Ramm, H.G. 1976b. The Church of St Mary Bishophill Senior, York: Excavation 1964, *YAJ* **48**, 35–68

Raybould, M. 1999. *A Study of Inscribed Material from Roman Britain*, Brit. Arch. Rep. Brit. Ser. **281**

Reece, R. 2002. *Coinage in Roman Britain*

Reynolds, P.J. 1979. *Iron Age Farm, The Butser Experiment*

Reynolds, P.J. and Langley, J.K. 1979. Romano-British corn-drying oven: an experiment, *Archaeol. J.* **136**, 27–42

RIB I: Collingwood, R.G. and Wright, R.P. 1965. *Roman Inscriptions of Britain* **1**

RIB II, 1: Frere, S.S., Roxan, M. and Tomlin, R.S.O. 1990. *Roman Inscriptions of Britain* **2**, Fasc. 1

RIB II, 2: Frere, S.S. and Tomlin, R.S.O. 1991. *Roman Inscriptions of Britain* **2**, Fasc. 2

RIB II, 4: Frere, S.S. and Tomlin, R.S.O. 1992. *Roman Inscriptions of Britain* **2**, Fasc. 4

RIB II, 5: Frere, S.S. and Tomlin, R.S.O. (eds) 1993. *Roman Inscriptions of Britain* **2**, Fasc. 5

RIB II, 7: Collingwood, R.G. and Wright, R.P. 1995. *Roman Inscriptions of Britain* **2**, Fasc. 7

RIB III: Tomlin, R.S.O., Wright, R.P. and Hassall, M.W.C. 2009. *The Roman Inscriptions of Britain* **3**

Richardson, K.M. 1959. Excavations in Hungate, York, *Archaeol. J.* **116**, 51–114

Rivet, A.L.F. and Smith, C. 1979. *The Place Names of Roman Britain*

Robertson, A.S. 2000. *An Inventory of Romano-British Coin Hoards*, Royal Numismatic Soc. Spec. Publ. **20**

Robinson, T. 2013a. *West Offices, Station Rise, York, Report on an Archaeological Investigation* **OSA11Ex02**

Robinson, T. 2013b. *Former North-eastern Railway Co Offices, Tanner Row, York, Report on a Programme of Archaeological Fieldwork*, **OSA08EX05**

Rogers, N.S.H. 2016. Non-ferrous metalwork, in Garner-Lahire 2016, 65–7

Rollason, D. 1998. *Sources for York History*, Archaeol. York **1**

Roskams, S. and Neal, C. 2020. *Landscape and Settlement in the Vale of York, Archaeological Investigations at Heslington East, York, 2003-13*, Res. Rep. Soc Ants London, 82

Russell, M. 2018. Facing up to Constantine: reassessing the Stonegate monumental head from York, *Britannia* **49**, 211–24

Rutledge, T. 2000. Roman cemetery excavations at the Royal York Hotel. *Yorkshire Archaeol. Soc. Roman Antiquities Section Bull.* **17**, 3–4

Saller, R.P. and Shaw, B.D. 1984. Tombstones and Roman family relations in the principate: civilians, soldiers and slaves, *J Roman Stud.* **74**, 124–56

Savine, B. 2017. *Archaeological Investigations at the Former Newington Hotel, Mount Vale, York*, YAT Archaeological Assessment Rep. **2017/76**

Scheidel, W. 2001. Roman age structure: evidence and models. *J. Roman Stud.* **91**, 1–26

Scheidel, W. 2012. Slavery, in Scheidel 2012, 89–113

Scheidel, W. (ed.) 2012. *The Cambridge Companion to the Roman Economy*

Sherlock, S. 2007. Roman forks, *Archaeol. J.* **164**, 249–67

Simpson, G. 1995. The samian pottery, in Philips and Heywood 1995, 272–90

Sitch, B.J. 1989. A small Roman port at Faxfleet near Broomfleet, in Halkon 1989, 10–14

Sitch, B.J. 1990. Faxfleet B, a Romano-British site near Broomfleet, in Ellis and Crowther 1990, 158–71

Spall and Toop, N.J. 2005a. *Blue Bridge House and Fishergate House, York, Report on Excavations: July 2000–July 2002*, published online at http://www.archaeologicalplanningconsultancy.co.uk/mono/001/index.html

Spall and Toop, N.J. 2005b. *Post-excavation Assessment, Mill Mount, York*, FAS Rep.

Stamp, D. 1955. *Man and the Land*

Stead, I.M. 1958. Excavations at the south corner tower of the Roman fortress at York, 1956, *YAJ* **39**, 515–38

Stead, I.M. 1968. An excavation at King's Square, York, 1957, *YAJ* **42**, 151–64

Steer, K.A. 1958. Roman and native in north Britain: the Severan re-organisation, in I. A Richmond (ed.) *Roman and Native in North Britain*, 91–111

Stewart, S. 2007. *Cosmetics and Perfume in the Roman World*

Stockwell, M. and Marwood, R. 1996. Observations in King's Square, in Ottaway 1996, 219–21

Storey, G.R. 1997. The population of ancient Rome, *Antiquity* **71**, 966–78

Sumpter, A.B. and Coll, S. 1977. *Interval Tower SW5 and the South-west Defences: Excavations 1972–75*, Archaeol. York **3/2**

Swan, V.G. 1994. Legio VI and its men: African legionaries in Britain, *J. Roman Pottery Stud.* **5**, 1–34

Swan, V.G. 2002. The Roman pottery of Yorkshire in its wider context, in Wilson and Price 2002, 35–79

Swan, V.G. and Monaghan, J. 1993. Head pots: a North African tradition in Roman York, *YAJ* **65**, 21–38

Swan, V.G. and McBride, R.M. 2002. A Rhineland potter at the legionary fortress of York, in M. Aldhouse-Green and P. Webster, *Artefacts and Archaeology. Aspects of the Celtic and Roman World*, 190–234

Todd, M. 1992. Jet in northern Gaul, *Britannia* **23**, 246–8

Tomlin, R.S.O. 2018. Britannia Romana: *Roman Inscriptions and Roman Britain*

Toop, N. 2008. Excavations at Moss Street Depot, Moss Street, York, *YAJ* **80**, 21–42

Toynbee, J. 1971. *Death and Burial in the Roman World*

Tufi, S.R. 1983. Corpus Signorum Imperii Romani (*Corpus of Sculpture of the Roman World*) *Great Britain, 1, fasc. 3, Yorkshire*

Turcan, R. 1996. *The Cults of the Roman Empire* (English trans.)

Tweddle, D. 1986. *Finds from Parliament Street and Other Sites in the City Centre*, Archaeol. York **17/4**

Tylecote, R.F. 1986. *The Prehistory of Metallurgy in the British Isles*

Tyler, D. 2000. *Kenning's Garage, Micklegate, an Archaeological Evaluation*, **OSA00EV01**

VCHY. Tillott, P.M. (ed.) 1961. *The Victoria County History of the County of Yorkshire: The City of York*

Wacher, J.S. 1969. *Excavations at Brough-on-Humber 1958–61*, Rep. Res. Comm. Soc. Antiq. London **25**

Wacher, J.S. 1995. *The Towns of Roman Britain* (second edn)

Wade, W.V. 1957. Coin list, in C. Dickinson and L.P. Wenham, Discoveries in the Roman cemetery on The Mount, York, *YAJ* **39**, 307–8

Wade, W.V. and Kent, J.P.C. 1968. The coins, in Wenham 1968b, 87–91

Walker, D.R. 1988. The Roman coins, in B. Cunliffe (ed.) *The Temple of Sulis Minerva at Bath, 2, The Finds from the Sacred Spring*, 281–358

Walsh, P.G. 1999. Introduction to Apuleius, *The Golden Ass* (Oxford World's Classic, Paperback edn)

Walton, P. 1995. An ivory weaving tablet, in Phillips 1995, 428–9

Walton Rogers, P. 2001. The re-appearance of an old Roman loom in medieval England, in P. Walton Rogers, L. Bender Jørgensen and A. Rast-Eicher (eds), *The Roman Textile Industry and its Influence*: *A Birthday Tribute to John Peter Wild*, 158–71

Ward-Perkins, J.B. 1981. *Roman Imperial Architecture* (Penguin edn)

Warwick, R. 1968. The skeletal remains, in Wenham 1968b, 113–216

Weatherhead, F.J. 1995. Roman wall-plaster from York Minster, in Phillips and Heywood 1995, 248–64

Wellbeloved, C. 1842. RCHME's *Eburacum, or York under the Romans*

Wells, C. 1992. *The Roman Empire* (2nd edn), Fontana History of the Ancient World

Wenham, L.P. 1957. Two discoveries of the Roman road between York and Tadcaster, *YAJ* **39**, 276–82

Wenham, L.P. 1958. Excavation of a Roman road in the Treasurer's House, 1954, *YAJ* **39**, 266

Wenham, L.P. 1960. Seven archaeological discoveries in Yorkshire, *YAJ* **40**, 298–328

Wenham, L.P. 1961. Excavations and discoveries adjoining the south-west wall of the Roman legionary fortress at Feasegate, York, 1955–57, *YAJ* **40**, 329–50

Wenham, L.P. 1962. Excavations and discoveries within the legionary fortress in Davygate, York 1955–8, *YAJ* **40**, 507–87

Wenham, L.P. 1965a. The south-west defences of the fortress of *Eboracum*, in M.G. Jarrett and B. Dobson (eds), *Britain and Rome*, 1–26

Wenham, L.P. 1965b. Blossom Street excavations, 1953–5, *YAJ* **41**, 524–90

Wenham, L.P. 1967. Two excavations, *YPSR 1967*, 41–60

Wenham, L.P. 1968a. Discoveries in King's Square, York, 1963, *YAJ* **42**, 165–8

Wenham, L.P. 1968b. *The Romano-British Cemetery at Trentholme Drive York*, Ministry of Public Buildings and Works Archaeol. Rep. **5**

Wenham, L.P. 1972. Excavations in Low Petergate, York, 1957–8, *YAJ* **44**, 65–113

Wenham, L.P. and Ottaway, P. in prep. Bishophill Junior, in Ottaway *et al.* in prep.

Wetzel, R.E. 1980. *Technical Examination of Painted Roman Plaster Excavated in the City of York*, unpubl. M.A. Diss., University of Bradford

Wheeler, M. 1954. *Archaeology from the Earth*

Wheeler, M. 1964. *Roman Art and Architecture*

Whitwell, J.B. 1976. *The Church Street Sewer and an Additional Building*, Archaeol. York **3/1**

Wiemer, K. 1993. *Early British Iron Edged Tools: A Metallurgical Study*, unpubl. PhD Cambridge Univ.

Wild, J.P. 1968. Clothing in the north-west provinces of the Roman Empire, *Bonner Jahrbuch* **168**, 166–240

Wild, J.P. 1976. Textiles, in D. Strong and D. Brown (eds), *Roman Crafts*, 167–77

Wild, J.P. 2002. The textile industries of Roman Britain, *Britannia* **33**, 1–42

Wilkinson, K and Stevens, C. 2003. *Environmental Archaeology: Approaches, Techniques and Applications*

Williams, D. 1979. The plant remains, in Kenward and Williams 1979, 52–62

Williams, D.F. 1990. Amphorae from York, in Perrin 1990, 342–62

Williams, D.F. 1995. Amphorae, in Phillips and Heywood 1995, 291–303

Williams, D.F. 1997. Amphorae, in Monaghan 1997, 967–73

Williams, D.F. and Carreras, C. 1995. North African amphorae in Roman Britain: a reappraisal, *Britannia* **26**, 231–52

Willis, S. 2016. The Iron Age tradition and Roman pottery, in Haselgrove 2016, 207–55

Wilmott, G.F. 1952–3. St Mary's Abbey, York, *Yorkshire Architectural and York Archaeol. Soc. Ann. Rep. and Summary of Proc.1952–3*, 8

Wilmott, G.F. 1953–4. Excavations at St Mary's Abbey, *Yorkshire Architectural and York Archaeol. Soc. Ann. Rep. and Summary of Proc. 1953–4*, 12–3

Wilson, P.R. and Price, J. (eds) 2002. *Aspects of Industry in Roman Yorkshire and the North*

Witt, R.E. 1971. *Isis in the Graeco-Roman World*

Index

Named Roman individuals, except emperors, are indexed under their family name (*nomen*), any praenomen is given in brackets. Emperors are indexed as they are commonly known. Street numbers for archaeological sites are given in brackets after the street name.

Aelia Aeliana (tombstone), 6, 189, 194–5, 202, 224–5
Aelia Severa (sarcophagus), 180–1, 246, 248
(Gaius) Aeresius Saenus, 29, 85, 247
Agriculture, 129–35
Aldborough, 63, 166
Amphitheatre, 53–4
Antonine Itinerary, 13, 54
Antonius Gargilianus (tomb monument), 83, 108, 168
Antoninus Pius, emperor, 64, 67
Appletree Farm, Heworth, 56, 140, 230, 240
Armour, 29, 71–2
Augustan History, 13, 40, 63, 67, 70, 73
(Marcus) Aurelius Lunaris (altar), 74, 128, 161, 211
Aurelius Mercurialis, 7–8, 10–11, 188–9

Baths, 40–3, 109–10, 113, 118, 121, 142, 144, 159, 196, 213–14
Bedern well, 25, 83, 120, 132, 152, 170, 200, 204

Bishophill Junior, 93, 95
Bishophill Senior (37), 116–20
Blake Street (9), 16, 60, 77, 79–80, 185
Blossom Street, 55, 186, 196, 226
Blossom Street (35–41), 231, 244–5
Boneworking, 147
Bootham Bar, 14, 34, 92, 225
Brigantes, 26–7, 63, 65, 137
Brigantian revolt, 65–6

Caecilius Musicus, 180–1, 246–8
Caerleon, 28, 30–1, 40, 52–4, 74, 168
Camps 31–2, 63
Canabae, 59–61, 86, 122–5
Candida Barita (tombstone), 173, 225, 247
Caracalla, emperor, 13, 70, 73–5, 87, 111, 162, 173, 218, 225, 234, 248
Cartimandua, 27, 160
Cassius Dio, 13, 67, 69, 70, 73, 234
Cattle, 25–6, 69, 106–107, 129, 133–5, 145, 150, 152, 201
Cemeteries, 229–33
    Baile Hill, 89

Castle Yard, 84, 230
Driffield Terrace, 16, 167, 169, 170, 178–9, 182, 226, 231, 235–6, 242, 244, 249
Old Station, 62
Railway Station, 108, 155, 176–8, 194–7, 215, 227–8, 231, 233, 236–40, 242, 244, 246, 248–50
The Mount, 29, 167, 181, 189, 217, 227, 231, 235, 241, 245–7, 249
Trentholme Drive, 60, 96, 153, 167–8, 176–8, 225, 226, 229, 232, 234–5, 237, 242, 248–9
Ceramic periods, 59–60, 86
Chester, 28, 30, 40, 52, 53–4, 74
Christians and Christianity, 5, 64, 83, 223, 240–1
Church Street (4–5), 41
Citizens and citizenship 10–11, 28–9, 62, 74, 86–7, 108, 166, 173, 179–81, 205, 211, 223, 228, 248
Claudius, emperor, 26, 64
Clementhorpe (Roman house), 76, 121
Clodius Albinus, 68–9, 74
Coinage, 57, 60, 161–3
Coffins, 83, 142, 194, 238–40, 245–6, 250
Colonia status, 74, 86–7, 108
Commodus, emperor, 11, 64, 67–8, 84, 162–3, 216–17
Coney Street (39–41), 26, 60–1, 122, 132, 153, 200
Cool, Hilary, 132
Constitutio Antoninano, 74, 87, 166, 248
Copmanthorpe, 23, 55
Coppergate (16–22), 124, 144, 223
Corellia Optata (tombstone), 169, 185–6, 233, 236
Cosmetics, 128, 159, 195

(Quintus) Creperius Marcus, 124

Decurions, 108–109
Dean's Park, 43, 45
Defences (fortress), 14, 15, 28, 30, 34–5, 43–53, 80–3, 88, 91, 252
Defences (town), 88–9
Drake, Francis, 15
Dress, 71, 147–8, 172, 187–90, 220, 246–7
Drink and drinking, 140, 149, 201–203, 225–6
Dringhouses, 23, 55, 125, 133, 152, 188, 233, 236

Ebor ware, 57, 138–40, 151, 175, 236
Elagabalus, emperor, 75–6
Ethnicity, 172–9

Flavia Augustina (tombstone), 29, 85, 148, 168, 183, 188–90, 224, 247
(Titus) Flavius Flavinus, 84, 246
Flavius Bellator, decurion, 108
Food, 6, 100, 106, 121, 126, 129, 131–2, 140, 149, 152, 196, 200–204, 225–6, 252
Forum 107–108
Foss, river, 23–4, 124
Friends Burial Ground, 89

Gardens, 120–1, 129
Geta, emperor, 70, 218
Gibbon, Edward, 64, 252
Glass:
  Jewellery, 197, 199
  Vessels, 41, 101, 157–61, 195–6, 202–203, 235–6, 249, 250
Glass making, 144, 149
Gods and goddesses:
  Arciacus, 84, 215–16

Attis, 6, 216–17
Bacchus, 212–13
Cupid, 226–7
Cybele, 6, 216
Fortuna, 61, 65, 111, 199, 209, 214
Genius loci, 76, 101, 124, 207, 209
Genius of *Eboracum*, 108
Hercules, 68, 123, 169, 213
Jupiter, 31, 38, 64, 124, 199, 206–207, 211, 213
Lares and Penates 10, 120
Mars, 199, 207, 212, 215
Mother goddesses (*Matres*), 85, 113, 214–15
Medusa, 148, 197, 226
Mercury, 11, 207, 212
Minerva, 145, 199, 211, 214
Mithras, 109, 188, 217–23, 237
Oceanus and Tethys, 206
Serapis, 68, 83, 112, 217–18, 237
Toutatis, 215
Venus, 11, 158, 206–207, 212, 226–7, 254
Gordian I, emperor, 75–7
Gordian III, emperor, 7, 77, 140
Grain, 29, 59–61, 102, 129, 131–2, 150, 153, 200–202
Grand Hotel, 107
Grave goods, 248–50

Hadrian, emperor, 36, 41, 45, 59, 62–3, 67, 137, 193
Hadrian's Wall, 32, 38, 40, 65–6, 69, 72, 215, 222
Hairstyles, 6–8, 70, 147, 184, 193–6, 212, 238, 247
Hargrove, William, 73
Head pots, 225–6
Herodian, 13, 69, 70, 73
Heslington East, 23, 56–8, 126, 131

Holgate (St Paul's Green and Holgate Cattle Dock), 94, 126
Home, Gordon, 15, 108, 170, 174
Houses, 113–20
Human remains, 167–71
Humber Estuary, 20, 23, 26–7, 85, 137, 150, 152
Hyginus, Gromaticus, 31–2

(Quintus) Isauricus, 61, 65

Jet, 147–9, 151, 194–7, 199, 204, 226
Jewellery, 70, 144, 151, 196–9, 245, 248, 250
Julia Brica (tombstone), 189, 190
Julia Domna, empress, 6, 70
Julia Velva, 1–3, 9–11, 169, 173, 175
Julia Victorina (sarcophagus), 83, 226, 230
Julius Caesar, 10, 27, 35, 183

King's Square, 34, 44

Leatherworking, 144–5
Legionary fortress:
    Barracks, 34–5, 77–9, 144, 146
    Baths, 35, 40–3, 142, 159, 196, 213–14
    Defences, 14, 15, 28, 30, 34–5, 43–53, 80–3, 88, 91, 252
    Headquarters, 34, 35–41, 62, 77, 108
    Intervallum, 34, 43, 77, 79
    Interval towers, 14, 35, 43, 45, 49–52, 83, 223
    Legate's house, 40
    Plan, 30–3
    Streets 34, 77
Literacy, 32, 184–6
(Lucius) Duccius Rufinus, 30

Marcus Aurelius, emperor, 31, 67
Maximinus, emperor, 76–7
Medicine, 121, 171
Metalworking, 116, 136, 138, 140–4, 149
Micklegate (1–9; Queen's Hotel), 109–10, 137
Miller, Stuart, 15, 51–2
(Marcus) Minucius Mudenus, river pilot, 85, 113, 214
Moraine (at York), 20, 23, 27
Mount, The, 3, 16, 20, 55, 231, 245, 247
Mount School, 60, 85, 235–6
Multangular Tower, 14, 45–53, 215

Naburn, 24, 56, 240
Neptune, 54
Nero, emperor, 26
Ninth legion, 27, 30–1, 44, 54, 62, 65, 136, 140, 165, 223, 236
Numeracy, 186–7

O'Connor, T.P., 133
Old station, 61–2, 75, 110–12, 144, 206, 218, 222, 240, 249
Ouse, river 20, 23–4, 84

Papinian, jurist, 70
Parliament Street, 82, 124, 127, 207, 209
Pertinax, emperor, 68, 83
Petillius Cerialis, 27
Pliny the Elder, 48, 119, 147, 201, 224, 226
Population size, 165–6
Pottery making, 138–40
Ptolemy, geographer, 13, 26
Pythagoras, 32, 224

Querns, 59, 132, 202

Rainfall (at York), 24
Rats, 204
RCHME's *Eburacum*, 15, 51–3, 69, 91, 122, 124, 196, 228–31
Richmond, Sir Ian, 69
Roads (Roman), 17, 54–6, 58, 89–92, 126
Rougier Street (5), 93, 100–103, 129, 212

St Leonard's Hospital, 52
St Leonard's Place, 14, 46, 50
St Mary Bishophill Junior (Roman building), 113–14
St Mary Bishophill Senior (Roman building), 116–20
St Mary's Abbey (Roman buildings), 125
Samian ware, 57, 62, 140, 154–5, 160–1, 173, 185–6, 205, 236
Scribonius Demetrius, 75
Septimius Lupianus, 83–4
Septimius Severus, emperor, 40, 68–73, 87, 123, 140, 162–3, 175, 216, 218, 234
Severus Alexander, emperor, 76, 125
Shoes, 191–3
Sixth Legion, 63–6, 68, 72, 74, 77–85
  Centurions, 83–4
  Legates, 64–5, 83
  Men, 84–5
Skeldergate (58–9), 25–6, 93, 96, 120, 157
Slaves and slavery, 8, 10, 41, 56, 59, 69, 70, 94, 120, 127, 132, 150, 166, 173, 180–3, 190, 202, 238
Sosia Juncina, 61–2, 209
South Shields, 44, 72, 150, 189
Sphinx, 227, 246
Spoons, 147, 174, 202
Stamford Bridge, 23, 56

Streets, 34, 77, 92–4
Suetonius Paullinus, 26
Swinegate (12–18), 41

Tacitus, Cornelius, 3, 12–13, 26–7, 30, 210, 234
Tanner Row (24–30), 16, 25, 65, 78, 103–107, 132–6, 141–2, 144–5, 147–8, 152, 155–8, 170–1, 191, 196, 200, 210–12
Territorium, 58–9, 126, 127, 136
Textiles, 145–7
Tiberius Claudius Paulinus, governor, 74
Tile-making, 140
Trade, 58, 86, 128, 150–63, 252–3
Trajan, emperor, 35, 44–5, 52, 60, 63, 137

Vale of York, 20, 23
Vespasian, emperor, 26–7, 60, 64, 71, 79
(Lucius) Viducius Placidus, 76, 128, 161, 173, 210
Vitruvius, architect, 38
Virgil, author of the *Aeneid*, 11, 13, 31, 64, 186, 224, 254
Virius Lupus, governor, 69

Wall plaster (painted), 78–80, 119
Water supply, 43, 86, 89, 94–6, 108, 118, 145
Wattle Syke, 59
Weaponry, 28, 71–2, 142
Wellbeloved, Charles, 15
Wells, Colin, 64
Wellington Row, 16, 43, 55, 89–90, 92–4, 97–101, 132, 136–7, 155
Wenham, Peter, 35, 65
Wheeler, Sir Mortimer, 36, 65–6
Wine, 140, 147, 149, 156–7, 160–1, 201, 209, 213
Women, status of, 183–4
Writing tablets, 185

York Archaeological Trust, 16
York Minster (archaeological excavation), 31, 34, 36, 38, 40, 60, 75, 77–8, 83, 108, 158, 185, 227, 246
York Minster library (archaeological excavation), 72, 77, 78, 133
Yorkshire Museum, 1, 15, 29, 30, 113, 145, 147, 163, 170, 197, 203, 212, 255